Praise for *Building Generative AI Services with FastAPI*

A masterclass in turning cutting-edge AI into real-world impact.
Ali distills the complexity of generative models and FastAPI into
an approachable, empowering guide for builders at every level.

—*Alan King, founder, AI Your Org*

A must-have for software developers and data scientists to learn to build
production-grade generative AI services with FastAPI. Ali's clear explanations and
depth of technical expertise will keep you ahead in this exciting and emerging field.

—*Joe Rowe, head of technical assurance & compliance,*
Applied Data Science Partners

This book is superb at taking complicated topics and explaining them in a simple,
easy-to-understand way for developers and non-developers alike. It's a fascinating
deep dive into using GenAI in your development projects, which is only going
to become more and more important as time goes on!

—*Lee Dalchow, software engineer*

A practical introduction to generative AI with valuable insights on building
real-world services. This book is a good starting point for aspiring AI developers.

—*Julian Brendel, senior Python developer, Vitol*

The book is well-structured, and the way it presents the topics gives you a
solid foundation in the subject. I've recommended it to my colleagues!

—*Daniel Saad, software engineer,*
Mercedes-Benz Tech Innovation

Building Generative AI Services with FastAPI

A Practical Approach to Developing
Context-Rich Generative AI Applications

Alireza Parandeh
Foreword by David Foster

O'REILLY®

Building Generative AI Services with FastAPI

by Alireza Parandeh

Published by O'Reilly Media, Inc., 1005 Gravenstein Highway North, Sebastopol, CA 95472.

O'Reilly books may be purchased for educational, business, or sales promotional use. Online editions are also available for most titles (*http://oreilly.com*). For more information, contact our corporate/institutional sales department: 800-998-9938 or *corporate@oreilly.com*.

Acquisitions Editor: Amanda Quinn	**Indexer:** WordCo Indexing Services, Inc.
Development Editor: Rita Fernando	**Interior Designer:** David Futato
Production Editor: Clare Laylock	**Cover Designer:** Karen Montgomery
Copyeditor: Kim Wimpsett	**Illustrator:** Kate Dullea
Proofreader: Vanessa Moore	

April 2025: First Edition

Revision History for the First Edition

2025-04-15: First Release

See *http://oreilly.com/catalog/errata.csp?isbn=9781098160302* for release details.

978-1-098-16030-2

[LSI]

Table of Contents

Part I.   Developing AI Services

Part III. Securing, Optimizing, Testing, and Deploying AI Services

Foreword

I remember the day Ali, our head of engineering at ADSP, walked confidently into the office and declared he wanted to write a book on building generative AI services. Knowing the mammoth-sized undertaking that is writing a technical book, I offered him a strong cup of coffee and regaled him with a few tales of my own late-night writing sessions, fueled by caffeine and the sheer will to meet a deadline. I might have even thrown in a cautionary whisper about the ever-present temptation to rewrite entire chapters at 3 a.m. But Ali was steadfast. He had that glint in his eye—a mix of determination and a clear vision. He knew he wanted to create something special, something that would demystify the complexities of generative AI and empower others to build.

Having now read *Building Generative AI Applications with FastAPI*, I can say he's done far more than that. Ali has crafted a truly indispensable guide for anyone looking to move beyond theoretical discussions about AI and into the realm of practical, real-world application. And somehow, he's made the whole process look deceptively easy.

As co-founder of an AI consultancy, I've seen firsthand the growing need for engineers who not only can understand how AI works but also build production-grade solutions with AI. We are in a period of profound transformation, where AI is rapidly changing how we live and work. It's no longer enough to be a passive consumer of AI-powered products. The future belongs to those who can harness the power of generative models to create, innovate, and solve real problems. This book is the perfect starting point for that journey.

Ali's technical expertise is evident on every page. He effortlessly blends complex concepts with clear, concise explanations and practical examples. The code snippets aren't just toy examples; they are building blocks for real applications. He guides you through the intricacies of FastAPI, authentication, authorization, and database integration with the confidence of a seasoned engineer who has spent countless hours wrestling with these challenges in the real world.

Building Generative AI Applications with FastAPI is a vital resource for any engineer looking to navigate the rapidly evolving landscape of AI. It's a testament to Ali's technical leadership and his remarkable ability to make the complex accessible. This book isn't just about building AI services; it's about empowering a new generation of engineers to shape the future. And that future, thanks to works like this, looks incredibly bright.

— David Foster
Partner at ADSP
Author of Generative Deep Learning
(O'Reilly, 2024)

Preface

Generative AI (GenAI) is taking the world by storm since the release of technologies like ChatGPT. This new type of AI can create content in various *modalities* (such as text, audio, video, etc.) by learning to mimic patterns from its training data. With the increased advancement in GenAI capabilities, many businesses are investing in off-the-shelf or custom AI tools. These tools require maintainable and scalable backend services that can adapt to high demand.

AI capabilities are exciting because they open the door to endless possibilities that unlock the potential for new tools. Before generative AI, developers had to write scripts and train optimization models to build automation and data pipelines for their processing of unstructured data like corpora of texts. This process could be tedious, error-prone, and applicable only to limited use cases. However, with the rise of GenAI models such as large language models (LLMs), we can now digest, compare, and summarize unstructured datasets and documents; reword complex ideas; and generate visualizations and illustrations.

While most generative models such as ChatGPT are excellent at what they do on their own, can you imagine the possibilities when we connect them to the internet, our own databases, and other services? If we can just "talk" to our services in natural language or give them some image, video, or audio and get them to do things for us, it opens up so many opportunities to create newly accessible and automated applications.

Chatbots are not the only apps that we can create with such generative models. There is so much more we can do. We can create backend service agents that can perform various complex tasks requiring comprehension, logical reasoning, and analysis of texts.

By connecting our generative models to existing services and the internet, we are giving our AI services additional data to enrich their understanding of the problem at hand. For instance, a company can use an open source, in-house, fine-tuned LLM to parse purchase orders, generate invoices, and validate data against their customer database before placing an order with a payment system. This is where generative models shine. Other use cases can include content management systems that can help users with generating content and website builders that can suggest imagery, icons, and user interface (UI) components to fast-track the site's design.

There is a catch. LLMs and other generative models require heavy processing power and memory to function, and it is not clear what deployment patterns and integration layers the developers should use to leverage these models. Building generative AI services is challenging because you need to balance scalability, security, performance, and data privacy. You'll also want the ability to moderate, retrain, and optimize these services for real-time inference. These challenges will be different for every organization, and how you build your generative AI services will depend on your existing software systems and services.

Existing resources and documentation provide the necessary information to get started with training custom models and fine-tuning large language models. However, most developers may continue to face challenges in packaging and deploying these novel generative models as part of existing software systems and services.

My aim with this book is to show you how to productionize GenAI by understanding the end-to-end process in building and deploying your own AI services with tools such as the FastAPI web framework.

Objective and Approach

The objective of this book is to help you explore the challenges of developing, securing, testing, and deploying generative AI as services integrated with your own external systems and applications.

This book centers on constructing modular, type-safe generative AI services in Fast-API with seamless database schema handling support and model integration to power backends that can generate new data.

The significance of these topics stems from the growing demand for building flexible services that can adapt to changing requirements, maintain high performance, and scale efficiently using the microservice pattern.

You will also learn the process of enriching your services with contextual data from a variety of sources such as databases, the web, external systems, and files uploaded by users.

A few generative models require heavy processing power and memory to function. You will explore how to handle these models in production and how to scale your services to handle the load. You will also explore how to handle long-running tasks such as model inference.

Finally, we will discuss authentication concepts, security considerations, performance optimization, testing, and deployment of production-ready generative AI services.

Prerequisites

This book assumes no prior knowledge of generative AI and won't require you to fully understand how generative models work. I will be covering the intuition of how such models generate data but will not dive into their underlying mathematics. However, if you want to learn more about building your own generative AI models in detail, I recommend *Generative Deep Learning* by David Foster (O'Reilly, 2024).

As this is a FastAPI book for generative AI applications, I do assume some familiarity with this web framework. If you need a refresher or would like to expand your understanding of FastAPI features, I recommend reading *FastAPI* by Bill Lubanovic (O'Reilly, 2023). However, this is not a requirement for following along with this book.

Furthermore, the book does assume some experience with Python, with Docker for deployment, with how the web works, and with communicating through the HTTP protocol.

To brush up on your Python skills, I highly recommend visiting realpython.org (*https://realpython.org*) for excellent tutorials on more advanced concepts. The official Docker website (*https://www.docker.com*) also provides an excellent practical tutorial on containerization and writing Dockerfiles.

I will not be covering the fundamentals of the web in this book, but I highly recommend MDN's documentation (*https://oreil.ly/vvwzI*) as a starting point.

Finally, the book won't require knowledge of deep learning frameworks such as Tensorflow and Keras. Where relevant, you'll be introduced to these frameworks. Instead, we will mostly work with pretrained models hosted on the Hugging Face model repository (*https://oreil.ly/vC0DA*).

Book Structure

The book is broken into three parts:

Part I, "Developing AI Services"
This part covers all the necessary steps to set up a FastAPI project that will power your GenAI service. You will learn to integrate various generative models into a type-safe FastAPI application and expose endpoints to interact with them.

- Chapter 1, "Introduction": This chapter discusses the importance of GenAI in the future and introduces the practical projects you'll build throughout the book.

- Chapter 2, "Getting Started with FastAPI": This chapter introduces FastAPI, a modern framework for building AI services. You will understand its features, limitations, and how it compares to other web frameworks. By the end of this chapter, you will be able to start creating FastAPI applications, progressively organize projects, and migrate from frameworks like Flask or Django.

- Chapter 3, "AI Integration and Model Serving": This chapter covers the full process of integrating and serving various GenAI models (including language, audio, vision, and 3D models) as a FastAPI service using application lifespan. We'll review various strategies for model serving like preloading, externalizing, and monitoring models with middleware.

- Chapter 4, "Implementing Type-Safe AI Services": This chapter introduces the concept of type-safety and how Python's type annotations and data validation tools like Pydantic can help validate and serialize data running past your AI services.

Part II, "Communicating with External Systems"

In this part, we'll integrate our AI services with external systems such as databases and learn how to serve concurrent users. We will also implement real-time streaming of model outputs.

- Chapter 5, "Achieving Concurrency in AI Workloads": This chapter introduces the concepts of concurrency and parallelism alongside comparing different strategies for solving concurrency problems. We'll review the purpose of asynchronous programming in handling long-running and blocking tasks and review the limitations of Python's Global Interpreter Lock (GIL) when handling these asynchronous processes. To practice, we'll implement a working "talk to the web and your documents" chatbot using a technique called *retrieval augmented generation* (RAG). Finally, we'll cover FastAPI's background tasks feature for tackling long-running operations.

- Chapter 6, "Real-Time Communication with Generative Models": In this chapter, we will focus on enabling real-time client-server communication with generative models. As part of this, we'll compare various mechanisms such as web sockets and server streaming events when streaming data to/from generative models with practical examples.

- Chapter 7, "Integrating Databases into AI Services": This chapter provides an overview of database technologies suitable for GenAI services. We'll cover best practices when working with databases using battle-tested tools such as SQLAlchemy ORM and Alembic for facilitating migrations. Finally, we'll introduce Prisma, an upcoming tool for generating a fully typed database client and automatic handling of migrations.

Part III, "Securing, Optimizing, Testing, and Deploying AI Services"

In this part, we focus on implementing the authentication layer for user management, alongside security and optimization enhancements. We'll then shift our focus on testing and finally deploying our AI service through containerization.

- Chapter 8, "Authentication and Authorization": In this chapter, we will cover the implementation of authentication layers for user management to secure, protect, and restrict access to AI services. We'll review and implement various authentication strategies including basic, token-based, and OAuth. We'll then introduce authorization models including role-based access control (RBAC) and explain the role of FastAPI's dependency graph in the process. This will include adding restrictive permissions for users based on roles where AI service interactions can be automatically moderated.

- Chapter 9, "Securing AI Services": This chapter provides an overview of common attack vectors for generative solutions. Here, we'll shift focus on implementing various security measures across our AI service, such as rate limiting and guardrails, to protect against toxic model outputs, common attacks, abuse, and misuse.

- Chapter 10, "Optimizing AI Services": This chapter covers various performance optimization techniques like batch processing, semantic caching, and prompt engineering for enhancing the quality and speed of AI services.

- Chapter 11, "Testing AI Services": This chapter covers the challenges and best practices in testing AI services. We'll review various testing concepts including testing phases, boundaries, and mocks and then implement mocks of external services, keeping test environments isolated. Finally, we'll introduce a novel approach to testing generative AI models even when they produce varying outputs across test runs.

- Chapter 12, "Deployment of AI Services": This chapter covers various deployment approaches including the use of virtual machines, cloud functions, managed app services, and containerization technologies like Docker. We'll then focus on containerization concepts, such as storage and networking, for deploying our AI service using Docker.

How to Read This Book

This book can be read cover to cover or used as a reference so you can dip into any chapter. In every chapter, I explain the concepts and compare approaches before we dive into practical code examples. Therefore, I recommend reading each chapter twice: once to understand the approach and then revisiting them to work through the code examples yourself using this book's accompanying code repository (*https:// github.com/Ali-Parandeh/building-generative-ai-services*).

I am a firm believer in explaining complex technical concepts with everyday analogies, diagrams, and stories that anyone can relate to. These are often used after a new complex concept is introduced. Look out for tip sections like this one to help improve your understanding of the concepts.

Ultimately, the best way to learn the concepts in this book is to get your hands on an open source generative model and then build a service around it using your own code. Above all, I hope you find it a useful and enjoyable read!

Hardware and Software Requirements

Running generative models is generally a compute-intensive task that requires a strong GPU. However, I've tried my best to provide code examples that use small open source generative models that won't require a GPU.

Only a few chapters will have code examples that require you to have access to a GPU to process concurrent operations or to run heavier models. In such cases, I recommend renting a virtual machine with CUDA-enabled NVIDIA GPUs from any cloud provider or to work from a CUDA-enabled GPU desktop with a minimum of 16 GB of VRAM.

Please refer to NVIDIA's CUDA installation instructions for Windows (*https://oreil.ly/fgwVk*) or Linux (*https://oreil.ly/3rMv2*).

Finally, to run models on a CUDA-enabled NVIDIA GPU, you will also need to install the torch package compiled for CUDA.

Conventions Used in This Book

The following typographical conventions are used in this book:

Italic
> Indicates new terms, URLs, email addresses, filenames, and file extensions.

`Constant width`
> Used for program listings, as well as within paragraphs to refer to program elements such as variable or function names, databases, data types, environment variables, statements, and keywords.

`Constant width italic`
> Shows text that should be replaced with user-supplied values or by values determined by context.

This element signifies a tip or suggestion.

This element signifies a general note.

This element indicates a warning or caution.

Using Code Examples

The book accompanies a code repository for the guided projects. This repository is available for download at *https://github.com/Ali-Parandeh/building-generative-ai-services*. You can also find additional resources, articles, and supporting materials on the book's companion website at *https://buildinggenai.com*.

After downloading and cloning the repository, you can perform a local installation. For example, if using `conda`, you can follow this setup to create your `genaiservice` environment:

```
conda create -n genaiservice python=3.11
conda activate genaiservice
```

You can then install all the necessary dependencies in your newly created Python environment:

```
pip install -r requirements.txt
```

There are around 170+ code examples scattered across the chapters. These code examples show you how to progressively build a production-ready generative AI service with the FastAPI web framework. We will walk through the code for each step-by-step, with clear signposts that show how the code implements the theory underpinning each technique.

The code repository contains several branches that map the state of application code to the start and end of each chapter as examples incrementally build on one another. The code examples are organized by branches instead of folders to avoid clutter and to provide you with a clean codebase to work from. The `main` branch contains the final state of the application code at the end of the book.

At the start of each chapter, check out the relevant `starter` branch to follow along with the code examples as you develop the application. For instance, at the start of Chapter 2, you can check out the `ch02-start` branch. If you get stuck or want to view the repository state at the end of each chapter, you can then check out the corresponding `end` branch (i.e., `ch02-end`) and compare your code with the code in the repository.

> The code repository contains instructions in the *README.md* file on the `main` branch on how to clone the repository and switch branches if you're not familiar with Git.

Each branch will also contain a *README.md* file to guide you with the practical elements of the chapter.

Throughout the book, I will provide additional tasks and exercises to help solidify your understanding of the concepts as part of the guided project. Look out for these sections for instructions on implementing these tasks. Solutions are provided within the code repository. However, I recommend trying to solve these tasks on your own before consulting the solutions. Please note that many solutions can exist for a given task.

If you have a technical question or a problem using the code examples, please send an email to *support@oreilly.com*.

This book is here to help you get your job done. In general, if example code is offered with this book, you may use it in your programs and documentation. You do not need to contact us for permission unless you're reproducing a significant portion of the code. For example, writing a program that uses several chunks of code from this book does not require permission. Selling or distributing examples from O'Reilly books does require permission. Answering a question by citing this book and quoting example code does not require permission. Incorporating a significant amount of example code from this book into your product's documentation does require permission.

We appreciate, but generally do not require, attribution. An attribution usually includes the title, author, publisher, and ISBN. For example, "*Building Generative AI Services with FastAPI* by Alireza Parandeh (O'Reilly). Copyright 2025 Ali Parandeh, 978-1-098-16030-2."

If you feel your use of code examples falls outside fair use or the permission given above, feel free to contact us at *permissions@oreilly.com*.

O'Reilly Online Learning

O'REILLY® For more than 40 years, *O'Reilly Media* has provided technology and business training, knowledge, and insight to help companies succeed.

Our unique network of experts and innovators share their knowledge and expertise through books, articles, and our online learning platform. O'Reilly's online learning platform gives you on-demand access to live training courses, in-depth learning paths, interactive coding environments, and a vast collection of text and video from O'Reilly and 200+ other publishers. For more information, visit *https://oreilly.com*.

How to Contact Us

Please address comments and questions concerning this book to the publisher:

O'Reilly Media, Inc.
1005 Gravenstein Highway North
Sebastopol, CA 95472
800-889-8969 (in the United States or Canada)
707-827-7019 (international or local)
707-829-0104 (fax)
support@oreilly.com
https://oreilly.com/about/contact.html

We have a web page for this book, where we list errata, examples, and any additional information. You can access this page at *https://oreil.ly/building-gen-ai-fastAPI*.

For news and information about our books and courses, visit *https://oreilly.com*.

Find us on LinkedIn: *https://linkedin.com/company/oreilly-media*.

Watch us on YouTube: *https://youtube.com/oreillymedia*.

Acknowledgments

Writing this book has been an incredible experience and journey for me. My deepest gratitude to my family for their unconditional support during the writing process. I would like to give special recognition to my sister, Tara Parandeh; my parents, Mansoureh Tahabaz and Mohammadreza Parandeh; and my partner, Cherry Waller.

I'm grateful to the friends, colleagues, collaborators, and ADSP folks who helped cultivate a supportive environment. Thank you to David Foster, Ross Witeszczak, Amy Bull, Zine Eddine, Joe Rowe, Jonathan Davies, Aneta Blazyczek, Giulia Scardovi,

Maddy Clements, Sarah Davies, Evelina Kireilyte, Khaleel Syed, Rob Foster, Mai Do, Bogdan Bija, Nicholas Rawitscher Torres, Snehan Sighat, and Leon Watson.

Specifically, I would like to thank my mentor, David Foster, author of *Generative Deep Learning* (O'Reilly), for inspiring me to write my own book. His book was a source of learning and inspiration on generative AI during the drafting process. In addition, I'm grateful to the close friends who played a role in shaping my career: Lee Dalchow, Isaac Cleave, and Rabah Tahraoui.

Working with O'Reilly was incredible. Special thanks to my wonderful editors Rita Fernando and Melissa Potter for their support during the writing process, enthusiasm, and excellent feedback. I could not have asked for better editors. Thanks to Clare Laylock for preparing early release chapters and fixing formatting issues during the process. Seeing these chapters on the O'Reilly platform and receiving positive feedback from readers was a significant motivator with writing. Also thanks to Nicole Butterfield and Amanda Quinn for their help in realizing this book and kick-starting the project.

Lastly, massive thanks to my technical reviewers, David Foster, Joe Rowe, and Julien Brendel, for their meticulous and detailed run-through of the book. Each reviewer contributed a different perspective to ensure all inconsistencies, inaccuracies, and gaps were addressed. Without their input, the quality of this book would have suffered.

## PART I

Developing AI Services

This part covers a gentle introduction to GenAI concepts and FastAPI with the necessary steps to set up a FastAPI project that will power your generative service. You will integrate various generative models into your FastAPI app and expose endpoints to interact with these models.

## CHAPTER 1

Introduction

Chapter Goals

In this chapter, you will learn about:

- Generative AI (GenAI) and its use cases
- Why GenAI services will power future applications
- The barriers to broader adoption of AI services
- How to build a GenAI service
- Why FastAPI is a good choice for building GenAI services
- The overview of the capstone project

By the end of this chapter, you should be able to identify the role of GenAI within the roadmap of your own applications and its associated challenges.

What Is Generative AI?

Generative AI is a subset of machine learning that focuses on creating new content using a model trained on a dataset. The *trained model*, which is a mathematical model representing patterns and distributions in the training data, can produce new data that is similar to the training dataset.

To illustrate these concepts, imagine training a model on a dataset containing images of butterflies. The model learns the complex relationships between pixels in images of butterflies. Once trained, you can sample from the model to create novel images of butterflies that didn't exist in the original dataset. These images will contain similarities with the original images of butterflies yet remain different.

> Using a trained generative model to create new content based on patterns learned from the training data is known as inference.

Figure 1-1 shows the full process.

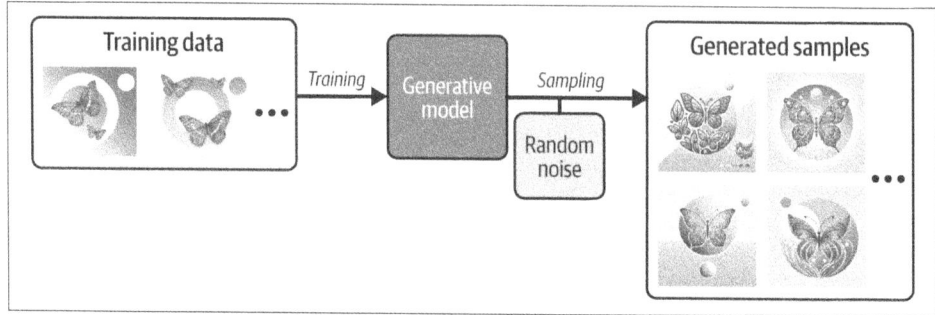

Figure 1-1. A generative model trained to create new photos of butterflies

Since we don't want to generate the same outputs as the training dataset, we add some random noise during the sampling process to create variations in the outputs. This random component that affects the generated samples makes the generative model *probabilistic*. It distinguishes a generative model from a fixed calculation function that as an example averages pixels of multiple images to create new ones.

When working on GenAI solutions, you may come across six families of generative models, including:[1]

Variational autoencoders (VAEs)
VAEs learn to encode data into a low-dimensional mathematical space (called a *latent space*—see Figure 1-2) to decode back to the original space when generating new data.

Generative adversarial networks (GANs)
GANs are a pair of neural networks (a discriminator and a generator) battling each other to learn patterns in the data during training. Once trained, you can use the generator to create new data.

Autoregressive models
These models learn to predict the next value in a sequence based on previous values.

---

1 You can learn more about these models in *Generative Deep Learning* by David Foster (O'Reilly, 2024).

Normalizing flow models

These models transform simple probability distributions (patterns in data) to more complex ones for generating new data.

Energy-based models (EBMs)

EBMs are based on statistical mechanics. They define an energy function that assigns lower energy to observed data and higher energy to other configurations, and they are trained to differentiate between these configurations.

Diffusion models

Diffusers learn to add noise to training data to create a pure noisy distribution. Then learn to incrementally remove noise from sampled points (from the pure noisy distribution) to generate new data.

Transformers

Transformers can model large sequential data like corpora of texts with extremely efficient parallelism. These models use a *self-attention* mechanism to capture the context and relationships between elements in a sequence. Given a new sequence, they can use the learned patterns to generate new sequences of data. Transformers are commonly used as *language models* to process and generate textual data as they better handle long-range relationships in text. OpenAI's ChatGPT is a language model referred to as a *generative pretrained transformer* (GPT).

Latent Space

VAEs can embed information into *latent spaces*, which are compressed mathematical versions of the input data containing the most important information needed to reconstruct the original input. The model's encoding layers compress/encode high-dimensional data in lower-dimensional space (i.e., latent space) for more efficient data manipulation, analysis, and reconstruction, as shown in Figure 1-2.

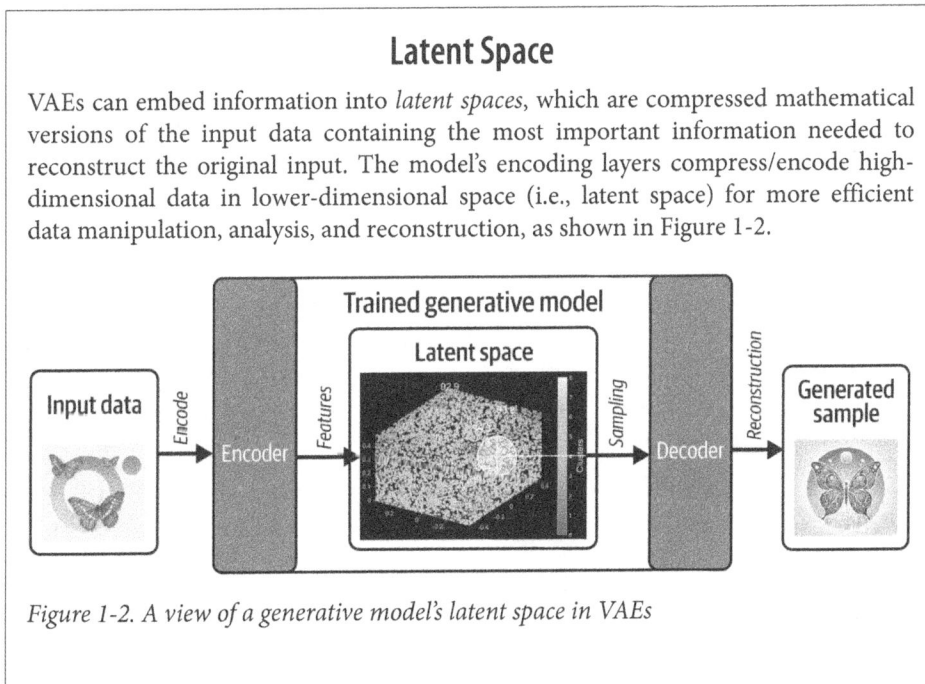

Figure 1-2. A view of a generative model's latent space in VAEs

Using this latent space, you can navigate this space (using some input data like a text or image prompt) to produce new content that never existed in the model's training data. Under the hood, the sampling process selects a data point to reconstruct that interpolates concepts in the learned information of the latent space.

One fact to note is that these generative models often can process only certain types of data or *modalities* such as text, images, audio, video, point clouds, or even 3D meshes. Some are even *multimodal,* like OpenAI's GPT-4o, that can natively process multiple modalities like text, audio, and images.

To explain these GenAI concepts, I will use an image generation use case as an example. Other use cases include language models being used as chatbots or document parsers, audio models used for music generation or speech synthesis, and video generators for creating AI avatars and deepfakes. You may have witnessed more than a handful of other use cases with hundreds more yet to be uncovered.

One fact remains for certain. GenAI services will power future applications. Let's see why.

Why Generative AI Services Will Power Future Applications

We use computers to automate solutions to everyday problems.

In the past, automating a process required manually coding business rules, which could be time-consuming and tedious, especially for complex problems such as spam detection when relying on handwritten rules. Nowadays, you can train a model to understand the nuances of the business process. Once trained, this model can outperform handwritten rules implemented as application code, resulting in replacing such rules.

This shift toward model-based automation has given rise to AI-powered applications in the market, solving a range of problems including price optimization, product recommendation, or weather forecasting. As part of this wave, generative models emerged that differed from other types of AI in their ability to produce multimedia content (text, code, images, audio, video, etc.), whereas traditional AI is more about prediction and classification.

As a software engineer, I believe these models have certain capabilities that will influence the development roadmap of future applications. They can:

- Facilitate the creative process
- Suggest contextually relevant solutions
- Personalize user experience

- Minimize delay in resolving customer queries
- Act as an interface to complex systems
- Automate manual administrative tasks
- Scale and democratize content generation

Let's look at each capability in more detail.

Facilitating the Creative Process

Mastering skills and acquiring knowledge are cognitively demanding. You can spend a long time studying and practicing something before you form your own original ideas for producing novel and creative content like an essay or a design.

During the creative process, you may have the writer's block—difficulties with imagining and visualizing scenes, navigating ideas, creating narratives, constructing arguments, and understanding relationships between concepts. The creative process requires a deep understanding of the purpose behind your creation and a clear awareness of sources for inspiration and ideas you intend to draw upon. Often, when you sit down to make something new like an original essay, you may find it difficult to start from a blank screen or piece of paper. You will need to have done extensive research on a topic to have formed your own opinions and the narrative you want to write about.

The creative process also applies to design, not just writing. For instance, when designing a user interface, you may need a few hours of design research by browsing design websites for ideas on the color palette, layout, and composition before you originate a design. Creating something truly original by looking at a blank canvas can feel like climbing a wall bare-handed. You will need inspiration and have to follow a creative process.

Producing original content requires creativity. Therefore, it is an extraordinary feat for humans to produce original ideas from scratch. New ideas and creations are often based on inspirations, connecting ideas and adaptations of other works. Creativity involves complex, nonlinear thinking and emotional intelligence that makes it challenging to replicate or automate with rules and algorithms. Yet it is now possible to mimic creativity with generative AI.

GenAI tools can help you to streamline the process by bridging various ideas and concepts from an extensive repository of human knowledge. Using these tools, you can stumble upon novel ideas that required understanding a large body of interconnected knowledge and the comprehension of the interactions between several concepts. Additionally, these tools can assist you with imagining hard-to-visualize scenes or concepts. To illustrate the point, try imagining the scene described in Example 1-1.

Example 1-1. Description of a scene that is hard to visualize for humans

```
An endless biomechanical forest where trees have metallic roots and glowing neon
leaves, each tree trunk embedded with rotating gears and digital screens
displaying alien glyphs; the ground is a mix of crystalline soil and pulsating
organic veins, while a surreal sky shifts between a digital glitch matrix and a
shimmering aurora made of liquid light.
```

This can be quite difficult to imagine unless you've been accustomed to imagining such concepts. However, with the help of a generative model, anyone can now visualize and communicate challenging concepts to others.

Providing the scene description in Example 1-1 to an image generation tool such as DALL-E 3 (OpenAI) (*https://oreil.ly/Z80Qm*) produces an output shown in Figure 1-3.

Figure 1-3. An image produced by DALL-E 3 (https://oreil.ly/Z80Qm)

It is fascinating to see how these GenAI tools can help you visualize and communicate challenging concepts. These tools allow you to expand your imagination and nudge your creativity. When you feel stuck or find it difficult to communicate or imagine novel ideas, you can turn to these tools for help.

In the future, I can see applications including similar features to help users in their creative process. If your applications give several suggestions for the user to build upon, it can help them get onboarded and build momentum.

Suggesting Contextually Relevant Solutions

Often you will find yourself facing niche problems that don't have a previously established solution. Solutions to these problems aren't obvious and require a lot of research, trial and error, consultation with other experts, and reading. Developers are familiar with this situation, as finding relevant solutions to programming problems can be tricky and not straightforward.

This is because developers must solve problems with a certain context in mind. A problem can't be defined without a thorough description of "circumstances," and the "situation" arises in the *context*.

Essentially, *context* narrows down the potential solutions to a problem.

The Role of Context-Rich Prompts in Generative Models

When you prompt a model with only a few keywords, you will get a response that may or may not satisfy your *intent*. To explain why, let's look at a search engine and how it works.

Google has invested a lot of capital into building a search engine that can infer your intent based on the few keywords you enter into the search bar. The search results then show you pages that closely match your intent.

The fewer keywords you provide, the harder it is for the search engine to infer what you want and to show you relevant results. For instance, if you search for "ties," the search engine has to make assumptions and infer that your intent was to shop for ties (clothing) versus learning about ties. If you instead search for "trinity tie" or "types of tie," there is an educational intent in your search query, and Google can show the appropriate results.

This is also true for generative models. When you provide little to no context as a prompt to the model, the model has to infer your intent and produce something highly likely correlated with your intent. A generic response would satisfy this type of query the most. And, that is why you would often get a generic output to a generic short-tailed keyword that consists of a small sequence of words.

The more detailed and contextually rich your queries are, the better and more relevant the responses from your model will be. That is why context-rich prompts are crucial to getting relevant, specific, and high-quality results when working with generative models.

With search engines, you look for sources of information with a few keywords that may or may not contain a relevant solution. When developers search for solutions, they paste error logs into Google and are directed to programming Q&A websites like Stack Overflow (*https://stackoverflow.com*). Developers must then hope to find someone who has encountered the same problem in the same context and that a solution has been provided. This method of finding solutions to programming problems is not very efficient. You may not always find the solution you're looking for as a developer on these websites.

Developers are now turning to generative AI to solve programming issues. By providing a prompt that describes the context of a problem, the AI can generate potential solutions. Even better, code editor integrations go a long way in providing this context to the language models, something not possible when searching in Google or Stack Overflow. These AI models can then generate solutions that are contextually relevant and based on a learned knowledge base sourced from online forums and several Q&A websites. With the proposed solution(s), you can then decide if any is appropriate.

Because of this, using GenAI coding tools is often quicker than searching for solutions on online forums and websites. Even the programming Q&A site, Stack Overflow (*https://oreil.ly/nOX_K*), has attributed an above-average traffic decrease (~14%) to developers trialing the GPT-4 language model and code generator after its release. This figure may be higher as several site power users have commented on the company's blog post that they feel user activity on the site has reduced dramatically. In fact, there has been a reported ~60% decline in questions asked and upvote activity on the site (*https://oreil.ly/P6Kur*), at the time of writing, when compared to 2018.

In any case, Stack Overflow still expects traffic to rise and fall in the future with the introduction of GenAI coding tools democratizing coding, expanding the developer community, and creating new programming challenges. The power of Q&A sites lies not just in finding the answer but also in understanding the surrounding discussions and the importance of referencing sources.[2] As a result, these sites will remain an invaluable resource to developers due to their communities of experts and human-curated content upholding trust in the correctness and quality of answers or solutions.[3]

Personalizing the User Experience

Customers and users of modern software expect a certain level of personalization and interactivity when they use modern applications.

By integrating generative models such as a language model into existing applications, you can innovate how users interact with the system. Instead of the traditional UI interaction where you have to click into several screens, you can converse in natural

---

2 Recent GenAI tools can now provide source references alongside the solution (e.g., phind.com).

3 Stack Overflow's 2024 Developer Survey (*https://oreil.ly/odPkB*) of 65,000 coders found that 72% of developers are favorable toward AI tools, but only 43% trust the accuracy of those tools.

text with a chatbot to ask for the information you seek or an action to be performed on your behalf. For example, when browsing a travel planning site, you can describe your ideal holiday and have the chatbot prepare an itinerary for you based on the platform's access to airlines, accommodation providers, and the database of package holiday deals. Or, if you've already booked a holiday, you can ask for sightseeing recommendations based on itinerary details from your account data. The chatbot can then describe the results back to you and ask for your feedback.

These language models can act as a personal assistant by asking relevant questions until they map your preferences and unique needs to a product catalog for generating personalized recommendations. These virtual assistant can understand your intent and suggest choices relevant to your situation. If you don't like the suggestions, you can provide some feedback to refine any suggestions to your liking.

In education, these GenAI models can be used to describe or visualize challenging concepts tailored to each student's learning preferences and abilities.

In gaming and virtual reality (VR), GenAI can be used to construct dynamic environments and worlds based on user interactions with the application. For instance, in role-playing games (RPGs), you can produce narratives and character stories on the fly, based on users' decisions and dialogue choices in real time using a baked-in large language model. This process creates a unique experience for the gamer and users of these applications.

Minimizing Delay in Resolving Customer Queries

Aside from personalized user assistants, businesses often need support in handling a large volume of customer service queries. Due to this volume, customers often have to wait in long queues or several business days before they hear back from businesses. Furthermore, as businesses grow in operational complexity and customers, resolving customer queries in a timely manner can become more expensive and require extensive staff training.

GenAI can streamline customer service processes for both the customers and the businesses. Customers can now chat or go on a call with a language model capable of accessing databases and relevant sources to resolve queries in a matter of minutes, not days. As customers describe their issues, the model can address these queries in accordance with business policies and can direct customers to relevant resources when necessary.

While traditional chatbots often relied on a set of handcrafted rules and predefined scripts, GenAI-powered chatbots can better:

- Understand conversation context
- Consider user preferences

- Form dynamic and personalized responses
- Accept and adjust to user feedback
- Handle unexpected queries, in particular over historical or larger conversations

These factors enable GenAI chatbots to have a more natural and varied interaction with the customer. These bots will be the first point of contact for customers who want their queries swiftly answered before cases are escalated to human agents. As a customer, you may also prefer talking to one of these GenAI chatbots first if it means avoiding long queues and achieving a quick resolution.

These examples only scratch the surface of all possible features that can be integrated into existing applications. This flexibility and agility of generative models opens up many possibilities for novel applications in the future.

Acting as an Interface to Complex Systems

Many people these days still face problems when interacting with complex systems such as databases or developer tools. Nondevelopers may need to access information or perform tasks without having the necessary skills to execute commands on these complex systems. LLMs and GenAI models can act as the interface between these systems and their users.

Users can provide a prompt in natural language, and GenAI models can write and execute queries on complex systems. For instance, an investment manager can ask a GenAI bot to aggregate the performance of the portfolio in the company's database without having to submit requests for reports to be produced by specialists. Another example is Photoshop's new generative fill tool that generates image layers and performs context-informed edits for users who have not mastered Photoshop's various tools.

Already, several AI startups have developed GenAI applications in which users interact with a language model in natural language to perform tool actions. Using language models, these startups are replacing complex workflows and clicking around in multiple UI screens.

While GenAI models can act as an interface to complex systems like databases or APIs, developers will still need to implement guardrails and security measures, as you will learn in Chapter 9 on AI security. These integrations will need to be handled carefully to avoid malicious queries and attack vectors via generative models on these systems.

Automating Manual Administrative Tasks

Across many large and long-standing companies, there are often several teams performing manual administrative tasks that are less visible to the front-house teams and their customers.

A typical administrative task involves manually processing documents with complex layouts, like invoices, purchase orders, and remittance slips. Until recently, these tasks have remained mostly manual since each document's layout and information arrangement can be visually unique, requiring human validation or sign-off. On top of this, any developed software to automate these processes could be fragile and held to a high level of accuracy and correctness, even in edge cases.

Now, language and other generative models can enable some parts of these manual processes to be further automated and enhanced for higher accuracy. If the existing automations fail to perform due to edge cases or changes in the process, language models can step in to check the outputs against some criteria and fill in the gaps or flag items for manual review.

Scaling and Democratizing Content Generation

People love new content and are always on the lookout for new ideas to explore. Writers can now research and ideate when writing a blog post with the help of GenAI tools. By conversing with a model, they can brainstorm ideas and generate outlines.

The productivity boost is enormous for content generation. You no longer have to perform low-level cognitive tasks of summarizing research or rewording sentences yourself. The time it takes to produce a quality blog post is slashed from days to hours. Instead of starting from scratch, you can focus on the outline, flow, and structure of the content before using GenAI to fill in the gaps. When you struggle with sequencing the right words for clarity and brevity, GenAI tools can shine. However, what makes a piece of writing interesting often isn't the content, but the style of writing and flow.

Many businesses have already started using these tools to explore ideas and draft documents, proposals, social media, and blog posts.

Overall, these are several reasons why I believe more developers will be integrating GenAI features into their applications in the future. The technology is still in its infancy, and there are still many challenges to overcome before GenAI can be widely adopted.

How to Build a Generative AI Service

Generative models need access to rich contextual information to provide more accurate and relevant responses. In some cases, they may also need access to tools to perform actions on the user's behalf—for instance, to place an order by running a custom function. As a result, you may need to build APIs around generative models (as wrappers) to take care of integrations with external data sources (i.e., databases, APIs, etc.) and controlling user access to the model.

To build these API wrappers, you can place generative models behind an HTTP web server and implement the required integrations, controls, and routers as shown in Figure 1-4.

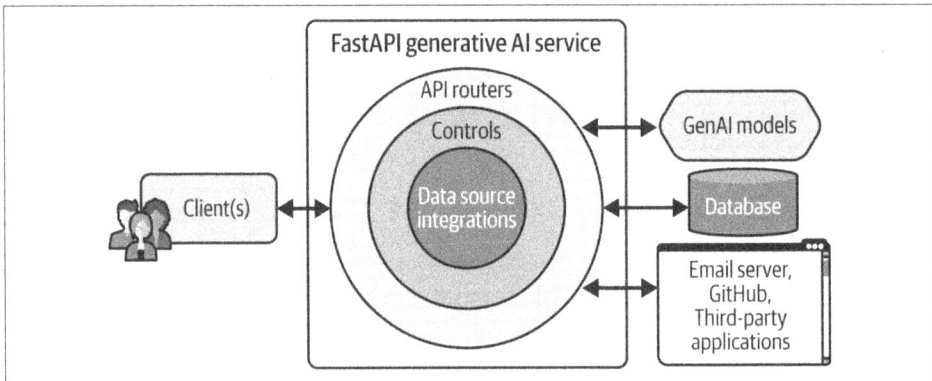

Figure 1-4. FastAPI web server with data source integrations that serve a generative model

The web server controls access to the data sources and the model. Under the hood, your server can query the database and external services to enrich user prompts with relevant information for generating more relevant outputs. Once outputs are generated, the control layer can then sanity-check while the routers return final responses to the user.

> You can even go one step further by configuring a language model to construct an instruction for another system and pass it off to another component to execute those commands such as to interact with a database or make an API call.

In summary, the web server acts as a crucial intermediary that manages data access, enriches user prompts, and quality controls the generated outputs before routing them to users. Alongside serving generative models to users, this layered approach enhances the relevance and reliability of responses from generative models.

Why Build Generative AI Services with FastAPI?

Generative AI services require performant web frameworks as backend engines powering event-driven services and applications. FastAPI, one of the most popular web frameworks in Python, can compete (*https://oreil.ly/LmEg7*) in performance with other popular web frameworks such as *gin (Golang)* or *express (Node.js)*, while holding onto the richness of Python's deep learning ecosystem. Non-Pythonic frameworks lack this direct integration required for working with a generative AI model within one service.

Within the Python ecosystem, there are several core web frameworks for building API services. The most popular options include:

Django
> A full-stack framework that comes with batteries included. It is a mature framework with a large community and a lot of support.

Flask
> A micro web framework that is lightweight and extensible.

FastAPI
> A modern web framework built for speed and performance. It is a full-stack framework that comes with batteries included.

FastAPI, despite its recent entry into the Python web framework space, has gained traction and popularity. As of this writing, FastAPI is the fastest growing Python web framework in terms of package downloads and the second most popular web framework on GitHub. It is on the trajectory to become more popular than Django based on its growing count of GitHub Stars (*https://oreil.ly/8fRO2*) (around 80,000 at the time of writing).

Among the frameworks mentioned, Flask leads in number of package downloads due to its reputation, community support, and extensibility. However, as a micro web framework, it ships with a limited number of default features, such as out-of-the-box support for schema validation.

Django is also popular for building APIs (via Django Rest Framework) and monolith applications following the model-view-controller (MVC) design pattern. But it has less mature support for asynchronous APIs with potential performance limitations, plus can add complexity and overhead to building lightweight APIs.

Compared to other web frameworks, FastAPI provides several features out of the box such as data validation, type safety, automatic documentation, and a built-in web server. Because of this, developers familiar with Python may be switching from opinionated and older frameworks like Django to FastAPI. I assume the exceptional developer experience, development freedom, excellent performance, and recent AI model-serving support via lifecycle events may be contributing to this.

This book covers the implementation details of developing generative AI services that can autonomously perform actions and interact with external services, all powered by the FastAPI web framework.

To learn the relevant concepts, I will be guiding you through a capstone project that you can work on as you read through the book. Let's take a look.

What Prevents the Adoption of Generative AI Services

Organizations face several challenges when adopting generative AI services. There are issues related to the inaccuracy, relevance, quality, and consistency of GenAI outputs. In addition, there are concerns about data privacy, cybersecurity, and potential abuse and misuse of the models if used in production. As a result, companies don't want to give full autonomy to these models yet. There is a hesitation in connecting them directly with sensitive systems like internal databases or payment systems.

Integrating the AI service with existing systems, such as internal databases, web interfaces, and external APIs, can pose a challenge. This integration can be difficult due to compatibility issues, the need for technical expertise, potential disruption of existing processes, malicious attempts on these systems, and similar concerns about data security and privacy.

Companies that want to use the service for customer-facing applications would want consistency and relevance in the model's responses and to ensure outputs are not offensive or inappropriate.

There are also limitations to producing original and high-quality content with these generative models. As covered before, these GenAI tools effectively bridge various ideas and concepts together within certain domains. But they can't produce totally unseen or novel ideas; rather, they recombine and rephrase existing information in a way that appears novel. Furthermore, they follow common patterns during generation, which can be generic, repetitive, and uninspiring to use out of the box. Finally, they may produce plausible-sounding outputs that are entirely incorrect and made up, not based on facts or reality.

Cases where GenAI models produce made-up facts and incorrect information are referred to as *hallucinations*.

The tendency of these models to hallucinate prevents their adoption in sensitive use cases that require highly accurate outputs such as medical diagnosis, legal advisory, and automated examinations.

Some challenges—such as data privacy and security issues—can be solved with software engineering best practices, which you will read more about in this book. Solutions to other challenges require optimizing inputs to the models or fine-tuning these models (adjusting their parameters through new examples in a particular use case) to improve the relevance, quality, coherence, and consistency of the outputs.

Overview of the Capstone Project

In this book, I will lead you through building a generative AI service using FastAPI as the underlying web framework.

The service will:

- Integrate with multiple models including a language model for text generation and chat, an audio model for text to speech, and a Stable Diffusion model for image generation
- Generate real-time responses to user queries as text, audio, or image
- Use the RAG technique to "talk" to uploaded documents using a vector database
- Scrape the web and communicate with internal databases, external systems, and APIs to gather sufficient information when responding to queries
- Record conversation histories in a relational database
- Authenticate users via token-based credentials and GitHub identity login
- Restrict responses based on user permission via authorization guards
- Provide sufficient protections against misuse and abuse using guardrails

As the focus of this book is on building API services, you will learn to use the Python Streamlit package and simple HTML for developing UIs. In real-world applications, you may interface your generative AI services with custom UIs built with libraries such as React or frameworks like Next.js for modularity, extensibility, and scalability.

Summary

In this chapter, you learned about the concept of generative AI and how it can create data across various modalities like text, audio, video, etc., using learned patterns in its training data. You also saw several practical examples and use cases of this technology and why most future applications will be powered by GenAI capabilities.

You also learned how GenAI can facilitate the creative process, eliminate intermediaries, personalize user experiences, and democratize access to complex systems and content generation. Further, you were introduced to several challenges preventing widespread adoption of GenAI alongside several solutions. Finally, you learned more about the GenAI API service that you will build with the FastAPI web framework as you follow the code examples in this book.

In the next chapter, you will learn about FastAPI, which will enable you to implement your own GenAI services.

## CHAPTER 2

Getting Started with FastAPI

Chapter Goals

In this chapter, you will learn about:

- What FastAPI is
- How to get started with creating your own FastAPI project
- FastAPI features and advantages
- How to structure FastAPI projects
- The onion/layered software design pattern
- Comparison of FastAPI to other frameworks
- FastAPI limitations
- Setting up a managed Python environment and tooling for your project

By the end of this chapter, you should feel comfortable using the FastAPI web framework, setting up FastAPI projects, and articulating your tech stack decisions for building GenAI services.

Introduction to FastAPI

FastAPI (*https://oreil.ly/2xcoR*) is an asynchronous gateway interface (ASGI) web framework that enables you to build lean APIs and backend web servers. Being an ASGI framework means that it can leverage concurrency to process web requests. It is fast comparable to modern frameworks (*https://oreil.ly/tgwEJ*) but also ships with strong Swagger/OpenAPI integrations for auto-documentation (*https://oreil.ly/WlwOC*), alongside built-in data validation and serialization features via Pydantic (*https://oreil.ly/5-EmU*).[1] Effectively, FastAPI is a wrapper over the Starlette framework (*https://oreil.ly/tyKtQ*), built by Encode, the same people who built the Django REST framework. It is light-weight and has a similar development experience.

Before we discuss FastAPI in more detail, let's set up your development environment with a running FastAPI application.

Setting Up Your Development Environment

Throughout the rest of this chapter, I will guide you through the installation process of FastAPI and its essential dependencies, enabling you to set up a basic web server. We will also install a selection of formatters, loggers, and linters that you can set up to enhance your development workflow.

> Code examples in this book have been tested against Python 3.11. Running code examples with other Python versions may result in issues. Furthermore, some deployment environments and package dependencies may not support the latest versions of Python.

You can now get started with setting up your FastAPI project.

Installing Python, FastAPI, and Required Packages

If you're on Windows, you can use conda to create a virtual Python environment:

```
conda create -n genaiservice python=3.11
conda activate genaiservice
```

If you're on a macOS or a Linux system, you can create a virtual Python environment using venv:

```
$ python3 -m venv .venv
```

venv creates your virtual environment in the .venv folder that you can activate by using this:

```
$ source .venv/bin/activate
```

Once the environment is activated, you can install the core packages needed to run the FastAPI server and serve requests from the OpenAI API:

```
$ pip install "fastapi[standard]" uvicorn openai
```

---

1 Large parts of Pydantic v2's data validation logic have been rewritten in Rust for significant performance improvements.

The uvicorn package is the bare-bones web server that FastAPI runs on. `fastapi` will also install its dependency packages such as `starlette` and `pydantic`.

Creating a Simple FastAPI Web Server

Once FastAPI and its dependencies are installed, you are ready to start your own web server. To create a simple web server that has one endpoint in FastAPI, all you have to write is 15 lines of code. Create a *main.py* file in the root of your directory, as shown in Example 2-1.

> For simplicity, Example 2-1 uses the OpenAI API. To run the code, you can get an API key from OpenAI (*https://oreil.ly/SZsuD*), which requires a credit card. However, rest assured that other code examples in this book will use open source models as much as possible.

Example 2-1. Starter code for a simple FastAPI web server serving GPT-4o requests

```
# main.py
from fastapi import FastAPI
from openai import OpenAI

app = FastAPI() ❶
openai_client = OpenAI(api_key="your_api_key") ❷

@app.get("/")
def root_controller():
    return {"status": "healthy"}

@app.get("/chat") ❸
def chat_controller(prompt: str = "Inspire me"): ❸
    response = openai_client.chat.completions.create( ❹
        model="gpt-4o",
        messages=[
            {"role": "system", "content": "You are a helpful assistant."},
            {"role": "user", "content": prompt},
        ],
    )
    statement = response.choices[0].message.content
    return {"statement": statement} ❺
```

❶ Create a FastAPI application object.

❷ You will need an API key (*https://oreil.ly/PP0nN*) to use the OpenAI API.

❸ Use the @app.get decorator to create a GET endpoint on the /chat path.

---

❹ Make an API call to the OpenAI Completions API to generate a response from the gpt-4o model.

❺ Any data returned by the decorated function will be returned when you hit the root endpoint.

You can now start the server using the fastapi dev command, as shown here:[2]

```
$ fastapi dev

>> server   Server started at http://127.0.0.1:8000
>> server   Documentation at http://127.0.0.1:8000/docs

>> INFO   Uvicorn running on http://127.0.0.1:8000 (Press CTRL+C to quit)
>> INFO   Started reloader process [4172] using WatchFiles
>> INFO   Started server process [11316]
>> INFO   Waiting for application startup.
>> INFO   Application startup complete.
```

Your web server is now accessible from http://127.0.0.1:8000 with two exposed endpoints at the root / and /chat routes.

If you visit http://127.0.0.1:8000 in your browser, you should see the {"status": "healthy"} message. Also, when you visit http://127.0.0.1:8000/chat, you should see an inspirational message from OpenAI's gpt-4o model.

Congratulations. You now have a fully working bare-bones generative AI service.

> As you started the server in a dev model using the fastapi dev command, a file watcher process is listening for changes in your project and auto-updates the service as you update the code.

Feel free to change the default prompt and refresh the browser to see your changes reflected in real time.

The app object—which is created from the FastAPI class—converts your Python function with a decorator into a Hypertext Transfer Protocol (HTTP) endpoint. You can trigger both endpoints by sending an HTTP request.

Under the hood, the uvicorn package takes the app object and starts a web server running your FastAPI service.

---

2 The fastapi dev command searches your project directories for a FastAPI app object. If you're having issues starting your FastAPI server, consult its documentation using fastapi dev --help.

In addition to getting a simple web server out of the box, you also get API documentation automatically generated for you. The documentation follows the OpenAPI standard and includes an `openapi.json` specification of your web service and a Swagger documentation page built from the same specification file.

You can access the auto-generated docs page by going to the `/docs` route of your server via `http://localhost:8000/docs`; you'll see a page similar to Figure 2-1.

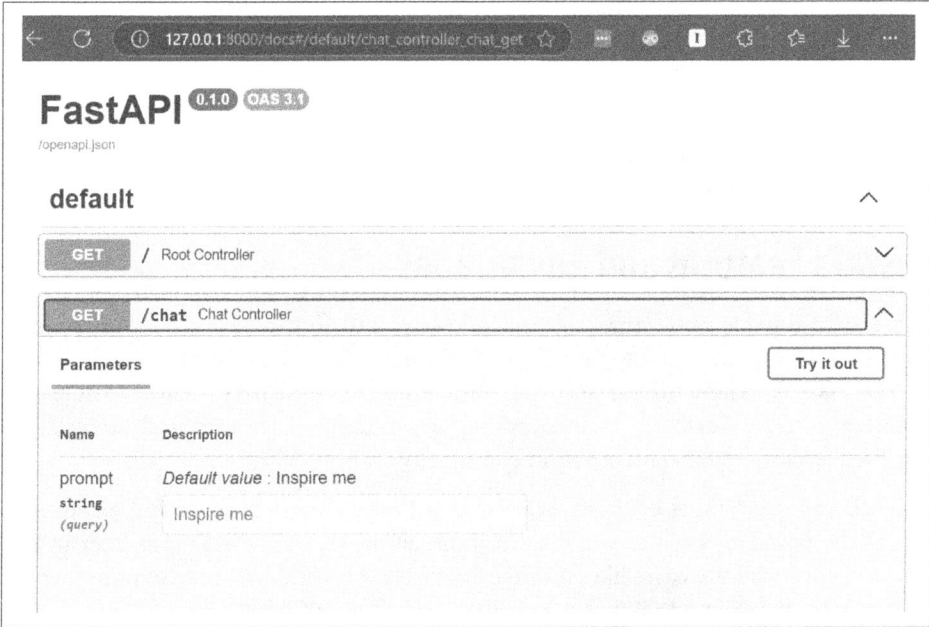

Figure 2-1. Auto-generated Swagger documentation of the API

From the Swagger docs page, you can send requests to your API to quickly test an endpoint. The docs page will also take care of sending the correct request headers, methods, and parameters.

What I love about the Swagger docs page is that you can quickly iterate over various implementations using the user interface, which can be quicker than writing tests when iterating over the design of your APIs. However, this does not replace the traditional testing that can check every endpoint when you make changes. As your application grows, it is still worth writing tests. Once your endpoint signatures are further established, you can write `pytest` tests to systematically test your web service from end to end.

In addition to auto-documentation, FastAPI ships with auto-serialization and validation of data. In Example 2-1, we returned a dictionary in the root controller as you visited `http://localhost:8000`. There is a bit of magic that must happen for data to show up in your browser. The data must first be serialized from a Python object such as a dictionary or a list into a JavaScript Object Notation (JSON) string first. Afterward, it's transferred over the web and deserialized back into a JavaScript object by your browser client once transmission is completed. This is effectively how applications around the web "talk" to each other.

> Serialization is required when using HTTP for data transmissions, as only text or binary data can be transferred via HTTP.

Now that you have a working FastAPI server, let's look at FastAPI's features and benefits that you can use in your project.

FastAPI Features and Advantages

You want a suitable web framework that allows you to effortlessly create your generative AI services, without any unnecessary struggles. This framework should include all the essential elements for security, authentication, and performance, while still granting you the flexibility to incorporate any additional features and integrations required as your application grows in complexity.

FastAPI can meet most of these criteria, as it hosts several features and advantages out of the box. However, as you'll learn more about FastAPI limitations later in this chapter, advanced use cases like resource-intensive AI workloads may require specialized web frameworks or solutions, as will be discussed in Chapter 3.

For now, let's review FastAPI's features and benefits before discussing its limitations in the context of building generative AI services.

Inspired by Flask Routing Pattern

In both Flask and FastAPI, you can create any route by decorating a function with a specialized decorator. You can then configure the routes to accept and validate headers, cookies, body, path, and query parameters to support your implementation.

Handling Asynchronous and Synchronous Operations

When building services, your service must be able to handle multiple requests by several users to increase usage efficiency as demand scales. FastAPI can seamlessly handle both synchronous and asynchronous functions in your application (*https://oreil.ly/gNYMg*) to enable concurrency from the get-go.

As we will discuss in detail in Chapter 5, if you define an asynchronous route using `async def`, FastAPI will run it on the main thread on the main event loop. On the other hand, if you define a synchronous route (not declared with the `async` keyword), FastAPI will run it on a *thread worker* for handling concurrent workloads.

> There is additional overhead to running threaded operations compared to running them asynchronously. Therefore, having many synchronous routes can still limit the scalability of your application.

As a result, concurrent requests won't block the main server thread. This is particularly useful when dealing with input/output operations, such as querying databases, exchanging data with a graphical processing units (GPU),[3] or making HTTP requests.

Built-In Support for Background Tasks

You can build routes capable of handling long-running tasks (e.g., sending emails) without the need of external libraries (e.g., `celery`). FastAPI includes a background tasks feature (*https://oreil.ly/aO6ml*)[4] for working with systems that need time to process data but you don't want them to delay returning the responses to requests.

Not all tasks can be responded to within the patience tolerance of your users. You do not want to keep them waiting while the process is continuing to finish. You can hand off the long-running operation to a background task running on a separate thread, after you respond to the client. As a response, you can then let clients know that your service has accepted and queued their request to process it in the background.

As an example, in GenAI services you can use background tasks to process large uploaded documents into a vector database without blocking the server. This allows the server to handle other requests while the document processing happens in the background.

You'll learn how to build such a system in Chapter 5.

Custom Middleware and CORS Support

FastAPI enables you to add middleware components (*https://oreil.ly/uvlLC*) to your app router to intercept the communication between your API endpoints and the clients. Each middleware, sitting in front of your endpoints, allows you to access the request and response objects to modify them as needed. You can add logic around

---

3 To perform model inference

4 Coming from the Starlette framework

how requests should be processed before they're handed off to the route handlers. Once the response is generated, you can then perform operations on the response—such as modifying headers, logging operations, and setting cookies—before sending it off to the client.

A common pattern in backend development is to use middleware to add extra headers to a response (*https://oreil.ly/Yfsqg*), perform basic checks on incoming requests, support CORS requests (*https://oreil.ly/6u1dI*), log and monitor communications, and much more. You can even take advantage of third-party and custom middleware (*https://oreil.ly/AJKJt*).

Freedom to Customize Any Service Layer

There are times when you may want to break away from the limitations of your current web framework. FastAPI provides a solution to this by allowing you to define custom classes that inherit base classes of Starlette—the underlying web framework. For instance, you can override default exception handlers (*https://oreil.ly/qgvgO*), add custom ASGI middleware (*https://oreil.ly/1A8OD*), or even create custom responses (*https://oreil.ly/jLXUf*).

With the power of Pydantic or FastAPI's encoders (*https://oreil.ly/MJmqJ*), you can also effortlessly create your own custom serializers (*https://oreil.ly/UnzRk*) to adjust how datetime objects are handled.

This enables you to implement features according to your preferences without having to struggle against FastAPI.

Data Validation and Serialization

For applications that handle large amounts of data, it is important that the data you are about to process is clean and in a known format.

As the complexity of your service grows, you will want to perform data validation and serialization. In FastAPI, you can use Pydantic to automatically serialize common data types (e.g., lists, dictionaries, primitives) when returning them in API routes. You can also define your own Pydantic schemas for request and response data to perform stricter data validation.

For instance, you can validate a user's password on account creation to match your security policies, as shown in Example 2-2.

Example 2-2. Validating user passwords in FastAPI using a Pydantic schema

```python
# main.py
from pydantic import BaseModel, Field, EmailStr

class UserCreate(BaseModel):
    username: str
    password: str

    @validator('password') ❶
    def validate_password(cls, value):
        if len(value) < 8:
            raise ValueError('Password must be at least 8 characters long')
        if not any(char.isdigit() for char in value):
            raise ValueError('Password must contain at least one digit')
        if not any(char.isupper() for char in value):
            raise ValueError('Password must contain at least one uppercase letter')
        return value ❷

app = FastAPI()

@app.post("/users")
async def create_user_controller(user: UserCreate):
    return {"name": user.name, "message": "Account successfully created"}

...
```

❶ Define a Pydantic model with custom data validation on the `password` field.

❷ Raise a `ValueError` if any of the password policies are not met.

This enables you to catch, handle, and protect your services from data issues that are not captured by static type checkers like `mypy`.

Pydantic validators also allow you to validate more complex data types at runtime like emails, URLs, UUIDs, and more. Chapter 4 will go into more detail on how to perform data validation using Pydantic.

Rich Ecosystem of Plug-Ins

Plug-ins are Python packages that hook into FastAPI internals and existing features. They are similar to any other Python package you install and import into your scripts, and they require minimal configurations after installation. Integrating them means extending the functionalities of your service without having to deal with order of integrations or compatibility issues. You can also remove them without breaking your app.

Some well-known plug-ins include FastAPI Filters, Auth Users, Rate Limiting and several others, which you can view at the Awesome FastAPI GitHub repository (*https://oreil.ly/nKbvP*).

Automatic Documentation

With FastAPI, Swagger UI documentation is auto-generated for you to view and test any routes you create, as you saw in Figure 2-1. During development, having an interactive docs page allows for easier and faster debugging and prototyping of your routes until you build and maintain your own test suites.

As you build new endpoints, you may often want to revisit the /docs page to test them.

You can configure a redirect from the base URL / to the /docs endpoint to facilitate quicker access to the documentation page, as shown in Example 2-3.

Example 2-3. Setting up redirect to the auto-generated docs page

```
# main.py
from fastapi.responses import RedirectResponse

@app.get("/", include_in_schema=False) ❶
def docs_redirect_controller():
    return RedirectResponse(url="/docs", status_code=status.HTTP_303_SEE_OTHER) ❷
```

❶ Set up a handler for the base root handler, but don't include it in OpenAPI specifications and the documentation page.

❷ Return a redirect response to the /docs page with a redirection status code for the browsers to perform the redirect.

With Example 2-3 implemented, you can access the /docs page during local development whenever you visit the base URL / of the service.

In production, unless your API is public, disable this redirection and hide the /docs routes by default for enhanced security.

> If your API is publicly accessible in production, you may expose unsecured endpoints and sensitive information about your API. Therefore, it is best practice to turn off the documentation page (*https://oreil.ly/Dk45G*).
>
> Instead, you can show the /docs page explicitly on selected environments only.

For public APIs, you can set the root handler / to return your API version instead of redirecting to the /docs page.

Dependency Injection System

Another powerful component of FastAPI is its dependency injection system (*https:// oreil.ly/eAIwR*) based on a development pattern called *inversion of control*. Using this pattern, you break down a function into a series of functions that you inject into other functions as *dependencies*.

In addition to helping structure your application logic, dependencies can help you reduce duplication. They let you share and reuse logic across your API, reuse open database connections, enforce security such as authentication or authorization requirements, and much more.

For example, you can specify common query parameters across API routes (e.g., for pagination and filtering), as shown in Example 2-4.

Example 2-4. Reducing duplication using a pagination dependency

```
from fastapi import FastAPI, Depends

app = FastAPI()

def paginate(skip: int = 0, limit: int = 10):
    return {"skip": skip, "limit": limit}

@app.get("/messages")
def list_messages_controller(pagination: dict = Depends(paginate)):
    return ...  # filter and paginate results using pagination params

@app.get("/conversations")
def list_conversations_controller(pagination: dict = Depends(paginate)):
    return ...  # filter and paginate results using pagination params
```

In FastAPI, dependencies are also cached within *the context of a single request* to prevent duplicate computations. This means a dependency function is executed only once per request, and its result is reused for the duration of that request if needed again. However, in a new request, the dependency function is executed again.

Having to manage database connections or checking user credentials in every route handler is tedious and violates the *Don't Repeat Yourself* (DRY) principles of programming. Another great use case of the dependency injection system is when you create a database connection and want to reuse that connection to perform multiple fetch requests while processing a single request.

You can create dependencies for your route controller functions, as shown in Example 2-5.

Example 2-5. Dependency injection in FastAPI

```
from fastapi import FastAPI, Depends

def get_db(): ❶
    db = ... # create a database session
    try:
        yield db ❷
    finally:
        db.close() ❸

app = FastAPI()

@app.get("users/{email}/messages")
def get_current_user_messages(email, db = Depends(get_db)): ❹
    user = db.query(...) # db is reused
    messages = db.query(...) # db is reused
    return messages ❺
```

❶ Implement a function to create and manage a database session, which can be used as a dependency in route handlers.

❷ Yield the open database session, making it available for any function that depends on get_db.

❸ Close the database session after the request is processed, preventing resource leaks.

❹ Inject the get_db dependency into the route handler to create and reuse the same database session during the request lifecycle. FastAPI will also automatically expose parameters within dependencies on your endpoint.

❺ Reuse the injected database session to perform multiple database operations within a single request to return a user's messages.

As shown in Example 2-5, you can inject these dependencies into other functions by passing them as parameters to Depends() for FastAPI to evaluate and cache your function outputs.

Here you define a utility function for creating a database session and then use it as a dependency of the get_current_user_messages function to inject the created database session.

Hierarchical Dependency Graph

You can also have dependencies injected into other dependencies to create a *hierarchical dependency graph*, which is extremely useful for building cached authentication and authorization flows (*https://oreil.ly/i_xHr*), nested data retrieval logic, or complex decision trees when implementing your application's business logic.

As an example, you can reuse the same database session creation or user fetching functions across different parts of your API, as shown in Figure 2-2.

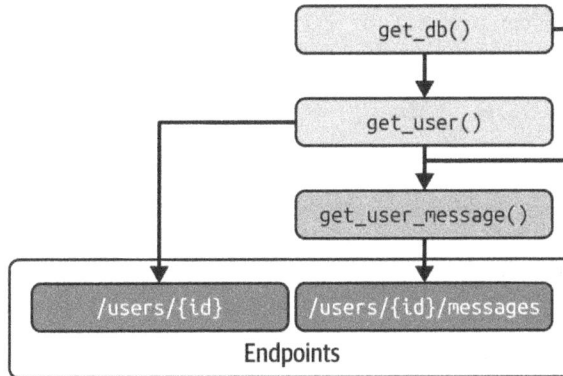

Figure 2-2. Dependency injection in FastAPI

In a hierarchical dependency graph, as shown in Figure 2-2, each dependency (and their subdependencies) can provide (inject) its results to another function that depends on it.

This dependency system is just one of many other features that ship with FastAPI that speed up and ease the process of building backend services.

Lifespan Events

FastAPI's lifespan events (*https://oreil.ly/Cn2DB*) are excellent for handling initialization and cleanup of your service when you need to set up resources that can be shared between requests.[5] During server startup, you can create database connection pools or load GenAI models into memory for reuse across requests. Afterward, before server shutdown, you can clean up by unloading AI models, closing connection pools, deleting temporary artifacts, and logging events.

---

5 FastAPI's new lifespan events replace the deprecated startup/shutdown events in older versions.

By using lifespan events, your FastAPI service performs long-running operations like model loading at the start, before serving requests, and keeps it loaded for reuse among requests. During server shutdown, you can then gracefully finish all remaining and queued requests before running any cleanup operations.

Security and Authentication Components

As with any other framework, you will need security and authentication components to secure your service. FastAPI doesn't lock you in a specific implementation of the security and authentication layer. It gives you a set of security components (*https://oreil.ly/zlAgl*) so you can protect your services based on your own needs.

You'll learn how to implement an authentication layer from scratch for your GenAI services in Chapter 8.

> If you don't want to implement an authentication layer from scratch, then you can also reach out for third-party plug-ins like FastAPI Users (*https://oreil.ly/eEtMe*) that automatically take care of that for you.

You can also integrate with third-party authentication providers for single sign-on flows in FastAPI (*https://oreil.ly/vIqCd*) in enterprise environments.

Bidirectional Web Socket, GraphQL, and Custom Response Support

When building services, you will often need to move beyond the standard *REST endpoints*.

REST Endpoints

Representational State Transfer (REST) is an architectural style for designing APIs where you use common HTTP methods like `GET`, `POST`, `PUT`, and `DELETE` to access and manipulate resources.

The following are common REST endpoint examples:

`GET endpoint /api/messages`
 Retrieve a list of messages.

`POST endpoint /api/messages`
 Create a new message.

`GET endpoint /api/messages/\{id}`
 Retrieve a specific message by ID.

```
PUT endpoint /api/messages/\{id}
    Update a specific message by ID.

PATCH endpoint /api/messages/\{id}
    Perform a partial update on a specific message by ID.

DELETE endpoint /api/messages/\{id}
    Delete a specific message by ID.
```

Most external APIs across the web are based on the REST architectural pattern due to its scalability, simplicity, and stateless nature (i.e., responses to each request can be independent of another).

If you're building a chat application, you may also need real-time client-server communication or longer-duration connections where data is streamed in a direction. WebSocket (WS) and server-sent events (SSE) endpoints can help you stream generative model outputs to the clients, as you will see in Chapter 6 on real-time communication with AI services.

In other cases, you may want to use GraphQL in FastAPI (*https://oreil.ly/SL62a*) to expose endpoints that can return dynamic schemas based on the request. FastAPI can use the strawberry package (*https://oreil.ly/wIzvi*)[6] to leverage GraphQL in using dynamic schemas for your API service so that clients can select fields they want from a resource to avoid over-fetching data from your service. However, we won't be covering GraphQL usage in this book.

Modern Python and IDE Integration with Sensible Defaults

Since the FastAPI tech stack is built on modern Python (e.g., with type annotations and doc-strings), all IDE linters and formatters can natively check and format your codebase. The defaults are also sufficient to get you started by importing and instantiating the FastAPI class. Because everything ties neatly with modern IDE and Python features, anyone can easily get started building, testing, debugging, and deploying their own FastAPI services.

FastAPI Project Structures

Often when you are working on a real-world project, you will end up building services that will span multiple modules, packages, and nested directories. The decision on how to structure your project is going to be totally up to you.

---

6 An external dependency

This is where most people will struggle and end up with a codebase too overwhelming to navigate. You will end up frustrated, having to understand the codebase and project structure before you can contribute to it. At some point, the complexity will grow so much that you will dread touching the project again.

Some files will end up too large to read with bloated functions, or there will be too many files scattered all over the place. You may also end up having millions of import errors or circular dependencies breaking your application.

Learning to structure larger applications will be even more important when working with generative AI models. These models often need dependencies and additional utility functions to support them. Therefore, you will have to add a layer of complexity for your models on top of existing applications layers.

> Compared to opinionated frameworks such as Django, you need to follow good practices for having success with larger projects in nonopinionated frameworks such as FastAPI.

Over the past few years working with FastAPI and data science applications, I have seen many developers come up with their own cookie-cutter templates for starting FastAPI projects. Some even recommend following a structure popularized by the Netflix Dispatch FastAPI project for larger API applications that has inspired other templates.

When it comes to building real-world applications, you must do everything you can to keep the codebase as structured as possible. This is for your own benefit—to help you and others in your team in understanding the code in the future.

You know you have a good project structure if you can find any function or component within your codebase. If you start questioning the purpose of a directory or spending hours searching for a piece of code, then your project structure might be unclear and too complex to understand.

In these instances, you can refer to a few common project structures that have recently become popular in the FastAPI community. There are a few project structures you can adopt: flat, nested, and modular.

Let us take a detailed look at each one.

Flat Structure

A flat structure is one in which the application files remain at the root of your project with no nested directories. You may group all your files under a single directory for better organization.

The main idea here is to keep all similar code in modules and placed together near the root of your project. For instance, put all your database models in *models.py* or your endpoints in *routes.py*.

By far, the most common project structure is flat due to its simplicity and ease of use. This structure is often great for building the first version of a service or a tiny microservices. Example 2-6 is what the structure could look like.

Example 2-6. A flat FastAPI project structure

```
flat-project
├── app
│   ├── services.py
│   ├── database.py
│   ├── models.py
│   ├── routers.py
│   └── main.py
├── requirements.txt
├── .env
├── .gitignore
```

You can see in the structure shown in Example 2-6 that you have a few files that contain the core of your application logic. If you are building a microservice with FastAPI, by definition, you will want to maintain a flat structure for simplicity.

The simplicity of the flat structure allows you to focus on the development rather than the structure. There are few files to worry about. You also don't need to care about coupling, decomposition, or reuse as there are few lines of codes to deal with.

On the other hand, the flat structure will be hard to maintain as your project grows in complexity. At this point, it makes sense to break down the global Python modules into packages of their own using the nested structure.

Nested Structure

The nested structure groups similar modules into packages—effectively creating a nested structure and hierarchy of modules. You group all modules under a package that are similar in nature irrespective of the feature they support. These are loosely coupled modules that contain similar logic for different entities in your project. For instance, the `models` package may contain `users` and `profiles` database models.

The nested structure is recommended for larger projects by the official FastAPI documentation.

You can see a project with nested structure in Example 2-7.

Example 2-7. Nested FastAPI project

```
nested-project
├── app
│     ├── main.py
│     ├── dependencies.py
│     └── services
│     │     ├── users.py
│     │     └── profiles.py
│     └── models
│     │     ├── users.py
│     │     └── profiles.py
│     └── routers
│           ├── users.py
│           └── profiles.py
├── requirements.txt
├── .env
├── .gitignore
```

As you add AI models and several external services and databases to your project, you can adopt a nested structure to manage the growing complexity.

The main pitfall with this project structure is the ambiguous coupling of modules. Changes in one module can cascade into other modules, and it can become difficult to understand the cascading effect of new changes. Over time, it can be challenging to maintain and change the code without performing many updates everywhere else. This is referred to as *shotgun updates*. Shotgun updates in the context of software development are when it is challenging to maintain and change the code without performing many updates everywhere else.

If you expect difficulty managing module coupling or expecting to deal with a large application, I would recommend using a modular structure.

Modular Structure

The modular structure—popularized by the Netflix Dispatch FastAPI project—is similar to the nested structure because you can place multiple modules within a package and subpackages. However, the core difference is in how you organize your project.

In the modular structure, modules that are closely related and refer to a specific domain are grouped together. This approach differs from the previously mentioned nested structure. An example could be the users package that contains user schemas, database services, dependencies and routers.

To understand this difference better, look at Example 2-8.

Example 2-8. Modular FastAPI project structure

```
modular-project
├── app
│   └── modules
│   │   ├── auth
│   │   │   ├── routers.py
│   │   │   ├── models.py
│   │   │   ├── dependencies.py
│   │   │   ├── guards.py
│   │   │   ├── services.py
│   │   └── users
│   │   │   ├── router.py
│   │   │   ├── models.py
│   │   │   ├── dependencies.py
│   │   │   ├── services.py
│   │   │   ├── mappers.py
│   │   │   ├── pipes.py
│   │   └── profiles
│   └── routers
│   │   └── users.py
│   └── providers
│   │   └── email.py
│   │   └── stripe.py
│   . . . . . . . . . . . .
│   ├── settings.py  # global configs
│   ├── middlewares.py  # global middleware
│   ├── models.py  # global models
│   ├── exceptions.py  # global exceptions
│   └── main.py
├── requirements.txt
├── .env
├── .gitignore
```

In modular project structure like the one shown in Example 2-8, you bring together closely interconnected components based on a feature or a global system they implement (e.g., authentication, payment processing, notifications, etc.) or the resource they interact with (e.g., users, profiles, messages, etc). This kind of encapsulation eliminates any uncertainty regarding the couplings in your code, resulting in improved scalability and maintainability.

If you need to include more features, you can create a new package that contains all the necessary code. Similarly, if you need to modify or delete code, you can easily determine where the changes should be made and expect how they will impact other parts of the code. This is possible because the structure of the codebase is transparent and well-encapsulated, making it clear where different components are connected.

Progressive Reorganization of Your FastAPI Project

A modular codebase allows you to add and remove components with ease. You can also reuse components across different parts of your system to avoid repetition.

When you first start your project, modularity is not as important. You can get started with just a single or a few Python files to build your services easily. However, as soon as you introduce AI models, external services, and complex business logic, you will want to consider modularizing your codebase.

You can achieve modularity by designing components of your system with re-usability and disposability in mind. Make sure the design of your modules and functions allow for usage in different environments and that you place them at the right place in your project directory. Selecting the best project structure is a matter of preference. However, you may be asking yourself, "Which project structure should I adopt for building generative AI services with FastAPI?"

I found that the best way to structure projects is to *progressively reorganize* your project from a flat to a modular structure as your service complexity grows:

1. *Flat*

   If you are starting with a new project and the complexity of your system is not yet clear, you can focus on writing all your FastAPI code in a single file before worrying about the project structure. You then extract your code into several files under the root directory. This is the initial structure you will adopt when experimenting on the first version of your service from scratch.

2. *Nested*

   As the number of files in your codebase and service complexity grows, you can adopt the nested structure. You can search for files based on logical grouping (models, routers, schemas, etc.) and do not have to worry too much about logical couplings in your code. As you make changes, only a handful of files are affected. At this point, you have an AI microservice.

3. *Modular*

   As you move from a microservice to a full backend service, you will want to adopt a modular structure. There is now an increasing number of modules, features, and complexity. You start grouping your code into packages based on *areas of concern*. Your code is now handling requests, authentication, external systems, etc., while serving an AI model.

I suggest restructuring your project as outlined. However, you have the flexibility to adopt any organizational scheme that makes sense to you and allows you to recall the location and purpose of your files.

Remember, if you cannot justify the file organization in your codebase to another developer, it is time to reconsider your existing structure.

As you build your GenAI service, you will inevitably end up with a large codebase and a complex application.

Thinking about the structure of your large FastAPI application is only the first step in building production-grade services. In the next step, you will learn more about a software design pattern that helps you manage the complexity of your AI services. This is called the *onion*, or *layered*, application design pattern, which we will talk about next.

Onion/Layered Application Design Pattern

If you plan on building a fully featured backend service for generative AI, you will benefit to know more about the onion, or layered, application design pattern, which can be implemented within the nested and modular project structures. The purpose of this pattern is to create a separation of concerns between the different parts of your application to simplify the process of adding, removing, and modifying features.

The onion design pattern has also influenced web frameworks in other languages such as Nest.js (*https://nestjs.com*).

The onion design consists of layers, each with a specific responsibility and dependency direction, shown in Figure 2-3. The innermost layer contains the domain models and business logic, while the outer layers contain route handling (in an API service) or user-interfacing code (when serving HTML templates).

The pattern is called "onion" because the layers build upon each other, with the domain model at the center, surrounded by layers of increasing abstraction promoting testability, maintainability, and flexibility in maintaining your AI services. The core of the application (domain model and business logic) is at the inner layers, and all other layers depend inwardly on it. This approach helps to manage dependencies, promote separation of concerns, and facilitate a more testable and maintainable codebase.

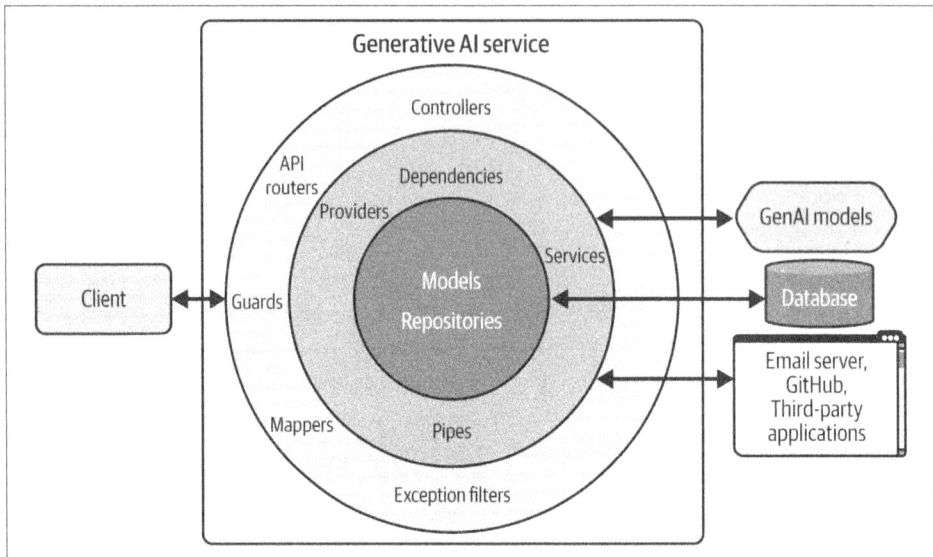

Figure 2-3. Onion design pattern

The main idea behind this pattern is the *dependency inversion principle*, which states that high-level modules should not directly depend on the implementation of low-level modules but declare what they need from low-level modules by leveraging the FastAPI dependency system. The dependency system can then inject the output of the low-level modules to avoid coupling between layers.

To implement this software design, you break down your service as an onion consisting of layers that go deeper and deeper. Each layer (as you move from outer to inner layers) introduces components that are responsible for a set of tasks:

API routers

Routers are responsible for grouping multiple controllers/route handlers to apply common logic across several controllers.

FastAPI provides the `APIRouter` class to help you with this.

Controllers/route handlers

Controllers are responsible for handling incoming *requests* and returning *responses* to the client via a logical execution of services or providers.

Good controller design always uses dependencies to inject required data or logic required for its execution. See Figure 2-4.

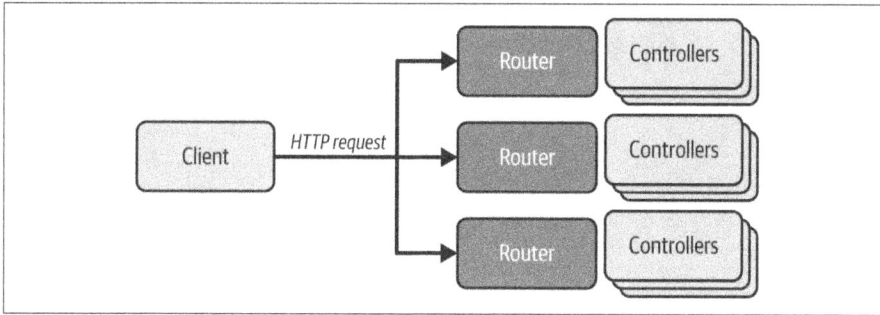

Figure 2-4. API routers and controllers

Services/providers

Services are responsible for combining or orchestrating multiple internal operations to implement a business logic (services), while providers implement the interface with external systems.

Services typically use repositories for data access to implement complex business logic rather than simple data retrieval and mutation operations. Each module of your application can have its own service.

Providers are similar to services but are specialized in interacting with external systems such as internal/third-party APIs. Examples of providers include clients for email servers, payment gateways, or other microservices.

Essentially, both providers and services support implementation of controller business logic by facilitating internal and external interactions.

Here is an example of how they work together within a route controller: the users database service fetches a user's record by email and then uses that information with a payment gateway and email server clients (providers) for processing payments and sending confirmation emails.

Repositories (data adapters)

A repository is a design pattern used when implementing the logic for data access and mutation operations with data sources (not to be confused with a Git repository).

Repositories use object-relational mapping (ORM) or raw SQL commands to execute queries on your infrastructure like a database, or a memory store for retrieving or mutating data.

You may implement an abstract interface in this layer to enforce consistent design across all your repositories—using the create, read, update, delete (CRUD) operations. See Figure 2-5.

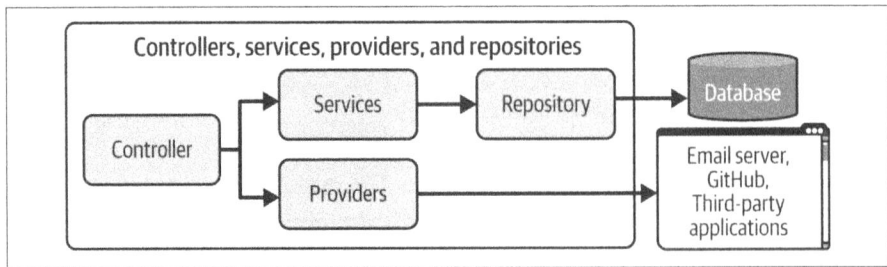

Figure 2-5. Services, providers, and repositories

Schemas/models

These are responsible for enforcing type-safety, structure, and validation logic on your data as it flows throughout your service.

You will also have components that span layers to support the whole application:

Middleware

This handles requests and responses before and after they are passed to the application controllers/route handlers (see Figure 2-6).

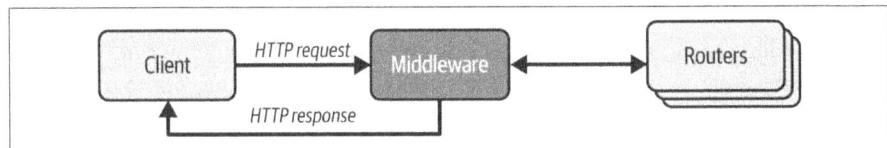

Figure 2-6. Middleware

Dependencies

These include reusable functions you define that can be injected into controllers to support a business logic. Dependencies can be cached and depend on other dependencies.

Pipes

These are data transformer functions that you can use across application layers. Examples include data aggregators, cleaners, parsers, translators, etc.

Mappers

These are data mappers from one schema into another, often passing data across layers such as from the `UserRequest` schema at a router layer to the `UserInDB` schema at the data access layer. See Figure 2-7.

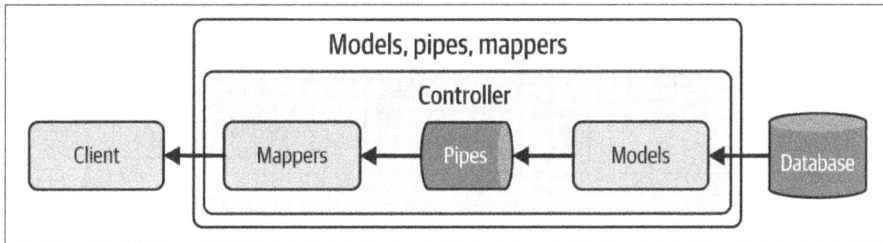

Figure 2-7. Models, pipes, and mappers

Exception filters

These consistently handle exceptions across the layers.

Guards

These secure and protect controllers from abuse. Authentication and authorization logic can be implemented as dependencies or middleware to act as guards (see Figure 2-8).

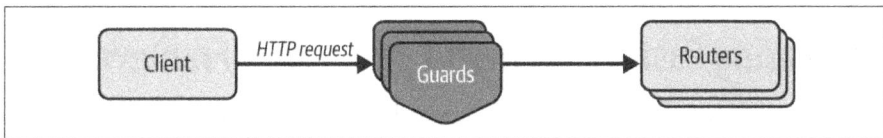

Figure 2-8. Guards

If you refer to the modular project structure shown in Example 2-8, you will now notice various elements of the onion design pattern in the modular project structure. Following this pattern can help you create a maintainable, testable, and scalable FastAPI generative AI service.

In the upcoming chapters, you'll use these patterns to build the GenAI service shown in Figure 2-9.

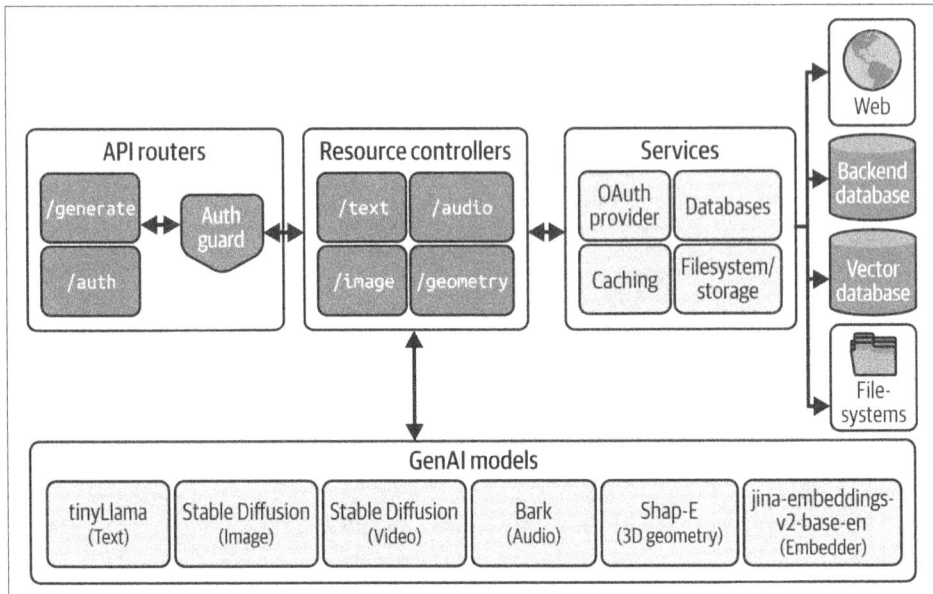

Figure 2-9. Generative AI service you'll build with FastAPI

Next, we will compare FastAPI with other frameworks.

Comparing FastAPI to Other Python Web Frameworks

Most Python web frameworks can provide you with tools for building REST, GraphQL, WebSocket, and other types of endpoints.

These frameworks are either opinionated, such as Django (Python) and Nestjs (Java-Script), while others are not. Flask or FastAPI (Python) and Express (JavaScript) give you the option to architect your service however you like.

Opinionated frameworks, such as Django (Python) and Nestjs (JavaScript), make decisions for you with certain assumptions about how you will be providing data to your components. Effectively, they provide structure while restricting what you are allowed to do. Opinionated frameworks are typically easier to use. On the other hand, nonopinionated frameworks such as Flask or FastAPI (Python) and Express (Java-Script) are more flexible but can give you too much freedom—many possibilities to achieve the same results.

Because nonopinionated frameworks such as FastAPI give you so much freedom in building services, you may feel some decision fatigue when choosing and integrating every single support package yourself. For instance, to work with a database, you will need to install and integrate several packages that work well together—one to access the database, one to migrate it, and another to act as an object relational mapper (ORM).

While doing that, you may run into compatibility issues with older packages during integration. This makes working with nonopinionated frameworks difficult, and often you may decide to use an opinionated framework such as Django, which ships with a tightly integrated and excellent ORM system for interacting with databases.

Django is a battery-included framework that markets itself as the "Python web framework for developers with deadlines." It ships with a fully integrated and feature-rich ORM system that takes care of your database migrations and data access needs when you provide the data models.

Additionally, it provides you with an administration panel, a credentials-based user authentication and authorization system, and several web security features out of the box, so you do not have to build these yourself. It has also been around for a long time, fostering an active community that has produced excellent documentation, tutorials, and other resources for the framework. In Django version 4.2, support for async requests has also been introduced—allowing you to build concurrency into your services. Django expects you to adopt the MVC architecture, requiring you to define data models and views. These views become routes serving templated HTML files, JSON responses, or any HTTP response out of the box, even without relying on `django-rest-framework`. Controller layers then will contain the core data processing and business logic.

This makes Django an excellent choice for monolith *progressive web applications* (PWA) that deploy as a single backend with a frontend. However, as businesses move toward building specialized teams for developing backends and frontends, microservice architectural patterns are becoming more popular. With microservices, you want to separate your backend and frontend services, build APIs instead of PWAs, and focus on keeping your services as lean as possible. Using Django you can also build APIs, but you can end up with a heavy application that slows you down during development, deployment, and scaling services. That is why nonopinionated frameworks such as Flask are rising in popularity.[7]

Flask ships with as little code as practically possible for building web servers. In comparison to FastAPI, Flask does not come packaged with data validation, auto-documentation, and a dependency injection system. The mentioned features are often required for building any backend service that is becoming complex or requires integration with databases and external services.

---

7 As is clear by their number of monthly downloads

A new web framework called Quart has tried to tackle this problem, which is a good contender to FastAPI. However, at the time of this writing, Quart is new, and compared to other frameworks it does not have a large community of users and documented resources to help if you get stuck on a problem.

Furthermore, Flask was released in 2010 and implements a communication protocol called *Web Server Gateway Interface* (WSGI) for web serving, meaning that requests are processed synchronously in comparison to ASGI, which is asynchronous in nature. Additionally, Flask is not designed for handling a large number of simultaneous connections (like an asynchronous framework would). However, this does not limit the number of parallel requests the server can handle on its own. In production, you can employ various strategies (like worker processes or threads) to handle multiple requests concurrently. Also, because Flask implements WSGI, it does not support WebSocket endpoints, which are used for maintaining a persistent, bidirectional communication channel between a client and a server. This is because WSGI does not natively support WebSocket. However, you can install Flask extensions to integrate WebSocket support.

Asynchronous Server Gateway Interface

ASGI-based frameworks can process multiple requests by running concurrent asynchronous operations on the main event loop, allowing it to handle a higher volume of requests at scale.

It can also use a thread pool (i.e., a pool of thread workers) to perform synchronous tasks concurrently without blocking the main server thread. Once tasks are finished, these threads return control to the main web server thread and share their results. When a thread raises an error, the web server gathers information from the worker thread and sends an error response to the client instead.

Modern web frameworks that implement the ASGI standard are not only more efficient but also provide backward compatibility for WSGI in case it's necessary.

Flask, relying on a WSGI server, will process each request synchronously, whereas FastAPI uses an event loop for concurrent workloads. Therefore, FastAPI is going to be much faster with input/output (I/O) heavy tasks—for instance, when communicating with an external API or data store, which would block an entire worker process in Flask.

In essence, I recommend Django and other frameworks if you want to build PWA monoliths, and Flask or Quart for simple APIs and frameworks in other languages if you have more experience with them.

However, if you're building a backend service that requires AI model support, connection to external systems, and some level of business logic complexity, I recommend considering FastAPI as the web framework of choice.

FastAPI Limitations

Given the aforementioned features and benefits, there are also several drawbacks and trade-offs you must consider if you are going to adopt FastAPI for your project. With AI use cases in mind, FastAPI falls short in several areas.

Inefficient Model Memory Management

FastAPI does provide built-in mechanisms for sharing model memory between multiple instances or processes of the same container. This means when scaling web workers horizontally, you need to load a whole new model instance into the container's memory. This creates a memory bottleneck and increases operational costs of high-traffic GenAI services.

Limited Number of Threads

There is a limit to the number of threads that FastAPI creates on application startup in the internal thread pool.[8]

This means there is also a limit to how much you can scale a single instance of FastAPI, especially with AI workloads that have heavy I/O as well as CPU/GPU-intensive operations.[9]

Restricted to Global Interpreter Lock

In Python, multithreading can produce unintuitive and often counterproductive results because of the *Global Interpreter Lock* (GIL).

FastAPI leverages multithreading via an internal thread pool to handle concurrent web requests hitting a synchronous route. However, even with asynchronous endpoints, the AI inference requests can still block the main event loop, preventing all other requests from being processed in the main web serving thread.

---

8 FastAPI relies on AnyIO (an asynchronous networking and concurrency library) to handle concurrency. AnyIO creates up to 40 threads by default on a dynamic internal thread pool and removes those that aren't used for a while.

9 Unless you run the GPU operations in another process (via multiprocessing) and await the operations

This is because AI inference workloads are CPU/GPU intensive. Non-I/O operations, such as serving an expensive model or aggregating large amounts of data on a worker, will cause other threads to wait as Python currently is not using multiple cores for threading.[10] Instead, as you'll learn more in Chapter 5, for these kinds of expensive compute operations, you'll need to use multiprocessing or a process pool instead.

Lack of Support for Micro-Batch Processing Inference Requests

Deep learning frameworks provide support for vectorization so that inferences can be batched together, efficiently computed, and parallelized. Unfortunately, prediction requests can't be batched together in FastAPI, and as a result, each compute-intensive model inference operation can block other requests.

When scaling services, a solution is to serve heavy models separately and use FastAPI to authenticate and manage the incoming and outgoing data.

Cannot Efficiently Split AI Workloads Between CPU and GPU

While the CPU mostly handles request transformation and validation operations, the GPU can run and parallelize compute-intensive model inference. In some specialized ML web frameworks (like BentoML), you can also efficiently split AI workloads between the CPU and GPU.

> When you split AI workloads across the CPU and GPU, data preparation and post-processing operations run on the CPU, while faster deep learning inference is performed on the GPU.

Unfortunately, FastAPI can't efficiently perform this split of the AI inference workload between these devices. This means your CPU can be blocked from processing requests even when inference processes are running on the GPU. As this is a big bottleneck when working with heavier models, it will require serving heavier models outside FastAPI for concurrent workloads.

We'll discuss solutions to this limitation in more detail in Chapter 5.

---

10 However, according to PEP 703 (*https://oreil.ly/_bRzj*), GIL will be made optional in CPython soon.

Dependency Conflicts

When you are deploying ML models, you will face unique challenges compared to deploying typical web applications. This is due to your model runtime's deep coupling with native libraries and hardware. Each deployment environment can operate on distinct hardware and may require you to use specific versions of native libraries and containerization commands.

Lack of Support for Resource-Intensive AI Workloads

Despite its incredible capabilities, FastAPI was developed before the rise of generative AI. As a result, it remains a general-purpose web framework with recent support for AI serving and ML workflows. However, for certain use cases, such as serving resource-intensive and complex billion-parameter models, it may be worth exploring other frameworks like *BentoML*.

BentoML: FastAPI-Inspired Framework for Running Resource-Intensive AI Models

BentoML is also built on top of Starlette and is designed with FastAPI patterns in mind but specifically for machine learning. Its architecture allows for scaling web requests separately from model inference, providing flexibility in computing distributions.

It addresses unique ML workflow challenges using its Runners, dependency management, and model versioning systems. Through its dependency management system, it can effectively speed up deployments by declaratively auto-generating Dockerfiles for you so that you do not have to debug complex Docker commands to install and use CUDA libraries for GPU inference.

Later in the book, I will present a FastAPI architecture for resource-intensive AI workflows that uses BentoML as the underlying AI server. In this architecture, model-serving tasks will be delegated to BentoML, while FastAPI will manage security, caching, and business logic for you.

In the following chapters, you'll learn how to build your own GenAI service with FastAPI.

But before moving forward, let's configure necessary Python tools like linters, formatters, and type checkers in your development environment for easier maintainability of your FastAPI project as we work on it together.

Setting Up a Managed Python Environment and Tooling

To maintain a stable and reproducible development environment, you may want to manage your Python environment and dependencies.

I recommend:

- Using a *requirements.txt* file with `pip` for simpler projects
- Using uv (*https://oreil.ly/Qxl7h*) or Conda (*https://oreil.ly/Kfsc4*) for `pip`-driven workflows
- Using Poetry (*https://oreil.ly/Rt04z*) for more complex projects

Aside from managing dependencies, Python also has several third-party packages that allow you to lint and format your codebase before shipping it into production.[11]

It is best practice for professional Python developers to use these tools to catch bugs during development and before adding changes to the code repository. In fact, I recommend that you run code checks with these tools against your codebase frequently to prevent bugs from appearing in your services.

Here is a nonexhaustive list of Python packages that I recommend integrating into any project you start:

Linters
These tools analyze source code to flag programming errors, stylistic errors, and unused code snippets:

- *Autoflake*: Removes unused imports and variables from code to improve readability
- *Flake8*: Checks against Python enhancement proposals (PEPs) and code styles

Formatters
These enable you to better see what you have written:

- *isort*: Sorts imports in Python modules
- *Black*: Formats Python code for readability
- *Ruff*: Rust-based linter and formatter that is extremely fast and can be used as a replacement for other tools such as `isort`, `black`, `flake8`, and possibly `bandit`[12]

---

11 Refer to Hypermodern's GitHub repository (*https://oreil.ly/6YWRN*) for tooling examples.

12 You can use `ruff` for faster checks in CI/CD pipelines, unless your development environment or CI/CD pipeline is tightly integrated with the other tools.

Loggers

Used in parts of the code that gets complex to debug and monitor your application:

- *Loguru*: Replacing Python's built-in logger module

Scanners

If you want confidence that you did not commit insecure code or passwords by chance:

- *Bandit*: Vulnerability scanning of your Python codebase with checking against common security issues such as hard-coded secrets
- *Safety*: Python dependency vulnerability scanner to detect packages with known vulnerabilities or malicious packages

Type checkers

To catch those bugs that normal linters do not catch. Also, great if you want confidence that changes in your schemas did not break your application:

- *Mypy*: A powerful static type checker that can help catch a lot of bugs in your code
- *Pylance*: A type checker that ships with Microsoft's Python extension for VS Code

As part of your development environment, it's also worthwhile to use version control systems like Git to track codebase changes, manage different versions of your project, and manage code contributions from other developers.

> When using Git, you can also add *.gitignore* files to help you manage files and directories that you want excluded from version control tracking.

Integrated development environments (IDEs) such as VS Code or JetBrains Pycharm provide plug-ins for running these tools as you type or save your work. They often require some configuration, but once done, you will get auto-formatting and linting set up and ready before you begin. In any case, I recommend having a script or precommit hooks that lints, checks, and formats your code before you commit to your codebase or deploy it to production.

> I've prepared a FastAPI blank template (*https://oreil.ly/j8lF7*) that includes integrations with common tools that you can use as a foundation for your projects.

These are fundamentals of Python programming and software engineering. They will become crucial when you start working with AI models that can produce probabilistic outputs as well as external services and databases that can change schemas at any time. Maintaining an AI application that changes schemas and prompts constantly without the aforementioned tools can definitively become a headache quite fast.

Summary

In this chapter, you learned about the FastAPI framework, including its capabilities and drawbacks compared to other frameworks.

You also learned how to set up your own FastAPI project from scratch, alongside a set of tools you can use to improve your development experience.

Then you were introduced to several project structures you can adopt when building your own FastAPI service. As part of this, you learned more about the onion/layered software design pattern to help manage project complexity.

Finally, we covered tools you can use to manage your Python environments and help maintain your FastAPI codebase as it grows in complexity.

You should now be comfortable starting your own FastAPI projects and managing the project complexity as it evolves over time.

In the next chapter, you will learn how to implement your own GenAI features in FastAPI for generating text, image, audio, and video. You will understand the inner workings of each model and the role of FastAPI lifecycle system in model serving, while leveraging NVIDIA GPUs for inference tasks. Finally, you will be introduced to the FastAPI background tasks system to offload long-running inference operations.

## CHAPTER 3

AI Integration and Model Serving

Chapter Goals

In this chapter, you will learn about:

- How different GenAI models work
- How to integrate and serve generative models into FastAPI
- How to work with text, image, audio, video, and 3D models
- How to quickly build a user interface for prototyping
- Several model-serving strategies in FastAPI
- How to leverage middleware for service monitoring

In this chapter, you will learn the mechanisms of various GenAI models and how to serve them in a FastAPI application. Additionally, using the Streamlit UI package (*https://oreil.ly/9BXmn*), you will create a simple browser client for interacting with the model-serving endpoints. We will explore differing model-serving strategies, how to preload models for efficiency, and how to use FastAPI features for service monitoring.

To solidify your learning in this chapter, we will progressively build a FastAPI service using open source GenAI models that generate text, images, audio, and 3D geometries, all from scratch. In later chapters, you'll build the functionality to parse documents and web content for your GenAI service so you can talk to them using a language model.

> In the previous chapter, you saw how to set up a fresh FastAPI project in Python. Make sure you have fresh installation ready before you read the rest of this chapter. Alternatively, you can clone or download the book's GitHub repository (*https://github.com/Ali-Parandeh/building-generative-ai-services*). Then once cloned, switch to the ch03-start branch, ready for the steps to follow.

By the end of this chapter, you will have a FastAPI service that serves various open source GenAI models that you can test inside the Streamlit UI. Additionally, your service will be capable of logging usage data to disk using middleware.

Serving Generative Models

Before you serve pretrained generative models in your application, it is worth learning how these models are trained and generate data. With this understanding, you can customize the internals of your application to enhance the outputs that you provide to the user.

In this chapter, I will show you how to serve models across a variety of modalities including:

- *Language* models based on the transformer neural network architecture
- *Audio* models in text-to-speech and text-to-audio services based on the aggressive transformer architecture
- *Vision* models for text-to-image and text-to-video services based on the Stable Diffusion and vision transformer architectures
- *3D* models for text-to-3D services based on the conditional implicit function encoder and diffusion decoder architecture

This list is not exhaustive and covers a handful of GenAI models. To explore other models, please visit the Hugging Face model repository (*https://oreil.ly/-4wlQ*).[1]

Language Models

In this section, we talk about language models, including transformers and recurrent neural networks (RNNs).

---

[1] Hugging Face provides access to a wide range of pretrained machine learning models, datasets, and applications.

Transformers versus recurrent neural networks

The world of AI was shaken with the release of the landmark paper "Attention Is All You Need."[2] In this paper, the authors proposed a completely different approach to natural language processing (NLP) and sequence modeling that differed from the existing RNN architectures.

Figure 3-1 shows a simplified version of the proposed transformer architecture from the original paper.

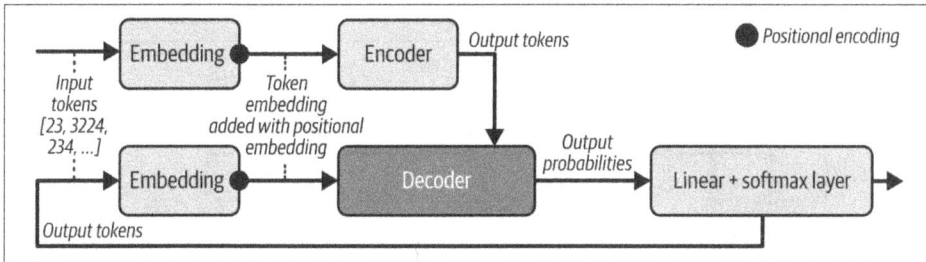

Figure 3-1. Transformer architecture

Historically, text generation tasks leveraged RNN models to learn patterns in sequential data such as free text. To process text, these models chunk text into small pieces such as a word or character called a *token* that can be sequentially processed.

RNNs maintain a memory store called a *state vector*, which carries information from one token to the next throughout the full text sequence, until the end. This means that by the time you get to the end of the text sequence, the impact of early tokens on the state vector is a lot smaller compared to the most recent tokens.

Ideally, every token should be as important as the other tokens in any text. However, as RNNs can only predict the next item in a sequence by looking at the items that came before, they struggle with this ideal in capturing long-range dependencies and modeling patterns in large chunks of texts. As a result, they effectively fail to remember or comprehend essential information or context in large documents.

With the invention of transformers, recurrent or convolutional modeling could now be replaced with a more efficient approach. Since transformers don't maintain a hidden state memory and leverage a new capability termed *self-attention*, they're capable of modeling relationships between words, no matter how far apart they appeared in a sentence. This self-attention component allows the model to "place attention" on contextually relevant words within a sentence.

---

2 A. Vaswani et al. (2017), "Attention Is All You Need" (*https://oreil.ly/sO33r*), arXiv preprint arXiv:1706.03762.

While RNNs model relationships between neighboring words in a sentence, transformers map pairwise relationships between every word in the text.

Figure 3-2 shows how RNNs process sentences in comparison to transformers.

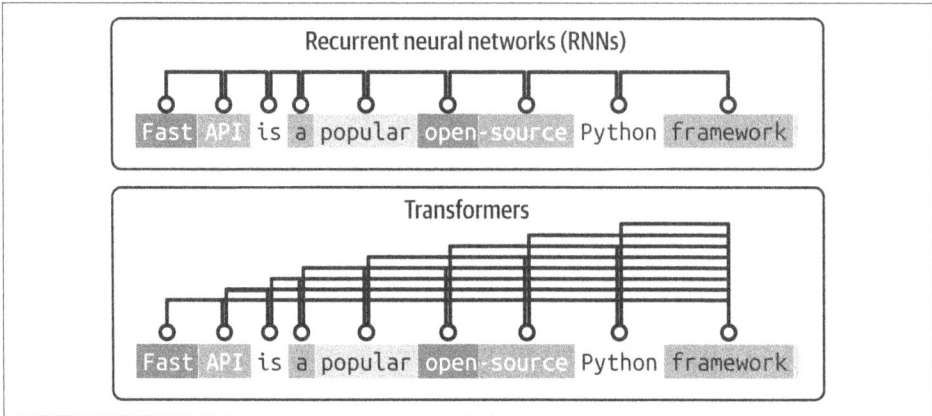

Figure 3-2. RNNs versus transformers in processing sentences

What powers the self-attention system are specialized blocks called *attention heads* that capture pairwise patterns between words as *attention maps*.

Figure 3-3 visualizes the attention map of an attention head.[3] Connections can be bidirectional with the thickness representing the strength of the relationship between words in the sentence.

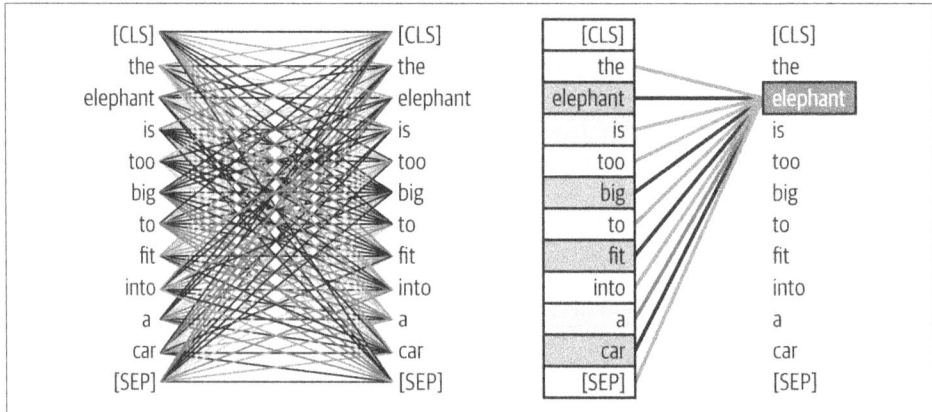

Figure 3-3. View of an attention map inside an attention head

---

3 A great tool for visualizing attention maps is BertViz (*https://oreil.ly/e2Q7X*).

A transformer model contains several attention heads distributed across its neural network layers. Each head computes its own attention map independently to capture relationships between words focusing on certain patterns in the inputs. Using multiple attention heads, the model can simultaneously analyze the inputs from various angles and contexts to understand complex patterns and dependencies within the data.

Figure 3-4 shows the attention maps for each head (i.e., independent set of attention weights) within each layer of the model.

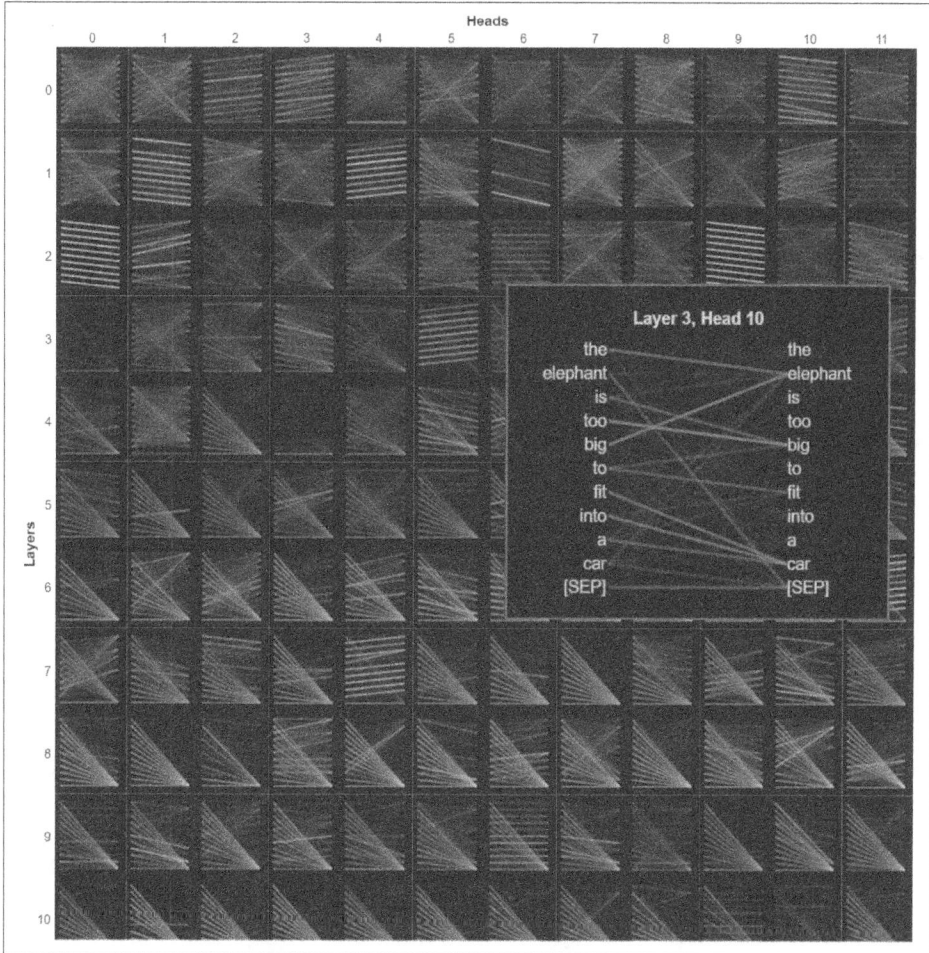

Figure 3-4. View of the attention maps within the model

RNNs also required extensive compute power to train, as the training process couldn't be parallelized on multiple GPU due to the sequential nature of their training algorithms. Transformers, on the other hand, process words nonsequentially, so they can run attention mechanisms in parallel on GPUs.

The efficiency of the transformer architecture means that these models are more scalable as long as there is more data, compute power, and memory. You can build language models with a corpus that spans libraries of books produced by humanity. All you would need is ample compute power and data to train an LLM. And, that is exactly what OpenAI did, the company behind the famous ChatGPT application that was powered by several of their proprietary LLMs including GPT-4o.

At the time of this writing, the implementation details behind OpenAI's LLMs remain a trade secret. While many researchers have a general understanding of OpenAI's methods, they may not necessarily have the resources to replicate them. However, several open source alternatives for research and commercial use have been released since, including Llama (Facebook), Gemma (Google), Mistral, and Falcon to name a few.[4] At the time of this writing, the model sizes vary between 0.05B and 480B parameters (i.e., model weights and biases) to suit your needs.

Hardware Requirements for Open Source LLMs

The biggest open source LLM at the time of this writing is the multilingual 480B-parameter *Snowflake Arctic* (*https://oreil.ly/DLukR*). The recommended hardware to run this massive model is a single AWS/Azure 8xH100 instance, which contains eight H100 data center GPU cards, each providing 80 GB of VRAM. Other flagship open LLMs such as the multilingual 405B-parameter Llama 3.1 also require similar hardware.

As of January 2024, one of the best consumer-grade GPU cards you can buy for AI workloads is NVIDIA 4090 RTX, which ships with only 24 GB of VRAM. A single consumer GPU like 4090 RTX may not be able to run model sizes above 30B due to memory constraints unless the model is quantized (i.e., compressed).

If you want to run a quantized 70B-Llama model, you may need a 64 GB VRAM GPU or multiple smaller cards (*https://oreil.ly/dJbKa*). Aside from power supply and cooling challenges with setting up a multi-GPU home server, you may still experience slow prediction rates when running models this size.

You will learn more about the quantization process and using quantized LLMs in Chapter 10.

---

4 You can find the up-to-date list of open source LLMs on the Open LLM GitHub repository (*https://oreil.ly/GZaEr*).

Serving LLMs still remains a challenge due to high memory requirements with requirements doubling if you need to train and fine-tune them on your own dataset. This is because the training process will require caching and reusing model parameters across training batches. As a result, most organizations may rely on lightweight (up to 3B) models or on APIs of LLM providers such as OpenAI, Anthropic, Cohere, Mistral, etc.

As LLMs grow in popularity, it becomes even more important to understand how they're trained and how they process data, so let's discuss underlying mechanisms next.

Tokenization and embedding

Neural networks can't process words directly as they're big statistical models that function on numbers. To bridge that gap between language and numbers, you need to use *tokenization*. With tokenization, you break down text into smaller pieces that a model can process.

Any piece of text must be first sliced into a list of *tokens* that represent words, syllables, symbols, and punctuations. These tokens are then mapped to unique numbers so that patterns can be numerically modeled.

By providing a vector of input tokens to a trained transformer, the network can then predict the next best token to generate text, one word at a time.

Figure 3-5 shows how the OpenAI tokenizer converts text into a sequence of tokens, assigning unique token identifiers to each.

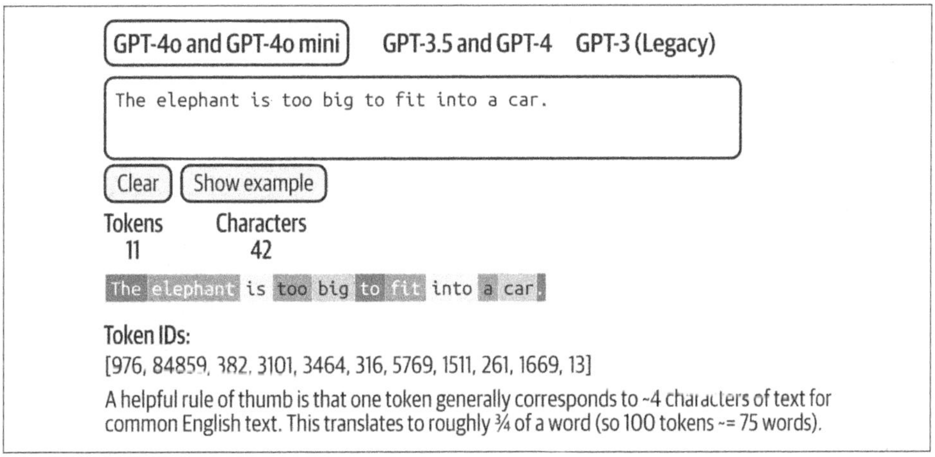

Figure 3-5. OpenAI tokenizer (Source: OpenAI (https://oreil.ly/S-a9M))

So what can you do after you tokenize some text? These tokens need to be processed further before a language model can process them.

After tokenization, you need to use an *embedder*[5] to convert these tokens into dense vectors of real numbers called *embeddings*, capturing semantic information (i.e., meaning of each token) in a continuous vector space. Figure 3-6 demonstrates these embeddings.

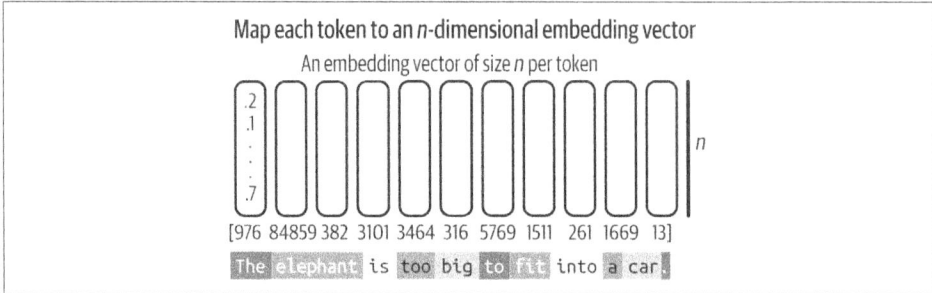

Map each token to an n-dimensional embedding vector

An embedding vector of size n per token

.2
.1
.
.
.7

[976 84859 382 3101 3464 316 5769 1511 261 1669 13]

The elephant is too big to fit into a car.

Figure 3-6. Assigning an embedding vector of size n to each token during the embedding process

These embedding vectors use small *floating-point numbers* (not integers) to capture nuanced relationships between tokens with more flexibility and precision. They also tend to be *normally distributed*, so language model training and inference can be more stable and consistent.

After the embedding process, each token is assigned an embedding vector filled with n numbers. Each number in the embedding vector focuses on a dimension that represents a specific aspect of the token's meaning.

Training transformers

Once you have a set of embedding vectors, you can train a model on your documents to update the values inside each embedding. During model training, the training algorithm updates the parameters of the embedding layers so that the embedding vectors describe the meaning of each token as close as possible within the input text.

---

5 An embedding model or an embedding layer such as in a transformer

Understanding how embedding vectors work can be challenging, so let's try a visualization approach.

Imagine you used a two-dimensional embedding vectors, meaning the vectors contained only two numbers. Then, if you plot these vectors, before and after model training, you will observe plots similar to Figure 3-7. The embedding vectors of tokens, or words, with similar meanings will be closer to each other.

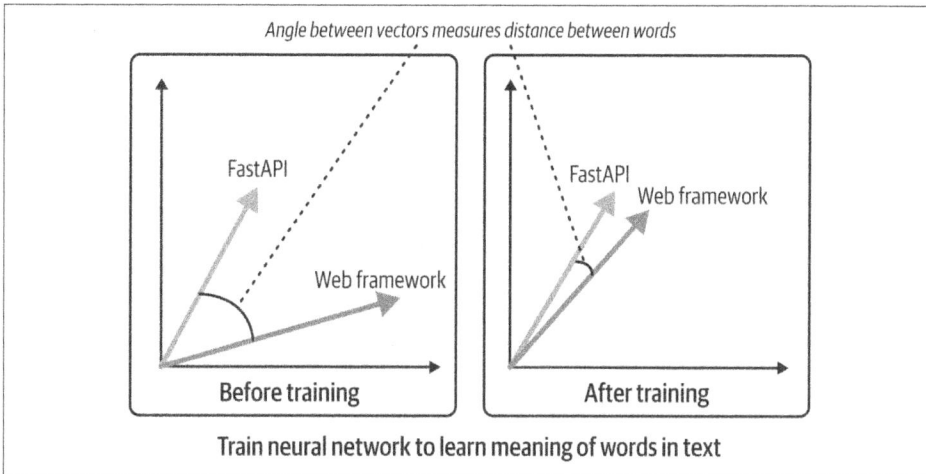

Figure 3-7. Training latent space of transformer network using embedding vectors

To determine the similarity between two words, you can compute the angle between vectors using a calculation known as *cosine similarity*. Smaller angles imply higher similarity, representing similar context and meaning. After training, the cosine similarity calculation of two embedding vectors with similar meanings will validate that those vectors are close to each other.

Figure 3-8 illustrates the full tokenization, embedding, and training process.

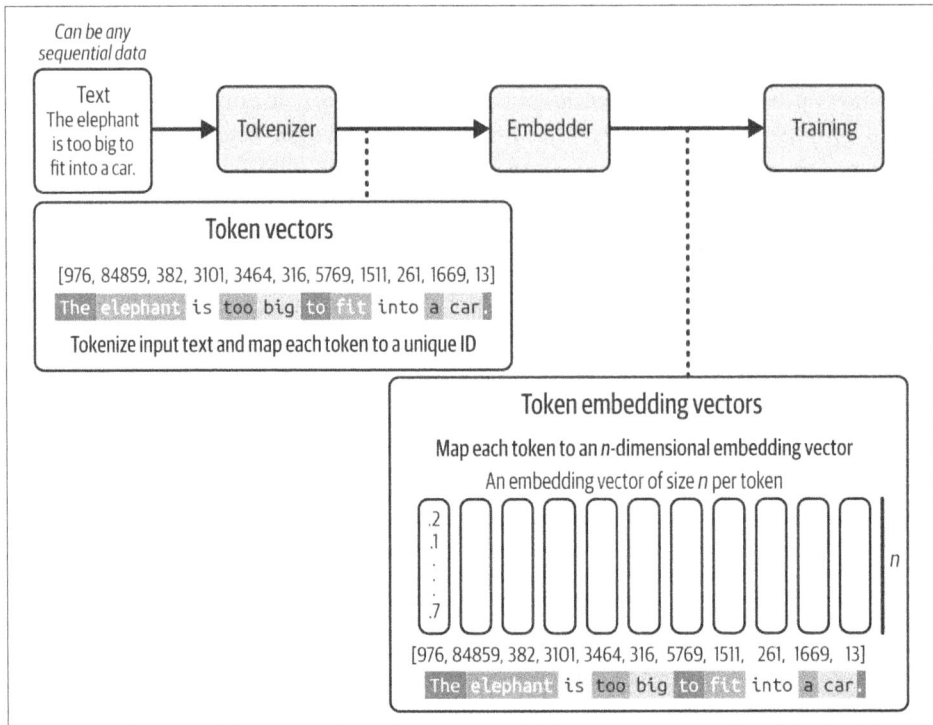

Figure 3-8. Processing sequential data like a piece of text into a vector of tokens and token embeddings

Once you have a trained embedding layer, you can now use it to embed any new input text to the transformer model shown in Figure 3-1.

Positional encoding

A final step before forwarding the embedding vectors to the attention layers in the transformer network is to implement *positional encoding*. The positional encoding process produces the positional embedding vectors that then are summed with the token embedding vectors.

Since transformers process words simultaneously rather than sequentially, positional embeddings are needed to record the word order and context within the sequential data, like sentences. The resultant embedding vectors capture both meaning and positional information of words in the sentences before they're passed to the attention mechanisms of the transformer. This process ensures attention heads have all the information they need to learn patterns effectively.

Figure 3-9 shows the positional encoding process where the positional embeddings are summed with token embeddings.

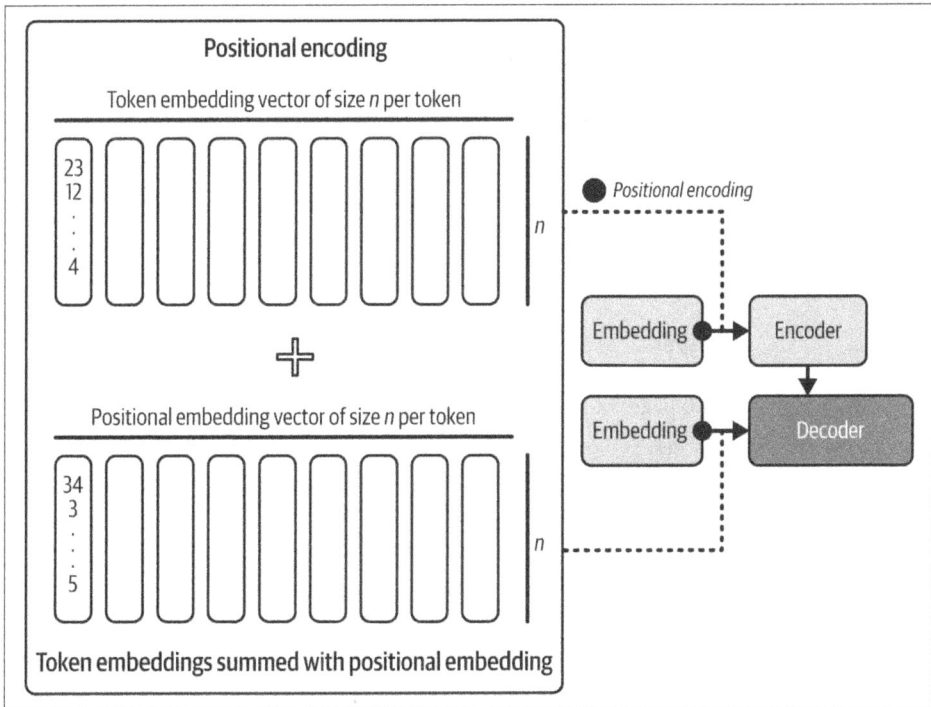

Figure 3-9. Positional encoding

Autoregressive prediction

The transformer is an autoregressive (i.e., sequential) model as future predictions are based on the past values, as shown in Figure 3-10.

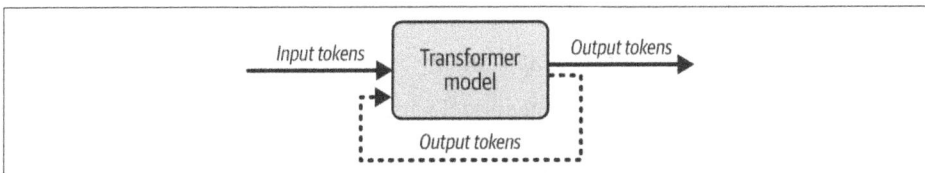

Figure 3-10. Autoregressive prediction

The model receives input tokens that are then embedded and passed through the network to make the next best token prediction. This process repeats until a `<stop>` or end of sentence `<eos>` token is generated.[6]

However, there is a limit to the number of tokens that the model can store in its memory to generate the next token. This token limit is referred to as the model's *context window*, which is an important factor to consider during the model selection stage for your GenAI services.

If the context window limit is reached, the model simply discards the least recently used tokens. This means it can *forget* the least recently used sentences in documents or messages in a conversation.

> At the time of writing, the context of the least expensive OpenAI `gpt-4o-mini` model is around ~128,000 tokens, equivalent to more than 300 pages of text.
>
> The largest context window as of March 2025 belongs to Magic.Dev LTM-2-mini (*https://oreil.ly/10Mj1*) with 100 million tokens. This equals ~10 million lines of code of ~750 novels.
>
> The context window of other models falls in the range of hundreds of thousands of tokens.

Short windows will lead to loss of information, difficulty maintaining conversations, and reduced coherence with the user query.

On the other hand, long context windows have larger memory requirements and can lead to performance issues or slow services when scaling to thousands of concurrent users who are using your service. In addition, you will need to consider the costs of relying on models with larger context windows as they tend to be more expensive due to increased compute and memory requirements. The correct choice will depend on your budget and user needs in your use case.

Integrating a language model into your application

You can download and use a language model within your application with a few lines of code. In Example 3-1, you will download a TinyLlama model that has 1.1 billion parameters and is pretrained on 3 trillion tokens.

---

6 This sequential token generation process can also limit scalability for long sequences, as each token relies on the previous one.

Installing TinyLlama Dependencies

To integrate TinyLlama into your application, you can use the Hugging Face `trans formers` library.[7] You will also need to install the Pytorch deep learning framework by installing the `torch` package. Both packages can be installed via `pip`.

On Windows, you will need to provide the `--index-url` flag to `pip` when installing `torch` that is compiled for a CUDA-enabled GPU.[8]

```
# Install `torch` with CUDA 12.4 and `transformers` packages for Windows.

$ pip install transformers torch \
    --index-url https://download.pytorch.org/whl/cu124
```

TinyLlama can't generate more than a few sentences at a time. You will also need around 3 GB of disk space and RAM to load this model onto memory for inference. I recommend running the model on a CUDA-enabled NVIDIA GPU (with the `torch` wheel compiled for CUDA) as CPU inference can be slow. Please refer to NVIDIA's CUDA installation instructions for Windows (*https://oreil.ly/LeA1O*) or Linux (*https://oreil.ly/qjNaO*).

Furthermore, to run Example 3-1 on Windows, you may need to install Visual Studio Build Tools 2022 with C++ and .NET development tools to resolve issues with missing DLL libraries and dependencies.

Example 3-1. Download and load a language model from the Hugging Face repository

```
# models.py

import torch
from transformers import Pipeline, pipeline

prompt = "How to set up a FastAPI project?"
system_prompt = """
Your name is FastAPI bot and you are a helpful
chatbot responsible for teaching FastAPI to your users.
Always respond in markdown.
"""

device = torch.device("cuda" if torch.cuda.is_available() else "cpu")  ❶

def load_text_model():
    pipe = pipeline(
```

---

7 The Hugging Face model repository (*https://huggingface.co*) is a resource for AI developers to publish and share their pretrained models.

8 See the Pytorch documentation (*https://pytorch.org*) for installation instructions.

```
        "text-generation",
        model="TinyLlama/TinyLlama-1.1B-Chat-v1.0", ❷
        torch_dtype=torch.bfloat16,
        device=device ❸
    )
    return pipe


def generate_text(pipe: Pipeline, prompt: str, temperature: float = 0.7) -> str:
    messages = [
        {"role": "system", "content": system_prompt},
        {"role": "user", "content": prompt},
    ] ❹
    prompt = pipe.tokenizer.apply_chat_template(
        messages, tokenize=False, add_generation_prompt=True
    ) ❺
    predictions = pipe(
        prompt,
        temperature=temperature,
        max_new_tokens=256,
        do_sample=True,
        top_k=50,
        top_p=0.95,
    ) ❻
    output = predictions[0]["generated_text"].split("</s>\n<|assistant|>\n")[-1] ❼
    return output
```

❶ Check if an NVIDIA GPU is available, and if so, set device to the current
  CUDA-enabled GPU. Otherwise, continue using the CPU.

❷ Download and load the TinyLlama model into memory with a float16 tensor
  precision data type.[9]

❸ Move the whole pipeline to GPU on the first load.

❹ Prepare the message list, which consists of dictionaries that have role and content
  key-value pairs. The order of the dictionaries dictates the order of messages from
  older to newer in a conversation. The first message is often a system prompt to
  guide the model's output in a conversation.

❺ Convert the list of chat messages into a list of integer tokens for the model. The
  model is then asked to generate output in textual format, not integer tokens
  tokenize=False. A generation prompt is also added to the end of chat messages

---

9 float16 tensor precision is more memory efficient in memory constraint environments. The computations
  can be faster but precision is lower compared to float32 tensor types. See the TinyLlama model card (*https://
  oreil.ly/rsmoB*) for more information.

(`add_generation_prompt=True`) so that the model is encouraged to generate a response based on the chat history.

❻ The prepared prompt is passed to the model with several inference parameters to optimize the text generation performance. A few of these key inference parameters include:

- `max_new_tokens`: Specifies the maximum number of new tokens to generate in the output.

- `do_sample`: Determines, when producing output, whether to pick a token randomly from a list of suitable tokens (`True`) or to simply choose the most likely token at each step (`False`).

- `temperature`: Controls the randomness of the output generation. Lower values make the model's outputs more precise, while higher values allow for more creative responses.

- `top_k`: Restricts the model's token predictions to the top K options. `top_k=50` means create a list of top 50 most suitable tokens to pick from in the current token prediction step.

- `top_p`: Implements *nucleus sampling* when creating a list of most suitable tokens. `top_p=0.95` means create a list of the top tokens until you're satisfied that your list has 95% of the most suitable tokens to pick from, for the current token prediction step.

❼ The final output is obtained from the `predictions` object. The generated text from TinyLlama includes the full conversation history, with the generated response appended to the end. The `</s>` stop token followed by `\n<|assistant|>\n` tokens are used to pick the content of the last message in the conversation, which is the model's response.

Example 3-1 is a good starting point; you can still load this model on your CPU and get responses within a reasonable time. However, TinyLlama may also not perform as well as its larger counterparts. For production workloads, you will want to use bigger models for better output quality and performance.

You can now use the `load_model` and `predict` functions inside a controller function[10] and then add a route handling decorator to serve the model via an endpoint, as shown in Example 3-2.

---

10 As we saw in Chapter 2, controllers are functions that handle an API route's incoming requests and return responses to the client via a logical execution of services or providers.

Example 3-2. Serving a language model via a FastAPI endpoint

```python
# main.py

from fastapi import FastAPI
from models import load_text_model, generate_text

app = FastAPI()

@app.get("/generate/text")  ❶
def serve_language_model_controller(prompt: str) -> str:  ❷
    pipe = load_text_model()  ❸
    output = generate_text(pipe, prompt)  ❹
    return output  ❺
```

❶ Create a FastAPI server and add a `/generate` route handler for serving the model.

❷ The `serve_language_model_controller` is responsible for taking the prompt from the request query parameters.

❸ The model is loaded into memory.

❹ The controller passes the query to the model to perform the prediction.

❺ The FastAPI server sends the output as an HTTP response to the client.

Once the FastAPI service is up and running, you can visit the Swagger documentation page located at `http://localhost:8000/docs` to test your new endpoint:

```
http://localhost:8000/generate/text?prompt="What is FastAPI?"
```

If you're running the code samples on a CPU, it will take around a minute to receive a response from the model, as shown in Figure 3-11.

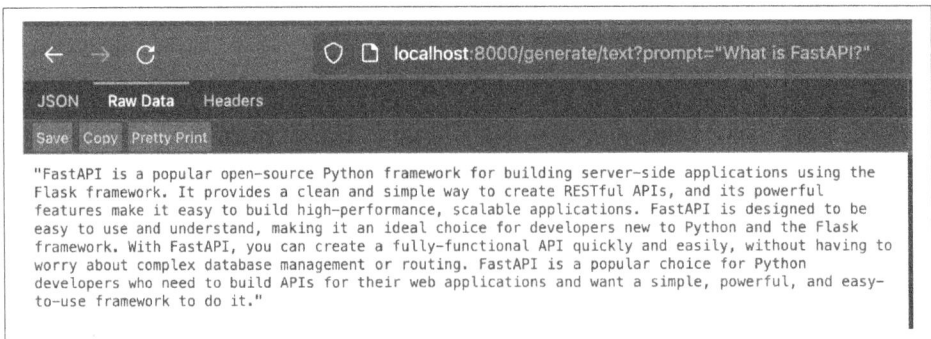

Figure 3-11. Response from TinyLlama

Not a bad response for a small language model (SLM) that runs on a CPU in your own computer, except that TinyLlama has *hallucinated* that FastAPI uses Flask. That is an incorrect statement; FastAPI uses Starlette as the underlying web framework, not Flask.

Hallucinations refer to outputs that aren't grounded in the training data or reality. Even though open source SLMs such as TinyLlama have been trained on impressive number of tokens (3 trillion), a small number of model parameters may have restricted their ability to learn the ground truth in data. Additionally, some unfiltered training data may also have been used, both of which can contribute to more instances of hallucinations.

> When serving language models, always let your users know to fact-check the outputs with external sources as language models may *hallucinate* and produce incorrect statements.

You can now use a web browser client in Python to visually test your service with more interactivity compared to using a command-line client.

A great Python package to quickly develop a user interface is Streamlit (*https://oreil.ly/9BXmn*), which enables you to create beautiful and customizable UIs for your AI services with little effort.

Connecting FastAPI with Streamlit UI generator

Streamlit allows you to easily create a chat user interface for testing and prototyping with models. You can install the streamlit package using pip:

```
$ pip install streamlit
```

Example 3-3 shows how to develop a simple UI to connect with your service.

Example 3-3. Streamlit chat UI consuming the FastAPI /generate endpoint

```
# client.py

import requests
import streamlit as st

st.title("FastAPI ChatBot") ❶

if "messages" not in st.session_state:
    st.session_state.messages = [] ❷

for message in st.session_state.messages:
    with st.chat_message(message["role"]):
```

```
        st.markdown(message["content"]) ❸

if prompt := st.chat_input("Write your prompt in this input field"): ❹
    st.session_state.messages.append({"role": "user", "content": prompt}) ❺

    with st.chat_message("user"):
        st.text(prompt) ❻

    response = requests.get(
        f"http://localhost:8000/generate/text", params={"prompt": prompt}
    ) ❼
    response.raise_for_status() ❽

    with st.chat_message("assistant"):
        st.markdown(response.text) ❾
```

❶ Add a title to your application that will be rendered to the UI.

❷ Initialize the chat and keep track of the chat history.

❸ Display the chat messages from the chat history on app rerun.

❹ Wait until the user has submitted a prompt via the chat input field.

❺ Add the user or assistant messages to the chat history.

❻ Display the user message in the chat message container.

❼ Send a GET request with the prompt as a query parameter to your FastAPI endpoint to generate a response from TinyLlama.

❽ Validate the response is OK.

❾ Display the assistant message in the chat message container.

You can now start your Streamlit client application:[11]

```
$ streamlit run client.py
```

You should now be able to interact with TinyLlama inside Streamlit, as shown in Figure 3-12. All of this was possible with a few short Python scripts.

---

11 Streamlit collects usage statistics by default, but you can turn this off using a configuration file (*https://oreil.ly/ m_Jix*).

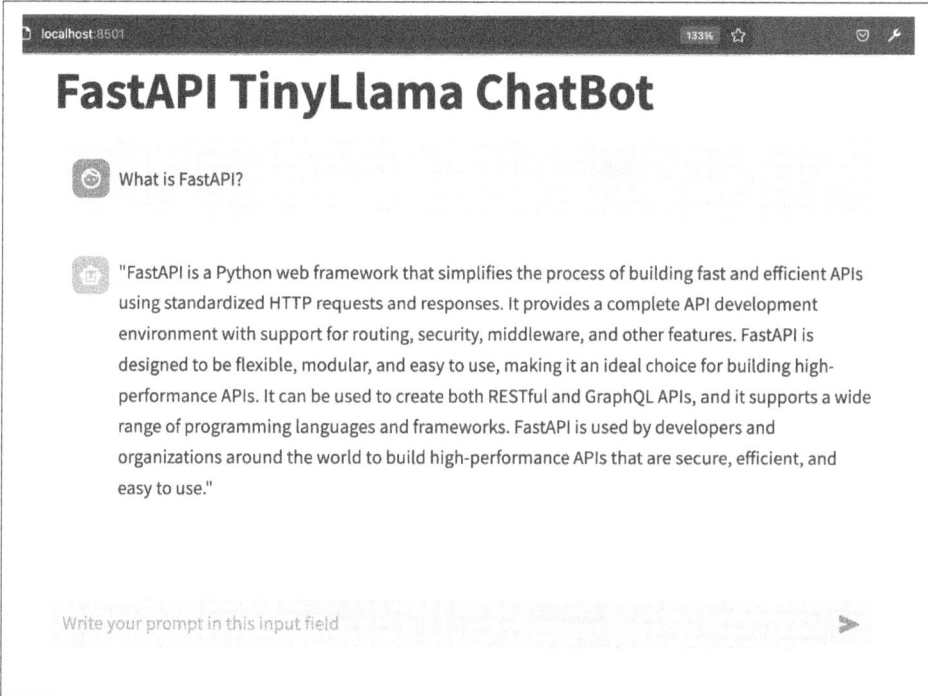

Figure 3-12. Streamlit client

Figure 3-13 shows the overall system architecture of the solution we've developed so far.

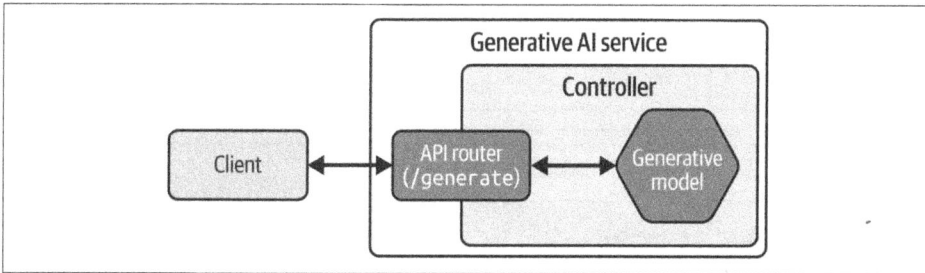

Figure 3-13. FastAPI service system architecture

While the solution in Example 3-3 is great for prototyping and testing models, it is not suitable for production workloads where several users would need simultaneous access to the model. This is because with the current setup, the model is loaded and unloaded onto memory every time a request is processed. Having to load/unload a large model to and from memory is slow and I/O blocking.

The TinyLlama service you've just built used a *decoder* transformer, optimized for conversational and chat use cases. However, the original paper on transformers (*https://oreil.ly/RqztC*) introduced an architecture that consisted of both an encoder and a decoder.

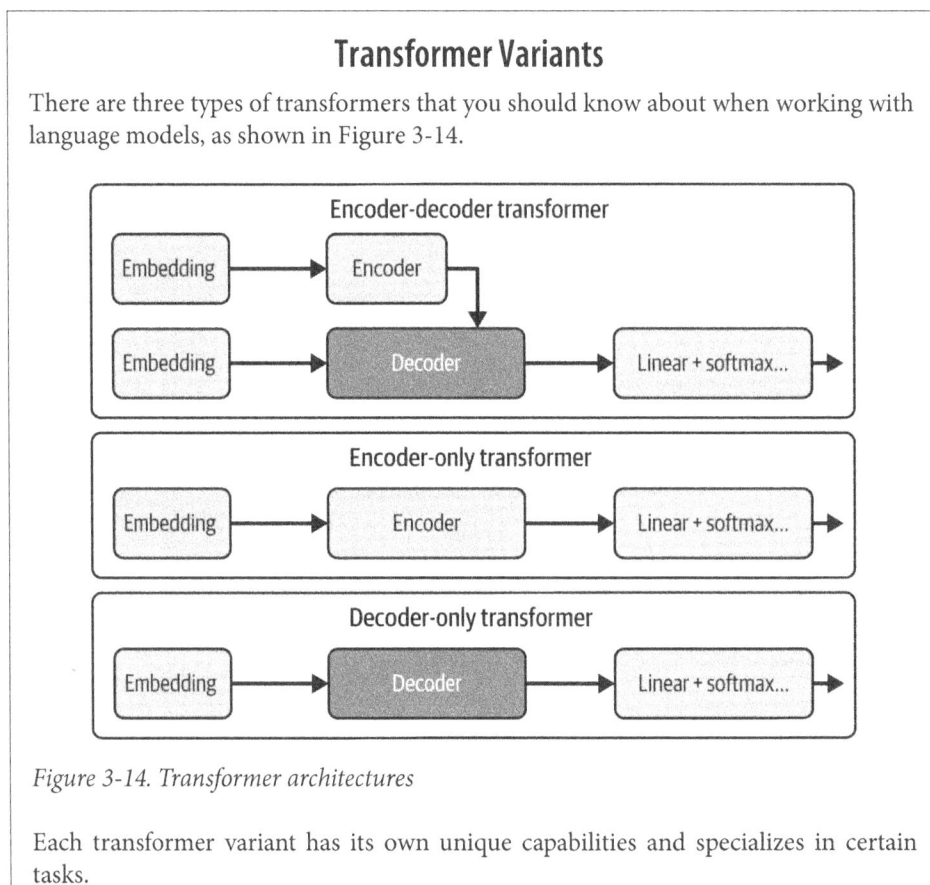

Transformer Variants

There are three types of transformers that you should know about when working with language models, as shown in Figure 3-14.

Figure 3-14. Transformer architectures

Each transformer variant has its own unique capabilities and specializes in certain tasks.

Encoder-decoder transformers
- Used for transforming one sequence of information into another
- Excel at translation, text summarization, question and answering tasks

Encoder-only transformers
- Used for understanding and representing the meanings of input sequences
- Specialize in sentiment analysis, entity extraction, and text classification tasks

Decoder-only transformers
- Used for predicting the next token in a sequence
- Outshine other transformers in text generation, conversational and language modeling tasks

In practice, you should select the appropriate transformer for your use case based on its specialization and capabilities.

You should now feel more confident in the inner workings of language models and how to package them in a FastAPI web server.

Language models represent just a fraction of all generative models. The upcoming sections will expand your knowledge to include the function and serving of models that generate audio, images, and videos.

We can start working with audio models first.

Audio Models

In GenAI services, audio models are important for creating interactive and realistic sounds. Unlike text models that you're now familiar with, which focus on processing and generating text, audio models can handle audio signals. With them, you can synthesize speech, generate music, and even create sound effects for applications like virtual assistants, automated dubbing, game development, and immersive audio environments.

One of the most capable text-to-speech and text-to-audio models is the Bark model created by Suno AI. This transformer-based model can generate realistic multilingual speech and audio including music, background noise, and sound effects.

The Bark model consists of four models chained together as a pipeline to synthesize audio waveforms from textual prompts, as shown in Figure 3-15.

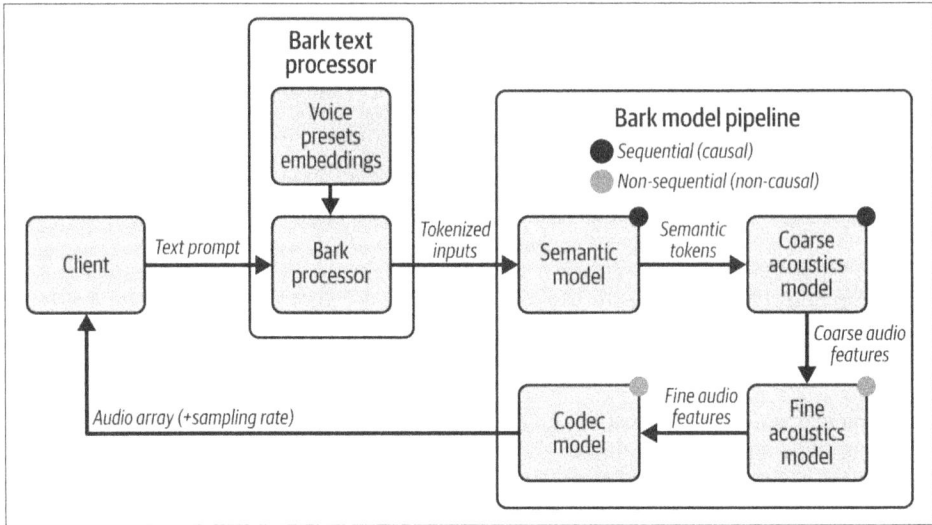

Figure 3-15. Bark synthesis pipeline

1. Semantic text model

A causal (sequential) autoregressive transformer model accepts tokenized input text and captures the meaning via semantic tokens. Autoregressive models predict future values in a sequence by reusing their own previous outputs.

2. Coarse acoustics model

A causal autoregressive transformer receives the semantic model's outputs and generates the initial audio features, which lack finer details. Each prediction is based on past and present information in the semantic token sequence.

3. Fine acoustics model

A noncausal auto-encoder transformer refines the audio representation by generating the remaining audio features. As the coarse acoustics model has generated the entire audio sequence, the fine model doesn't need to be casual.

4. Encodec audio codec model

The model decodes the output audio array from all previously generated audio codes.

Bark synthesizes the audio waveform by decoding the refined audio features into the final audio output in the form of spoken words, music, or simple audio effects.

Example 3-4 shows how to use the small Bark model.

Example 3-4. Download and load the small Bark model from the Hugging Face repository

```
# schemas.py

from typing import Literal

VoicePresets = Literal["v2/en_speaker_1", "v2/en_speaker_9"] ❶

# models.py
import torch
import numpy as np
from transformers import AutoProcessor, AutoModel, BarkProcessor, BarkModel
from schemas import VoicePresets

device = torch.device("cuda" if torch.cuda.is_available() else "cpu")

def load_audio_model() -> tuple[BarkProcessor, BarkModel]:
    processor = AutoProcessor.from_pretrained("suno/bark-small", device=device) ❷
    model = AutoModel.from_pretrained("suno/bark-small", device=device) ❸
    return processor, model


def generate_audio(
    processor: BarkProcessor,
    model: BarkModel,
    prompt: str,
    preset: VoicePresets,
) -> tuple[np.array, int]:
    inputs = processor(text=[prompt], return_tensors="pt",voice_preset=preset) ❹
    output = model.generate(**inputs, do_sample=True).cpu().numpy().squeeze() ❺
    sample_rate = model.generation_config.sample_rate ❻
    return output, sample_rate
```

❶ Specify supported voice preset options using a Literal type.

❷ Download the small Bark processor, which prepares the input text prompt for the core model.

❸ Download the Bark model, which will be used to generate the output audio. Both objects will be needed for audio generation later.

❹ Preprocess the text prompt with a speaker voice preset embedding and return a Pytorch tensor array of tokenized inputs using return_tensors="pt".

❺ Generate an audio array that contains amplitude values of the synthesized audio signal over time.

❻ Get the sampling rate from model generating configurations, which can be used to produce the audio.

When you generate audio using a model, the output is a sequence of floating-point numbers that represent the *amplitude* (or strength) of the audio signal at each point in time.

To play back this audio, it needs to be converted to a digital format that can be sent to the speakers. This involves sampling the audio signal at a fixed rate and quantizing the amplitude values to a fixed number of bits. The soundfile library can help you here by generating the audio file using a *sampling rate*. The higher the sampling rate, the more samples that are taken, which enhances the audio quality but also increases the file size.

You can install the soundfile audio library for writing audio files using pip:

```
$ pip install soundfile
```

Example 3-5 shows how you can stream the audio content to the client.

Example 3-5. FastAPI endpoint for returning generated audio

```
# utils.py

from io import BytesIO
import soundfile
import numpy as np

def audio_array_to_buffer(audio_array: np.array, sample_rate: int) -> BytesIO:
    buffer = BytesIO()
    soundfile.write(buffer, audio_array, sample_rate, format="wav")  ❶
    buffer.seek(0)
    return buffer  ❷


# main.py

from fastapi import FastAPI, status
from fastapi.responses import StreamingResponse

from models import load_audio_model, generate_audio
from schemas import VoicePresets
from utils import audio_array_to_buffer

@app.get(
    "/generate/audio",
    responses={status.HTTP_200_OK: {"content": {"audio/wav": {}}}},
    response_class=StreamingResponse,
) ❸
def serve_text_to_audio_model_controller(
    prompt: str,
```

```
    preset: VoicePresets = "v2/en_speaker_1",
):
    processor, model = load_audio_model()
    output, sample_rate = generate_audio(processor, model, prompt, preset)
    return StreamingResponse(
        audio_array_to_buffer(output, sample_rate), media_type="audio/wav"
    ) ❹
```

❶ Install the soundfile library to write the audio array to memory buffer using its sampling rate.

❷ Reset the buffer cursor to the start of the buffer and return the iterable buffer.

❸ Create a new audio endpoint that returns the audio/wav content type as Stream ingResponse. StreamingResponse is typically used when you want to stream the response data, such as when returning large files or when generating the response data. It allows you to return a generator function that yields chunks of data to be sent to the client.

❹ Convert the generated audio array to an iterable buffer that can be passed to streaming response.

In Example 3-5, you generated an audio array using the small Bark model and streamed the memory buffer of the audio content. Streaming is more efficient for larger files as the client can consume the content as it is being served. In previous examples, we didn't use streaming responses, as generated images or text can be fairly small compared to audio or video content.

> Streaming audio content directly from a memory buffer is faster and more efficient than writing the audio array to a file and streaming the content from the hard drive.
>
> If you need the memory available for other tasks, you can write the audio array to a file first and then stream from it using a file reader generator. You will be trading off latency for memory.

Now that you have an audio generation endpoint, you can update your Streamlit UI client code to render audio messages. Update your Streamlit client code as shown in Example 3-6.

Example 3-6. Streamlit audio UI consuming the FastAPI /audio generation endpoint

```
# client.py

for message in st.session_state.messages:
    with st.chat_message(message["role"]):
        content = message["content"]
        if isinstance(content, bytes):
            st.audio(content)
        else:
            st.markdown(content)


if prompt := st.chat_input("Write your prompt in this input field"):
    response = requests.get(
        f"http://localhost:8000/generate/audio", params={"prompt": prompt}
    )
    response.raise_for_status()
    with st.chat_message("assistant"):
        st.text("Here is your generated audio")
        st.audio(response.content) ❶
```

❶ Update the Streamlit client code to render audio content.

With Streamlit, you can swap components to render any type of content including images, audio, and video.

You should now be able to generate highly realistic speech audio in your updated Streamlit UI, as shown in Figure 3-16.

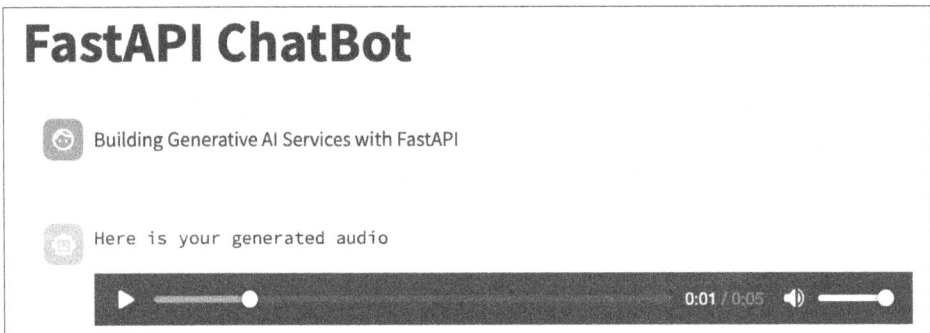

Figure 3-16. Rendering audio responses in the Streamlit UI

Bear in mind that you're using the compressed version of the Bark model, but with the light version, you can generate speech and music audio fairly quickly even on a single CPU. This is in exchange for some audio generation quality.

You should now feel more comfortable serving larger content to your users via streaming responses and working with audio models.

So far, you've been building conversational and text-to-speech services. Now let's see how to interact with a vision model to build an image generator service.

Vision Models

Using vision models, you can generate, enhance, and understand visual information from prompts.

Since these models can produce very realistic outputs faster than any human and can understand and manipulate existing visual content, they're extremely useful for applications like image generators and editors, object detection, image classification and captioning, and augmented reality.

One of the most popular architectures used to train image models is called *Stable Diffusion* (SD).

SD models are trained to encode input images into a latent space. This latent space is the mathematical representation of patterns in the training data that the model has learned. If you try to visualize an encoded image, all you would see is a white noise image, similar to the black and white dots you would see on your TV screen when it loses signal.

Figure 3-17 shows the full process for training and inference and visualizes how images are encoded and decoded via the forward and reverse diffusion processes. A text encoder using text, images, and semantic maps assists in controlling the output via the reverse diffusion.

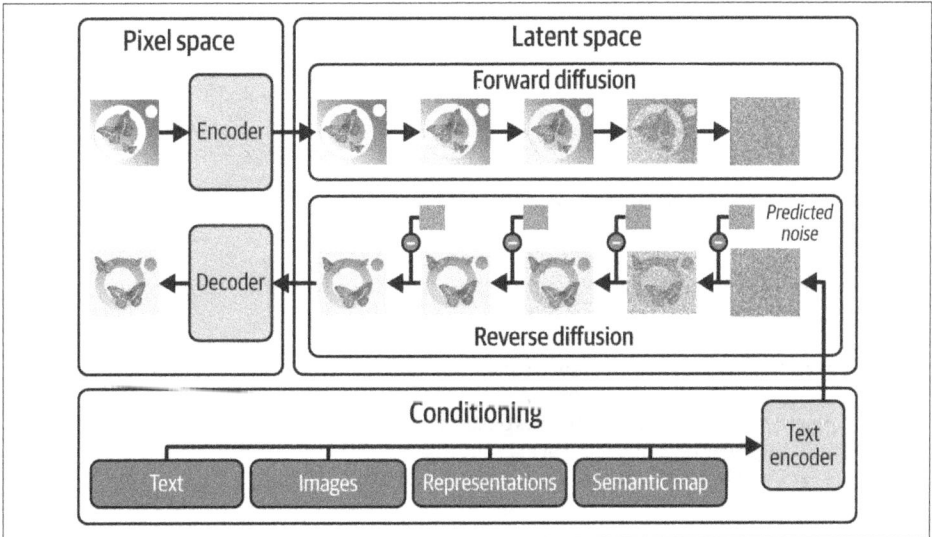

Figure 3-17. Stable Diffusion training and inference

What makes these models magical is their ability to decode noisy images back into original input images. Effectively, the SD models also learn to remove white noise from an encoded image to reproduce the original image. The model performs this denoising process over several iterations.

However, you don't want to re-create images you already have. You will want the model to create new, never-before-seen images. But how can an SD model achieve this for you? The answer lies in the latent space where the encoded noisy images live. You can change the noise in these images so that when the model denoises them and decodes them back, you get a whole new image that the model has never seen before.

A challenge remains: how can you control the image generation process so that the model doesn't produce random images? The solution is to also encode image descriptions alongside the image. The patterns in the latent space are then mapped to textual image descriptions of what is seen in each input image. Now, you use textual prompts to sample the noisy latent space such that the produced output image after the denoising process is what you want.

This is how SD models can generate new images that they've never seen before in their training data. In essence, these models navigate a latent space that contains encoded representations of various patterns and meanings.[12] The model iteratively refines this noise through a denoising process to produce a novel image not present in its training dataset.

To download an SD model, you will need to have the Hugging Face `diffusers` library installed:

```
$ pip install diffusers
```

Example 3-7 shows how to load an SD model into memory.

Example 3-7. Download and load an SD model from the Hugging Face repository

```
# models.py

import torch
from diffusers import DiffusionPipeline, StableDiffusionInpaintPipelineLegacy
from PIL import Image

device = torch.device("cuda" if torch.cuda.is_available() else "cpu")

def load_image_model() -> StableDiffusionInpaintPipelineLegacy:
    pipe = DiffusionPipeline.from_pretrained(
        "segmind/tiny-sd", torch_dtype=torch.float32,
```

---

12 The latent space of a trained model when visualized may look like white noise but will contain structured representations that the model has learned to encode and decode.

```
        device=device
    ) ❶
    return pipe

def generate_image(
    pipe: StableDiffusionInpaintPipelineLegacy, prompt: str
) -> Image.Image:
    output = pipe(prompt, num_inference_steps=10).images[0] ❷ ❸
    return output ❹
```

❶ Download and load the TinySD model into memory with the less memory efficient `float32` tensor type. Using `float16`, which has limited precision for large
and complex models, leads to numerical instability and loss of accuracy. Additionally, hardware support for `float16` is limited, so trying to run an SD model
on your CPU with the `float16` tensor type may not be possible. Source: Hugging
Face (*https://oreil.ly/rzw8P*).

❷ Pass the text prompt to the model to generate a list of images and pick the first
one. Some models allow you to generate multiple images in a single inference
step.

❸ The `num_inference_steps=10` specifies the number of diffusion steps to perform
during inference. In each diffusion step, a stronger noisy image is produced from
previous diffusion steps. The model generates multiple noisy images by undertaking multiple diffusion steps. With these images, the model can better understand the patterns of noise that are present in the input data and learn to remove
them more effectively. The more inference steps, the better results you will get,
but at the cost of computing power needed and longer processing times.

❹ The generated image will be a Python Pillow image type, so you have access to a
variety of Pillow's image methods for post-processing and storage. For instance,
you can call the `image.save()` method to store the image in your filesystem.

Vision models are extremely resource hungry. To load and use a
small vision model such as TinySD on CPU, you will need around
5 GB of disk space and RAM. However, you can install `accelerate`
using `pip install accelerate` to optimize resources required so
that the model pipeline uses lower CPU memory usage.

When serving video models, you will need to use a GPU. Later in
this chapter, I will show you how to leverage GPUs for video
models.

You can now package this model into another endpoint as similar to Example 3-2, with the difference being that the returned response will be an image binary (not text). Refer to Example 3-8.

Example 3-8. FastAPI endpoint for returning a generated image

```python
# utils.py

from typing import Literal
from PIL import Image
from io import BytesIO

def img_to_bytes(
    image: Image.Image, img_format: Literal["PNG", "JPEG"] = "PNG"
) -> bytes:
    buffer = BytesIO()
    image.save(buffer, format=img_format)
    return buffer.getvalue() ❶

# main.py

from fastapi import FastAPI, Response, status
from models import load_image_model, generate_image
from utils import img_to_bytes

...

@app.get("/generate/image",
        responses={status.HTTP_200_OK: {"content": {"image/png": {}}}}, ❷
        response_class=Response) ❸
def serve_text_to_image_model_controller(prompt: str):
    pipe = load_image_model()
    output = generate_image(pipe, prompt) ❹
    return Response(content=img_to_bytes(output), media_type="image/png") ❺
```

❶ Create an in-memory buffer, save the image to this buffer in a given format, and then return the raw byte data from the buffer.

❷ Specify the media content type and status codes for the auto-generated Swagger UI documentation page.

❸ Specify the response class to prevent FastAPI from adding `application/json` as an additional acceptable response media type.

❹ The response returned from the model will be Pillow image format.

❺ We will need to use the FastAPI `Response` class to send a special response carrying image bytes with a PNG media type.

Figure 3-18 shows the results of testing the new `/generate/image` endpoint via Fast-API Swagger docs with the text prompt `A cosy living room with trees in it.`

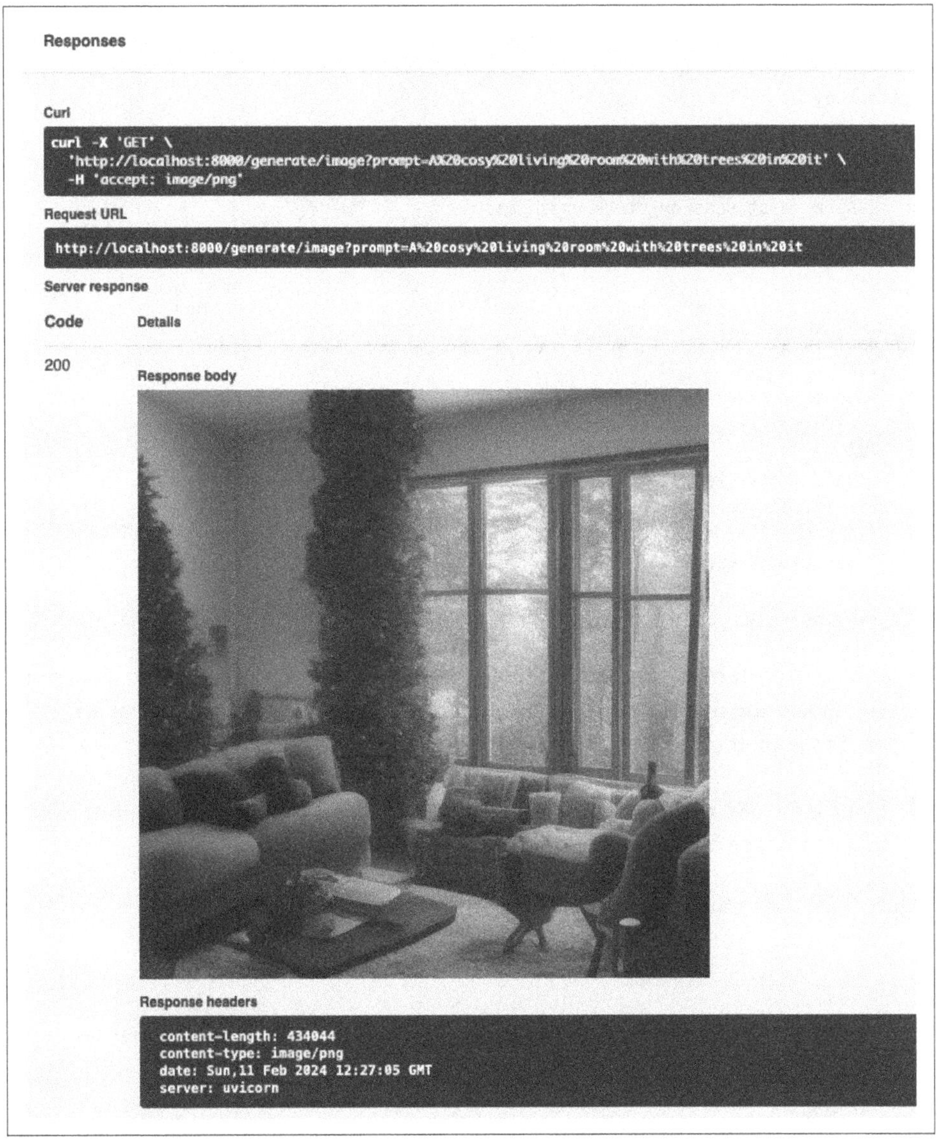

Figure 3-18. *TinySD FastAPI service*

Now, connect your endpoint to a Streamlit UI for prototyping, as shown in Example 3-9.

Example 3-9. Streamlit Vision UI consuming the FastAPI /image generation endpoint

```
# client.py

...

for message in st.session_state.messages:
    with st.chat_message(message["role"]):
        st.image(message["content"]) ❶
...

if prompt := st.chat_input("Write your prompt in this input field"):
    ...
    response = requests.get(
        f"http://localhost:8000/generate/image", params={"prompt": prompt}
    ) ❷
    response.raise_for_status()
    with st.chat_message("assistant"):
        st.text("Here is your generated image")
        st.image(response.content)

    ...
```

❶ Images transferred over the HTTP protocol will be in binary format. Therefore, we update the display function to render binary image content. You can use the st.image method to display images to the UI.

❷ Update the GET request to hit the /generate/image endpoint. Then, render a textual and image message to the user.

Figure 3-19 shows the final results of the user experience with the model.

Figure 3-19. Rendering image messages in the Streamlit UI

Running XL Models

You now see how to implement model-serving endpoints with FastAPI and Streamlit to generate text or images. We used tiny versions of these models so that you can run the examples on your CPU. However, your hardware requirements significantly increase if you need to use the XL versions for better quality. As an example, to run the SDXL model, you will require both 16 GB of CPU RAM and 16 GB of GPU VRAM to generate an image. This is because you will first need to load the model onto your CPU from disk and then move it to your GPU for inference. We will cover this process in more detail when discussing model-serving strategies.

We saw how even with a tiny SD model, you can generate reasonable looking images. The XL versions can produce even more realistic images but still have their own limitations.

At the time of writing, the current open source SD models do have certain limitations:

Coherency
    The models can't produce every detail described in the prompts and complex compositions.

Output size
    The output images can only be predefined sizes such as 512×512 or 1024×1024 pixels.

Composability
    You can't fully control the generated image and define composition in the image.

Photorealism
    The generated outputs do show details that give away they've been generated by AI.

Legible text
    Some models cannot generate legible texts.

The `tinysd` model you worked with is an early phase model that has undergone the *distillation* process (i.e., compression) from the larger V1.5 SD model. As a result, the generated outputs may not meet production standards or be entirely cohesive and could fail to incorporate all the concepts mentioned in the text prompts. However, the distilled models may perform well if you *fine-tune* them using *Low-Rank Adaptation* (LoRA) (*https://oreil.ly/Nqtkm*) on specific concepts/styles.

Low-Rank Adaptation in Fine-Tuning Generative Models

LoRA is a training strategy that introduces a minimal number of trainable parameters to each layer in a model. The majority of the original model's parameters remain fixed.

By limiting the number of parameters that need to be trained, LoRA greatly decreases the GPU memory needed for training. This is quite useful when fine-tuning or training large-scale models, where memory constraints are typically a major challenge to customization.

You can now build both text- and image-based GenAI services. However, you may be wondering how to build text-to-video services based on video models. Let's learn more about video models, how they work, and how to build an image animator service with them next.

Video Models

Video models are some of the most resource-hungry generative models and often require a GPU to produce a short snippet of good quality. These models have to generate several tens of frames to produce a single second of video, even without any audio content.

Stability AI has released several open source video models based on the SD architecture on Hugging Face. We will work with the compressed version of their image-to-video model for a faster image animation service.

To get started, let's get a small image-to-video model running using Example 3-10.

> To run Example 3-10, you may need access to a CUDA-capable NVIDIA GPU.
>
> Also, for commercial use of the `stable-video-diffusion-img2vid` model, please refer to its model card (*https://oreil.ly/DM-0p*).

Example 3-10. Download and load the Stability AI's img2vid model from the Hugging Face repository

```
# models.py

import torch
from diffusers import StableVideoDiffusionPipeline
from PIL import Image

device = torch.device("cuda" if torch.cuda.is_available() else "cpu")
```

```
def load_video_model() -> StableVideoDiffusionPipeline:
    pipe = StableVideoDiffusionPipeline.from_pretrained(
        "stabilityai/stable-video-diffusion-img2vid",
        torch_dtype=torch.float16,
        variant="fp16",
        device=device,
    )
    return pipe

def generate_video(
    pipe: StableVideoDiffusionPipeline, image: Image.Image, num_frames: int = 25
) -> list[Image.Image]:
    image = image.resize((1024, 576))  ❶
    generator = torch.manual_seed(42)  ❷
    frames = pipe(
        image, decode_chunk_size=8, generator=generator, num_frames=num_frames
    ).frames[0]  ❸
    return frames
```

❶ Resize the input image to a standard size expected by model input. Resizing will also protect against large inputs.

❷ Create a random tensor generator with the seed set to 42 for reproducible video frame generation.

❸ Run the frame generation pipeline to produce all video frames at once. Grab the first batch of generated frames. This step requires significant video memory. num_frames specifies the number of frames to generate, while decode_chunk_size specifies how many frames to generate at once.

With the model loading functions in place, you can now build the video-serving endpoint.

However, before you proceed with declaring the route handler, you do need a utility function to process the video model outputs from frames into a streamable video using an I/O buffer.

To export a sequence of frames to videos, you need to encode them into a video container using a video library such as av, which implements Python bindings to the popular ffmpeg video processing library.

You can install the av library via:

```
$ pip install av
```

Now you can use Example 3-11 to create streamable video buffers.

Example 3-11. Exporting video model output from frames to a streamable video buffer using the av library

```python
# utils.py

from io import BytesIO
from PIL import Image
import av

def export_to_video_buffer(images: list[Image.Image]) -> BytesIO:
    buffer = BytesIO()
    output = av.open(buffer, "w", format="mp4")  ❶
    stream = output.add_stream("h264", 30)  ❷
    stream.width = images[0].width
    stream.height = images[0].height
    stream.pix_fmt = "yuv444p"  ❸
    stream.options = {"crf": "17"}  ❹
    for image in images:
        frame = av.VideoFrame.from_image(image)
        packet = stream.encode(frame)    ❺
        output.mux(packet)  ❻
    packet = stream.encode(None)
    output.mux(packet)
    return buffer  ❼
```

❶ Open a buffer for writing an MP4 file and then configure a video stream with AV's video multiplexer.[13]

❷ Set the video encoding to h264 at 30 frames per second and make sure the frame dimensions match the frames provided to the function.

❸ Set the pixel format of the video stream to yuv444p so that each pixel has the full resolution for the y (luminance or brightness) and both u and v (chrominance or color) components.

❹ Configure the stream's constant rate factor (CRF) to control the video quality and compression. Set the CRF to 17 to output a lossless high-quality video with minimal compression.

❺ Encode the input frames into encoded packets with the configured stream video multiplexer.

❻ Add the encoded frames into the opened video container buffer.

---

13 *Multiplexing* is the process of combining multiple streams (such as audio, video, and subtitles) into a single file or stream in a synchronized manner.

❼ Flush any remaining frames in the encoder and combine the resulting packet into the output file before returning the buffer containing the encoded video.

To use image prompts with the service as file uploads, you must install the python-multipart library:[14]

```
$ pip install python-multipart
```

Once installed, you can set up the new endpoint using Example 3-12.

Example 3-12. Serving generated videos from the image-to-video model

```
# main.py

from fastapi import status, FastAPI, File
from fastapi.responses import StreamingResponse
from io import BytesIO
from PIL import Image

from models import load_video_model, generate_video
from utils import export_to_video_buffer

...

@app.post(
    "/generate/video",
    responses={status.HTTP_200_OK: {"content": {"video/mp4": {}}}},
    response_class=StreamingResponse,
)
def serve_image_to_video_model_controller(
    image: bytes = File(...), num_frames: int = 25 ❶
):
    image = Image.open(BytesIO(image)) ❷
    model = load_video_model()
    frames = generate_video(model, image, num_frames)
    return StreamingResponse(
        export_to_video_buffer(frames), media_type="video/mp4" ❸
    )
```

❶ Use the File object to specify image as a form file upload.

❷ Create a Pillow Image object by passing the image bytes transferred to the service. The model pipeline expects a Pillow image format as input.

---

14 The python-multipart library is used for parsing multipart/form-data, which is commonly used encoding in file upload form submissions.

❸ Export the generated frames as a MP4 video and stream it to the client using an iterable video buffer.

With the video endpoint set up, you can now upload images to your FastAPI service to animate them as videos.

There are other video models available on the hub that allow you to generate GIFs and animations. For additional practice, you can try building a GenAI service with them. While open source video models can produce videos at ample quality, Open-AI's announcement of a new large vision model (LVM) called Sora has shaken the video generation industry.

OpenAI Sora

Text-to-video models are limited in their generation capabilities. Apart from the immense computational power needed to sequentially generate coherent video frames, training these models can be challenging due to:

- *Maintaining temporal and spatial consistency across frames* to achieve realistic undistorted video outputs.
- *Lack of training data* with high-quality caption and metadata needed to train video models.
- *Captioning challenges* when captioning the content of videos clearly and descriptively is time-consuming and moves beyond drafting short pieces of text. Captioning must describe the narrative and scenes for each sequence for the model to learn and map the rich patterns contained in the video to text.

Because of these reasons, there has not been a breakthrough with video generation models until the announcement of OpenAI's Sora model.

Sora is a generalist large vision diffusion transformer model capable of generating videos and images spanning diverse durations, aspect ratios, and resolutions, up to a full minute of high-definition video. Its architecture is based on the transformers commonly used in LLMs and the diffusion process. Whereas LLMs use text tokens, Sora uses visual patches.

> The Sora model combines elements and principles of the transformer and SD architectures, while in Example 3-10, you used Stability AI's SD model to generate videos.

So what makes Sora different?

Transformers have demonstrated remarkable scalability across language models, computer vision, and image generation, so it made sense for Sora architecture to be based on transformers to handle diverse inputs like text, images, or video frames. Also, since transformers can understand complex patterns and long-range dependencies in sequential data, Sora as a vision transformer can also capture fine-grained temporal and spatial relationships between video frames to generate coherent frames with smooth transitions between them (i.e., exhibiting temporal consistency).

Furthermore, Sora borrows capabilities of the SD models to generate high-quality and visually coherent video frames with precise controls using the iterative noise reduction process. Using the diffusion process lets Sora generate images with fine detail and desirable properties.

By combining both sequential reasoning of transformers with iterative refinement of SD, Sora can generate high-resolution, coherent, and smooth videos from multimodal inputs like text and images that contain abstract concepts.

Sora's network architecture is also designed to reduce dimensionality through a U-shape network where high-dimensional visual data is compressed and encoded into a latent noisy space. Sora can then generate patches from the latent space through the denoising diffusion process.

The diffusion process is similar to image-based SD models. Instead of having a 2D U-Net normally used for images, OpenAI has trained a 3D U-Net where the third dimension is a sequence of frames across time (making a video), as shown in Figure 3-20.

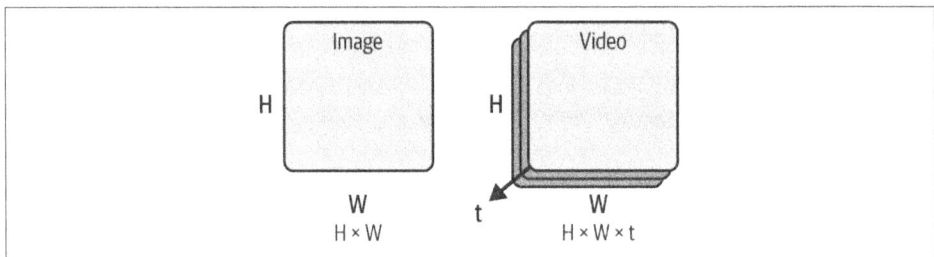

Figure 3-20. A sequence of images forms a video

OpenAI has demonstrated that by compressing videos into patches, as shown in Figure 3-21, the model can achieve scalability of learning high-dimensional representations when training on diverse types of videos and images varying in resolution, durations, and aspect ratios.

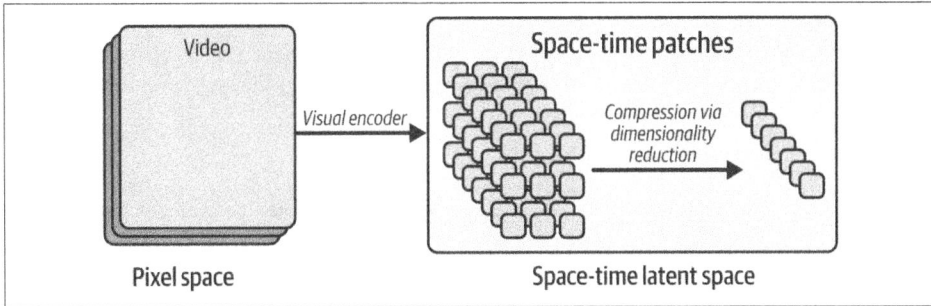

Figure 3-21. Video compression into space-time patches

Through the diffusion process, Sora crunches input noisy patches to generate clean videos and images in any aspect ratio, size, and resolution for devices directly in their native screen sizes.

While a text transformer is predicting the next token in a text sequence, Sora's vision transformer is predicting the next patch to generate an image or a video, as shown in Figure 3-22.

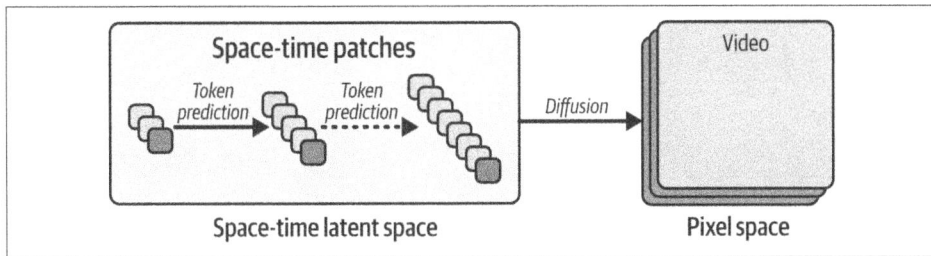

Figure 3-22. Token prediction by the vision transformer

Through training on various datasets, OpenAI overcame the previously mentioned challenges of training vision models such as lack of quality captions, high dimensionality of video data, etc., to name a few.

What is fascinating about Sora and potentially other LVMs is the emerging capabilities they exhibit:

3D consistency
　　Objects in the generated scenes remain consistent and adjust to perspective even when the camera moves and rotates around the scene.

Object permanence and large range coherence
　　Objects and people that are occluded or leave a frame at a location will persist when they reappear in the field of view. In some cases, the model effectively remembers how to keep them consistent in the environment. This is also referred to as *temporal consistency* that most video models struggle with.

World interaction

Actions simulated in generated videos realistically affect the environment. For instance, Sora understands the action of eating a burger should leave a bite mark on it.

Simulating environments

Sora can also simulate worlds—real or fictional environments like in games—while adhering to the rules of interactions in those environments, such as playing a character in a *Minecraft* level. In other words, Sora has learned to be a data-driven physics engine.

Figure 3-23 illustrates these capabilities.

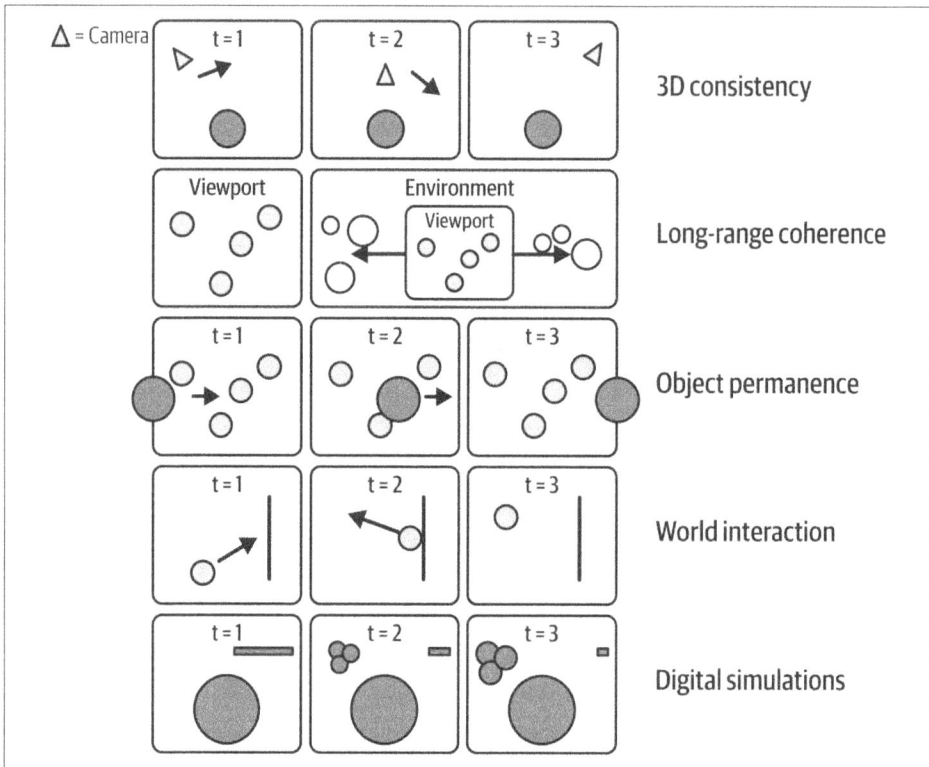

Figure 3-23. Sora's emergent capabilities

At the time of this writing, Sora has not yet been released as an API, but open source alternatives have already emerged. A promising large vision model called "Latte" allows you to fine-tune the LVM on your own visual data.

You can't yet commercialize some open source models, including Latte, at the time of writing. Always check the model card and the license to ensure any commercial use is allowed.

Combining transformers with diffusers to create LVMs is a promising area of research for generating complex outputs like videos. However, I imagine the same process can be applied for generating other types of high-dimensional data that can be represented as multidimensional arrays.

You should now feel more comfortable building services with text, audio, vision, and video models. Next, let's take a look at another set of models capable of generating complex data such as 3D geometries by building a 3D asset generator service.

3D Models

You now understand how previously mentioned models use transformers and diffusers to generate any form of textual, audio, or visual data. Producing 3D geometries requires a different approach than image, audio, and text generation because you must account for spatial relationships, depth information, and geometric consistency, which add layers of complexity not present in other data types.

For 3D geometries, *meshes* are used to define the shape of an object. Software packages like Autodesk 3ds Max, Maya, and SolidWorks can be used to produce, edit, and render these meshes.

Meshes are effectively a collection of *vertices*, *edges*, and *faces* that reside in a 3D virtual space. Vertices are points in space that connect to form edges. Edges form faces (polygons) when they enclose on a flat surface, often in the shape of triangles or quadrilaterals. Figure 3-24 shows the differences between vertices, edges, and faces.

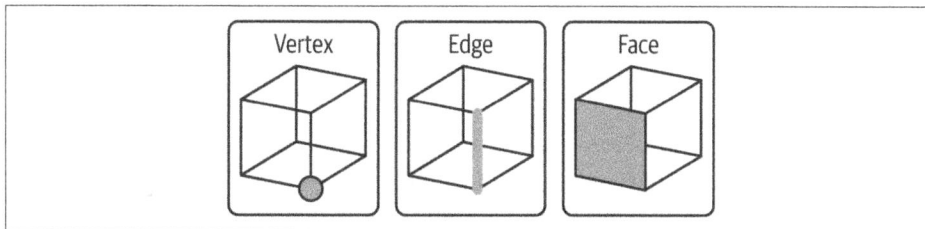

Figure 3-24. Vertices, edges, and faces

You can define vertices by their coordinates in a 3D space, usually determined by a Cartesian coordinate system (x, y, z). Essentially, the arrangement and connection of vertices form surfaces of a 3D mesh that define a geometry.

Figure 3-25 shows how these features combine to define a mesh of a 3D geometry such as a monkey's head.

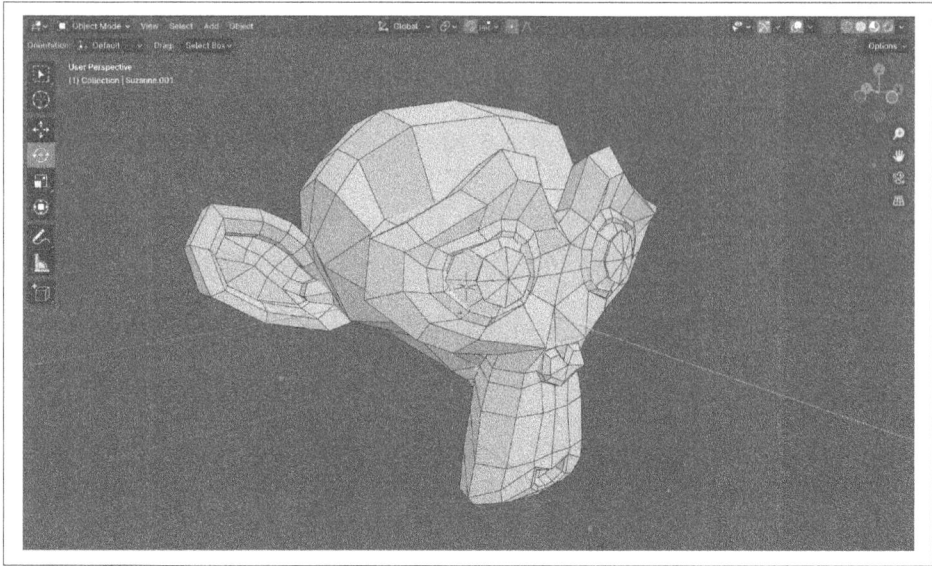

Figure 3-25. Mesh for 3D geometry of a monkey head using both triangular and quadrilateral polygons (shown in Blender, open source 3D modeling software)

You can train and use a transformer model to predict the next token in a sequence where the sequence is coordinates of vertices on a 3D mesh surface. Such a generative model can produce 3D geometries by predicting the next set of vertices and faces within a 3D space that form the desired geometry. However, the geometry would require thousands of vertices and faces to achieve a smooth surface.

This means for each 3D object, you need to wait for a long time for the generation to complete, and the results may still remain low fidelity. Because of this, the most capable models (i.e., OpenAI's Shap-E) in producing 3D geometry train functions (with many parameters) to implicitly define surfaces and volumes in a 3D space.

Implicit functions are useful for creating smooth surfaces or handling intricate details that are challenging for discrete representations like meshes. A trained model can consist of an encoder that maps patterns to an implicit function. Instead of explicitly generating sequences of vertices and faces for a mesh, *conditional* 3D models can evaluate the trained implicit functions across a continuous 3D space. As a result, the generation process has a high degree of freedom, control, and flexibility in producing high-fidelity outputs, becoming suitable for applications that require detailed and intricate 3D geometries.

Once the model's encoder is trained to produce implicit functions, it leverages the *neural radiance fields* (NeRF) rendering technique, as part of the decoder, to construct 3D scenes. NeRF maps a pair of inputs—a 3D spatial coordinate and a 3D viewing direction—to an output consisting of an object density and RGB color via the implicit functions. To synthesize new views in a 3D scene, the NeRF method considers the viewport as a matrix of rays. Each pixel corresponding to a ray, originates from the camera position, and then extends in the viewing direction. The color of each ray and associated pixel is computed by evaluating the implicit function along the ray and integrating the results to calculate the RGB color.

Once the 3D scene is computed, *signed distance functions* (SDFs) are used to generate meshes, or wireframes of 3D objects by calculating the distance and color of any point to the nearest surface of the 3D object. Think of SDFs as a way to describe a 3D object by telling you how far away every point in space is from the object's surface. This function gives a number for each point: if the point is inside the object, the number is negative; if it's on the surface, the number is zero; and if it's outside, the number is positive. The surface of the object is where all points have the number zero. SDFs help to turn this information into a 3D mesh.

Despite the use of implicit functions, the quality of outputs is still inferior to human-created 3D assets and may feel cartoonish. However, with 3D GenAI models, you can generate the initial 3D geometries to iterate over concepts and refine 3D assets quickly.

OpenAI Shap-E

Shap-E (developed by OpenAI) is an open source model "conditioned" on input 3D data (descriptions, parameters, partial geometries, colors, etc.) to generate specific 3D shapes. You can use Shap-E to create an image or text-to-3D services.

As usual, you start by downloading and loading the model from Hugging Face, as shown in Example 3-13.

Example 3-13. Downloading and loading OpenAI's Shap-E model

```
# models.py
import torch
from diffusers import ShapEPipeline

device = torch.device("cuda" if torch.cuda.is_available() else "cpu")

def load_3d_model() -> ShapEPipeline:
    pipe = ShapEPipeline.from_pretrained("openai/shap-e", device=device)
    return pipe

def generate_3d_geometry(
    pipe: ShapEPipeline, prompt: str, num_inference_steps: int
```

```
):
    images = pipe(
        prompt, ❶
        guidance_scale=15.0, ❷
        num_inference_steps=num_inference_steps, ❸
        output_type="mesh", ❹
    ).images[0] ❺
    return images
```

❶ This specific Shap-E pipeline accepts textual prompts, but if you want to pass image prompts, you need to load a different pipeline.

❷ Use the `guidance_scale` parameter to fine-tune the generation process to better match the prompt.

❸ Use the `num_inference_steps` parameter to control the output resolution in exchange for additional computation. Requesting a higher number of inference steps or increasing the guidance scale can elongate the rendering time in exchange for higher-quality outputs that better follow the user's request.

❹ Set the `output_type` parameter to produce `mesh` tensors as output.

❺ By default, the Shap-E pipeline will produce a sequence of images that can be combined to generate a rotating GIF animation of the object. You can export this output to either GIFs, videos, or OBJ files that can be loaded in 3D modeling tools such as Blender.

Now that you have a model loading and 3D mesh generation functions, let's export the mesh into a buffer using Example 3-14.

open3d is an open source library for processing 3D data such as point clouds, meshes, and color images with depth information (i.e., RGB-D images). You will need to install open3d to run Example 3-14:

```
$ pip install open3d
```

Example 3-14. Exporting a 3D tensor mesh to a Wavefront OBJ buffer

```
# utils.py

import os
import tempfile
from io import BytesIO
from pathlib import Path
import open3d as o3d
import torch
```

```
from diffusers.pipelines.shap_e.renderer import MeshDecoderOutput

def mesh_to_obj_buffer(mesh: MeshDecoderOutput) -> BytesIO:
    mesh_o3d = o3d.geometry.TriangleMesh() ❶
    mesh_o3d.vertices = o3d.utility.Vector3dVector(
        mesh.verts.cpu().detach().numpy() ❷
    )
    mesh_o3d.triangles = o3d.utility.Vector3iVector(
        mesh.faces.cpu().detach().numpy() ❷
    )

    if len(mesh.vertex_channels) == 3:  # You have color channels
        vert_color = torch.stack(
            [mesh.vertex_channels[channel] for channel in "RGB"], dim=1
        ) ❸
        mesh_o3d.vertex_colors = o3d.utility.Vector3dVector(
            vert_color.cpu().detach().numpy()
        ) ❹

    with tempfile.NamedTemporaryFile(delete=False, suffix=".obj") as tmp:
        o3d.io.write_triangle_mesh(tmp.name, mesh_o3d, write_ascii=True)
        with open(tmp.name, "rb") as f:
            buffer = BytesIO(f.read()) ❺
        os.remove(tmp.name) ❻

    return buffer
```

❶ Create an Open3D triangle mesh object.

❷ Convert the generated mesh from the model into an Open3D triangle mesh object. To do so, grab vertices and triangles from the generated 3D mesh by moving the mesh vertices and faces tensors to the CPU and converting them to numpy arrays.

❸ Check if the mesh has three vertex color channels (indicating RGB color data) and stack these channels into a tensor.

❹ Convert mesh color tensor to a format compatible with Open3D for setting the vertex colors of the mesh.

❺ Use a temporary file to create and return a data buffer.

❻ Windows doesn't support NameTemporaryFile's delete=True option. Instead, manually remove the created temporary file just before returning the in-memory buffer.

Finally, you can build the endpoints, as shown in Example 3-15.

Example 3-15. Creating the 3D model-serving endpoint

```
# main.py

from fastapi import FastAPI, status
from fastapi.responses import StreamingResponse
from models import load_3d_model, generate_3d_geometry
from utils import mesh_to_obj_buffer

...

@app.get(
    "/generate/3d",
    responses={status.HTTP_200_OK: {"content": {"model/obj": {}}}}, ❶
    response_class=StreamingResponse,
)
def serve_text_to_3d_model_controller(
    prompt: str, num_inference_steps: int = 25
):
    model = load_3d_model()
    mesh = generate_3d_geometry(model, prompt, num_inference_steps)
    response = StreamingResponse(
        mesh_to_obj_buffer(mesh), media_type="model/obj"
    )
    response.headers["Content-Disposition"] = (
        f"attachment; filename={prompt}.obj"
    ) ❷
    return response
```

❶ Specify the OpenAPI specification for a successful response to include `model/obj` as the media content type.

❷ Indicate to clients that the content of streaming response should be treated as an attachment.

If you send a request to the `/generate/3d` endpoint, the download of the 3D object as a Wavefront OBJ file should start as soon as generation is complete.

You can import the OBJ file into any 3D modeling software such as Blender to view the 3D geometry. Using prompts such as `apple`, `car`, `phone`, and `donut` you can generate the 3D geometries shown in Figure 3-26.

Figure 3-26. 3D geometries of a car, apple, phone, and donut imported into Blender

If you isolate an object like the apple and enable the wireframe view, you can see all the vertices and edges that make up the apple's mesh, represented as triangular polygons, as shown in Figure 3-27.

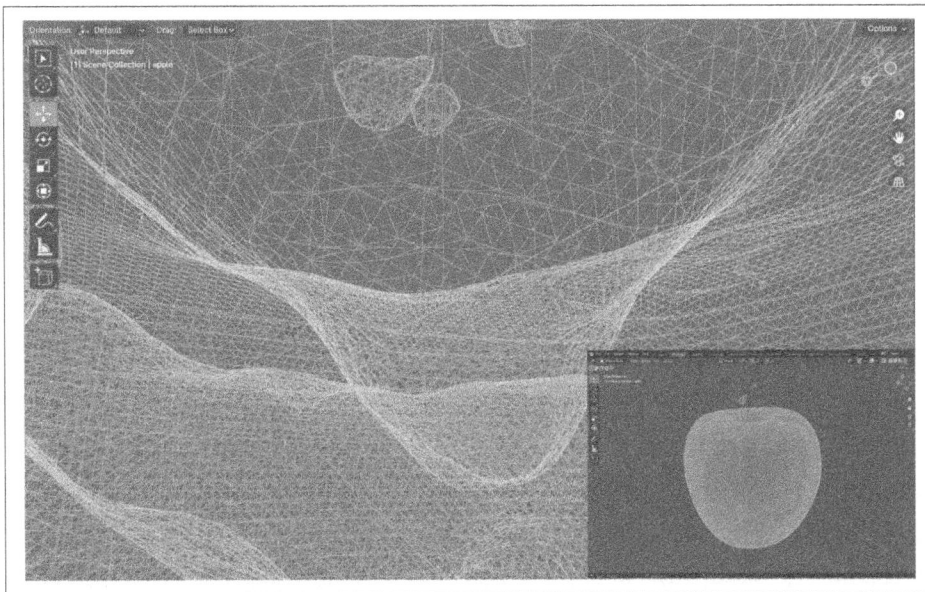

Figure 3-27. Zooming in on the generated 3D mesh to view triangular polygons; inset: viewing the generated apple geometry mesh (including vertices and edges)

Shap-E supersedes another older model called *Point-E* that generates *point clouds* of 3D objects. This is because Shap-E, compared to Point-E, converges faster and reaches comparable or better generation shape quality despite modeling a higher-dimensional, multirepresentation output space.

Point clouds (often used in the construction industry) are a large collection of point coordinates that closely represent a 3D object (such as a building structure) in a real-world space. Environment scanning devices including LiDAR laser scanners produce point clouds to represent objects within a 3D space at approximate measurements close to the real-world environment.

As 3D models improve, it may be possible to generate objects that closely represent their real counterparts.

Strategies for Serving Generative AI Models

You now should feel more confident building your own endpoints that serve a variety of models from the Hugging Face model repository. We touched upon a few different models, including those that generate text, image, video, audio, and 3D shapes.

The models you used were small, so they could be loaded and used on a CPU with reasonable outputs. However, in a production scenarios, you may want to use larger models to produce higher-quality results that may run only on GPUs and require a significant amount of video random access memory (VRAM).

In addition to leveraging GPUs, you will need to pick a model-serving strategy from several options:

Be model agnostic
    Load models and generate outputs on every request (useful for model swapping).

Be compute efficient
    Use the FastAPI lifespan to preload models that can be reused for every request.

Be lean
    Serve models externally without frameworks or work with third-party model APIs and interact with them via FastAPI.

Let's take a look at each strategy in detail.

Be Model Agnostic: Swap Models on Every Request

In the previous code examples, you defined the model loading and generation functions and then used them in route handler controllers. Using this serving strategy, FastAPI loads a model into RAM (or VRAM if using a GPU) and runs a generation process. Once FastAPI returns the results, the model is then unloaded from RAM. The process repeats for the next request.

As the model is unloaded after use, the memory is released to be used by another process or model. With this approach, you dynamically swap various models in a single request if processing time isn't a concern. This means other concurrent requests must wait before the server responds to them.

When serving requests, FastAPI will queue incoming requests and process them in a first in first out (FIFO) order. This behavior will lead to long waiting times as a model needs to be loaded and unloaded every time. In most cases, this strategy is not recommended, but if you need to swap between multiple large models and you don't have sufficient RAM, then you can adopt this strategy for prototyping. However, in production scenarios, you should never use this strategy for obvious reasons—your users will want to avoid the long wait times.

Figure 3-28 shows this model service strategy.

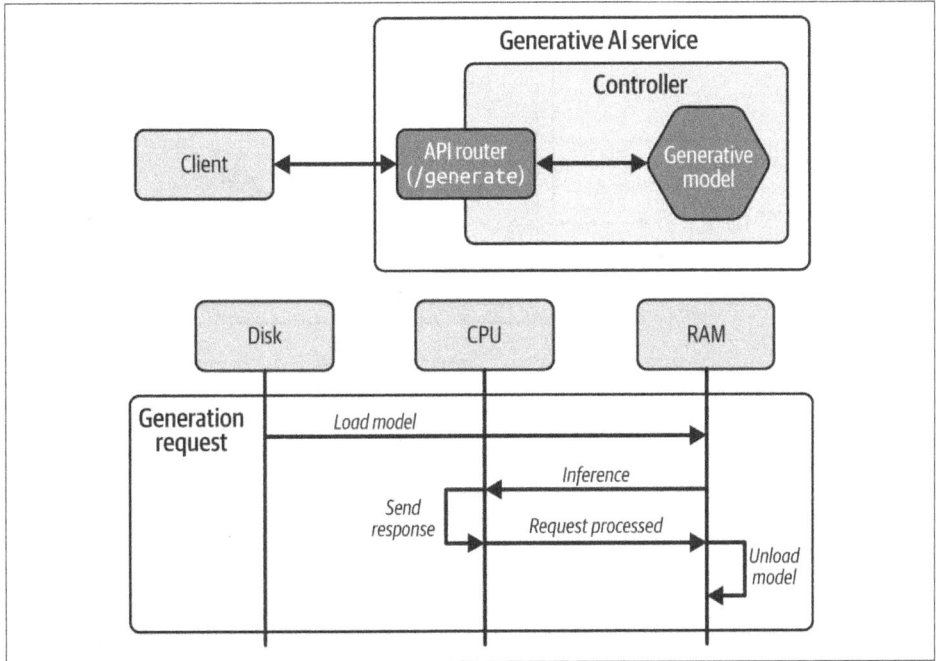

Figure 3-28. Loading and using models on every request

If you need to use different models in each request and have limited memory, this method can work well for quickly trying things on a less powerful machine with just a few users. The trade-off is significantly slower processing time due to model swapping. However, in production scenarios, it is better to get larger RAM and use the model preloading strategy with FastAPI application lifespan.

Be Compute Efficient: Preload Models with the FastAPI Lifespan

The most compute-efficient strategy for loading models in FastAPI is to use the application lifespan. With this approach, you load models on application startup and unload them on shutdown. During shutdown, you can also undertake any cleanup steps required, such as filesystem cleanup or logging.

The main benefit of this strategy compared to the first one mentioned is that you avoid reloading heavy models on each request. You can load a heavy model once and then make generations on every request coming using a preloaded model. As a result, you will save several minutes in processing time in exchange for a significant chunk of your RAM (or VRAM if using GPU). However, your application user experience will improve considerably due to shorter response times.

Figure 3-29 shows the model-serving strategy that uses application lifespan.

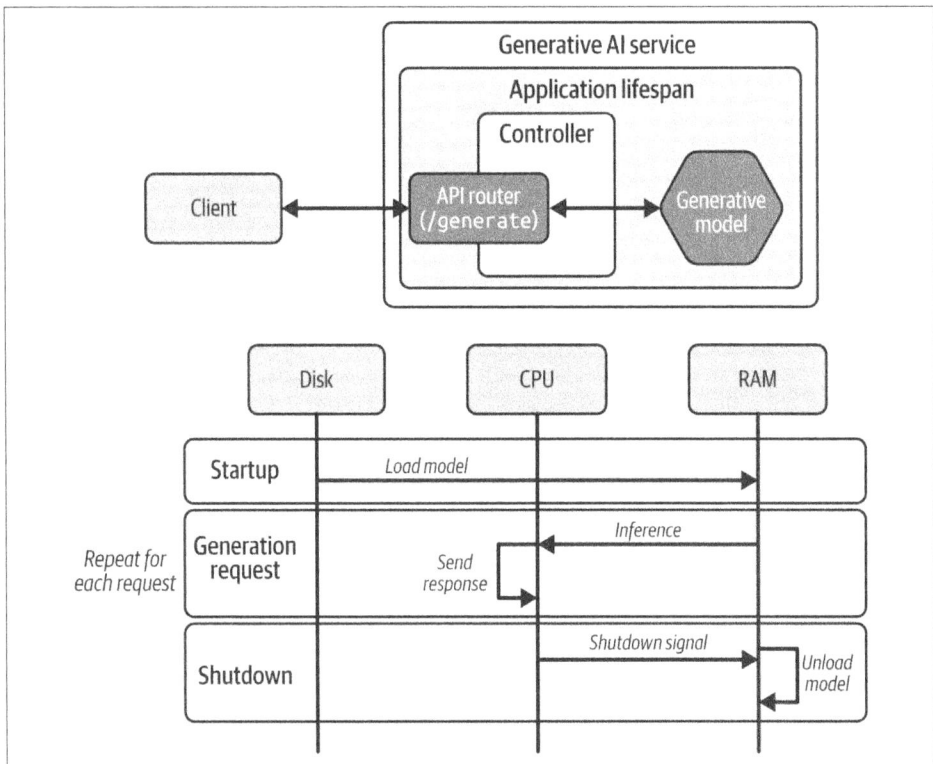

Figure 3-29. Using the FastAPI application lifespan to preload models

You can implement model preloading using the application lifespan, as shown in Example 3-16.

Example 3-16. Model preloading with application lifespan

```python
# main.py

from contextlib import asynccontextmanager
from typing import AsyncIterator
from fastapi import FastAPI, Response, status
from models import load_image_model, generate_image
from utils import img_to_bytes

models = {}  ❶

@asynccontextmanager  ❷
async def lifespan(_: FastAPI) -> AsyncIterator[None]:
    models["text2image"] = load_image_model()  ❸

    yield  ❹

    ... # Run cleanup code here

    models.clear()  ❺

app = FastAPI(lifespan=lifespan)  ❻

@app.get(
    "/generate/image",
    responses={status.HTTP_200_OK: {"content": {"image/png": {}}}},
    response_class=Response,
)
def serve_text_to_image_model_controller(prompt: str):
    output = generate_image(models["text2image"], prompt)  ❼
    return Response(content=img_to_bytes(output), media_type="image/png")
```

❶ Initialize an empty mutable dictionary at the *global* application scope to hold one or multiple models.

❷ Use the `asynccontextmanager` decorator to handle startup and shutdown events as part of an async context manager:

- The context manager will run code before and after the `yield` keyword.
- The `yield` keyword in the decorated `lifespan` function separates the startup and shutdown phases.
- Code prior to the `yield` keyword runs at application startup before any requests are handled.
- When you want to terminate the application, FastAPI will run the code after the `yield` keyword as part of the shutdown phase.

❸ Preload the model on startup onto the `models` dictionary.

❹ Start handling requests as the startup phase is now finished.

❺ Clear the model on application shutdown.

❻ Create the FastAPI server and pass it the lifespan function to use.

❼ Pass the global preloaded model instance to the generation function.

If you start the application now, you should immediately see model pipelines being loaded onto memory. Before you applied these changes, the model pipelines used to load only when you made your first request.

> You can preload more than one model into memory using the lifespan model-serving strategy, but this isn't practical with large GenAI models. Generative models can be resource hungry, and in most cases you'll need GPUs to speed up the generation process. The most powerful consumer GPUs ship with only 24 GB of VRAM. Some models require 18 GB of memory to perform inference, so try to deploy models on separate application instances and GPUs instead.

Startup and Shutdown Events

Before the introduction of lifespan async context managers in FastAPI 0.93.0 for handling the application lifespan, separate startup and shutdown event handler functions were commonly used. Example 3-17 shows an example usage.

Example 3-17. Startup and shutdown events

```python
# main.py
from models import load_image_model

models = {}
app = FastAPI()

@app.on_event("startup")
def startup_event():
    models["text2image"] = load_image_model()

@app.on_event("shutdown")
def shutdown_event():
    with open("log.txt", mode="a") as logfile:
        logfile.write("Application shutdown")
```

A few resources across the web may use this alternative and legacy approach, so it is worth knowing.

Be Lean: Serve Models Externally

Another strategy to serve GenAI models is to package them as external services via other tools. You can then use your FastAPI application as the logical layer between your client and the external model server. In this logical layer, you can handle coordination between models, communication with APIs, management of users, security measures, monitoring activities, content filtering, enhancing prompts, or any other required logic.

Cloud providers

Cloud providers are constantly innovating serverless and dedicated compute solutions that you can use to serve your models externally. For instance, Azure Machine Learning Studio now provides a PromptFlow tool that you can use to deploy and customize OpenAI or open source language models. Upon deployment, you will receive a model endpoint run on your Azure compute ready for usage. However, there is a steep learning curve in using PromptFlow or similar tools as they may require particular dependencies and nontraditional steps to be followed.

BentoML

Another great contender for serving models external to FastAPI is BentoML. BentoML is inspired by FastAPI but implements a different serving strategy, purpose built for AI models.

A huge improvement over FastAPI for handling concurrent model requests is BentoML's ability to run different requests on different worker processes. It can parallelize CPU-bound requests without you having to directly deal with Python multiprocessing. On top of this, BentoML can also batch model inferences such that the generation process for multiple users can be done with a single model call.

I covered BentoML in detail in Chapter 2.

> To run BentoML, you will need to install a few dependencies first:
>
> ```
> $ pip install bentoml
> ```

You can see how to start a BentoML server in Example 3-18.

Example 3-18. Serving an image model with BentoML

```
# bento.py
import bentoml
from models import load_image_model
```

```
@bentoml.service(
    resources={"cpu": "4"}, traffic={"timeout": 120}, http={"port": 5000}
) ❶
class Generate:
    def __init__(self) -> None:
        self.pipe = load_image_model()

    @bentoml.api(route="/generate/image") ❷
    def generate(self, prompt: str) -> str:
        output = self.pipe(prompt, num_inference_steps=10).images[0]
        return output
```

❶ Declare a BentoML service with four allocated CPUs. The service should time out in 120 seconds if the model doesn't generate in time and should run from port 5000.

❷ Declare an API controller for undertaking the core model generation process. This controller will hook to BentoML's API route handler.

You can then run the BentoML service locally:

```
$ bentoml serve service:Generate
```

Your FastAPI server can now become a client with the model being served externally. You can now make HTTP POST requests from within FastAPI to get a response, as shown in Example 3-19.

Example 3-19. BentoML endpoints via FastAPI

```
# main.py

import httpx
from fastapi import FastAPI, Response

app = FastAPI()

@app.get(
    "/generate/bentoml/image",
    responses={status.HTTP_200_OK: {"content": {"image/png": {}}}},
    response_class=Response,
)
async def serve_bentoml_text_to_image_controller(prompt: str):
    async with httpx.AsyncClient() as client: ❶
        response = await client.post(
            "http://localhost:5000/generate", json={"prompt": prompt}
        ) ❷
    return Response(content=response.content, media_type="image/png")
```

❶ Create an asynchronous HTTP client using the `httpx` library.

❷ Send a `POST` request to the BentoML image generation model endpoint.

Model providers

Aside from BentoML and cloud providers, you can also use external model service providers such as OpenAI. In this case, your FastAPI application becomes a service wrapper over OpenAI's API.

Luckily, integrating with model provider APIs such as OpenAI is quite straightforward, as shown in Example 3-20.

> To run Example 3-20, you must get an API key and set the `OPENAI_API_KEY` environment variable to this key, as recommended by OpenAI.

Example 3-20. Integrating with OpenAI service

```python
# main.py

from fastapi import FastAPI
from openai import OpenAI

app = FastAPI()
openai_client = OpenAI()
system_prompt = "You are a helpful assistant."

@app.get("/generate/openai/text")
def serve_openai_language_model_controller(prompt: str) -> str | None:
    response = openai_client.chat.completions.create(  ❶
        model="gpt-4o",
        messages=[
            {"role": "system", "content": f"{system_prompt}"},
            {"role": "user", "content": prompt},
        ],
    )
    return response.choices[0].message.content
```

❶ Use the `gpt-4o` model to chat with the model via the OpenAI API.

And now you should be able to get outputs via external calls to the OpenAI service.

LangChain

You can use the `langchain` library to switch integration with any LLM providers. The library also provides excellent tools working with LLMs, which we will cover later in the book. First, install the library:

```
$ pip install langchain langchain-openai
```

Once `langchain` is installed, follow Example 3-21 to integrate with external model APIs such as OpenAI.

Example 3-21. Integrating with external provider APIs with LangChain

```python
# main.py

from fastapi import FastAPI
from langchain.chains.llm import LLMChain
from langchain_core.prompts import PromptTemplate
from langchain_openai import OpenAI

llm = OpenAI(openai_organization="YOUR_ORGANIZATION_ID")  ❶
template = """
Your name is FastAPI bot and you are a helpful
chatbot responsible for teaching FastAPI to your users.
Here is the user query: {query}
"""
prompt = PromptTemplate.from_template(template)  ❷
llm_chain = LLMChain(prompt=prompt, llm=llm)  ❸

app = FastAPI()

@app.get("/generate/text")
def generate_text_controller(query: str):
    return llm_chain.run(query)  ❹
```

❶ Create the OpenAI client with the organization ID.

❷ Construct a prompt template.

❸ Construct the OpenAI `llm_chain` object from the prompt template.

❹ Run the text generation process by passing in the user query.

When using external services, be mindful that data will be shared with third-party service providers. In this case, you may prefer self-hosted solutions if you value data privacy and security. With self-hosting, the trade-off will be an increased complexity in deploying and managing your own model servers.

If you really want to avoid serving large models yourself, cloud providers can provide managed solutions where your data is never shared with third parties. An example is Azure OpenAI, which at the time of writing provides snapshots of OpenAI's best LLMs and image generator.

You now have a few options for model serving. One final system to implement before we wrap up this chapter is logging and monitoring of the service.

The Role of Middleware in Service Monitoring

You can implement a simple monitoring tool where prompts and responses can be logged alongside their request and response token usage. To implement the logging system, you can write a few logging functions inside your model-serving controller. However, if you have multiple models and endpoints, you may benefit from leveraging the FastAPI middleware mechanism.

Middleware is an essential block of code that runs before and after a request is processed by any of your controllers. You can define custom middleware that you then attach to any API route handlers. Once the requests reach the route handlers, the middleware acts as an intermediary, processing the requests and responses between the client and server controller.

Excellent uses cases for middleware include logging and monitoring, rate limiting, content filtering, and cross-origin resource sharing (CORS) implementations.

Example 3-22 shows how you can monitor your model-serving handlers.

Usage logging via custom middleware in production

Don't use Example 3-22 in production as the monitoring logs can disappear if you run the application from a Docker container or a host machine that can be deleted or restarted without a mounted persistent volume or logging to a database.

In Chapter 7, you will integrate the monitoring system with a database to persist logs outside the application environment.

Example 3-22. Using middleware mechanisms to capture service usage logs

```python
# main.py

import csv
import time
from datetime import datetime, timezone
from uuid import uuid4
from typing import Awaitable, Callable
from fastapi import FastAPI, Request, Response

# preload model with a lifespan
...

app = FastAPI(lifespan=lifespan)

csv_header = [
    "Request ID", "Datetime", "Endpoint Triggered", "Client IP Address",
    "Response Time", "Status Code", "Successful"
]


@app.middleware("http") ❶
async def monitor_service(
    req: Request, call_next: Callable[[Request], Awaitable[Response]]
) -> Response: ❷
    request_id = uuid4().hex ❸
    request_datetime = datetime.now(timezone.utc).isoformat()
    start_time = time.perf_counter()
    response: Response = await call_next(req)
    response_time = round(time.perf_counter() - start_time, 4) ❹
    response.headers["X-Response-Time"] = str(response_time)
    response.headers["X-API-Request-ID"] = request_id ❺
    with open("usage.csv", "a", newline="") as file:
        writer = csv.writer(file)
        if file.tell() == 0:
            writer.writerow(csv_header)
        writer.writerow( ❻
            [
                request_id,
                request_datetime,
                req.url,
                req.client.host,
                response_time,
                response.status_code,
                response.status_code < 400,
            ]
        )
    return response


# Usage Log Example
```

```
"""
Request ID: 3d15d3d9b7124cc9be7eb690fc4c9bd5
Datetime: 2024-03-07T16:41:58.895091
Endpoint triggered: http://localhost:8000/generate/text
Client IP Address: 127.0.0.1
Processing time: 26.7210 seconds
Status Code: 200
Successful: True
"""

# model-serving handlers
...
```

❶ Declare a function decorated by the FastAPI HTTP middleware mechanism. The function must receive the `Request` object and `call_next` callback function to be considered valid `http` middleware.

❷ Pass the request to the route handler to process the response.

❸ Generate a request ID for tracking all incoming requests even if an error is raised in `call_next` during request processing.

❹ Calculate the response duration to four decimal places.

❺ Set custom response headers for the processing time and request ID.

❻ Log the URL of the endpoint triggered, request datetime and ID, client IP address, response processing time, and status code into a CSV file on disk in `append` mode.

In this section, you captured information about endpoint usage including processing time, status code, endpoint path, and client IP.

Middleware is a powerful system for executing blocks of code before requests are passed to the route handlers and before responses are sent to the user. You saw an example of how middleware can be used to log model usage for any model-serving endpoint.

Accessing request and response bodies in middleware

If you need to track interactions with your models, including prompts and the content they generate, using middleware for logging is more efficient than adding individual loggers to each handler. However, you should take into account data privacy and performance concerns when logging request and response bodies as the user could submit sensitive or large data to your service, which will require careful handling.

Summary

We covered a lot of concepts in this chapter, so let's quickly review everything we've discussed.

You saw how you can download, integrate, and serve a variety of open source GenAI models from the Hugging Face repository in a simple UI using the Streamlit package, within a few lines of code. You also reviewed several types of models and how to serve them via FastAPI endpoints. The models you experimented with were text, image, audio, video, and 3D-based, and you saw how they process data. You also learned the model architectures and the underlying mechanisms powering these models.

Then, you reviewed several different model-serving strategies including model swapping on request, model preloading, and finally model serving outside the FastAPI application using other frameworks such as BentoML or using third-party APIs.

Next, you noticed that the larger models could take some time to generate responses. Finally, you implemented a service monitoring mechanism for your models that leverage the FastAPI middleware system for every model-serving endpoint. You then wrote the logs to disk for future analysis.

You should now feel more confident building your own GenAI services powered by a variety of open source models.

In the next chapter, you will learn more about type safety and its role in eliminating application bugs and reducing uncertainty when working with external APIs and services. You will also see how to validate requests and response schemas to make your services even more reliable.

Additional References

- "Bark" (*https://oreil.ly/HKT8O*), in "Transformers" documentation, *Hugging Face*, accessed on 26 March 2024.

- Borsos, Z., et al. (2022). "AudioLM: A Language Modeling Approach to Audio Generation" (*https://oreil.ly/8YZBr*). arXiv preprint arXiv:2209.03143.

- Brooks, T., et al. (2024). "Video Generation Models as World Simulators" (*https://oreil.ly/52duF*). OpenAI.

- Défossez, A., et al. (2022). "High-Fidelity Neural Audio Compression" (*https://oreil.ly/p4_-5*). arXiv preprint arXiv:2210.13438.

- Jun, H. & Nichol, A. (2023). "Shap-E: Generating Conditional 3D Implicit Functions" (*https://oreil.ly/LzLy0*). arXiv preprint arXiv:2305.02463.

- Kim, B.-K., et al. (2023). "BK-SDM: A Lightweight, Fast, and Cheap Version of Stable Diffusion" (*https://oreil.ly/uErOQ*). arXiv preprint arXiv:2305.15798.

- Liu, Y., et al. (2024). "Sora: A Review on Background, Technology, Limitations, and Opportunities of Large Vision Models" (*https://oreil.ly/Zr6bJ*). arXiv preprint arXiv:2402.17177.

- Mildenhall, B., et al. (2020). "NeRF: Representing Scenes as Neural Radiance Fields for View Synthesis" (*https://oreil.ly/hBiBV*). arXiv preprint arXiv:2003.08934.

- Nichol, A., et al. (2022). "Point-E: A System for Generating 3D Point Clouds from Complex Prompts" (*https://oreil.ly/FW-wT*). arXiv preprint arXiv:2212.08751.

- Vaswani, A., et al. (2017). "Attention Is All You Need" (*https://oreil.ly/N4MkH*). arXiv preprint arXiv:1706.03762.

- Wang, C., et al. (2023). "Neural Codec Language Models are Zero-Shot Text to Speech Synthesizers" (*https://oreil.ly/h1D0e*). arXiv preprint arXiv:2301.02111.

- Zhang, P., et al. (2024). "TinyLlama: An Open-Source Small Language Model" (*https://oreil.ly/Idi1B*). arXiv preprint arXiv:2401.02385.

## CHAPTER 4

Implementing Type-Safe AI Services

Chapter Goals

In this chapter, you will learn about:

- Why it is essential to have fully typed services

- How to correctly define and implement type safety for GenAI services

- Similarities and differences between dataclasses and Pydantic data models

- How to validate the content of requests and responses in GenAI services using Pydantic models

- How to build custom field and data model validators with Pydantic to prevent incorrect data from passing through your service

- How to use the Pydantic Settings package to load and validate your application environment variables

- How to reduce uncertainty when working with external systems that change schemas

- How to manage changes as the complexity grows to avoid introducing unintended bugs

When working with complex codebases that continuously change by multiple contributors and when interacting with external services such as APIs or databases, you will want to follow best practices such as type safety in building your applications.

This chapter focuses on the importance of type safety when building backend services and APIs. You will learn how to implement type safety using Python's built-in dataclasses and then Pydantic data models, and you will see their similarities and differences. In addition, you will explore how to use Pydantic data models with custom

---

validators to protect against bad user input or incorrect data, and you will learn how to use Pydantic Settings for loading and validating environment variables. Finally, you will discover strategies for dealing with schema changes in external systems and managing complexity in evolving codebases to prevent bugs.

By the end of this chapter, you will have a fully typed GenAI service that is less prone to bugs when dealing with changes, bad user inputs, and inconsistent model responses.

To follow along, you can find the starting code for this chapter by switching to the ch04-start branch (*https://github.com/Ali-Parandeh/building-generative-ai-services/tree/ch04-start*).

Introduction to Type Safety

Types in programming specify what values can be assigned to variables and operations that can be performed on those variables.

In Python, common types include the following:

Integer
    Representing whole numbers

Float
    Representing numbers with fractional parts

String
    Representing sequences of characters

Boolean
    Representing True or False values

> You can use the typing package to import special types as you saw in other code examples in Chapter 3.

Type safety is a programming practice that ensures variables are only assigned values compatible with their defined types. In Python, you can use types to check the usage of variables across a codebase, in particular if the codebase grows in complexity and size. Type checking tools (e.g., mypy) can then use these types to catch incorrect variable assignments or operations.

Static and Dynamically Typed Languages

Python is one of the few languages that are *dynamically typed*, meaning types are checked only when you run the code, not in advance. Also, you don't have to explicitly declare types as they can be inferred as you assign values to variables. However, as soon as your codebase becomes complex and your services start interacting with other systems like a filesystem, a database, or external services, you will face several reliability issues.

Using typing, you can catch errors more quickly. Without typing, you must rely on tests, and insufficient test coverage can lead to production crashes due to mistakes. At best, you remain unaware of minor issues and nuances affecting the user. At worst, you risk data corruption or incur massive server costs, only discovering the damage when it is too late.

Static languages enforce the use of typing on developers for greater code reliability and execution speed, potentially at the cost of development speed. On the other hand, in Python, typing isn't enforced to offer flexibility, so you can build applications faster. But the static type analysis in Python has evolved heavily with tools like mypy.

You can enforce type constraints by declaring fully typed variables and functions as shown in Example 4-1.

Example 4-1. Using types in Python

```
from datetime import datetime

def timestamp_to_isostring(date: int) -> str:
    return datetime.fromtimestamp(date).isoformat()

print(timestamp_to_isostring(1736680773))
# 2025-01-12T11:19:52.876758

print(timestamp_to_isostring("27 Jan 2025 14:48:00"))
# error: Argument 1 to "timestamp_to_isostring" has incompatible type "str";
# expected "int" [arg-type]
```

Code editors and IDEs (e.g., VS Code or JetBrains PyCharm) can also use type checking extensions, as shown in Figure 4-1, to raise warnings on type violations as you write code.

```
42 4-1.py   1 ●

42 4-1.py > ...
  1    from datetime import datetime
  2
  3    def timestamp_to_isostring(date: int) -> str:
  4        return datetime.fromtimestamp(date).isoformat()
  5
  6    print(timestamp_to_isostring(1736680773))
  7    # 2025-01-12T11:19:52.876758
  8
  9    |    Argument 1 to "timestamp_to_isostring" has incompatible type "str"; expected "int"
 10    print(timestamp_to_isostring("27 Jan 2025 14:48:00"))
 11
```

Figure 4-1. Catching type errors in VS Code mypy extension

In a complex codebase, it is easy to lose track of variables, their states, and constantly changing schemas. For example, you might forget that the timestamp_to_isostring function accepts numbers as input and mistakenly pass a timestamp as a string, as shown in Figure 4-1.

Types are also extremely useful when package maintainers or external API providers update their code. Type checkers can immediately raise warnings to help you address such changes during development. This way, you will be immediately directed to sources of potential errors without having to run your code and test every endpoint. As a result, type safety practices can save you time with early detection and prevent you from dealing with more obscure runtime errors.

Finally, you can go one step further to set up automatic type checks in your deployment pipeline to prevent pushing breaking changes to production environments.

Type safety at first seems like a burden. You have to explicitly type each and every function you write, which can be a hassle and slow you down in the initial phases of development.

Some people skip typing their code for rapid prototyping and to write less boilerplate code. The approach is more flexible and easier to use, and Python is powerful enough to infer simple types. Also, some code patterns (such as functions with multitype arguments) can be so dynamic that it is easier to avoid implementing strict type safety when still experimenting. However, it will come to save you hours of development as inevitably your services become complex and continuously change.

The good news is some of these types can be auto-generated using tools such as Prisma, when working with databases, or client generators, when working with external APIs. For external APIs, you can often find official SDKs containing clients with type hints (i.e., fully typed client) specifying expected types of inputs and outputs for using the API. If not, you can inspect the API to create your own fully typed client. I will cover Prisma and API client generators in more detail later in the book.

When you don't use types, you open yourself to all sorts of bugs and errors that might occur because other developers unexpectedly updated the database tables or API schemas that your service interacts with. In other cases, you may update a database table—drop a column for instance—and forget to update the code interacting with that table.

Without types, you may never notice breaking changes due to updates. This can be challenging to debug as unhandled downstream errors might not pinpoint the broken component or general issues around unhandled edge cases from your own development team. As a result, what might have taken a minute to resolve can last half a day or even longer.

You can always prevent a few disasters in production with extensive testing. However, it's much easier to avoid integration and reliability issues if you start using types from the start.

Developing good programming habits

If you haven't been typing your code in the past, it is never too late to start getting into the habit of typing all your variables, function parameters, and return types.

Using types will make your code more readable, help you catch bugs early on, and save you a lot of time when you revisit complex codebases to quickly understand how data flows.

Implementing Type Safety

Since Python 3.5, you can explicitly declare types for your variables, function parameters, and return values. The syntax that allows you to declare these types is *type annotation*.

Type Annotations

Type annotations don't affect the runtime behavior of your application. They help catch type errors, particularly in complex larger applications where multiple people are working together. Tools for static type checking, such as `mypy`, `pyright`, or `pyre`, alongside code editors, can validate that the data types stored and returned from functions, match the expected types.

In Python applications, type annotations are used for:

- *Code editor auto-complete support*
- *Static type checks* using tools like `mypy`

FastAPI also leverages types hints to:

- *Define handler requirements* including path and query parameters, bodies, headers, and dependencies, etc.
- *Convert data* whenever needed
- *Validate data* from incoming requests, databases, and external services
- *Auto-update the OpenAPI specification* that powers the generated documentation page

You can install `loguru` using `pip`:

```
$ pip install loguru
```

Example 4-2 shows several examples of type annotation.

Example 4-2. Using type annotation to reduce future bugs as code changes occur

```python
# utils.py

from typing import Literal, TypeAlias
from loguru import logger
import tiktoken

SupportedModels: TypeAlias = Literal["gpt-3.5", "gpt-4"]
PriceTable: TypeAlias = dict[SupportedModels, float] ❶ ❷
price_table: PriceTable = {"gpt-3.5": 0.0030, "gpt-4": 0.0200} ❸

def count_tokens(text: str | None) -> int: ❹
    if text is None:
        logger.warning("Response is None. Assuming 0 tokens used")
        return 0 ❺
    enc = tiktoken.encoding_for_model("gpt-4o")
    return len(enc.encode(text)) ❻

def calculate_usage_costs(
    prompt: str,
    response: str | None,
    model: SupportedModels,
) -> tuple[float, float, float]: ❼
    if model not in price_table:
        # raise at runtime - in case someone ignores type errors
        raise ValueError(f"Cost calculation is not supported for {model} model.") ❽
    price = price_table[model] ❾
    req_costs = price * count_tokens(prompt) / 1000
    res_costs = price * count_tokens(response) / 1000 ❿
    total_costs = req_costs + res_costs
    return req_costs, res_costs, total_costs ⓫
```

❶ Use the `Literal` from Python's `typing` module included in its standard library.[1] Declare literals `gpt-3.5` and `gpt-4` and assign them to `SupportedModel` *type alias*. The `PriceTable` is also a simple type alias that defines a dictionary with keys limited to `SupportedModel` literals and with values of type `float`.

❷ Mark type aliases with `TypeAlias` to be explicit that they're not a normal variable assignment. Types are also normally declared using CamelCase as a best practice to differentiate them from variables. You can now reuse the `PriceTable` type alias later.

❸ Declare the pricing table dictionary and assign the `PriceTable` type to explicitly limit what keys and values are allowed for in the pricing table dictionary.

❹ Type the `count_tokens` function to accept strings or `None` types and always return an integer. Implement exception handling in case someone tries to pass in anything other than strings or `None` types. When defining `count_tokens`, code editor and static checkers will raise warnings if `count_tokens` doesn't return an integer even if it receives a `None` and raises errors if any other types other than string or `None`.

❺ Return `0` even if a `None` type is passed to ensure you comply with function typing.

❻ Tokenize the given text using OpenAI's `tiktoken` library using the same encoding that was used for the `gpt-4o` model.[2]

❼ Type the `calculate_usage_costs` function to always take a text prompt and the prespecified literals for `model` parameter. Pass the `price_table` with the previously declared `PriceTable` type alias. The function should return a tuple of three floats.

❽ Type checkers will raise warnings when an unexpected model literal is passed in, but you should always check for incorrect inputs to functions and raise errors at runtime if an unexpected model parameter is passed in.

❾ Grab the correct price from the pricing table. No need to worry about exception handling, as there is no chance a `KeyError` can be raised here if an unsupported

---

1 A `Literal` type (*https://oreil.ly/69Pmn*) can be used to indicate to type checkers that the annotated object has a value equivalent to one of the provided literals.

2 OpenAI's `tiktoken` uses the *Byte-Pair Encoding* (BPE) algorithm (*https://oreil.ly/l67GS*) to tokenize text. Different models use different encodings to convert text into tokens.

model is passed in. If the pricing table is not updated, the function will raise a `ValueError` early on. Catch the `KeyError`, issue a warning that pricing table needs updating and then reraise the `KeyError` so that full details of the issue are still printed to the terminal, as you can't make assumptions about prices.

⑩ Use `count_tokens` function to calculate the LLM request and response costs. If for any reason the LLM doesn't return a response (returns `None`), the `count_tokens` can handle it and assume zero tokens.

⑪ Return a tuple of three floats as per function typing.

In a complex codebase, it can be challenging to guess which data types are being passed around, especially if you make lots of changes everywhere. With typed functions, you can be confident that unexpected parameters aren't passed to functions that don't yet support it.

As you can see from Example 4-2, typing your code assists in catching unexpected bugs as you make updates to your code. For instance, if you start using a new LLM model, you can't yet calculate costs for the new model. To support cost calculation for other LLM models, you first should update the pricing table, related typing, and any exception handling logic. Once done, you can be pretty confident that your calculation logic is now extended to work with new model types.

Using Annotated

In Example 4-2, you can use `Annotated` instead of type aliases. `Annotated` is a feature of the `typing` module—introduced in Python 3.9—and is similar to type aliases for reusing types, but it allows you to also define *metadata* for your types.

The metadata doesn't affect the type checkers but is useful for code documentation, analysis, and runtime inspections.

Since its introduction in Python 3.9, you can use `Annotated` as shown in Example 4-3.

Example 4-3. Using `Annotated` to declare custom types with metadata

```
from typing import Annotated, Literal

SupportedModels = Annotated[
    Literal["gpt-3.5-turbo", "gpt-4o"], "Supported text models"
]
PriceTableType = Annotated[
    dict[SupportedModels, float], "Supported model pricing table"
]
```

```
prices: PriceTableType = {
    "gpt-4o": 0.000638,
    # error: Dict entry 1 has incompatible type "Literal['gpt4-o']" [dict-item]
    "gpt4-o": 0.000638,
    # error: Dict entry 2 has incompatible type "Literal['gpt-4']" [dict-item]
    "gpt-4": 0.000638,
}
```

The FastAPI documentation (*https://oreil.ly/mtGcY*) recommends the use of Annotated instead of type aliases for reusability, for enhanced type checks in the code editor, and for catching issues during runtime.

> Keep in mind that the Annotated feature requires a minimum of two arguments to work. The first should be the type passed in, and the other arguments are the annotation or metadata you want to attach to the type such as a description, validation rule, or other metadata, as shown in Example 4-3.

Typing, while beneficial by itself, doesn't address all aspects of data handling and structuring. Thankfully, Python's *dataclasses* from the standard library help to extend the typing system.

Let's see how you can leverage dataclasses to improve typing across your application.

Dataclasses

Dataclasses were introduced in Python 3.7 as part of the standard library. If you need custom data structures, you can use dataclasses to organize, store, and transfer data across your application.

They can help with avoiding code "smells" such as function parameter bloat, where a function is hard to use because it requires more than a handful of parameters. Having a dataclass allows you to organize your data in a custom-defined structure and pass it as a single item to functions that require data from different places.

You can update Example 4-2 to leverage dataclasses, as shown in Example 4-4.

Example 4-4. Using dataclasses to enforce type safety

```
# utils.py

from dataclasses import dataclass
from typing import Literal, TypeAlias
from utils import count_tokens

SupportedModels: TypeAlias = Literal["gpt-3.5", "gpt-4"]
PriceTable: TypeAlias = dict[SupportedModels, float]
```

```
prices: PriceTable = {"gpt-3.5": 0.0030, "gpt-4": 0.0200}

@dataclass ❶
class Message:
    prompt: str
    response: str | None ❷
    model: SupportedModels

@dataclass
class MessageCostReport:
    req_costs: float
    res_costs: float
    total_costs: float

# Define count_tokens function as normal
...

def calculate_usage_costs(message: Message) -> MessageCostReport: ❸
    if message.model not in prices :
        # raise at runtime - in case someone ignores type errors
        raise ValueError(
            f"Cost calculation is not supported for {message.model} model."
        )
    price = prices[message.model]
    req_costs = price * count_tokens(message.prompt) / 1000
    res_costs = price * count_tokens(message.response) / 1000
    total_costs = req_costs + res_costs
    return MessageCostReport(
        req_costs=req_costs, res_costs=res_costs, total_costs=total_costs
    )
```

❶ Use dataclasses to decorate the Message and MessageCost classes as special classes for holding data.

❷ Type the response attribute to be either a str or None. This is similar to using Optional[str] from the typing module. This new syntax is available in Python 3.10 and later, using the new union operator: |.

❸ Change the signature of the calculate_usage_costs function to use the predefined dataclasses. This change simplifies the function signature.

You should aim to leverage dataclasses when your code accumulates code smells and becomes difficult to read.

The primary benefit of using dataclasses in Example 4-4 was to group related parameters to simplify the function signature. In other scenarios, you may use dataclasses to:

- Eliminate code duplication
- Shrink down code bloat (large classes or functions)
- Refactor data clumps (variables that are commonly used together)
- Prevent inadvertent data mutation
- Promote data organization
- Promote encapsulation
- Enforce data validation

They can also be used to implement many other code enhancements.

Dataclasses are an excellent tool to improve data organization and exchange anywhere in your application. However, they don't natively support several features when building API services:

Automatic data parsing
Parsing ISO datetime-formatted strings to datetime objects on assignment

Field validation
Performing complex checks on assignment of values to fields, such as checking if a string is too long

Serialization and deserialization
Converting between JSON and Pythonic data structures, especially when using uncommon types

Field filtering
Removing fields of objects that are unset or contain None values

None of the mentioned limitations would force you to move away from using dataclasses. You should use dataclasses rather than normal classes when you need to create data-centric classes with minimal boilerplate code, as they automatically generate special methods, type annotations, and support for default values, reducing potential errors. However, libraries such as pydantic support these features if you don't want to implement your own custom logic (e.g., serializing datetime objects).

> FastAPI also supports dataclasses through Pydantic, which implements its own version of dataclasses with support for the aforementioned features, enabling you to migrate codebases that heavily use dataclasses.

Let's take a look at Pydantic next and what makes it great for building GenAI services.

Pydantic Models

Pydantic is the most widely used data validation library with support for custom validators and serializers. Pydantic's core logic is controlled by type annotations in Python and can emit data in JSON format, allowing for seamless integration with any other tools.

In addition, the core data validation logic in Pydantic V2 has been rewritten in Rust to maximize its speed and performance, positioning it as one of the fastest data validation libraries in Python. As a result, Pydantic has heavily influenced FastAPI and 8,000 other packages in the Python ecosystem including Hugging Face, Django, and LangChain. It is a battle-tested toolkit used by major tech companies with 141 million downloads a month at the time of writing, making it a suitable candidate for adoption in your projects in replacement for dataclasses.

Pydantic provides an extensive toolset for data validation and processing using its own `BaseModel` implementation. Pydantic models share many similarities with dataclasses but differ in subtle areas. When you create Pydantic models, a set of initialization hooks are called that add data validation, serialization, and JSON schema generation features to the models that vanilla dataclasses lack.

FastAPI tightly integrates with Pydantic and leverages its rich feature set under the hood for data processing. Type checkers and code editors can also read Pydantic models similar to dataclasses to perform checks and provide auto-completions.

How to Use Pydantic

You can install Pydantic into your project using the following:

```
$ pip install pydantic
```

Pydantic at its core implements a `BaseModel`, which is the primary method for defining models. *Models* are simply classes that inherit from `BaseModel` and define fields as annotated attributes using type hints. Any models can then be used as schemas to validate your data.

Aside from grouping data,[3] Pydantic models let you specify the request and response requirements of your service endpoints and validate incoming untrusted data from external sources. You can also go as far as filter your LLM outputs using Pydantic models (and validators, which you will learn more about shortly).

You can create your own Pydantic models as shown in Example 4-5.

---

3 Structs in C-like languages and dataclasses in Python can also be used to group and pass data around.

Example 4-5. Creating Pydantic models

```python
from typing import Literal
from pydantic import BaseModel

class TextModelRequest(BaseModel):  ❶
    model: Literal["gpt-3.5-turbo", "gpt-4o"]
    prompt: str
    temperature: float = 0.0 ❷
```

❶ Define the `TextModelRequest` model inheriting the Pydantic `BaseModel`.

❷ Set defaults if an explicit value isn't provided. For instance, set the `temperature` field to `0.0` if a value is not provided on initialization.

Example 4-5 also shows how you can switch your dataclasses into Pydantic models to leverage its many features.

Compound Pydantic Models

With Pydantic models, you can declare data *schemas*, which define data structures supported in the operations of your service. Additionally, you can also use inheritance for building compound models, as shown in Example 4-6.

Example 4-6. Creating Pydantic models

```python
# schemas.py

from datetime import datetime
from typing import Annotated, Literal
from pydantic import BaseModel

class ModelRequest(BaseModel):  ❶
    prompt: str

class ModelResponse(BaseModel):  ❷
    request_id: str
    ip: str | None
    content: str | None
    created_at: datetime = datetime.now()

class TextModelRequest(ModelRequest):
    model: Literal["gpt-3.5-turbo", "gpt-4o"]
    temperature: float = 0.0

class TextModelResponse(ModelResponse):
    tokens: int

ImageSize = Annotated[tuple[int, int], "Width and height of an image in pixels"]
```

```
class ImageModelRequest(ModelRequest):  ❸
    model: Literal["tinysd", "sd1.5"]
    output_size: ImageSize
    num_inference_steps: int = 200

class ImageModelResponse(ModelResponse):  ❹
    size: ImageSize
    url: str
```

❶ Define the `ModelRequest` model inheriting the Pydantic `BaseModel`.

❷ Define the `ModelResponse`. If the data for the `ip` optional field is not provided, then use the defaults of `None`. The `content` field can be both bytes (for image images) or string (for text models).

❸ Define the `TextModelRequest` and `ImageModelRequest` models by inheriting `ModelRequest`. The optional temperature field by default is set to 0.0. The `num_inference_steps` field for the `ImageModelRequest` model is optional and set to 200. Both of these models will now require the prompt string field to be provided.

❹ Define the `ImageModelResponse` and `TextModelResponse` models by inheriting the `ModelResponse` model. For `TextModelResponse`, provide the count of tokens, and with `ImageModelResponse`, provide an image size in pixels alongside the remote URL for downloading the image.

With the models shown in Example 4-6, you have schemas needed to define the requirements of your text and image generation endpoints.

Field Constraints and Validators

Aside from support for standard types, Pydantic also ships with *constrained types* such as `EmailStr`, `PositiveInt`, `UUID4`, `AnyHttpUrl`, and more that can perform data validation out of the box during model initialization for common data formats. The full list of Pydantic types is available in the official documentation (*https://oreil.ly/ xNbXX*).

> Some constrained types such as `EmailStr` will require dependency packages to be installed to function but can be extremely useful for validating common data formats such as emails.

To define more custom and complex field constraints on top of Pydantic-constrained types, you can use the Field function from Pydantic with the Annotated type to introduce validation constraints such as a valid input range.

Example 4-7 replaces the standard type hints in Example 4-6 with constrained types and Field functions to implement stricter data requirements for your endpoints based on model constraints.

Example 4-7. Using constrained fields

```
# schemas.py

from datetime import datetime
from typing import Annotated, Literal
from uuid import uuid4
from pydantic import BaseModel, Field, HttpUrl, IPvAnyAddress, PositiveInt

class ModelRequest(BaseModel):
    prompt: Annotated[str, Field(min_length=1, max_length=10000)]  ❶

class ModelResponse(BaseModel):
    request_id: Annotated[str, Field(default_factory=lambda: uuid4().hex)]  ❷
    # no defaults set for ip field
    # raise ValidationError if a valid IP address or None is not provided
    ip: Annotated[str, IPvAnyAddress] | None  ❸
    content: Annotated[str | None, Field(min_length=0, max_length=10000)]  ❹
    created_at: datetime = datetime.now()

class TextModelRequest(ModelRequest):
    model: Literal["gpt-3.5-turbo", "gpt-4o"]
    temperature: Annotated[float, Field(ge=0.0, le=1.0, default=0.0)]  ❺

class TextModelResponse(ModelResponse):
    tokens: Annotated[int, Field(ge=0)]

ImageSize = Annotated[  ❻
    tuple[PositiveInt, PositiveInt], "Width and height of an image in pixels"
]

class ImageModelRequest(ModelRequest):
    model: Literal["tinysd", "sd1.5"]
    output_size: ImageSize  ❻
    num_inference_steps: Annotated[int, Field(ge=0, le=2000)] = 200  ❼

class ImageModelResponse(ModelResponse):
    size: ImageSize  ❻
    url: Annotated[str, HttpUrl] | None = None  ❽
```

❶ Replace the `str` standard type with `Field` and `Annotated` to bound the string length to a range of characters.

❷ Generate a new request UUID by passing a callable to `default_factory` that will be called to generate a new UUID.

❸ Constrain the optional `ip` field to any valid IPv4 or IPv6 address ranges. `None` is also a valid entry if the client's IP can't be determined. This optional field doesn't have a default value, so if a valid IP or `None` is not provided, Pydantic will raise a `ValidationError`.

❹ Constrain the `content` field to 10,000 characters or bytes.

❺ Constrain the temperature between `0.0` and `1.0` with a default value of `0.0`.

❻ Reuse an `Annotated` constrain on the `output_size` field to positive integers using the `PositiveInt` constrained type. The `lte` and `gte` keywords refer to *less than equal* and *greater than equal*, respectively.

❼ Constrain the `num_inference_steps` field with `Field` between `0` and `2000` and a default of `200`.

❽ Constrain the optional `url` field to any valid HTTP or HTTPS URL, where the hostname and top-level domain (TLD) are required.

With the models defined in Example 4-7, you can now perform validation on incoming or outgoing data to match the data requirements you have. In such cases, FastAPI will leverage Pydantic to automatically return error responses when data validation checks fail during a request runtime, as shown in Example 4-8.

Example 4-8. FastAPI error response on data validation failure

```
$ curl -X 'POST' \
  'http://127.0.0.1:8000/validation/failure' \
  -H 'accept: application/json' \
  -H 'Content-Type: application/json' \
  -d '{
  "prompt": "string",
  "model": "gpt-4o",
  "temperature": 0
}'

{
  "detail": [
```

```
    {
      "type": "literal_error",
      "loc": [
        "body",
        "model"
      ],
      "msg": "Input should be 'tinyllama' or 'gemma2b'",
      "input": "gpt-4o",
      "ctx": {
        "expected": "'tinyllama' or 'gemma2b'"
      }
    }
  ]
}
```

Custom Field and Model Validators

Another excellent feature of Pydantic for performing data validation checks is *custom field validators*. Example 4-9 shows how both types of custom validators can be implemented on the ImageModelRequest.

Example 4-9. Implementing custom field and model validators for ImageModelRequest

```
# schemas.py

from typing import Annotated, Literal
from pydantic import (
    AfterValidator,
    BaseModel,
    Field,
    PositiveInt,
    validate_call,
)

ImageSize = Annotated[
    tuple[PositiveInt, PositiveInt], "Width and height of an image in pixels"
]
SupportedModels = Annotated[
    Literal["tinysd", "sd1.5"], "Supported Image Generation Models"
]

@validate_call ❶
def is_square_image(value: ImageSize) -> ImageSize: ❷
    if value[0] / value[1] != 1:
        raise ValueError("Only square images are supported")
    if value[0] not in [512, 1024]:
        raise ValueError(f"Invalid output size: {value} - expected 512 or 1024")
    return value

@validate_call ❶
def is_valid_inference_step(
```

```
    num_inference_steps: int, model: SupportedModels
) -> int:
    if model == "tinysd" and num_inference_steps > 2000: ❸
        raise ValueError(
            "TinySD model cannot have more than 2000 inference steps"
        )
    return num_inference_steps

OutputSize = Annotated[ImageSize, AfterValidator(is_square_image)] ❹
InferenceSteps = Annotated[ ❹
    int,
    AfterValidator(
        lambda v, values: is_valid_inference_step(v, values["model"])
    ),
]

class ModelRequest(BaseModel):
    prompt: Annotated[str, Field(min_length=1, max_length=4000)]

class ImageModelRequest(ModelRequest):
    model: SupportedModels
    output_size: OutputSize ❺
    num_inference_steps: InferenceSteps = 200 ❻
```

❶ In addition to static type checks, raise a runtime validation error if incorrect parameters have been passed to both the is_square_image and is_valid_ inference_step functions.

❷ The tinysd model can generate square images in certain sizes only. Asking for a nonsquare image size (an aspect ratio other than 1) should raise a ValueError.

❸ Raise a ValueError if the user asks for a large number of inference steps for the tinysd model.

❹ Create reusable and more readable validators using the annotated pattern for both OutputSize and InferenceSteps.

❺ Attach the OutputSize field validator to the output_size field to check for incorrect values after the model is initialized.

❻ Attach the InferenceSteps validator to the ImageModelRequest model to perform checks on the model field values *after* the model is initialized.

With custom field validators, as shown in Example 4-9, you can now be confident that your image generation endpoints will be protected from incorrect configurations provided by users.

You can also use the decorator pattern to validate model fields. Special methods can be associated with model fields to execute conditional data checks by employing the @field_validator or @model_validator decorator.

While @field_validator accesses a value of a single field to perform checks, the @model_validator decorator allows for checks that involve multiple fields.

With after validators, you can perform extra checks or modify the data after Pydantic has completed its parsing and validation.

Computed Fields

Similar to dataclasses, Pydantic also allows you to implement methods to compute fields derived from other fields.

You can use the @computed_field decorator to implement a computed field for calculating count of tokens and cost, as shown in Example 4-10.

Example 4-10. Using computed fields to automatically count the total number of tokens

```python
# schemas.py

from typing import Annotated
from pydantic import computed_field, Field
from utils import count_tokens

...

class TextModelResponse(ModelResponse):
    model: SupportedModels
    price: Annotated[float, Field(ge=0, default=0.01)]
    temperature: Annotated[float, Field(ge=0.0, le=1.0, default=0.0)]

    @property
    @computed_field
    def tokens(self) -> int:
        return count_tokens(self.content)

    @property
    @computed_field
    def cost(self) -> float:
        return self.price * self.tokens
```

Computed fields are useful for encapsulating any field computation logic inside your Pydantic models to keep code organized. Bear in mind that computed fields are only accessible when you convert a Pydantic model to a dictionary using .model_dump() or via serialization when a FastAPI API handler returns a response.

Model Export and Serialization

As Pydantic models can serialize to JSONs, the models you defined in Example 4-7 can also be dumped into (or be loaded from) JSON strings or Python dictionaries while maintaining any compound schemas, as shown in Example 4-11.

Example 4-11. Exporting and serializing the `TextModelResponse` model

```
>> response = TextModelResponse(content="FastAPI Generative AI Service", ip=None)
>> response.model_dump(exclude_none=True)
{'content': 'FastAPI Generative AI Service',
 'cost': 0.06,
 'created_at': datetime.datetime(2024, 3, 7, 20, 42, 38, 729410),
 'price': 0.01,
 'request_id': 'a3f18d85dcb442baa887a505ae8d2cd7',
 'tokens': 6}

>> response.model_dump_json(exclude_unset=True)
'{"ip":null,"content":"FastAPI Generative AI Service","tokens":6,"cost":0.06}'
```

Exporting Pydantic Models to Dictionaries or JSON Strings

When you create a Pydantic model, you also get access to type hints for the associated fields and can later export your model to Python dictionaries or JSON strings. Pydantic will also allow you to exclude fields based on their values. For instance, you can run `model.dict(exclude_none=True)` to return a dictionary without any of the fields that had been set to None. Other options for excluding fields during export include:

exclude_unset
: Only return the fields that were explicitly set during the model creation.

exclude_defaults
: Only return the optional fields that were set to default values.

exclude_None
: Only return fields that were set to None.

You can mix and match these conditions when exporting your models. These options are extremely useful when working with models that have a large number of fields such as filters. For example, if the client doesn't specify certain filters as query parameters to your endpoint, you can exclude all unset filtering fields from your request filter model.

You can also use the same field exclusion features when exporting your Pydantic models to JSON strings using `model.json_dump(exclude_unset=True)`.

Parsing Environment Variables with Pydantic

Alongside the `BaseModel`, Pydantic also implements a `Base` class for parsing settings and secrets from files. This feature is provided in an optional Pydantic package called `pydantic-settings`, which you can install as a dependency:

```
$ pip install pydantic-settings
```

The `BaseSettings` class provides optional Pydantic features for loading a settings or config class from environment variables or secret files. Using this feature, the settings values can be set in code or overridden by environment variables.

This is useful in production where you don't want to expose secrets inside the code or the container environment.

When you create a model inheriting from `BaseSettings`, the model initializer will attempt to set values of each field using provided defaults. If unsuccessful, the initializer will then read the values of any unset fields from the environment variables.

Given a dotenv environment file (ENV):

```
APP_SECRET=asdlkajdlkajdklaslkldjkasldjkasdjaslk
DATABASE_URL=postgres://sa:password@localhost:5432/cms
CORS_WHITELIST=["https://xyz.azurewebsites.net","http://localhost:3000"]
```

An ENV is an environment variable file that can use a shell script syntax for key-value pairs.

Example 4-12 shows parsing environment variables using `BaseSettings` in action.

Example 4-12. Using Pydantic BaseSettings to parse environment variables

```
# settings.py

from typing import Annotated
from pydantic import Field, HttpUrl, PostgresDsn
from pydantic_settings import BaseSettings, SettingsConfigDict

class AppSettings(BaseSettings):  ❶
    model_config = SettingsConfigDict(
        env_file=".env", env_file_encoding="utf-8"  ❷
    )

    port: Annotated[int, Field(default=8000)]
    app_secret: Annotated[str, Field(min_length=32)]
    pg_dsn: Annotated[
        PostgresDsn,
        Field(
            alias="DATABASE_URL",
            default="postgres://user:pass@localhost:5432/database",
        ),
```

```
    ] ❸
    cors_whitelist_domains: Annotated[
        set[HttpUrl],
        Field(alias="CORS_WHITELIST", default=["http://localhost:3000"]),
    ] ❹


settings = AppSettings()
print(settings.model_dump()) ❺
"""
{'port': 8000
 'app_secret': 'asdlkajdlkajdklaslkldjkasldjkasdjaslk',
 'pg_dsn': MultiHostUrl('postgres://sa:password@localhost:5432/cms'),
 'cors_whitelist_domains': {Url('http://localhost:3000/'),
                           Url('https://xyz.azurewebsites.net/')},
}
"""
```

❶ Declare AppSettings inheriting from the BaseSettings class from the pydantic_settings package.

❷ Configure AppSettings to read environment variables from the ENV file at the root of a project with the UTF-8 encoding. By default, the snake_case field names will map to environment variables names that are an uppercase version of those names. For instance, app_secret becomes APP_SECRET.

❸ Validate that the DATABASE_URL environment variable has a valid Postgres connection string format. If not provided, set the default value.

❹ Check that the CORS_WHITELIST environment variable has a unique list of valid URLs with hostname and TLDs. If not provided, set the default to a set with a single value of http://localhost:3000.

❺ We can check the AppSettings class is working by printing a dump of the model.

> You can switch environment files when using the _env_file argument:
>
> ```
> test_settings = AppSettings(_env_file="test.env")
> ```

Dataclasses or Pydantic Models in FastAPI

Even though dataclasses support serialization of only the common types (e.g., `int`, `str`, `list`, etc.) and won't perform field validation at runtime, FastAPI can still work with both Pydantic models and Python's dataclasses. For field validation and additional features, you should use Pydantic models. Example 4-13 shows how dataclasses can be used in FastAPI route handlers.

Example 4-13. Using dataclasses in FastAPI

```
# schemas.py

from dataclasses import dataclass
from typing import Literal

@dataclass
class TextModelRequest:  ❶
    model: Literal["tinyLlama", "gemma2b"]
    prompt: str
    temperature: float

@dataclass
class TextModelResponse:  ❶
    response: str
    tokens: int

# main.py

from fastapi import Body, FastAPI, HTTPException, status
from models import generate_text, load_text_model
from schemas import TextModelRequest, TextModelResponse
from utils import count_tokens

# load lifespan
...

app = FastAPI(lifespan=lifespan)

@app.post("/generate/text")
def serve_text_to_text_controller(
    body: TextModelRequest = Body(...),
) -> TextModelResponse:  ❷ ❹
    if body.model not in ["tinyLlama", "gemma2b"]:  ❸
        raise HTTPException(
            detail=f"Model {body.model} is not supported",
            status_code=status.HTTP_400_BAD_REQUEST,
        )
    output = generate_text(models["text"], body.prompt, body.temperature)
    tokens = count_tokens(body.prompt) + count_tokens(output)
    return TextModelResponse(response=output, tokens=tokens)  ❹
```

❶ Define models for text model request and response schemas.

❷ Convert the handler to serve POST requests with a body. Then, declare the request body as TextModelRequest and the response as TextModelResponse. Static code checkers like mypy will read the type annotations and raise warnings if your controller doesn't return the expected response model.

❸ Explicitly check whether the service supports the model parameter provided in the request body. If not, return a bad request HTTP exception response to the client.

❹ FastAPI converts vanilla dataclasses to Pydantic dataclasses to serialize/deserialize and validate the request and response data.

In Example 4-13, you have leveraged type annotations by refactoring the text model controller to be resilient to new changes and bad user input. Static type checkers can now help you catch any data-related issues as changes occur. In addition, FastAPI used your type annotations to validate request and responses alongside the auto-generation of an OpenAPI documentation page, as shown in Figure 4-2.

You now see that FastAPI leverages Pydantic models under the hood for data handling and validation, even if you use vanilla dataclasses. FastAPI converts your vanilla dataclasses to Pydantic-flavored dataclasses to use its data validation features. This behavior is intentional because if you have projects with several pre-existing dataclass type annotations, you can still migrate them over without having to rewrite them into Pydantic models for leveraging data validation features. However, if you're starting a fresh project, it is recommended to use Pydantic models directly in replacement for Python's built-in dataclasses.

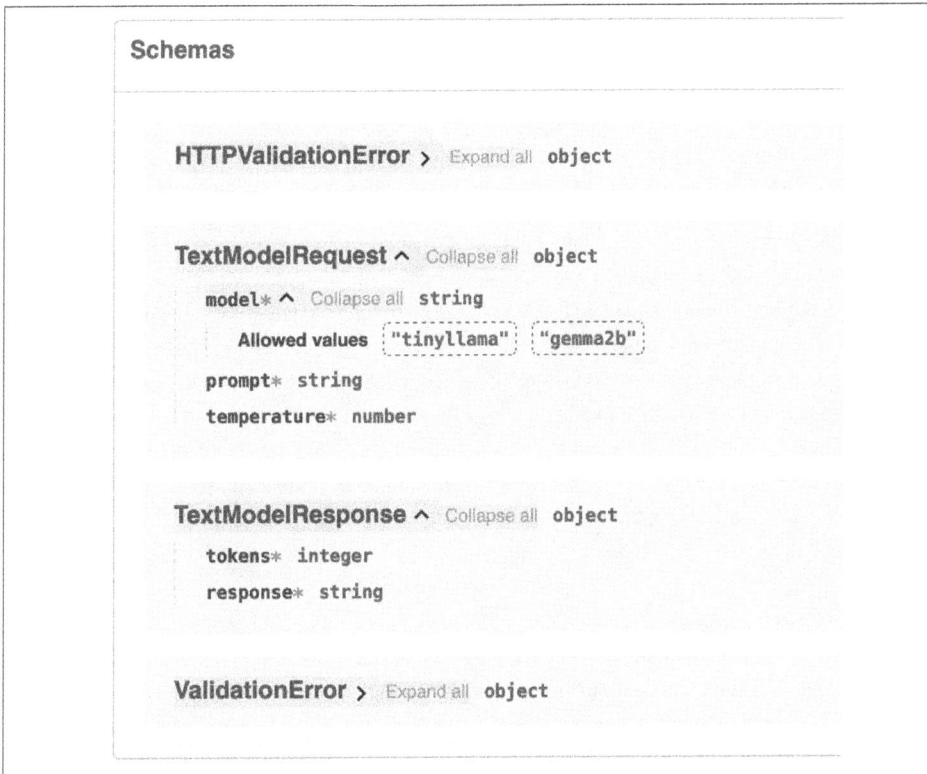

```
Schemas

    HTTPValidationError  >  Expand all  object


    TextModelRequest  ^  Collapse all  object
        model*  ^  Collapse all  string
            Allowed values   "tinyllama"   "gemma2b"
        prompt*  string
        temperature*  number


    TextModelResponse  ^  Collapse all  object
        tokens*  integer
        response*  string


    ValidationError  >  Expand all  object
```

Figure 4-2. Automatic generation of validation schemas using vanilla dataclasses

Now let's see how you can replace dataclasses with Pydantic in your FastAPI application. See Example 4-14.

Example 4-14. Using Pydantic to model request and response schemas

```
# main.py

from fastapi import Body, FastAPI, HTTPException, Request, status
from models import generate_text
from schemas import TextModelRequest, TextModelResponse  ❶

# load lifespan
...

app = FastAPI(lifespan=lifespan)

@app.post("/generate/text")  ❷
def serve_text_to_text_controller(
    request: Request, body: TextModelRequest = Body(...)
) -> TextModelResponse:
```

```
if body.model not in ["tinyLlama", "gemma2b"]: ❸
    raise HTTPException(
        detail=f"Model {body.model} is not supported",
        status_code=status.HTTP_400_BAD_REQUEST,
    )
output = generate_text(models["text"], body.prompt, body.temperature)
return TextModelResponse(content=output, ip=request.client.host) ❹
```

❶ Import Pydantic models for text model request and response schemas.

❷ Convert the handler to serve POST requests with a body. Then, declare the request
    body as TextModelRequest and the response as TextModelResponse. Static code
    checkers like mypy will read the type annotations and raise warnings if your con-
    troller doesn't return the expected response model.

❸ Explicitly check whether the service supports the model parameter provided in
    the request body. If not, return a bad request HTTP exception response to the
    client.

❹ Return the TextModelResponse Pydantic model as per the function typing.
    Access the client's IP address using the request object via request.client.host.
    FastAPI will take care of serializing your model using .model_dump() under the
    hood. As you also implemented the computed fields for tokens and cost proper-
    ties, these will automatically will be included in your API response without any
    additional work.

> As shown in Example 4-13, if you use dataclasses instead of Pydan-
> tic models, FastAPI will convert them to Pydantic dataclasses to
> serialize/deserialize and validate the request and response data.
> However, you may not be able to leverage advanced features such
> as field constraints and computed fields with dataclasses.

As you can see in Example 4-14, Pydantic can provide exceptional developer experience by helping in type checks, data validation, serialization, code editor auto-
completions, and computed attributes.

FastAPI can also use your Pydantic models to auto-generate an OpenAPI specification and documentation page so that you can manually test your endpoints
seamlessly.

Once you start the server, you should see an updated documentation page with the
new Pydantic models and the updated constrained fields, as shown in Figure 4-3.

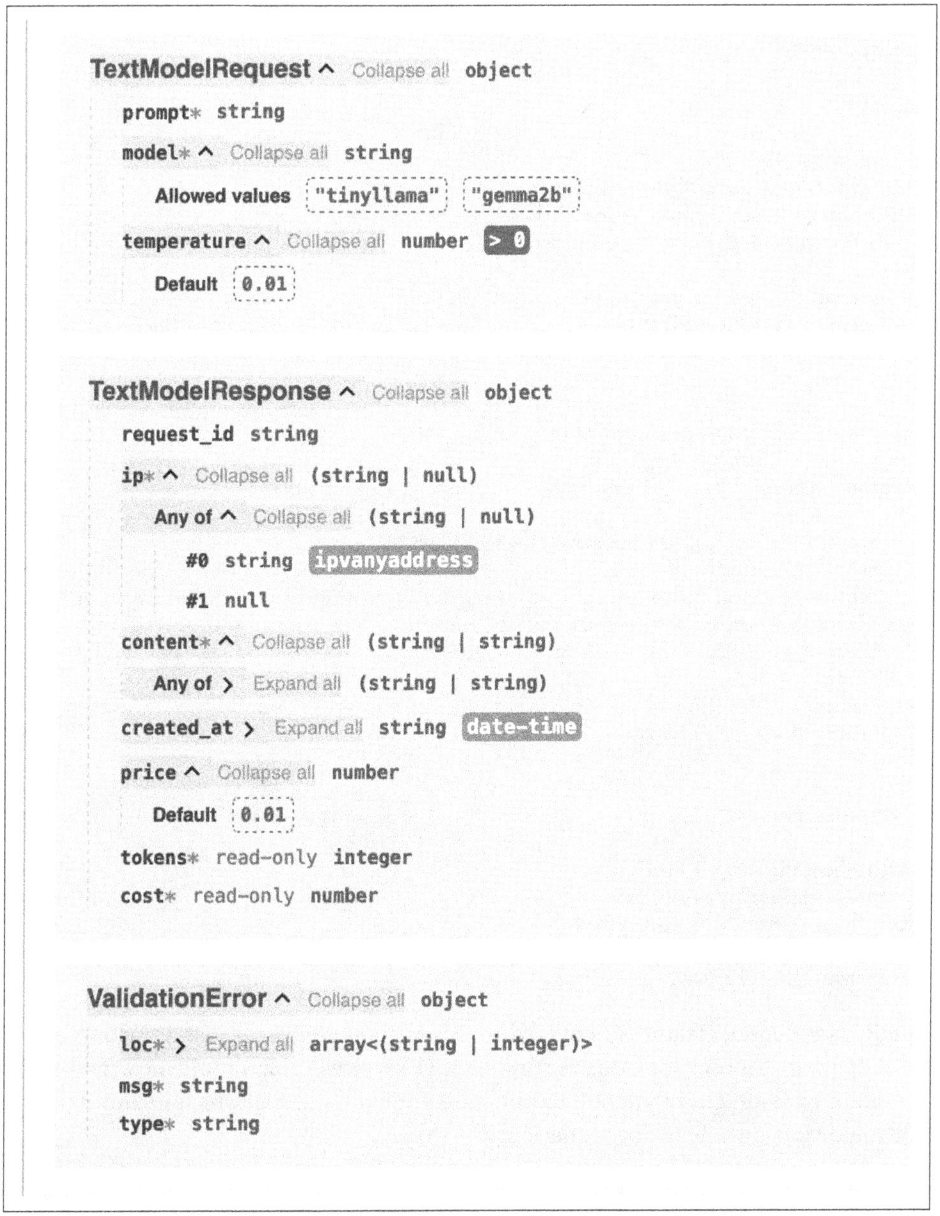

```
TextModelRequest ∧  Collapse all  object

  prompt* string

  model* ∧  Collapse all  string

    Allowed values  "tinyllama"   "gemma2b"

  temperature ∧  Collapse all  number  > 0

    Default  0.01


TextModelResponse ∧  Collapse all  object

  request_id string

  ip* ∧  Collapse all  (string | null)

    Any of ∧  Collapse all  (string | null)

      #0  string  ipvanyaddress

      #1  null

  content* ∧  Collapse all  (string | string)

    Any of >  Expand all  (string | string)

  created_at >  Expand all  string  date-time

  price ∧  Collapse all  number

    Default  0.01

  tokens* read-only integer

  cost* read-only number


ValidationError ∧  Collapse all  object

  loc* >  Expand all  array<(string | integer)>

  msg* string

  type* string
```

Figure 4-3. Automatic generation of FastAPI docs using Pydantic models

If you send a request to the /generate/text endpoint, you should now see the prepopulated fields via the TextModelResponse Pydantic model, as shown in Example 4-15.

Example 4-15. Automatic population of the response fields via the `TextModelResponse`
Pydantic model

```
Request

curl -X 'POST' \
    'http://localhost:8000/generate/text' \
    -H 'accept: application/json' \
    -H 'Content-Type: application/json' \
    -d '{
    "prompt": "What is your name?",
    "model": "tinyllama",
    "temperature": 0.01
}'

http://localhost:8000/generate/text

>> Response body
{
    "request_id": "7541204d5c684f429fe43ccf360f33dc",
    "ip": "127.0.0.1",
    "content": "I am not a person. However, I can provide you with information
        about my name. My name is fastapi bot.",
    "created_at": "2024-03-07T16:06:57.492039",
    "price": 0.01,
    "tokens": 25,
    "cost": 0.25
}

>> Response headers

content-length: 259
content-type: application/json
date: Thu, 07 Mar 2024 16:07:01 GMT
server: uvicorn
x-response-time: 22.9243
```

The Pydantic model features I covered in this chapter represent just a fraction of the
tools at your disposal for constructing GenAI services. You should now feel more
confident in leveraging Pydantic to annotate your own services to improve its reliability and your own developer experience.

Summary

In this chapter, you learned the importance of creating fully typed services for GenAI models. You now understand how to implement type safety with standard and constrained types, how to use Pydantic models for data validation, and how to implement your own custom data validators across your GenAI service. You also discovered strategies for validating request and response content and managing application settings with Pydantic to prevent bugs and to improve your development experience. Overall, by following along with the practical examples, you learned how to implement a robust, less error-prone GenAI service.

The next chapter covers asynchronous programming in AI workloads, discussing performance and parallel operations. You will learn more about I/O-bound and CPU-bound tasks and understand the role and limitations of FastAPI's background tasks with concurrent workflows.

## PART II

Communicating with External Systems

In this part, you will build endpoints that are capable of handling concurrent AI workloads and processing real-time data generated by AI models. This is also where you will handle the application's lifecycle, long-running tasks such as AI model inference, and integrating databases with AI services.

## CHAPTER 5

Achieving Concurrency in AI Workloads

Chapter Goals

In this chapter, you will learn about:

- The role and benefits of multithreading, multiprocessing, and asynchronous programming in enhancing AI application performance and scalability
- The role of the thread pool and event loop in a FastAPI server
- How to avoid blocking the server when processing requests
- Using asynchronous programming to interact with external systems such as databases, AI models, and web content by building a web scraper and a RAG module
- The model-serving strategies and LLM memory-optimization strategies to reduce memory-bound blocking operations
- Strategies for handling long-running AI inference tasks

In this chapter, you will learn more about the role and benefits of asynchronous programming in boosting the performance and scalability of your GenAI services. As part of this, you'll learn to manage concurrent user interactions and interface with external systems such as databases, implement RAG, and read web pages to enrich the context of model prompts. You'll acquire techniques for effectively dealing with I/O-bound and CPU-bound operations, especially when dealing with external services or handling long-running inference tasks.

We will also dive into strategies for efficiently handling long-running Generative AI inference tasks, including the use of FastAPI event loop for background tasks execution.

Optimizing GenAI Services for Multiple Users

AI workloads are computationally expensive operations that can inhibit your GenAI services from serving multiple simultaneous requests. In most production scenarios, multiple users will be using your applications. Therefore, your services will be expected to serve requests *concurrently* such that multiple overlapping tasks can be executed. However, if you're interfacing with GenAI models and external systems such as databases, the filesystem, or the internet, there will be operations that can block other tasks from executing on your server. Long-running operations that can halt the program execution flow are considered *blocking*.

These blocking operations can be twofold:

Input/output (I/O) bound
> Where a process has to wait because of data input/output operation, which can come from a user, file, database, network, etc. Examples include reading or writing a file to a disk, making network requests and API calls, sending or receiving data from databases, or waiting for user input.

Compute bound
> Where a process has to wait because of a compute-intensive operation on CPU or GPU. Compute-bound programs push the CPU or GPU cores to their limit by performing intensive computations, often blocking them from performing other tasks.[1] Examples include data processing, AI model inference or training, 3D object rendering, running simulations, etc.

You have a few strategies to serve multiple users:

System optimization
> For I/O-bound tasks like fetching data from a database, working with files on disk, making network requests, or reading web pages

Model optimization
> For memory- and compute-bound tasks such as model loading and inference

Queuing system
> For handling long-running inference tasks to avoid delays in responding

---

[1] A core is an individual processing unit within a CPU or GPU that executes instructions. Modern CPUs and GPUs have multiple cores to perform tasks simultaneously.

In this section, we will look at each strategy in more detail. To help solidify your learning, we will also implement several features together that leverage the aforementioned strategies:

- Building a *web page scraper* for bulk fetching and parsing of HTTP URLs pasted in the chat, so that you can ask your LLM about the content of web pages

- Adding a *retrieval augmented generation* (RAG) module to your service with a self-hosted vector database such as `qdrant` so that you can upload and talk to your documents via your LLM service

- Adding a *batch image generation system* so that you can run image generation workloads as background tasks

Before I can show you how to build the aforementioned features, we should dive deeper into the topic of *concurrency* and *parallelism* as understanding both concepts will help you identify the correct strategies to use for your own use cases.

Concurrency refers to the ability of a service in handling multiple requests or tasks at the same time, without completing one after another. During concurrent operations, the timeline of multiple tasks can overlap and may start and end at different times.

In Python, you can implement concurrency with a single CPU core by switching between tasks on a single thread (via asynchronous programming) or across different threads (via multithreading).

Time Slicing

Time slicing is a scheduling mechanism in multithreading and asynchronous programming where a process allocates CPU time between tasks to give the illusion of concurrent execution.

In Python, the CPU time can be allocated to only one task at any moment because of Python's *Global Interpreter Lock* (GIL). Python's GIL allows only one thread (i.e., execution flow in a Python process) to control the Python interpreter for executing code. This means that only one thread can be in a state of execution at any point in time.[2]

The GIL was originally implemented to simplify Python's development, ease memory management between threads in a Python process, and prioritize the performance of single-threaded programs. It was also added to Python to ensure *thread-safety* within the process, preventing race conditions that could lead to data corruption when working with shared resources between threads.

---

2 Multithreading in most languages is parallel (running on multiple cores) and not concurrent. Python is changing over the next coming versions to do the same (free-threaded Python).

However, the addition of the GIL to Python also means that true parallel execution of threads in a single Python process is not possible. When a task is waiting for an I/O operation to finish, the CPU can quickly switch to another task to avoid blocking other operations. The paused tasks save their state and can resume once the I/O operations are done.

With multiple cores, you can also implement a subset of concurrency called *parallelism* where tasks are split among several independent workers (via multiprocessing), with each executing tasks simultaneously on their own isolated resources and separate processes.

> Although there are plans to remove the GIL from Python soon, at the time of this writing it is not possible for multiple threads to simultaneously work through tasks. Therefore, concurrency on a single core can give an illusion of parallelism even though there is one process doing all the work. The single process can only multitask by switching active threads to minimize waiting times of I/O blocking operations.
>
> You can only achieve true parallelism with multiple workers (in multiprocessing).

Even though concurrency and parallelism have many similarities, they aren't exactly the same concepts. The big difference between them is that concurrency can help you manage multiple tasks by interleaving their execution, which is useful for I/O-bound tasks. Parallelism, on the other hand, involves executing multiple tasks simultaneously, typically on multicore machines, which is more useful for CPU-bound tasks.

You can implement concurrency using approaches like threading or asynchronous programming (i.e., time-slicing on a single-core machine, where tasks are interleaved to give the appearance of simultaneous execution).

Figure 5-1 shows the relationship between concurrency and parallelism.

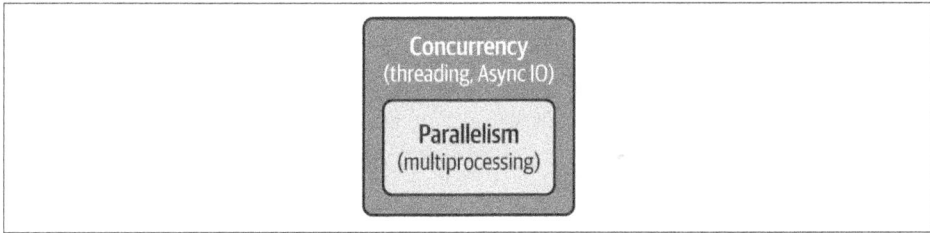

Figure 5-1. Concurrency and parallelism

In most scalable systems, you can witness both concurrency and parallelism.

Imagine that you're visiting a fast-food restaurant and placing an order. In a concurrent system, you'll see the restaurant owner taking orders while cooking burgers, attending to each task time to time, and effectively multitasking by switching between tasks. In a parallel system, you'll see multiple staff members taking orders and a few others cooking the burgers at the same time. Here different workers handle each task simultaneously.

Without any multithreading or asynchronous programming in a single-threaded process, the process has to wait for blocking operations to finish before it can start new tasks. Without multiprocessing implementing parallelism on multiple cores, computationally expensive operations can block the application from starting other tasks.

Figure 5-2 shows the distinctions between nonconcurrent execution, concurrent execution without parallelism (single core), and concurrent execution with parallelism (multiple cores).

The three Python execution models shown in Figure 5-2 are as follows:

No concurrency (synchronous)
    A single process (on one core) executes tasks sequentially.

Concurrent and non-parallel
    Multiple threads in a single process (on a core) handle tasks concurrently but not in parallel due to Python's GIL.

Concurrent and parallel
    Multiple processes on multiple cores perform the tasks in parallel, making the most of multicore processors for maximum efficiency.

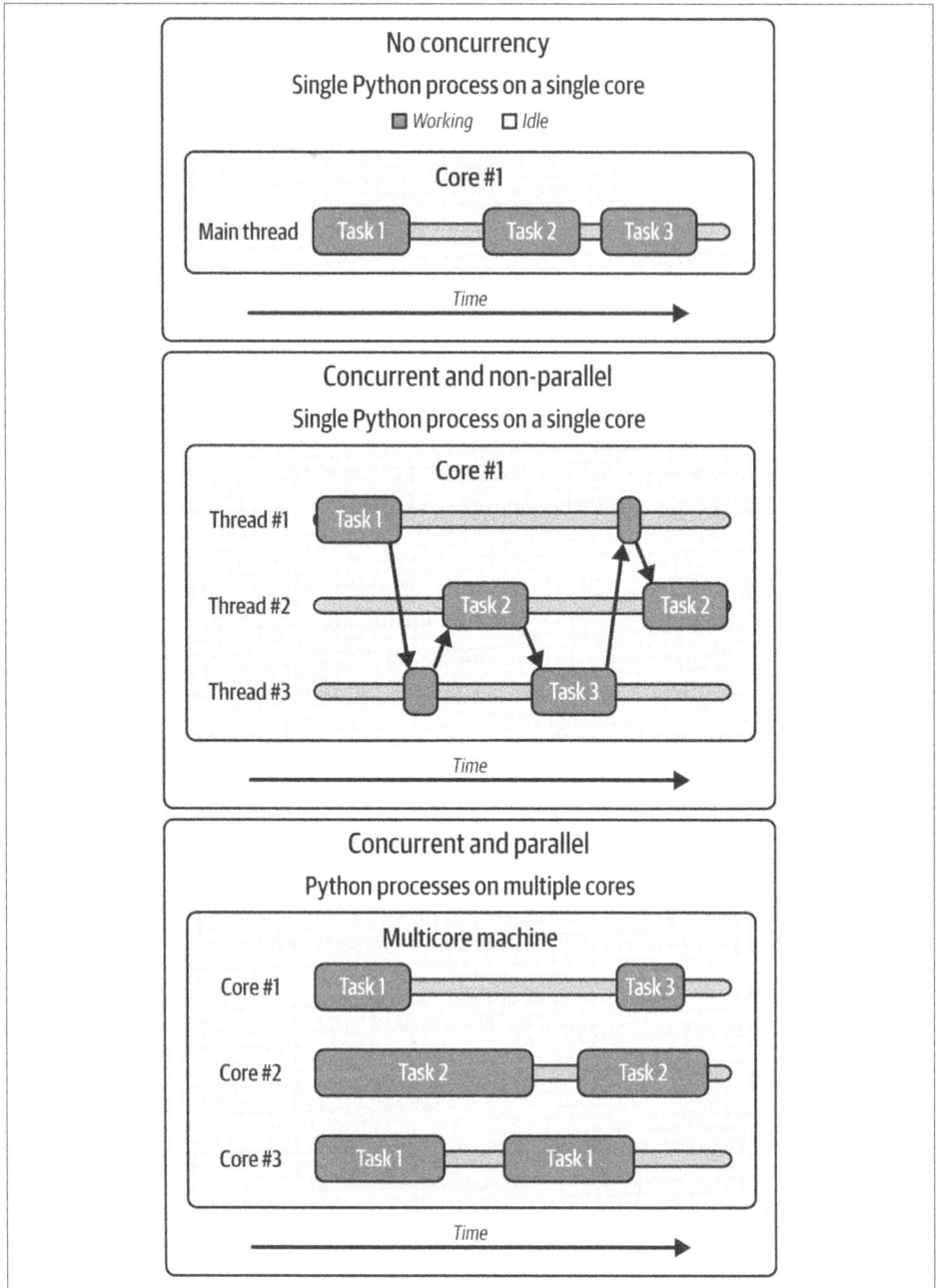

Figure 5-2. Concurrency with and without parallelism

In multiprocessing, each process has access to its own memory space and resources to complete a task in isolation from other processes. This isolation can make processes more stable—since if a process crashes, it won't affect others—but makes interprocess communication more complex compared to threads, which share the same memory space, as shown in Figure 5-3.

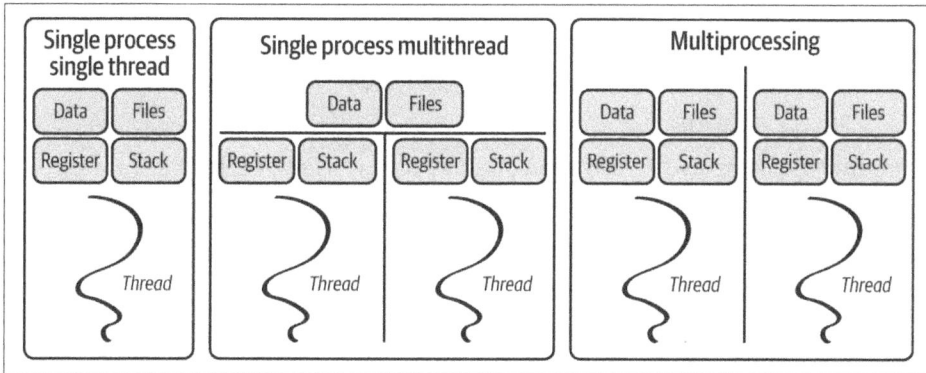

Figure 5-3. Resource sharing in multithreading and multiprocessing

Distributed workloads often use a managing process that coordinates the execution and collaboration of these processes to avoid issues such as data corruption and duplicating work. A good example of multiprocessing is when you serve requests with a load balancer managing traffic to multiple containers, each running an instance of your application.

Both multithreading and asynchronous programming reduce wait time in I/O tasks because the processor can do other work while waiting for I/O. However, they don't help with tasks that require heavy computation, like AI inference, because the process is busy with computing some results. Therefore, to serve a large self-hosted GenAI model to multiple users, you should either scale services with multiprocessing or use algorithmic model optimizations (via specialized model inference servers like vLLM).

Your first instinct when working with slow models may be to adopt parallelism by creating multiple instances of your FastAPI service (multiprocessing) in a single machine to serve requests in parallel.

Unfortunately, multiple workers running in separate processes will not have access to a shared memory space. As a result, you can't share artifacts—like a GenAI model—loaded in memory between separate instances of your app in FastAPI. Sadly, a new instance of your model will also need to be loaded, which will significantly eat up your hardware resources. This is because FastAPI is a general-purpose web server that doesn't natively optimize serving GenAI models.

The solution is not parallelism on its own, but to adopt the external model-serving strategy, as discussed in Chapter 3.

The only instance where you can treat AI inference workloads as I/O-bound, instead of compute-bound, is when you're relying on third-party AI provider APIs (e.g., OpenAI API). In this case, you're offloading the compute-bound tasks to the model provider through network requests.

On your side, the AI inference workloads become I/O-bound through network requests, allowing for the use of concurrency through time slicing. The third-party provider has to worry about scaling their services to handle model inferences—that are compute-bound—across their hardware resources.

You can externalize the serving and inference of larger GenAI models such as an LLM, with specialized servers like vLLM, Ray Serve, or NVIDIA Triton.

Later in this chapter, I will detail how these servers maximize inference efficiency of compute-bound operations during model inference while minimizing the model's memory footprint during the data generation process.

To help you digest what was discussed so far, have a look at the comparison table of concurrency strategies in Table 5-1 to understand when and why to use each.

Table 5-1. Comparison of concurrency strategies

Strategy	Features	Challenges	Use cases
No concurrency (synchronous)	• Simple, readable, easy-to-understand code to debug • A single CPU core and thread	• Potential long waiting times depending on I/O or CPU blocking operations halting the process execution • Can't serve multiple users simultaneously	• Single user applications where users can wait for tasks to finish • Infrequently used services or applications
Async IO (asynchronous)	• A single CPU core and thread • Multitasking managed by an event loop within the Python process • Thread-safe as the Python process manages tasks • Maximizes the CPU utilization rate • Faster than multithreading and multiprocessing for I/O tasks	• Harder to implement in code and can make debugging harder • Requires libraries and dependencies that use Async IO features • Easy to make mistakes that block the main process (and event loop)	Applications that have blocking I/O tasks

Strategy	Features	Challenges	Use cases
Multithreading	• A single CPU core but multiple threads within the same process • Threads share data and resources • Simpler than Async IO to implement in code • Multitasking across threads orchestrated by the OS	• Difficult to lock resources for each thread to avoid thread-safety issues that can lead to nonreproducible bugs and data corruption • Threads can block each other indefinitely (deadlocks) • Concurrent access to resources can cause inconsistent results (race conditions) • A thread can be denied resources by monopolizing threads (starvation) • Creating and destroying threads is computationally expensive	Applications or services that have blocking I/O tasks
Multiprocessing	• Multiple processes running on several CPU cores • Each process is allocated a CPU core and isolated resources • Work can be distributed across CPU cores and managed by an orchestrator process using tools like Celery	• Sharing hardware resources and objects like a large AI model or data between processes can be complex and requires inter-process communication (IPC) mechanisms or a dedicated shared memory • Difficult to keep multiple isolated processes in sync • Creating and destroying processes is computationally expensive	• Applications or services that have blocking compute-bound tasks • Divide-and-conquer type of tasks where processing can be done in isolated chunks • Distributing workloads or processing requests across multiple CPU cores

Now that we've explored various concurrency strategies, let's continue by enhancing your services with asynchronous programming to efficiently manage I/O-bound operations. Later we'll focus on optimizing compute-bound tasks, specifically model inference via specialized servers.

Optimizing for I/O Tasks with Asynchronous Programming

In this section, we'll explore the use of asynchronous programming to prevent blocking the main server process with I/O-bound tasks during AI workloads. You'll also learn about the `asyncio` framework that enables writing asynchronous applications in Python.

Synchronous Versus Asynchronous (Async) Execution

What is considered an asynchronous application? To answer the question, let's compare both synchronous and asynchronous programs.

An application is considered *synchronous* when tasks are performed in a sequential order with each task waiting for the previous one to complete before starting. For applications that run infrequently and take only a few seconds to process, synchronous code rarely causes a problem and can make implementations faster and easier. However, if you need concurrency and want the efficiency of your services to be maximized on every core, your services should multitask without waiting for blocking operations to complete. That's where implementing *asynchronous* (async) concurrency can help.

Let's look at a few examples of synchronous and async functions to understand how much of a performance boost an async code can give you. In both examples, I will use sleeping to simulate I/O blocking operation, but you can imagine other I/O tasks being performed in real-world scenarios.

Example 5-1 shows an example of a synchronous code that simulates an I/O blocking operation with the blocking `time.sleep()` function.

Example 5-1. Synchronous execution

```
import time

def task():
    print("Start of sync task")
    time.sleep(5) ❶
    print("After 5 seconds of sleep")

start = time.time()
for _ in range(3): ❷
    task()
duration = time.time() - start
print(f"\nProcess completed in: {duration} seconds")
"""
Start of sync task
After 5 seconds of sleep
Start of sync task
After 5 seconds of sleep
Start of sync task
After 5 seconds of sleep

Process completed in: 15.014271020889282 seconds
"""
```

❶ Use `sleep()` to simulate an I/O blocking operation such as sending a network request.

❷ Call the `task()` three times, sequentially. The loop simulates sending multiple network requests, one after another.

Calling `task()` three times in Example 5-1 takes 15 seconds to complete as Python waits for the blocking operation `sleep()` to complete.

To develop async programs in Python, you can use the `asyncio` package as part of the standard library of Python 3.5 and later versions. Using `asyncio`, asynchronous code looks similar to sequential synchronous code but with additions of `async` and `await` keywords to perform nonblocking I/O operations.

Example 5-2 shows how you can use `async` and `await` keywords with `asyncio` to run Example 5-1 asynchronously.

Example 5-2. Asynchronous execution

```
import time
import asyncio

async def task(): ❶
    print("Start of async task")
    await asyncio.sleep(5) ❷
    print("Task resumed after 5 seconds")

async def spawn_tasks():
    await asyncio.gather(task(), task(), task()) ❸

start = time.time()
asyncio.run(spawn_tasks()) ❹
duration = time.time() - start

print(f"\nProcess completed in: {duration} seconds")
"""
Start of async task
Start of async task
Start of async task
Task resumed after 5 seconds
Task resumed after 5 seconds
Task resumed after 5 seconds

Process completed in: 5.0057971477508545 seconds ❺
"""
```

❶ Implement a `task` coroutine that cedes control to the event loop on blocking operations.

② The nonblocking five-second sleep signals to the event loop to run another task while waiting.

③ Use `asyncio.create_task` to spawn task instances to chain (or gather) and run them concurrently using `asyncio.gather`.

④ Create an event loop to schedule async tasks with via the `asyncio.run` method.

⑤ Execution time is 1/3 of the synchronous example since the Python process wasn't blocked this time.

After running Example 5-2, you will notice that the `task()` function was concurrently called three times. On the other hand, the code in Example 5-1 calls the `task()` function three times sequentially. The async function ran inside the `asyncio`'s event loop, which was responsible for executing the code without waiting.

In any async code, the `await` keyword flags the I/O blocking operations to Python so that they're executed in a *nonblocking* manner (i.e., they can run without blocking the main process). By being made aware of blocking operations, Python can go and do something else while waiting for blocking operations to finish.

Example 5-3 shows how to use the `async` and `await` keywords to declare and run async functions.

Example 5-3. How to use async and await keywords

```
import asyncio

async def main():
    print("Before sleeping")
    await asyncio.sleep(3) ①
    print("After sleeping for 3 seconds")

asyncio.run(main()) ②

"""
Before sleeping
After sleeping for 3 seconds ③
"""
```

① Simulate a nonblocking I/O operation by `await`ing the `asyncio.sleep()` so that Python can go and do other things while waiting.

❷ You need to call `main()` inside the `asyncio.run()` to execute it as it's an async function. Otherwise, it will not be executed and returns a *coroutine* object instead. I will cover coroutines shortly.

❸ If you run the code, the second statement will be printed 3 seconds after the first one. In this instance, as there are no other operations to run beyond sleeping, Python runs in idle until the sleep operation is completed.

In Example 5-3, I used sleeping as a way to simulate I/O blocking operations such as making network requests.

> You can only use the `await` keyword inside a function declared with `async def`. Using `await` outside of an `async` function will raise a `SyntaxError` in Python. Another common pitfall is using blocking code that's not asynchronous within an `async` function that will inadvertently prevent Python from doing other tasks while waiting.

So, you now understand that in async programs, to keep the main process from being blocked, Python switches between functions as soon as it hits a blocking operation. You now may be wondering:

- How does Python leverage `asyncio` to pause and resume functions?
- What is the mechanism that Python's `asyncio` uses to move from one function to another without forgetting about those that are suspended?
- How can functions be paused or resumed without losing their state?

To answer the aforementioned questions, let's dive deeper into the underlying mechanisms within `asyncio`, as understanding the answers to these questions will help you significantly to debug async code in your services.

At the heart of `asyncio` lies a first-class object called an *event loop*, responsible for efficient handling of I/O events, system events, and application context changes.

Figure 5-4 shows how the `asyncio` event loop undertakes task orchestration in Python.

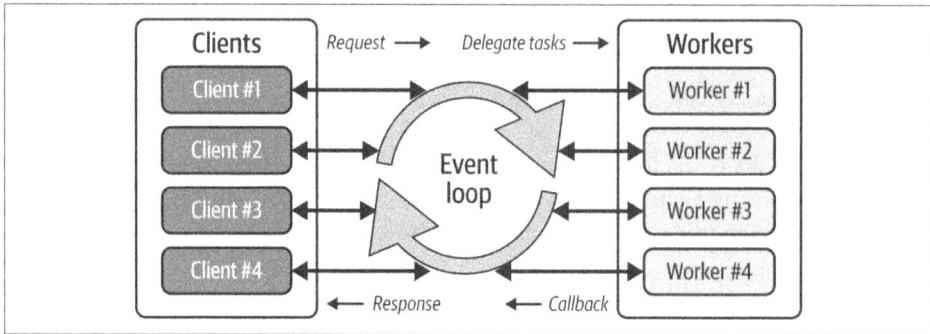

Figure 5-4. Async IO event loop

The event loop can be compared to a while True loop that watches for events or messages emitted by *coroutine functions* within the Python process and dispatches events to switch between functions while waiting for I/O blocking operations to complete. This orchestration allows other functions to execute asynchronously without interruption.

Coroutine Functions

Coroutine functions are specialized functions that yield control back to the caller without losing their state (i.e., they can be paused and resumed at a later time). The mechanism for yielding back control to the event loop relies on coroutines.

The ability to pause and resume operations without losing state makes coroutines similar to generator functions. In fact, you could implement coroutines using generators prior to Python 3.5 when there was no native support for coroutine functions. Similar to generators, simply calling a coroutine function will not execute it.

To run coroutines, you will need to use asyncio.run() or await them via the await keyword in Python 3.5 or later versions.

Aside from coroutines, the asyncio package also implements other concurrency primitives such as *futures*, *semaphores*, and *locks*.

Async Programming with Model Provider APIs

All three examples I've shown you so far are considered to be the "Hello World" examples of async programming. Now, let's look at a real-world scenario related to building GenAI services where you need to use a model provider's API—such as OpenAI, Anthropic, or Mistral—since it may be more expensive to serve LLMs yourself.

Additionally, if you stress test the generation endpoints you created in Chapter 3 by sending multiple requests in a short timeframe, you will notice long waiting times before each request is processed. This is because you were preloading and hosting the model in the same Python process and CPU core that the server is running on. When you send the first request, the whole server becomes blocked while the inference workload is complete. Since during inference the CPU is working as hard as it can, the inference/generation process is a CPU-bound blocking operation. However, it doesn't have to be.

When you use a provider's API, you no longer have CPU-bound AI workloads to worry about since they become I/O-bound for you, and you offload the CPU-bound workloads to the provider. Therefore, it makes sense to know how to leverage async programming to concurrently interact with the model provider's API.

The good news is API owners will often release both synchronous and asynchronous *clients* and *software development kits* (SDKs) to reduce the work needed to interact with their endpoints.

> If you need to make requests to other external services, fetch some data from databases, or ingest content from files, you will add other I/O blocking tasks to the process. These blocking tasks can force the server to keep waiting if you don't leverage asynchronous programming.
>
> However, any synchronous code can be made async using a process or thread pool executor (*https://oreil.ly/hIDNI*) to avoid running the task within the event loop. Instead, you run the asynchronous task on a separate process or thread to prevent blocking the event loop.
>
> You can also verify any async support by checking library documentation or source code for mentions of `async` or `await` keywords. Otherwise, you can try testing whether the tool can be used within an async function without raising a `TypeError` when you use `await` on it.
>
> If a tool, such as a database library, only has a synchronous implementation, then you can't implement asynchronicity with that tool. The solution will be to switch the tool to an asynchronous equivalent so that can you can use them with the `async` and `await` keywords.

In Example 5-4, you will interact with OpenAI GPT-3.5 API via both synchronous and asynchronous OpenAI clients to understand the performance difference between the two.

You will need to install the openai library:

```
$ pip install openai
```

Example 5-4. Comparing synchronous and asynchronous OpenAI clients

```python
import os
from fastapi import FastAPI, Body
from openai import OpenAI, AsyncOpenAI

app = FastAPI()

sync_client = OpenAI(api_key=os.environ.get("OPENAI_API_KEY"))
async_client = AsyncOpenAI(api_key=os.environ.get("OPENAI_API_KEY"))

@app.post("/sync")
def sync_generate_text(prompt: str = Body(...)):
    completion = sync_client.chat.completions.create(
        messages=[
            {
                "role": "user",
                "content": prompt,
            }
        ],
        model="gpt-3.5-turbo",
    )
    return completion.choices[0].message.content

@app.post("/async")
async def async_generate_text(prompt: str = Body(...)):
    completion = await async_client.chat.completions.create(
        messages=[
            {
                "role": "user",
                "content": prompt,
            }
        ],
        model="gpt-3.5-turbo",
    )
    return completion.choices[0].message.content
```

The difference between the sync and async clients is that with the async version, FastAPI can start processing user inputs in parallel without waiting for a response from the OpenAI API for the previous user input.

By leveraging asynchronous code, you can get a massive boost in throughput and scale to a larger volume of concurrent requests. However, you must be careful when writing asynchronous (async) code.

Here are some common pitfalls and problems you might face with async code:

- Understanding and debugging errors can be more complex due to the nonlinear execution flow of concurrent tasks.

- Some libraries, like `aiohttp`, require nested async context managers for proper implementation. This can get confusing pretty fast.

- Mixing asynchronous and synchronous code can negate any performance benefits, such as if you forget to mark functions with the `async` and `await` keywords.

- Not using async-compatible tools and libraries can also cancel out any performance benefits; for example, using the `requests` package instead of `aiohttp` for making async API calls.

- Forgetting to await coroutines within any async function or awaiting non-coroutines can lead to unexpected behavior. All `async` keywords must be followed by an `await`.

- Improperly managing resources (e.g., open API/database connections or file buffers) can cause memory leaks that freeze your computer. You can also leak memory if you don't limit the number of concurrent operations in async code.

---

3 You can also find a custom implementation in OpenAI Cookbook on GitHub (*https://oreil.ly/8E7GQ*).

- You might also run into concurrency and race condition issues where the thread-safety principle is violated, causing deadlocks on resources leading to data corruption.

This list is not exhaustive, and as you can see, there are several pitfalls to using asynchronous programming. Therefore, I recommend starting with writing synchronous programs first, to understand the basic flow and logic of your code, before dealing with the complexities of migrating to an async implementation.

Event Loop and Thread Pool in FastAPI

Under the hood, FastAPI can handle both async and sync blocking operations. It does this by running sync handlers in its *thread pool* so that blocking operations don't stop the *event loop* from executing tasks.

As I mentioned in Chapter 2, FastAPI runs on the ASGI web framework via Starlette. If it didn't, the server would effectively run synchronously, so you would have to wait for each process to finish before it could serve the next. However, using ASGI, the FastAPI server supports concurrency via both multithreading (via a thread pool) and asynchronous programming (via an event loop) to serve multiple requests in parallel, while keeping the main server process from being blocked.

FastAPI sets up the thread pool by instantiating a collection of threads at application startup to reduce the runtime burden of thread creation.[4] It then delegates background tasks and synchronous workloads to the thread pool to prevent the event loop from being blocked by any blocking operations inside the synchronous handlers. The event loop is also referred to as the main FastAPI server thread that is responsible for orchestrating the processing of requests.

As I mentioned, the event loop is the core component of every application built on top of `asyncio`, including FastAPI that implements concurrency. Event loops run asynchronous tasks and callbacks, including performing network I/O operations, and running subprocesses. In FastAPI, the event loop is also responsible for orchestrating the asynchronous processing of requests.

If possible, you should run handlers on the event loop (via asynchronous programming) as it can be even more efficient than running them on the thread pool (via multithreading). This is because each thread in the thread pool has to acquire the GIL before it can execute any code bytes, and that requires some computational effort.

Imagine if multiple concurrent users were using both the synchronous and asynchronous OpenAI GPT-3.5 handlers (endpoints) of your FastAPI service, as shown in

---

4 The cost of setting up the threads is still incurred; it's just done early to avoid doing it on the fly later.

Example 5-4. FastAPI will run the async handler requests on the event loop since that handler uses a nonblocking async OpenAI client. On the other hand, FastAPI has to delegate the synchronous handler requests to the thread pool to protect the event loop from blocking. Since delegating requests (to threads) and switching between threads in a thread pool is more work, the synchronous requests will finish later than their async counterparts.

> Remember that all of this work—processing both synchronous and async handler requests—is running on a single CPU core within the same FastAPI Python process.
>
> This is so that the CPU idle time is minimized while waiting for responses from OpenAI API.

The differences in performance are shown in Figure 5-5.

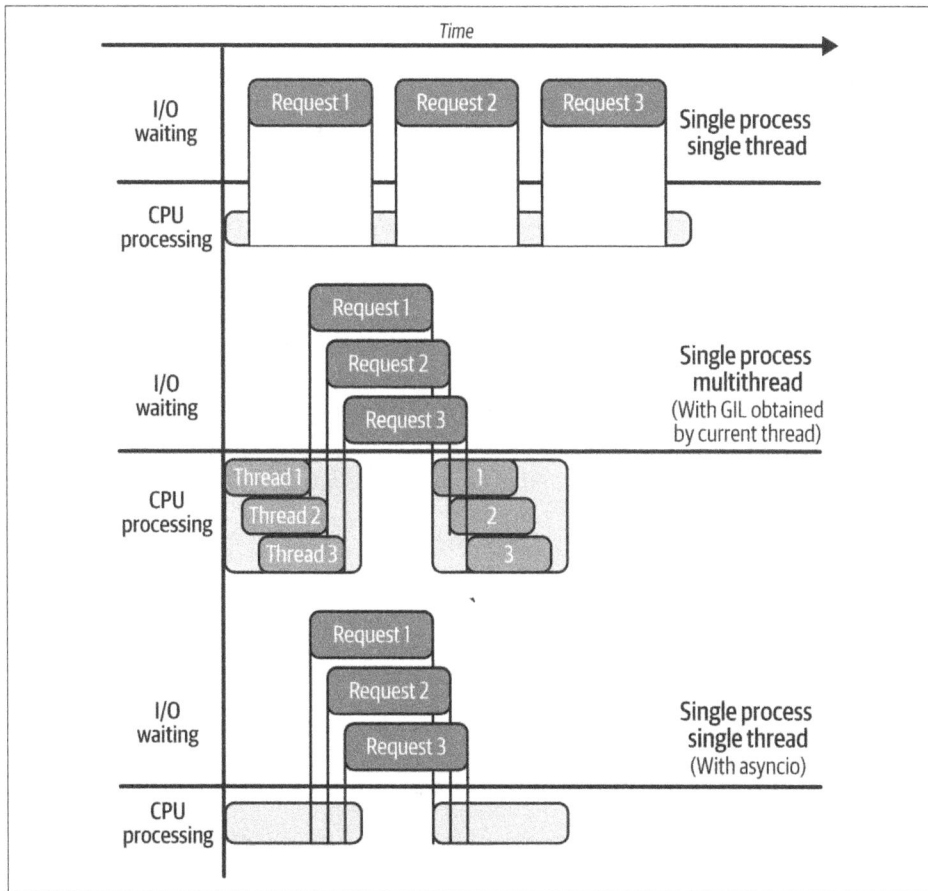

Figure 5-5. How multithreading and Async IO handle I/O blocking operations

Figure 5-5 shows that with I/O-bound workloads, async implementations are faster and should be your preferred method if you need concurrency. However, FastAPI does still do a solid job of serving multiple concurrent requests even if it has to work with a synchronous OpenAI client. It simply sends the synchronous API calls within threads of the thread pool to implement some form of concurrency for you. That's why the FastAPI official documentation tells you to not worry too much about declaring your handler functions as `async def` or `def`.

However, keep in mind that when you declare handlers with `async def`, FastAPI trusts you with performing only nonblocking operations. When you break that trust and execute blocking operations inside `async` routes, the event loop will be blocked and can no longer continue with executing tasks until the blocking operation is finished.

Blocking the Main Server

If you're using the `async` keyword when defining your functions, make sure you're also using the `await` keyword somewhere inside your function and that none of the package dependencies you use inside the function are synchronous.

Avoid declaring route handler functions as `async` if their implementation is synchronous. Otherwise, requests to the affected route handlers will block the main server from processing other requests while the server is waiting for the blocking operation to complete. It won't matter if the blocking operation is I/O-bound or compute-bound. Therefore, any calls to databases or AI models can still cause the blockage if you're not careful.

This is an easy mistake to make. For instance, you may use a synchronous dependency inside handlers you've declared as async, as shown in Example 5-5.

Example 5-5. Incorrect implementation of asynchronous handlers in FastAPI

```
import os
from fastapi import FastAPI
from openai import AsyncOpenAI, OpenAI

app = FastAPI()

@app.get("/block")
async def block_server_controller():
    completion = sync_client.chat.completions.create(...) ❶
    return completion.choices[0].message.content

@app.get("/slow")
def slow_text_generator():
    completion = sync_client.chat.completions.create(...) ❷
    return completion.choices[0].message.content
```

```
@app.get("/fast")
async def fast_text_generator():
    completion = await async_client.chat.completions.create(...) ❸
    return completion.choices[0].message.content
```

❶ I/O blocking operation to get ChatGPT API response. Because the route handler is marked async, FastAPI trusts us to not run blocking operations, but as we are, the request will block the event loop (main server thread). Other requests are now blocked until the current request is processed.

❷ A simple synchronous route handler with blocking operation that doesn't leverage asynchronous features. Sync requests are handed off to the thread pool to run in the background so that the main server is not blocked.

❸ An asynchronous route that is nonblocking.

The request won't block the main thread and doesn't need to be handed off to the thread pool. As a result, the FastAPI event loop can process the request much faster using the async OpenAI client.

You now should feel more comfortable implementing new features in your FastAPI service that require performing I/O-bound tasks.

To help solidify your understanding of the I/O concurrency concepts, in the next few sections you will build several new features using concurrency into your FastAPI service. These features include:

Talk to the web
    Build and integrate a web scraper module that allows you to ask questions to your self-hosted LLM about the content of a website by providing an HTTP URL.

Talk to documents
    Build and integrate a RAG module to process documents into a vector database. A vector database stores data in a way that supports efficient similarity searches. You can then use semantic search, which understands the meaning of queries, to interact with uploaded documents using your LLM.

Both projects will give you a hands-on experience interacting asynchronously with external systems such as websites, a database, and a filesystem.

Project: Talk to the Web (Web Scraper)

Companies often host a series of internal web pages for manuals, processes, and other documentation as HTML pages. For longer pages, your users may want to provide URLs when asking questions and expect your LLM to fetch and read the content. This is where having a built-in web scraper can come in handy.

There are many ways to build a web scraper for your self-hosted LLM. Depending on your use case, you can use a combination of the following methods:

- Fetch web pages as HTML and feed the raw HTML (or inner text content) to your LLM to parse the content into your desired format.

- Use *web scraping frameworks* such as `BeautifulSoup` and `ScraPy` to parse the content of web pages after fetching.

- Use *headless web browsers* such as Selenium and Microsoft Playwright to dynamically navigate nodes in pages and parse content. Headless browsers are great for navigation single-page applications (SPAs).

> You or your users should avoid LLM-powered web scraping tools for illegal purposes. Make sure you have permission before extracting content from URLs:
>
> - Review each website's terms of use, especially if there is a mention of web scraping.
>
> - Use APIs when possible.
>
> - Ask website owners for permission directly if unsure.

For this mini-project, we will only fetch and feed raw inner text of HTML pages to our LLM since implementing a production-ready scraper can become a book of its own.

The process for building a simple asynchronous scraper is as follows:

1. Develop a function to match URL patterns using regex on user prompts to the LLM.

2. If found, loop over the list of provided URLs and asynchronously fetch the pages. We will use an asynchronous HTTP library called `aiohttp` instead of the `requests` since `requests` can only make synchronous network requests.

3. Develop a parsing function to extract the textual content from fetched HTML.

4. Feed the parsed page content to the LLM alongside the original user prompt.

Example 5-6 demonstrates how you can implement the aforementioned steps.

> You will need to install a few additional dependencies to run this example:
>
> ```
> $ pip install beautifulsoup lxml aiohttp
> ```

Example 5-6. Building an asynchronous web scraper

```python
# scraper.py

import asyncio
import re

import aiohttp
from bs4 import BeautifulSoup
from loguru import logger

def extract_urls(text: str) -> list[str]:
    url_pattern = r"(?P<url>https?:\/\/[^\s]+)"  ❶
    urls = re.findall(url_pattern, text)  ❷
    return urls


def parse_inner_text(html_string: str) -> str:
    soup = BeautifulSoup(html_string, "lxml")
    if content := soup.find("div", id="bodyContent"):  ❸
        return content.get_text()
    logger.warning("Could not parse the HTML content")
    return ""


async def fetch(session: aiohttp.ClientSession, url: str) -> str:
    async with session.get(url) as response:  ❹
        html_string = await response.text()
        return parse_inner_text(html_string)


async def fetch_all(urls: list[str]) -> str:
    async with aiohttp.ClientSession() as session:  ❺
        results = await asyncio.gather(
            *[fetch(session, url) for url in urls], return_exceptions=True
        )
    success_results = [result for result in results if isinstance(result, str)]
    if len(results) != len(success_results):  ❻
        logger.warning("Some URLs could not be fetched")
    return " ".join(success_results)
```

❶ A simple regex pattern that captures the URLs into a named group called `url` and matches both `http` and `https` protocols. For simplicity, this pattern matches more loosely defined URLs and doesn't validate the structure of a domain name or path, nor does it account for query strings or anchors in a URL.

❷ Find all nonoverlapping matches of the regex pattern in the text.

❸ Use the bs4 Beautiful Soup package to parse the HTML string. In Wikipedia pages, the article content is nested within a div container with the id="bodyCon tent", so the parsing logic assumes only Wikipedia URLs will be passed in. You can change this logic for other URLs or just use soup.getText() to grab any text content nested within the HTML. However, bear in mind that there will be lots of noise in the parsed content if you parse the raw HTML like that, which can confuse the LLM.

❹ Given an aiohttp session and a URL, perform an asynchronous get request. Create a response async context manager and await the response within this context manager.

❺ Given a list of URLs, create a client session async context manager to asynchronously perform multiple fetch calls. Since fetch() is a coroutine function (i.e., it uses the await keyword), fetch_all() will need to run multiple fetch() coroutines inside the asyncio.gather() to be scheduled for asynchronous execution on the event loop.

❻ Check that all URLs have been fetched successfully and, if not, raise a warning.

You now have the utility scraper functions you need to implement the web scraping feature in your /generate/text endpoint.

Next, upgrade the text-to-text handler to use the scraper functions via a dependency in an asynchronous manner, as shown in Example 5-7.

Example 5-7. Injecting web scraper functionality as a dependency into the FastAPI LLM handler

```
# dependencies.py

from fastapi import Body
from loguru import logger

from schemas import TextModelRequest
from scraper import extract_urls, fetch_all

async def get_urls_content(body: TextModelRequest = Body(...)) -> str: ❶
    urls = extract_urls(body.prompt)
    if urls:
        try:
            urls_content = await fetch_all(urls)
            return urls_content
```

```
        except Exception as e:
            logger.warning(f"Failed to fetch one or several URLs - Error: {e}")
    return ""
```

```python
# main.py

from fastapi import Body, Depends, Request
from dependencies import construct_prompt
from schemas import TextModelResponse

@app.post("/generate/text", response_model_exclude_defaults=True)  ❷
async def serve_text_to_text_controller(
    request: Request,
    body: TextModelRequest = Body(...),
    urls_content: str = Depends(get_urls_content)  ❸
) -> TextModelResponse:
    ... # rest of controller logic
    prompt = body.prompt + " " + urls_content
    output = generate_text(models["text"], prompt, body.temperature)
    return TextModelResponse(content=output, ip=request.client.host)
```

❶ Implement a get_urls_content FastAPI dependency that gets a user prompt
  from the request body and finds all URLs. It then returns the content of all URLs
  as a long string. The dependency has exception handling built in to handle any
  I/O errors by returning an empty string and logging a warning on the server.

❷ When using aiohttp inside FastAPI, you don't need to manage the event loop
  yourself because FastAPI, as an asynchronous framework, handles the event loop.
  You can define your endpoint as an async function and use aiohttp to make
  asynchronous HTTP requests within the handler or via a dependency like in this
  example.

❸ Inject the results of the get_urls_content dependency call to the handler via the
  FastAPI's Depends class. Using a FastAPI dependency here kept the controller
  logic small, clean, and readable.

Now, run the Streamlit client in the browser and try your shiny new feature.
Figure 5-6 shows my experiment.

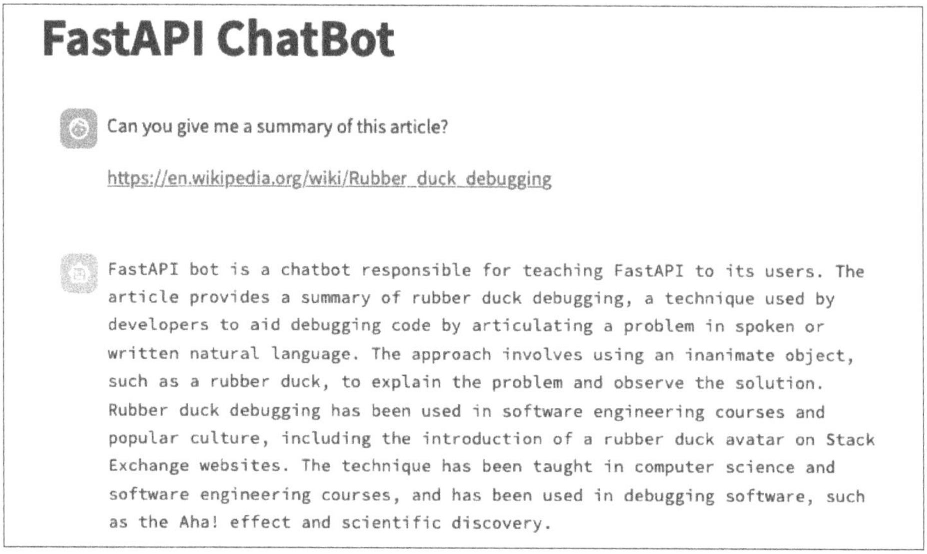

FastAPI ChatBot

Can you give me a summary of this article?

https://en.wikipedia.org/wiki/Rubber_duck_debugging

FastAPI bot is a chatbot responsible for teaching FastAPI to its users. The article provides a summary of rubber duck debugging, a technique used by developers to aid debugging code by articulating a problem in spoken or written natural language. The approach involves using an inanimate object, such as a rubber duck, to explain the problem and observe the solution. Rubber duck debugging has been used in software engineering courses and popular culture, including the introduction of a rubber duck avatar on Stack Exchange websites. The technique has been taught in computer science and software engineering courses, and has been used in debugging software, such as the Aha! effect and scientific discovery.

Figure 5-6. Asking the self-hosted TinyLlama model to summarize a Wikipedia article

Congratulations! You've learned how to build a simple nonblocking web scraper to work with your own LLM. In this mini-project, you leveraged re package to match URL patterns in the user prompt and then used the aiohttp library to asynchronously fetch multiple pages concurrently. You then used the BeautifulSoup package to parse the content of Wikipedia articles by grabbing the text content of the div container with the ID of bodyContent within the fetched HTML string. For other websites or internal company web pages, you can always alter the parsing logic for appropriate parsing. Finally, you wrapped the whole scraping logic inside a FastAPI dependency with exception handling built-in to make use of dependency injection while upgrading the text model-serving handler.

Bear in mind that your scraper can't handle complex pages with dynamic layouts that are server-rendered. In such cases, you can add a headless browser to your web scraper for navigating dynamic pages.

Additionally, fetching content of external sites will be challenging since most sites may implement anti-scraping protections such as *IP blocking* or *CAPTCHAs* as common deterrents. Maintaining *data quality* and *consistency* with external websites is also an ongoing challenge as you may need to update your scraping scripts regularly to ensure accurate and reliable extraction.

You should now feel more comfortable building GenAI-powered services that need to interact with the web via making asynchronous network requests.

Next, we will look at other I/O asynchronous interactions such as those with databases and the filesystem by building a *talk to your documents* feature.

This functionality allows users to upload documents through the Streamlit interface to your service. The content of the uploaded documents is then extracted, processed, and saved in a database. Subsequently, during user interactions with the LLM, an asynchronous retrieval system retrieves semantically relevant content from the database, which is then used to augment the context provided to the LLM.

This process is referred to as RAG, which we will build as a module for your LLM next.

Project: Talk to Documents (RAG)

In this project, we will build a RAG module into your GenAI service to give you a hands-on experience interacting asynchronously with external systems such as a database and a filesystem.

You might be curious about the purpose of a RAG module and its necessity. RAG is simply a technique for augmenting the context of LLM prompts with custom data sources for knowledge-intensive tasks.[5] It is an effective technique to ground LLM responses in facts contained within data without the need for complex and expensive LLM fine-tuning.

Organizations are eager to implement RAG with their own LLMs since it allows their employees to engage with their massive internal knowledge bases via the LLM. With RAG, businesses expect that the internal knowledge bases, systems, and procedures will be made accessible and readily available to anyone who needs them to answer questions, just when they need it. This accessibility to the company's body of information is expected to enhance productivity, cut costs and time looking for information, and boost profits for any business.

However, LLMs are susceptible to generating responses that don't adhere to the instructions given by the user. In other words, the LLM can *hallucinate* responses with information or data that is not based on facts or reality.

These hallucinations can occur due to the model's reliance on patterns in the data it was trained on rather than direct access to external, up-to-date, and factual data. LLMs can manifest hallucinations with confidently presented yet incorrect or nonsensical answers, fabricated stories, or claims without a basis in truth.

Therefore, for more complex and knowledge-intensive tasks, you will want your LLM to access external knowledge sources to complete tasks. This enables more factual consistency and improves the reliability of the generated responses. Figure 5-7 shows the full process.

---

5 P. Lewis et al. (2022), "Retrieval-Augmented Generation for Knowledge-Intensive NLP Tasks" (*https://oreil.ly/ GCk08*), arXiv preprint arXiv:2005.11401.

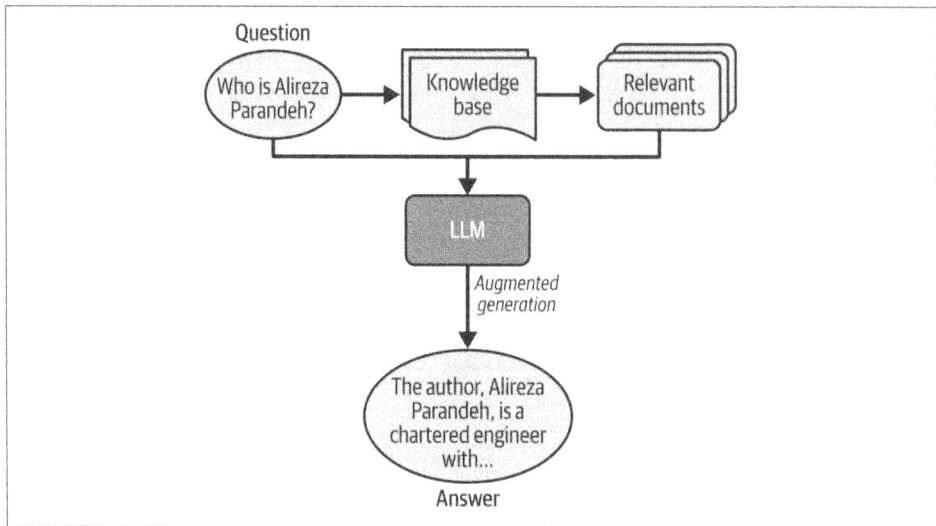

Figure 5-7. RAG

In this project, you will build a simple RAG module for your LLM service such that users can upload and talk to their documents.

> There is a lot to know about RAG. It's enough to fill several textbooks with new papers being published every day for new techniques and algorithms.
>
> I recommend checking out other publications on LLMs to learn about the RAG process and advanced RAG techniques.

The pipeline for RAG consists of the following stages:

1. *Extraction* of documents from a filesystem to load the textual content in chunks onto memory.

2. *Transformation* of the textual content by cleaning, splitting, and preparing them to be passed into an embedding model to produce embedding vectors that represent a chunk's semantic meaning.

3. *Storage* of embedding vectors alongside metadata, such as the source and text chunk, in a vector store such as Qdrant.

4. *Retrieval* of semantically relevant embedding vectors by performing a semantic search on the user's query to the LLM. The original text chunks—stored as metadata of the retrieved vectors—are then used to augment (i.e., enhance the context within) the initial prompt provided to the LLM.

5. *Generation* of LLM response bypassing both the query and retrieved chunks (i.e., context) to the LLM for getting a response.

You can see the full pipeline in Figure 5-8.

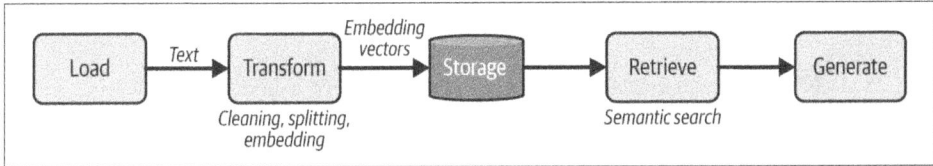

Figure 5-8. RAG pipeline

You can take the pipeline shown in Figure 5-8 and build it to your existing service. Figure 5-9 shows the system architecture of a "talk to your documents" service enabled with RAG.

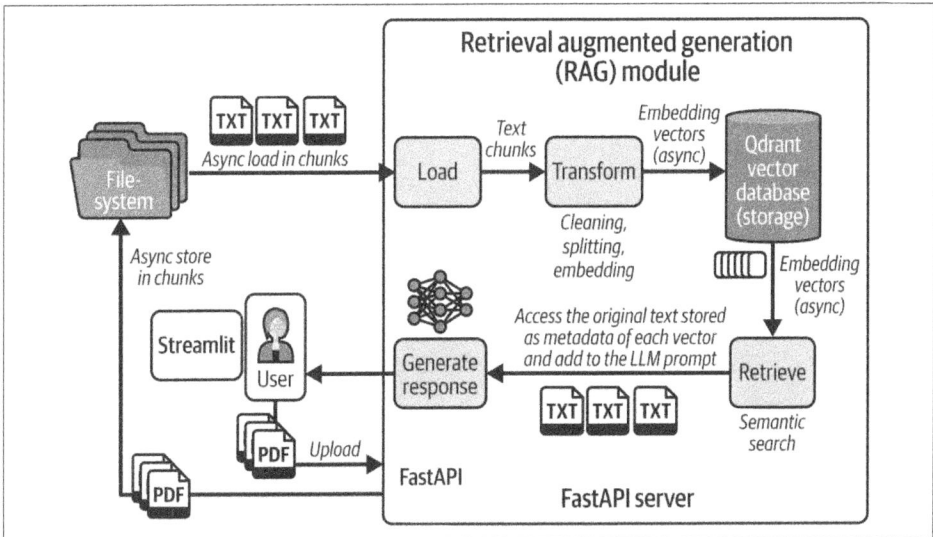

Figure 5-9. Talk to your documents system architecture

Figure 5-9 outlines how the documents uploaded by users via the Streamlit interface are stored and then fetched for processing and storage into the database for later retrieval to augment the LLM prompts.

The first step before implementing the RAG system in Figure 5-9 is to include a file upload functionality in both the Streamlit client and your backend API.

Using FastAPI's `UploadFile` class, you can accept documents from users in chunks and save them into the filesystem or any other file storage solution such as a blob

---

storage. The important item to note here is that this I/O operation is nonblocking through asynchronous programming, which FastAPI's `UploadFile` class supports.

> Since users may upload large documents, FastAPI's `UploadFile` class supports *chunking* to store the uploaded documents, one piece at a time.
>
> This will prevent your service's memory from being clogged up. You will also want to protect your service by disallowing users from uploading documents above a certain size.

Example 5-8 shows how to implement an asynchronous file upload functionality.

> You will need to install `aiofiles` package to asynchronously upload files alongside `python-multipart` to receive uploaded files from HTML forms:
>
> ```
> $ pip install aiofiles python-multipart
> ```

Example 5-8. Implementing an asynchronous file upload endpoint

```python
# upload.py

import os
import aiofiles
from aiofiles.os import makedirs
from fastapi import UploadFile

DEFAULT_CHUNK_SIZE = 1024 * 1024 * 50  # 50 megabytes

async def save_file(file: UploadFile) -> str:
    await makedirs("uploads", exist_ok=True)
    filepath = os.path.join("uploads", file.filename)
    async with aiofiles.open(filepath, "wb") as f:
        while chunk := await file.read(DEFAULT_CHUNK_SIZE):
            await f.write(chunk)
    return filepath

# main.py

from fastapi import FastAPI, HTTPException, status, File
from typing import Annotated
from upload import save_file

@app.post("/upload")
async def file_upload_controller(
    file: Annotated[UploadFile, File(description="Uploaded PDF documents")]
):
    if file.content_type != "application/pdf":
```

```python
        raise HTTPException(
            detail=f"Only uploading PDF documents are supported",
            status_code=status.HTTP_400_BAD_REQUEST,
        )
    try:
        await save_file(file)
    except Exception as e:
        raise HTTPException(
            detail=f"An error occurred while saving file - Error: {e}",
            status_code=status.HTTP_500_INTERNAL_SERVER_ERROR,
        )
    return {"filename": file.filename, "message": "File uploaded successfully"}

# client.py

import requests
import streamlit as st

st.write("Upload a file to FastAPI")
file = st.file_uploader("Choose a file", type=["pdf"])

if st.button("Submit"):
    if file is not None:
        files = {"file": (file.name, file, file.type)}
        response = requests.post("http://localhost:8000/upload", files=files)
        st.write(response.text)
    else:
        st.write("No file uploaded.")
```

You should now be able to upload files via the Streamlit UI, as you can see in Figure 5-10.

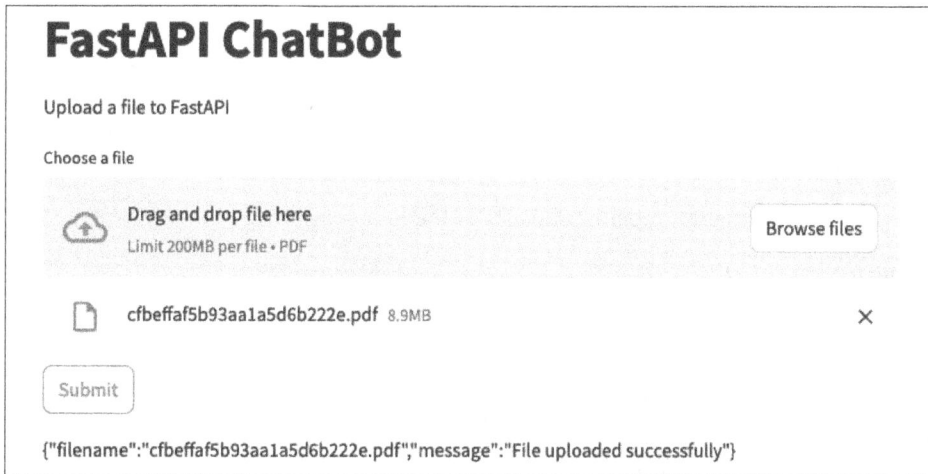

Figure 5-10. Uploading files via Streamlit to the FastAPI service

With upload functionality implemented, you can now turn your attention to building the RAG module. Figure 5-11 shows the detailed pipeline, which opens up the data transformation component in Figure 5-9.

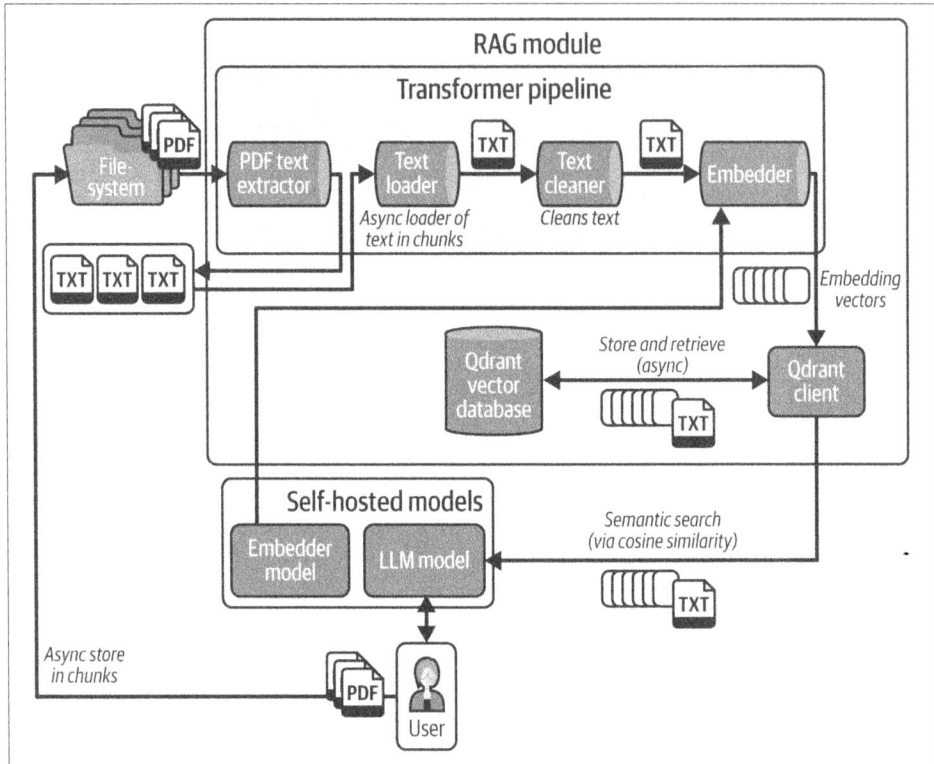

Figure 5-11. Detailed RAG data processing pipeline

As you can see in Figure 5-11, you need to asynchronously fetch the stored files from the hard disk and pass them through a data transformation pipeline prior to storage via an asynchronous database client.

The data transformation pipeline consists of the following parts:

Extractor
    Extract content of PDFs and store in text files back onto the hard disk.

Loader
    Asynchronously load a text file into memory in chunks.

Cleaner
    Remove any redundant whitespace or formatting characters from text chunks.

Embedder

Use a pretrained and self-hosted embedding model to convert text into embedding vectors.

Embeddings

Embeddings are high-dimensional vectors that capture semantic meanings and relationships between words and phrases in texts. Semantically similar texts have a smaller distance between them.

Using embedding models, you can encode text and images into embedding representations as points within a continuous vector space. These transformed data points can subsequently be used for a myriad of downstream applications, such as information retrieval in RAG as well as clustering and classification tasks.

Please refer to Chapter 3 for more information on embedding vectors.

Once users upload their PDF files onto your server's filesystem via the process shown in Example 5-8, you can immediately convert them into text files via the `pypdf` library. Since there is no asynchronous library for loading binary PDF files, you will want to convert them into text files first.

Example 5-9 shows how to load PDFs, extract and process their content, and then store them as text files.

> You will need to install several packages to run the upcoming examples:
>
> ```
> $ pip install qdrant_client aiofiles pypdf loguru
> ```

Example 5-9. RAG PDF-to-text extractor

```
# rag/extractor.py

from pypdf import PdfReader

def pdf_text_extractor(filepath: str) -> None:
    content = ""
    pdf_reader = PdfReader(filepath, strict=True) ❶
    for page in pdf_reader.pages:
        page_text = page.extract_text()
        if page_text:
            content += f"{page_text}\n\n" ❷
    with open(filepath.replace("pdf", "txt"), "w", encoding="utf-8") as file: ❸
        file.write(content)
```

❶ Use the pypdf library to open a stream pointer to a PDF file with strict=True so that any read errors are logged to the terminal. Note that there is no asynchronous implementation of the pypdf library, so the function is declared with a normal def keyword. It is important to avoid using this function within an asynchronous function to avoid blocking the event loop that runs the main server thread. You will see how FastAPI background tasks can help solve this problem.

❷ Loop over every page in the PDF document, and extract and append all text content into a long string.

❸ Write the content of the PDF document into a text file for downstream processing. Specify encoding="utf-8" to avoid problems on platforms like Windows.

The text extractor will convert the PDF files into simple text files that we can stream into memory in chunks using an asynchronous file loader. Each chunk can then be cleaned and embedded into an embedding vector using an open source embedding model such as jinaai/jina-embeddings-v2-base-en, available to download from the Hugging Face model hub (*https://oreil.ly/gI74r*).

I selected the Jina base embedder since it matches the performance of OpenAI's proprietary text-embedding-ada-002 model.

Example 5-10 shows the implementation of the RAG data transformation pipeline including the async text loader, cleaner, and embedding functions.

Example 5-10. RAG data transformation functions

```
# rag/transform.py

import re
from typing import Any, AsyncGenerator

import aiofiles
from transformers import AutoModel

DEFAULT_CHUNK_SIZE = 1024 * 1024 * 50  # 50 megabytes

embedder = AutoModel.from_pretrained(
    "jinaai/jina-embeddings-v2-base-en", trust_remote_code=True  ❶
)
```

```
async def load(filepath: str) -> AsyncGenerator[str, Any]:
    async with aiofiles.open(filepath, "r", encoding="utf-8") as f: ❷
        while chunk := await f.read(DEFAULT_CHUNK_SIZE): ❸
            yield chunk ❹

def clean(text: str) -> str:
    t = text.replace("\n", " ")
    t = re.sub(r"\s+", " ", t)
    t = re.sub(r"\. ,", "", t)
    t = t.replace("..", ".")
    t = t.replace(". .", ".")
    cleaned_text = t.replace("\n", " ").strip()
    return cleaned_text ❺

def embed(text: str) -> list[float]:
    return embedder.encode(text).tolist() ❻
```

❶ Download and use the open source `jina-embeddings-v2-base-en` model to embed text strings into embedding vectors. Set `trust_remote_code=True` to download model weights and tokenizer configurations. Without this parameter set to `True`, the downloaded model weights will be initialized with random values instead of trained values.

❷ Use the `aiofiles` library to open an asynchronous connections to a file on the filesystem.

❸ Load the content of text documents in chunks for memory-efficient I/O operation.

❹ Instead of returning a chunk, yield it so that the `load()` function becomes an *asynchronous generator*. Asynchronous generators can be iterated with `async for` loops so that blocking operations within them can be `awaited` to let the event loop start/resume other tasks. Both async `for` loops and normal `for` loops, iterate sequentially over the iterable but async `for` loops allow for iteration over an async iterator.

❺ Clean the text by removing any extra spaces, commas, dots, and line breaks.

❻ Use the Jina embedding model to convert a text chunk to an embedding vector.

Once the data is processed into embedding vectors, you can store them into the *vector database*.

Unlike conventional alternatives such as relational databases, a vector database is specifically designed for handling data storage and retrieval operations optimized for *semantic searching*, which yields better results compared to keyword searches that can return suboptimal or incomplete results.

Performing a Semantic Search

Semantic search uses a mathematical operation called *cosine similarity* between the user query's embedding vector and the embedding vectors (i.e., embedded documents) stored in the database to retrieve the most relevant items.

Cosine similarity calculation performs a normalized dot product computation between two vectors to return a number between –1 and 1.[6] The normalization ensures the result is between –1 and 1.

A score of 1 means the vectors are aligned and share a similar semantic meaning, while a score of –1 implies they're diametrically opposed, signifying opposite meanings.

A score of 0 indicates no semantic correlation between the vectors, suggesting that these vectors can be excluded from search results.

The returned results from the database are a collection of ordered embedding vectors that contain metadata including the original text. You can inject these text snippets directly into user prompts to augment them with relevant context before forwarding to the LLM.

Semantic search results retrieved from the database are sorted in descending order by similarity scores. This ordering, referred to as *context ranking*, is important since research has shown that LLMs are more sensitive to the words that appear earlier in the prompt than later.

This makes sense since we humans also have better comprehension and attention, in a single reading session, earlier within large documents rather than in the middle or the end. That's why we have sections such as an "Executive Summary" in large reports to communicate the most important content of the report to readers.

---

6 A dot product operation multiplies components of two vectors and then sums the results. It can be used to calculate the cosine of the angle between the vectors to quantify their similarity in direction (i.e., alignment). Vector databases use it to perform semantic search on document embeddings.

The following code examples require you to run a local instance of the qdrant vector database on your local machine for the RAG module. Having a local database setup will give you the hands-on experience of working asynchronously with production-grade vector databases. To run the database in a container, you should have Docker installed on your machine and then pull and run the qdrant vector database container.[7] If you aren't familiar with Docker, don't worry. You will learn more about Docker and containerization in Chapter 12.

```
$ docker pull qdrant/qdrant ❶
$ docker run -p 6333:6333 -p 6334:6334 \  ❷
    -v $(pwd)/qdrant_storage:/qdrant/storage:z \ ❸
    qdrant/qdrant
```

❶ Download the qdrant vector database image from the qdrant repository in the Docker registry.

❷ Run the qdrant/qdrant image, and then expose and map container ports 6333 and 6334 to the same ports on the host machine.

❸ Mount the qdrant database storage to the host machine filesystem at your project's root directory.

Since database storage and retrieval are I/O operations, you should use an asynchronous database client. Thankfully, qdrant provides an asynchronous database client to work with.

> You can use other vector database providers such as Weaviate, Elastic, Milvus, Pinecone, Chroma, or others in replacement of Qdrant. Each has a set of features and limitations to consider for your own use case.
>
> If you're picking another database provider, make sure there is an asynchronous database client available that you can use.

Instead of writing several functions to store and retrieve data from the database, you can use the repository pattern mentioned in Chapter 2. With the repository pattern, you can abstract low-level create, read, update, and delete database operations with defaults that match your use case.

---

7 Refer to the Docker documentation (*https://oreil.ly/V4itQ*) for installation instructions.

Example 5-11 shows the repository pattern implementation for the Qdrant vector database.

Example 5-11. Vector database client setup using the repository pattern

```
# rag/repository.py

from loguru import logger
from qdrant_client import AsyncQdrantClient
from qdrant_client.http import models
from qdrant_client.http.models import ScoredPoint


class VectorRepository:  ❶
    def __init__(self, host: str = "localhost", port: int = 6333) -> None:
        self.db_client = AsyncQdrantClient(host=host, port=port)

    async def create_collection(self, collection_name: str, size: int) -> bool:  ❷
        vectors_config = models.VectorParams(
            size=size, distance=models.Distance.COSINE  ❸
        )
        response = await self.db_client.get_collections()

        collection_exists = any(
            collection.name == collection_name
            for collection in response.collections
        )
        if collection_exists:  ❹
            logger.debug(
                f"Collection {collection_name} already exists - recreating it"
            )
            await self.db_client.delete_collection(collection_name)
            return await self.db_client.create_collection(
                collection_name,
                vectors_config=vectors_config,
            )

        logger.debug(f"Creating collection {collection_name}")
        return await self.db_client.create_collection(
            collection_name=collection_name,
            vectors_config=models.VectorParams(
                size=size, distance=models.Distance.COSINE
            ),
        )

    async def delete_collection(self, name: str) -> bool:
        logger.debug(f"Deleting collection {name}")
        return await self.db_client.delete_collection(name)

    async def create(
        self,
```

```
        collection_name: str,
        embedding_vector: list[float],
        original_text: str,
        source: str,
    ) -> None:
        response = await self.db_client.count(collection_name=collection_name)
        logger.debug(
            f"Creating a new vector with ID {response.count} "
            f"inside the {collection_name}"
        )
        await self.db_client.upsert(
            collection_name=collection_name,
            points=[
                models.PointStruct(
                    id=response.count,
                    vector=embedding_vector,
                    payload={
                        "source": source,
                        "original_text": original_text,
                    },
                )
            ],
        )

    async def search(
        self,
        collection_name: str,
        query_vector: list[float],
        retrieval_limit: int,
        score_threshold: float, ❺
    ) -> list[ScoredPoint]:
        logger.debug(
            f"Searching for relevant items in the {collection_name} collection"
        )
        response = await self.db_client.query_points(
            collection_name=collection_name,
            query_vector=query_vector,
            limit=retrieval_limit,
            score_threshold=score_threshold,
        )
        return response.points
```

❶ Use the repository pattern to interact with the vector database via an asynchronous client. Normally, in the repository pattern you will implement the create, get, update, and delete methods. But for now let's implement the create_collection, delete_collection, create, and search methods.

❷ Vectors need to be stored in a collection. A collection is a named set of points that you can use during a search. Collections are similar to tables in a relational database.

❸ Let the database know that any vectors in this collection should be compared via the cosine similarity calculation that calculates distances between vectors.

❹ Check whether a collection exists before creating a new one. Otherwise, re-create the collection.

❺ Set the `retrieval_limit` and `score_threshold` to limit the number of items in the search results.

The `VectorRepository` class should now make it easier to interact with the database.

When storing vector embeddings, you will also store some *metadata* including the name of the source document, the location of the text within source, and the original extracted text. RAG systems rely on this metadata to augment the LLM prompts and to show source information to the users.

> Currently, converting text to embedding vectors is an irreversible process. Therefore, you will need to store the text that created the embedding with the embedding vector as metadata.

You can now extend the `VectorRepository` and create the `VectorService` that allow you to chain together the data processing and storage pipeline, as shown in Example 5-12.

Example 5-12. Vector database service

```
# rag/service.py

import os

from loguru import logger
from .repository import VectorRepository
from .transform import clean, embed, load


class VectorService(VectorRepository):  ❶
    def __init__(self):
        super().__init__()

    async def store_file_content_in_db(  ❷
        self,
        filepath: str,
        chunk_size: int = 512,
        collection_name: str = "knowledgebase",
        collection_size: int = 768,
```

```
) -> None:
    await self.create_collection(collection_name, collection_size)
    logger.debug(f"Inserting {filepath} content into database")
    async for chunk in load(filepath, chunk_size):  ❸
        logger.debug(f"Inserting '{chunk[0:20]}...' into database")

        embedding_vector = embed(clean(chunk))
        filename = os.path.basename(filepath)
        await self.create(
            collection_name, embedding_vector, chunk, filename
        )


vector_service = VectorService()  ❹
```

❶ Create the VectorService class by inheriting the VectorRepository class so that you can use and extend common database operation methods from Example 5-11.

❷ Use the store_file_content_in_db service method to asynchronously load, transform, and store raw text documents into the database in chunks.

❸ Use an asynchronous generator load() to load text chunks from a file asynchronously.

❹ Create an instance of the VectorService to import and use across the application.

The final step in the RAG data processing and storage pipeline is to run the text extraction and storage logic within the file_upload_controller as background tasks. The implementation is shown in Example 5-13 so that the handler can trigger both operations in the background after responding to the user.

Example 5-13. Update the upload handler to process and store PDF file content in the vector database

```
# main.py

from fastapi import (
    BackgroundTasks,
    FastAPI,
    File,
    UploadFile,
    status,
    HTTPException,
)
from typing import Annotated
from rag import pdf_text_extractor, vector_service
```

```
@app.post("/upload")
async def file_upload_controller(
    file: Annotated[UploadFile, File(description="A file read as UploadFile")],
    bg_text_processor: BackgroundTasks, ❶
):
    ... # Raise an HTTPException if data upload is not a PDF file
    try:
        filepath = await save_file(file)
        bg_text_processor.add_task(pdf_text_extractor, filepath) ❷
        bg_text_processor.add_task( ❸
            vector_service.store_file_content_in_db,
            filepath.replace("pdf", "txt"),
            512,
            "knowledgebase",
            768,
        )

    except Exception as e:
        raise HTTPException(
            detail=f"An error occurred while saving file - Error: {e}",
            status_code=status.HTTP_500_INTERNAL_SERVER_ERROR,
        )
    return {"filename": file.filename, "message": "File uploaded successfully"}
```

❶ Inject the FastAPI background tasks feature into the handler for processing file uploads in the background. FastAPI background tasks will be executed in order shortly after the handler sends a response to the client.

❷ Run the PDF text-extraction function in the background after retuning a response to the client. Since the pdf_text_extractor is a synchronous function, FastAPI will run this function on a separate thread within the thread pool to avoid blocking the event loop.

❸ Run the vector_service.store_file_content_in_db asynchronous function in the background on the FastAPI managed event loop as soon as the pdf_text_extractor has finished processing. Set the function to load content of the text document in chunks of 512 characters and store them in the knowledge base vector collection, which accepts vectors of size 768.

After building the RAG data storage pipeline, you can now focus on the search-and-retrieval system, which will allow you to augment the user prompts to the LLM, with knowledge from the database. Example 5-14 integrates the RAG search-and-retrieval operations with the LLM handler to augment the LLM prompts with additional context.

Example 5-14. RAG integration with the LLM-serving endpoint

```python
# dependencies.py

from rag import vector_service
from rag.transform import embed
from schemas import TextModelRequest, TextModelResponse

async def get_rag_content(body: TextModelRequest = Body(...)) -> str: ❶
    rag_content = await vector_service.search( ❷
        "knowledgebase", embed(body.prompt), 3, 0.7
    )
    rag_content_str = "\n".join( ❸
        [c.payload["original_text"] for c in rag_content]
    )

    return rag_content_str
```

```python
# main.py

... # other imports
from dependencies import get_rag_content, get_urls_content

@app.post("/generate/text", response_model_exclude_defaults=True)
async def serve_text_to_text_controller(
    request: Request,
    body: TextModelRequest = Body(...),
    urls_content: str = Depends(get_urls_content),
    rag_content: str = Depends(get_rag_content), ❹
) -> TextModelResponse:
    ... # Raise HTTPException for invalid models
    prompt = body.prompt + " " + urls_content + rag_content
    output = generate_text(models["text"], prompt, body.temperature)
    return TextModelResponse(content=output, ip=request.client.host)
```

❶ Create the `get_rag_content` dependency function for injection into the LLM-serving handler. This dependency has access to the request body and subsequently the user `prompt`.

❷ Use the `vector_service` to search the database for content relevant to the user `prompt`. Convert the user `prompt` to an embedding using the `embed` function when passing to the `vector_service.search` function. Only retrieve the three most relevant items if their cosine similarity score is above `0.7` (or 70%).

❸ Merge the text payload of the top three most relevant retrieved items as `rag_content_str` and return it.

❹ Inject the results of the `get_rag_content` dependency function into the LLM handler to augment the final prompt to the LLM with content from the vector database knowledgebase. The LLM handler can now fetch content of web pages and the RAG vector database.

If you now visit your browser and upload a PDF document, you should be able to ask questions about it to your LLM. Figure 5-12 shows my experiment with the service by uploading a sample of this book in its raw form and asking the LLM to describe who I am.

> Depending on the model and size of the inputs, you may observe performance degradations or exceptions like token length limit issues.

FastAPI ChatBot

Upload a file to FastAPI

Choose a file

⬆ **Drag and drop file here**
Limit 200MB per file • PDF   Browse files

📄 cfbeffaf5b93aa1a5d6b222e.pdf 8.9MB   ✕

Submit

◉ Who is ali parandeh?

🖥 The author, Ali Parandeh, is a chartered engineer with the UK engineering council and a certified developer with Microsoft Azure and Google Cloud. He has led engineering teams both at large multinational consultancies and at tech startups. He has published books on building generative AI services with FastAPI, which is a practical approach to developing context-rich generative AI applications. The book is published by O'Reilly Media and has a copyright of 2025 by the author. The book's ISBN is 978-1-098-16030-2. The book's publisher is O'Reilly Media, Inc., and the author's email address is permissions@oreilly.com. The book's title is "Building Generative AI Services with FastAPI" and it is available for purchase from O'Reilly Online Learning.

Figure 5-12. Leveraging RAG to provide answers in response to user queries

Congratulations! You now have a fully working RAG system enabled by open source models and a vector database.

This longer project served as a hands-on tutorial for learning concepts related to asynchronous programming and I/O operations with the filesystem and a vector database by building a RAG module for your LLM system. Note that the RAG system we just built together still has many limitations:

- Text splitting may split words in half leading to poor retrieval and LLM confusion.
- The LLM may still produce hallucinations and inconsistent outputs even with the augmented prompts.
- The search-and-retrieval system may perform poorly in certain instances.
- The augmented prompts may exceed the LLM context window.
- The retrieved information from the database may lack the relevant facts due to an outdated or incomplete knowledge base, ambiguous queries, or poor retrieval algorithm.
- The retrieved context may not be ordered based on relevance to the user query.

You can work on improving the RAG module further by implementing various other techniques, which I will not cover in this book:

- Optimize text splitting, chunk sizing, cleaning and embedding operations.
- Perform query transformations using the LLM to aid the retrieval and augmentation system via techniques such as prompt compression, chaining, refining, and aggregating, etc., to reduce hallucinations and improve LLM performance.
- Summarize or break down large augmented prompts to feed the context into the models using a sliding window approach.
- Enhance retrieval algorithms to handle ambiguous queries and implement fallback mechanisms for incomplete data.
- Enhance the retrieval performance with methods such as *maximal marginal relevance* (MMR) to enrich the augmentation process with more diverse documents.
- Implement other advanced RAG techniques like retrieval reranking and filtering, hierarchical database indices, RAG fusion, retrieval augmented thoughts (RAT), etc., to improve the overall generation performance.

I'll let you research these techniques in more detail and implement them as additional exercises on your own.

In the next section, well review other techniques for optimizing your GenAI services to avoid blocking the server with compute-bound operations such as model inference.

Optimizing Model Serving for Memory- and Compute-Bound AI Inference Tasks

So far, we've looked at optimizing the operations of our service that are I/O bound. You learned to leverage asynchronous programming to interact with the web, databases, and files by building a web scraper and a RAG module.

Using async tools and techniques, your service remained responsive when interacting with the web, the filesystem, and databases. However, if you're self-hosting the model, switching to async programming techniques won't fully eliminate the long waiting times. This is because the bottleneck will be model inference operations.

Compute-Bound Operations

You can speed up the inference by running models on GPUs to massively parallelize computations. Modern GPUs have staggering compute power measured by the number of *floating-point* operations per second (FLOPS), with modern GPUs reaching teraflops (NVIDIA A100) or petaflops (NVIDIA H100) of compute. However, despite their significant power and parallelization capabilities, modern GPU cores are often underutilized under concurrent workloads with larger models.

When self-hosting models on GPUs, model parameters are loaded from disk to RAM (I/O bound) and then moved from RAM to the GPU high-bandwidth memory by the CPU (memory bound). Once model parameters are loaded on the GPU memory, inference is performed (compute bound).

Counterintuitively, model inference for larger GenAI models such as SDXL and LLMs is not I/O- or compute-bound, but rather memory-bound. This means it takes more time to load 1 MB of data into GPU's compute cores than it takes for those compute cores to process 1 MB of data. Inevitably, to maximize the concurrency of your service, you will need to *batch* the inference requests and fit the largest batch size you can into the GPU high-bandwidth memory.

Therefore, even when using async techniques and latest GPUs, your server can be blocked waiting for billions of model parameters to be loaded to the GPU high-bandwidth memory during each request. To avoid blocking the server, you can decouple the memory-bound model-serving operations from your FastAPI server by externalizing model serving, as we touched upon in Chapter 3.

Let's see how to delegate model serving to another process.

Externalizing Model Serving

You have several options available to you when externalizing your model-serving workloads. You can either host models on another FastAPI server or use specialized model inference servers.

Specialized inference servers support only a limited set of GenAI model architectures. However, if your model architecture is supported, you will save a lot of time not having to implement inference optimizations yourself. For instance, if you need to self-host LLMs, LLM-serving frameworks can perform several inference optimizations for you such as batch processing, tensor parallelism, quantization, caching, streaming outputs, GPU memory management, etc.

Model Optimization Techniques

You have several model compression techniques you can try to improve inference performance:

- *Quantization* to compress models
- *Pruning* to summarize model parameters
- *Distillation* to create "student" models significantly smaller than their "teacher" counterparts
- *Fine-tuning* small models to specialize them for your use case

If you're serving transformer-based models, you can further optimize model inference using the following techniques:

- *Fast attention* to optimize attention map calculations on GPUs
- *KV caching* to leverage in-memory caching techniques to speed up inference by reusing the results of computed attention maps
- *Paged attention* to optimize KV cache memory usage after attention computation
- *Request batching*, including simple and continuous batching, to maximize GPU utilization rates

Chapter 10 will delve into more details of model optimization techniques.

Since we've been mostly working with LLMs in this chapter, I will show you how to integrate vLLM, an open source LLM server that can start a FastAPI server for you matching the OpenAI API specification. vLLM also has seamless integration with popular open source Hugging Face model architectures including GPT, Llama, Gemma, Mistral, Falcon, etc.

At the time of writing, other LLM hosting servers you can use include NVIDIA Triton Inference Server, Ray Serve, Hugging Face Inference, and OpenLLM, among others.

There are features, benefits, and drawbacks to using each including the supported model architectures. I recommend researching these servers prior to adopting them in your own use cases.

You can start your own vLLM FastAPI server via a single command, as shown in Example 5-15. To run the code in Example 5-15, you will need to install vllm using:

```
$ pip install vllm
```

At the time of writing, vLLM only supports Linux platforms (including WSL) with NVIDIA-compatible GPUs to run CUDA toolkit dependencies. Unfortunately, you can't install vLLM on Mac or Windows machines for local testing.

vLLM is designed for production inference workloads on NVIDIA GPUs in Linux environments where the server can delegate requests to multiple GPU cores via *tensor parallelism*. It does also support distributed computing when scaling services beyond a single machine via its Ray Serve dependency.

Please consult vLLM documentation for more details related to distributed inference and serving.

Example 5-15. Starting the vLLM FastAPI OpenAI API server for TinyLlama on a Linux machine with 4x 16 GB NVIDIA T4 GPUs

```
$ python -m vllm.entrypoints.openai.api_server \ ❶
--model "TinyLlama/TinyLlama-1.1B-Chat-v1.0" \
--dtype float16 \ ❷
--tensor-parallel-size 4 \ ❸
--api-key "your_secret_token" ❹
```

❶ Start an OpenAI-compatible API server with FastAPI to serve the TinyLlama model.

❷ Use the float16 medium precision data type. float16 is compatible with GPU hardware, whereas bfloat16 is generally compatible with CPU hardware.

❸ Leverage vLLM tensor parallelism feature to run the API server on four GPUs.

❹ Set a secret token for basic authentication to secure the LLM server. This is useful for secure machine-to-machine communication, for instance, to directly communicate with your current FastAPI service.

With the vLLM FastAPI server up and running, you can now replace the model-serving logic in your current service with network calls to the vLLM server. Refer to Example 5-16 for implementation details.

Example 5-16. Replace model serving with asynchronous API calls to the new vLLM server

```python
# models.py

import os
import aiohttp
from loguru import logger

async def generate_text(prompt: str, temperature: float = 0.7) -> str:
    system_prompt = "You are an AI assistant"
    messages = [
        {"role": "system", "content": system_prompt},
        {"role": "user", "content": prompt},
    ]
    data = {"temperature": temperature, "messages": messages}
    headers = {"Authorization": f"Bearer {os.environ.get('VLLM_API_KEY')}"}
try:
    async with aiohttp.ClientSession() as session:  ❶
        response = await session.post(
            "http://localhost:8000/v1/chat", json=data, headers=headers
        )
        predictions = await response.json()
except Exception as e:
    logger.error(f"Failed to obtain predictions from vLLM - Error: {e}")
    return (
        "Failed to obtain predictions from vLLM - "
        "See server logs for more details"
    )
try:
    output = predictions["choices"][0]["message"]["content"]  ❷
    logger.debug(f"Generated text: {output}")
    return output
except KeyError as e:
    logger.error(f"Failed to parse predictions from vLLM - Error: {e}")
    return (
        "Failed to parse predictions from vLLM - "
        "See server logs for more details"
    )
```

❶ Use `aiohttp` to create an asynchronous session for sending POST requests to the vLLM FastAPI server. This logic replaces the Hugging Face model pipeline inference logic on the current FastAPI server.

❷ Since the vLLM server is OpenAI compatible, you can access the output content by following the OpenAI API specification.

Next, remove the code related to the FastAPI lifespan so that your current service won't load the TinyLlama model. You can achieve this by following the code in Example 5-17.

Example 5-17. Remove the FastAPI lifespan and update the text generation handler to be asynchronous

```
# main.py

from fastapi import FastAPI, Request
from schemas import TextModelRequest, TextModelResponse
from models import generate_text

# Remove the asynccontextmanager to remove TinyLlama from FastAPI ❶
# @asynccontextmanager
# async def lifespan(app: FastAPI):
#     models["text"] = load_text_model()
#     yield
#     models.clear()

# Remove the `lifespan` argument from `FastAPI()`
app = FastAPI()

@app.post("/generate/text")
async def serve_text_to_text_controller(
    request: Request, body: TextModelRequest
) -> TextModelResponse: ❷
    ... # controller logic
    output = await generate_text(body.prompt, body.temperature)
    return TextModelResponse(content=output, ip=request.client.host)
```

❶ There is no need to use FastAPI `lifespan` anymore since the model is now served by an external vLLM FastAPI server.

❷ Make `serve_text_to_text_controller` an async route handler as it is now performing I/O operations to the vLLM server. It is no longer running synchronous compute-bound model inference operations as those are delegated to the vLLM server to manage.

Congratulations, you've now achieved concurrency with your AI inference workloads. You implemented a form of multiprocessing on a single machine by moving your LLM inference workloads to another server. Both servers are now running on separate cores with your LLM server delegating work to multiple GPU cores, leveraging parallelism.

This means your main server is now able to process multiple incoming requests and do other tasks than processing one LLM inference operation at a time.

Bear in mind that any concurrency you've achieved so far has been limited to a single machine.

To support more concurrent users, you may need more machines with CPU and GPU cores. At that point, distributed computing frameworks like Ray Serve and Kubernetes can help to scale and orchestrate your services beyond a single worker machine using parallelism.

Before integrating vLLM, you would experience long waiting times between requests because your main server was too busy running inference operations. With vLLM, there is now a massive reduction in latency and increase in throughput of your LLM service.

Latency and Throughput

Latency in the context of LLMs refers to the time taken from when a request is made to the model until the first response is received. It's a measure of the delay experienced during the processing of a single request. *Throughput*, on the other hand, is the number of requests that an LLM can process within a given time frame and indicates the server's capacity to handle concurrent or sequential requests over time. Latency can be measured in *delay seconds* and throughput in *tokens per minute* (TPM).

As a developer, you will want your service to have the lowest latency and the highest throughput possible. However, there is a trade-off between the model size and quality versus these two metrics. Normally, LLMs with larger number of parameters achieve higher quality but also increased latency and reduced throughput.

Research is currently underway to use model compression techniques such as *distillation*, *quantization*, and *pruning* to keep language models small while maintaining high quality, throughput, and small latency in AI inference services.

In addition to model compression mechanisms like quantization, vLLM uses other optimization techniques including continuous request batching, cache partitioning (paged attention), reduced GPU memory footprint via memory sharing, and streaming outputs to achieve smaller latency and high throughput.

Let's look at both the request batching and paged attention mechanisms in more detail to understand how to further optimize LLM inference.

Request batching and continuous batching

As we discussed in Chapter 3, LLMs produce the next token prediction in an autoregressive manner, as you can see in Figure 5-13.

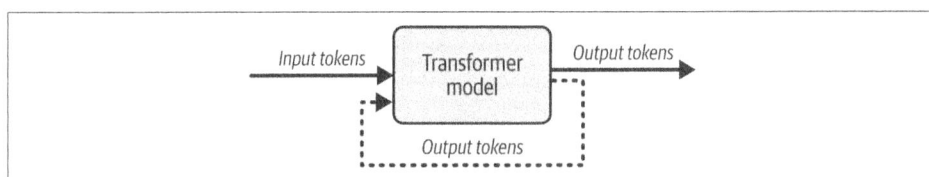

Figure 5-13. Autoregressive prediction

This means the LLMs must perform several inference iterations in a loop to produce a response, and each iteration produces a single output token. The input sequence grows as each iteration's output token is appended to the end, and the new sequence is forwarded to the model in the next iteration step. Once the model generates an end-of-sequence token, the generation loop stops. Essentially, the LLM produces a sequence of completion tokens, stopping only after producing a stop token or reaching a maximum sequence length.

The LLM must calculate several attention maps for each token in the sequence so that it can iteratively make the next token predictions.

Fortunately, GPUs can parallelize the attention map calculations for each iteration. As you learned, these attention maps are capturing the meaning and context of each token within the input sequence and are expensive to calculate. Therefore, to optimize inference, LLMs use *key-value* (KV) *caching* to store calculated maps in the GPU memory.

> The attention map formula computes a *value (V)* based on a given *query (Q)* and a *key (K)*.
>
> $$Q = KV$$
>
> This calculation has to be done for each token in the sequence but luckily can be vectorized using large matrix multiplication operations on a GPU.

However, storing parameters on the GPU memory for reuse between iterations can consume huge chunks of GPU memory. For instance, a 13B-parameter model consumes nearly 1 MB of state for each token in a sequence on top of all those 13B model parameters. This means there is a limited number of tokens you can store in memory for reuse.

If you're using a higher-end GPU, such as the A100 with 40 GB RAM, you can only hold 14 K tokens in memory at once, while the rest of the memory is used up for storing 26 GB of model parameters. In short, the GPU memory consumed scales with the base model size plus the length of the token sequence.

To make matters worse, if you need to serve multiple users concurrently by batching requests, your GPU memory has to be shared between multiple LLM inferences. As a result, you have less memory to store longer sequences, and your LLM is constrained to a shorter context window. On the other hand, if you want to maintain a large context window, then you can't handle more concurrent users. As an example, a sequence length of 2048 means that your batch size will be limited to 7 concurrent requests (or 7 prompt sequences). Realistically, this is an upper-bound limit and doesn't leave room for storing intermediate computations, which will reduce the aforementioned numbers even further.

What this all means is that LLMs are failing to fully saturate the GPU's available resources. The primary reason is that a significant portion of the GPU's memory bandwidth is consumed in loading the model parameters instead of processing inputs.

The first step to reduce the load on your services is to integrate the most efficient models. Often, smaller and more compressed models could do the job you're asking of them, with a similar performance to their larger counterparts.

Another suitable solution to the GPU underutilization problem is to implement *request batching* where the model processes multiple inputs in groups, reducing the overhead of loading model parameters for each request. This is more efficient in using the chip's memory bandwidth, leading to higher compute utilization, higher throughput, and less expensive LLM inference. LLM inference servers like vLLM take advantage of batching plus fast attention, KV caching, and paged attention mechanisms to maximize throughput.

You can see the difference of response latency and throughput with and without batching in Figure 5-14.

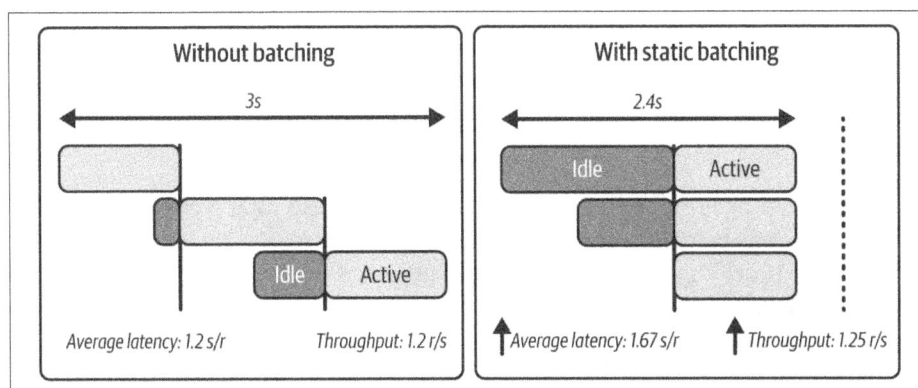

Figure 5-14. LLM server response latency and throughput with and without batching

There are two ways to implement batching:

Static batching
    The size of the batch remains constant.

Dynamic or continuous batching
    The size of batch is determined based on demand.

In *static batching*, we wait for a predetermined number of incoming requests to arrive before we batch and process them through the model. However, since requests can finish at any time in a batch, we're effectively delaying responses to every request—and increasing latency—until the whole batch is processed.

Releasing the GPU resource can also be tricky when processing a batch and adding new requests to the batch that may be at different completion states. As a result, the GPU remains underutilized as the generated sequences within a batch vary and don't match the length of the longest sequence in that batch.

Figure 5-15 illustrates static batching in the context of LLM inference.

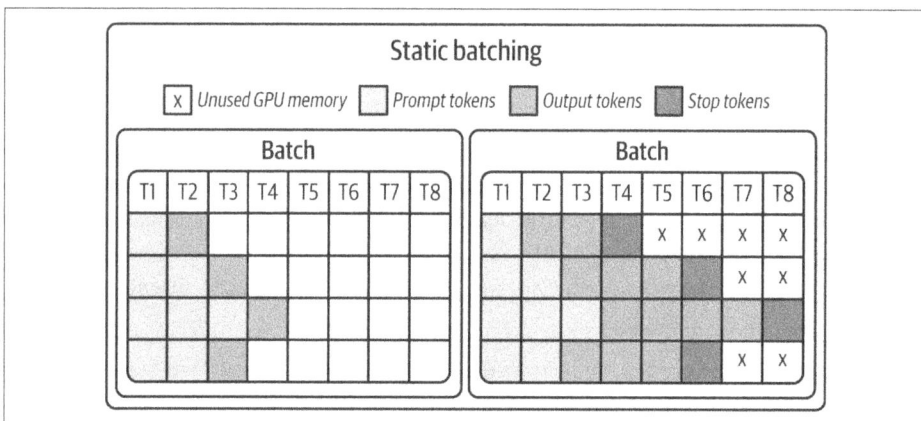

Figure 5-15. Static batching with fixed batch size

In Figure 5-15 you will notice the white blocks representing underutilized GPU computation time. Only one input sequence in the batch saturated the GPU across the batch's processing timeline.

Aside from adding unnecessary waiting times and not saturating the GPU utilization, what makes static batching problematic is that users of an LLM-powered chatbot service won't be providing fixed-length prompts or expect fixed-length outputs. The variance in generation outputs could cause massive underutilization of GPUs.

A solution is to avoid assuming fixed input or output sequences and instead set dynamic batch sizes during the processing of a batch. In *dynamic* or *continuous batching*, the size of batch can be set based on the incoming request sequence length and the available GPU resource. With this approach, new generation requests can be inserted in a batch by replacing completed requests to yield higher GPU utilization than static batching.

Figure 5-16 shows how dynamic or continuous batching can fully saturate the GPU resource.

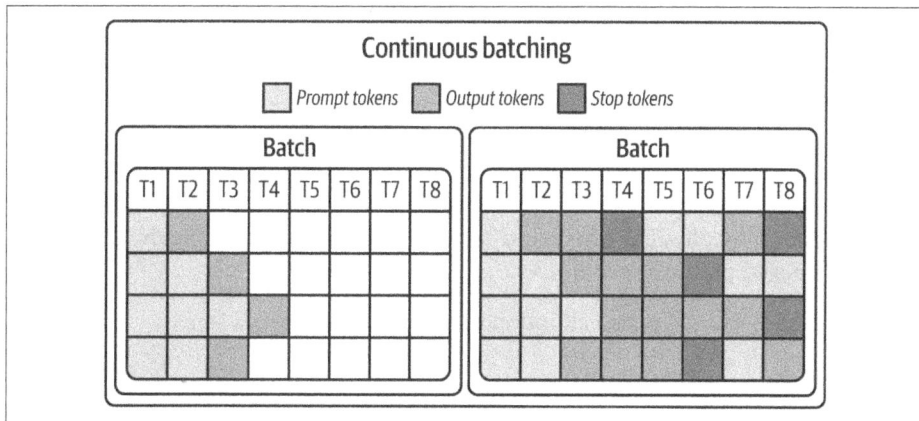

Figure 5-16. Dynamic/continuous batching with variable batch size

While the model parameters are loaded, requests can keep flowing in, and the LLM inference server schedules and insert them into the batch to maximize GPU usage. This approach leads to higher throughput and reduced latency.

If you're building a LLM inference server, you will probably want to bake in the continuous batching mechanism into your server. However, the good news is that the vLLM server already provides continuous batching out of the box with its FastAPI server, so you don't have to implement all of that yourself. Additionally, it also ships with another important GPU optimization feature, which sets it apart from other alternative LLM inference frameworks: paged attention.

Paged attention

Efficient memory usage is a critical challenge for systems that handle high-throughput serving, particularly for LLMs. For faster inference, today's models rely on *KV caches* to store and reuse attention maps, which grow exponentially as input sequence lengths increase.

Paged attention is a novel solution designed to minimize the memory demands of these KV caches, subsequently enhancing the memory efficiency of LLMs and making them more viable for use on devices with limited resources. In transformer-based LLMs, attention key and value tensors are generated for each input token to capture essential context. Instead of recalculating these tensors at every step, they're saved in the GPU memory as a KV cache, which serves as the model's memory. However, the KV cache can grow to enormous sizes, such as 40 GB for a model with 13B parameters, posing a significant challenge for efficient storage and access, particularly on hardware with constrained resources.

Paged attention introduces a method that breaks down the KV cache into smaller, more manageable segments called *pages*, each holding a KV vector for a set number of tokens. With this segmentation, paged attention can efficiently load and access KV caches during the attention computations. You can compare this technique to how the virtual memory is managed by operating systems, where the logical arrangement of data is separated from its physical storage. Essentially, a block table maps the logical blocks to physical ones, allowing for dynamic allocation of memory as new tokens are processed. The core idea is to avoid memory fragmentation by leveraging logical blocks (instead of physical ones) and use a mapping table to quickly access data stored in a paged physical memory.

You can break down the paged attention mechanism into several steps:

Partitioning the KV cache
    The cache is split into fixed-size pages, with each containing a portion of the key-value pairs.

Building the lookup table
    A table is created to map query keys to their corresponding pages, facilitating quick allocation and retrieval.

Selective loading
    Only the necessary pages for the current input sequence are loaded during inference, reducing the memory footprint.

Attention computation
    The model computes attention using the key-value pairs from the loaded pages. This approach aims to make LLMs more accessible by addressing the memory bottleneck, potentially enabling their deployment on a wider range of devices.

The aforementioned steps enable the vLLM server to maximize memory usage efficiency through the mapping of physical and logical memory blocks so that the KV cache is efficiently stored and retrieved during generation.

In a blog post published on Anyscale.com (*https://oreil.ly/WgRfJ*), the authors have researched and compared the performance of various LLM-serving frameworks during inference. The authors concluded that leveraging both paged attention and continuous batching mechanisms are so powerful in optimizing GPU memory usage that the vLLM server was able to reduce latencies by 4 times and throughput by up to 23 times.

In the next section, we will turn our attention to GenAI workloads that can take a long time to process and are compute-bound. This is mostly the case with large non-LLM models such as SDXL where performing batch inferences (such as batch image generation) for multiple users may prove challenging.

Managing Long-Running AI Inference Tasks

With the ability to host models in a separate process outside the FastAPI event loop, you can turn your attention to blocking operations that take a long time to complete.

In the previous section, you leveraged specialized frameworks such as vLLM to externally host and optimize the inference workloads of your LLMs. However, you may still run into models that can take significant time to generate results. To prevent your users from waiting, you should manage tasks that generate models and take a long time to complete.

Several GenAI models such as Stable Diffusion XL may take several minutes, even on a GPU, to produce results. In most cases, you can ask your users to wait until the generation process is complete. But if users are using a single model simultaneously, the server will have to queue these requests. When your users work with generative models, they need to interact with it several times to guide the model to the results they want. This usage pattern creates a large backlog of requests, and users at the end of the queue will have to wait a long time before they see any results.

If there was a way to handle long-running tasks without making the users wait, that would be perfect. Luckily, FastAPI provides a mechanism for solving these kinds of problems.

FastAPI's *background tasks* is a mechanism you can leverage to respond to users while your models are busy processing the request. You've been briefly introduced to this feature while building the RAG module where a background task was populating a vector database with the content of the uploaded PDF documents.

Using background tasks, your users can continue sending requests or carry on with their day without having to wait. You can either save the results to disk or a database for later retrieval or provide a polling system so that their client can ping for updates as the model processes the requests. Another option is to create a live connection between the client and the server so that their UI is updated with the results as soon as it becomes available. All these solutions are doable with FastAPI's background tasks.

Example 5-18 shows how to implement background tasks to handle long-running model inferences.

Example 5-18. Using background tasks to handle long-running model inference (e.g., batch generating images)

```
# main.py

from fastapi import BackgroundTasks
import aiofiles

...

async def batch_generate_image(prompt: str, count: int) -> None:
    images = generate_images(prompt, count) ❶
    for i, image in enumerate(images):
        async with aiofiles.open(f"output_{i}.png", mode='wb') as f:
            await f.write(image) ❷

@app.get("/generate/image/background")
def serve_image_model_background_controller(
    background_tasks: BackgroundTasks, prompt: str, count: int ❸
):
    background_tasks.add_task(batch_generate_image, prompt, count) ❹
    return {"message": "Task is being processed in the background"} ❺
```

❶ Generate multiple images in a batch using an external model-serving API like Ray Serve (*https://oreil.ly/NjlV4*).

❷ Loop over the generated images and asynchronously save each to disk using the `aiofiles` library. In production, you can also save output images to cloud storage solutions that clients can directly fetch from.

❸ Enable the controller to perform background tasks.

❹ Pass the `batch_generate_image` function definition to a FastAPI background tasks handler with the required arguments.

❺ Return a generic success message to the client before processing the background task so that the user is not kept waiting.

In Example 5-18, you're allowing FastAPI to run inference operations in the background (via an external model server API) such that the event loop remains unblocked to process other incoming requests. You can even run multiple tasks in the background, such as generating images in batches (in separate processes) and sending notification emails. These tasks are added to a queue and processed sequentially without blocking the user. You can then store the generated images and expose an additional endpoint that clients can use to poll for status updates and to retrieve the inference results.

Background tasks run in the same event loop. They won't provide true parallelism; they only provide concurrency.

If you run heavy CPU-bound operations like AI inference in background tasks, it'll block the main event loop until all background tasks are completed. Similarly, be careful with async background tasks. If you don't await the blocking I/O operations, the task will block the main server from responding to other requests, even if it runs in the background. FastAPI runs nonasync background tasks in an internal thread pool.

While FastAPI's background tasks are a wonderful tool for handling simple batch jobs, it doesn't scale and can't handle exceptions or retries as well as specialized tools. Other ML-serving frameworks like Ray Serve, BentoML, and vLLM may handle model serving better at scale by providing features such as request batching. More sophisticated tools like Celery (a queue manager), Redis (a caching database), and RabbitMQ (a message broker) can also be used in combination to implement a more robust and reliable inference pipeline.

Summary

This chapter explored the complex aspects of applying concurrency in AI systems.

You were introduced to concurrency and parallelism concepts, including several types of blocking operations that prevent you from simultaneously serving users. You discovered concurrency techniques such as multithreading, multiprocessing, and asynchronous programming alongside their differences, similarities, benefits, and drawbacks in various use cases.

Next, you learned about thread pools and event loops, particularly in a FastAPI server environment, and understood their roles in processing requests concurrently. This involved understanding how and why the server can be blocked if you're not careful how you declare your route handlers.

Later, you discovered how to implement asynchronous programming to manage I/O blocking operations. Through hands-on examples, you developed a deeper understanding of asynchronous interactions with databases and the web content, constructing both a web scraper and a RAG module.

Furthermore, you saw why larger GenAI models can be memory hungry and create memory-bound blocking operations. As part of this, you were introduced to memory optimization techniques such as continuous batching and paged attention in serving LLMs to minimize memory-related bottlenecks.

Finally, you learned about approaches for handling long-running AI inference processes, ensuring your service remains responsive over prolonged operations.

With your knowledge from this chapter, you're now prepared to apply concurrency principles to your own services, crafting resilient, scalable, and high-performing AI applications.

The ability to handle multiple users simultaneously is a significant milestone. But there are additional optimizations you can perform to improve the user experience of your GenAI services even further. You can provide real-time updates via streaming technologies to progressively show near real-time results to users during generation. This is particularly useful for LLMs that may have longer generation times in conversation scenarios.

The upcoming chapter will explore AI streaming workloads, detailing the use of real-time communication technologies like server-sent events (SSE) and WebSocket (WS). You will learn the difference between these technologies and how to implement model streaming by building endpoints for real-time text-to-text, text-to-speech, and speech-to-text interactions.

Additional References

- Kwon, W., et al. (2023). "Efficient Memory Management for Large Language Model Serving with PagedAttention" (*https://oreil.ly/PtCqL*). arXiv preprint arXiv:2309.06180.
- Lewis, P., et al. (2022). "Retrieval-Augmented Generation for Knowledge-Intensive NLP Tasks" (*https://oreil.ly/r5yVL*). arXiv preprint arXiv:2005.11401.

## CHAPTER 6

Real-Time Communication with Generative Models

Chapter Goals

In this chapter, you will learn about:

- When to implement real-time communication in AI workflows

- Web communication mechanisms by comparing their features, differences, and similarities

- Real-time communication mechanisms including server-sent events (SSE) and WebSocket (WS)

- Selecting the correct streaming technology for your use case

- Implementing mocked streaming endpoints from scratch for testing and proto-typing

- Implementing real-time API endpoints with both SSE and WebSocket mechanisms

- How to gracefully handle exceptions and close streaming connections

- API design patterns to simplify streaming endpoints

This chapter will explore AI streaming workloads such as chatbots, detailing the use of real-time communication technologies like SSE and WebSocket. You will learn the difference between these technologies and how to implement model streaming by building endpoints for real-time text-to-text interactions.

Web Communication Mechanisms

In the previous chapter, you learned about implementing concurrency in AI work-flows by leveraging asynchronous programming, background tasks, and continuous batching. With concurrency, your services become more resilient to matching increased demand when multiple users access your application simultaneously. Concurrency solves the problem of allowing simultaneous users to access your service and helps to decrease the waiting times, yet AI data generation remains a resource-intensive and time-consuming task.

Up until this point, you've been building endpoints using the conventional HTTP communication where the client sends a request to the server. The web server processes the incoming requests and responds via HTTP messages.

Figure 6-1 shows the client-server architecture.

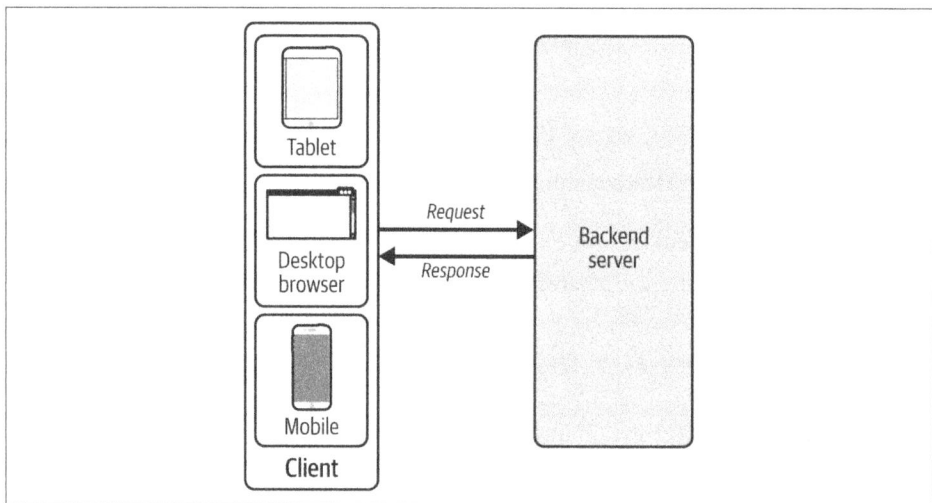

Figure 6-1. The client-server architecture (Source: scaleyourapp.com)

Since the HTTP protocol is stateless, the server treats each incoming request completely independent and unrelated from other requests. This means that multiple incoming requests from differing clients wouldn't affect how the server responds to each one. As an example, in a conversational AI service that doesn't use a database, each request may provide the full conversation history and receive the correct response from the server.

The *HTTP request-response* model is a widely adopted API design pattern used across the web due to its simplicity. However, this approach becomes inadequate as soon as the client or the server needs real-time updates.

In the standard HTTP request-response model, your services typically respond to the user's request once it has been entirely processed. However, if the data generation process is lengthy and sluggish, your users will wait a long time and subsequently be inundated with lots of information at once. Imagine chatting to a bot that takes several minutes to reply, and once it does, you're shown overwhelming blocks of text.

Alternatively, if you provide the data to the client as it's being generated, rather than holding off until the entire generation process is complete, you can mitigate lengthy delays and deliver the information in digestible chunks. This approach not only enhances user experience but also maintains user engagement during the ongoing processing of their request.

There will be cases where implementing real-time features can be overkill and escalate the development burden. For instance, some open source models or APIs lack the real-time generation capability. Furthermore, adding data streaming endpoints can add to the complexity of your system on both sides, the server and the client. It means having to handle exceptions differently and manage concurrent connections to the streaming endpoints to avoid memory leakage. If the client disconnects during a stream, there may be a chance for data loss or state drift between the server and the client. And, you may need to implement complex reconnection and state management logic to handle cases where the connection drops.

Maintaining many concurrent open connections can also put a burden on your servers and lead to an increase in hosting and infrastructure costs.

Equally important, you also need to consider the scalability of handling a large number of concurrent streams, your application's latency requirements, and browser compatibilities with your chosen streaming protocol.

> Compared to traditional web applications that have some form of I/O or data processing latency, AI applications also have AI model inference latency, depending on the model you're using.
>
> Since this latency can be significant, your AI services should be able to handle longer waiting times on both the server and client sides, including managing the user experience.

If your use case does benefit from real-time features, then you have a few architectural design patterns you can implement:

- Regular/short polling
- Long polling
- SSE
- WS

The choice depends on your requirements for user experience, scalability, latency, development cost, and maintainability.

Let's explore each option in more detail.

Regular/Short Polling

A method to benefit from semi-real-time updates is to use *regular/short polling*, as shown in Figure 6-2. In this polling mechanism, the client periodically sends HTTP requests to the server to check for updates at preconfigured intervals. The shorter the intervals, the closer you get to real-time updates but also the higher the traffic you will have to manage.

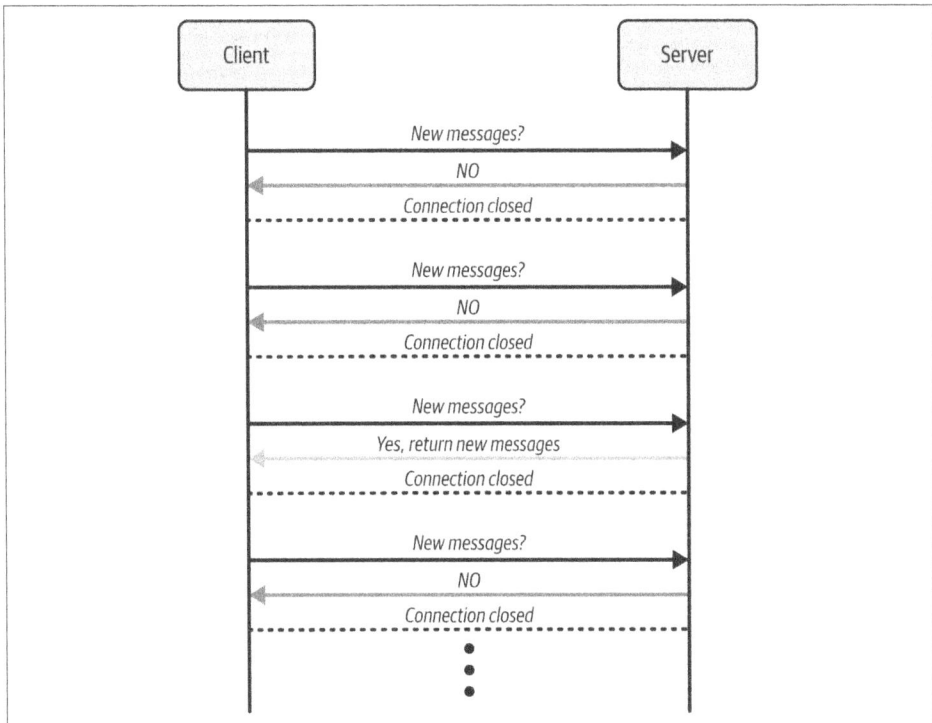

Figure 6-2. Regular/short polling

You can use this technique if you're building a service to generate data such as images in batches. The client simply submits a request to start the batch job and is given a unique job/request identifier. It then periodically checks back with the server to confirm the status and outputs of the requested job. The server then responds with new data or provides an empty response (and perhaps a status update) if outputs are yet to be computed.

As you can imagine with short polling, you'll end up with an excessive number of incoming requests that the server needs to respond to, even when there's no new information. If you have multiple concurrent users, this approach can quickly overwhelm the server, which limits your application's scalability. However, you can still reduce server load by using cached responses (i.e., executing status checks on the backend at a tolerable frequency) and implementing rate limiting, which you will learn more about in Chapters 9 and 10.

A potential use case for short polling in AI services is when you have some in-progress batch or inference jobs. You can expose endpoints for your clients to use short polling to keep up-to-date with the status of these jobs. And, fetch the results when they're completed.

An alternative is to leverage long polling instead.

Long Polling

If you want to reduce the burden on your server while continuing to leverage a real-time polling mechanism, you can implement *long polling* (see Figure 6-3), an improved version of regular/short polling.

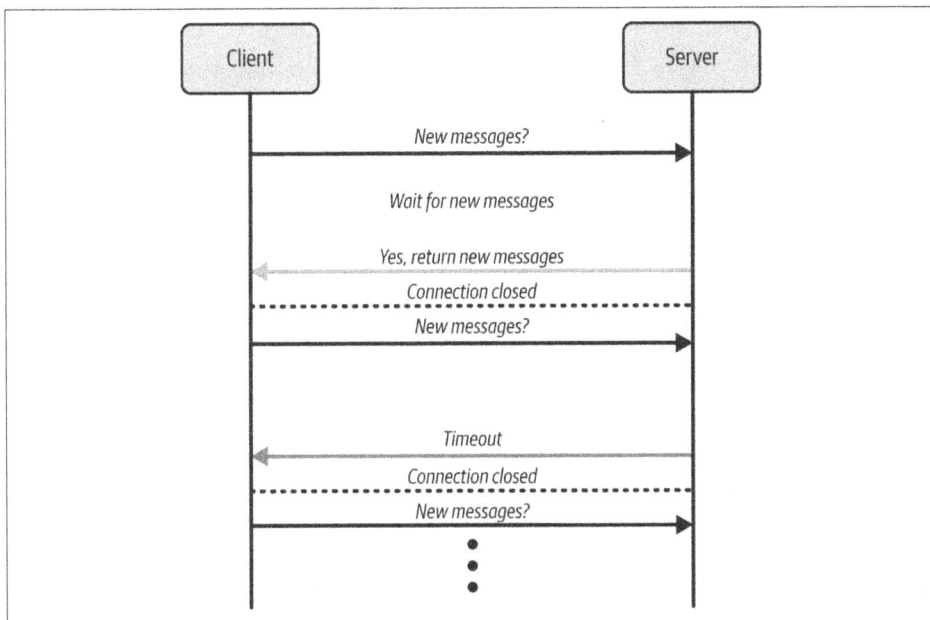

Figure 6-3. Long polling

With long polling, both the server and the client are configured to prevent *timeouts* (if possible) that occur when either the client or the server gives up on the prolonged request.

Timeouts are observed more often in a typical HTTP request-response cycle when a request takes an extended time to resolve or when there are network issues.

To implement long polling, the server keeps the incoming requests open (i.e., hanging) until there is data available to send back. For instance, this can be useful when you have an LLM with unpredictable processing times. The client is instructed to wait for an extended period of time and avoid aborting and repeating the requests prematurely.

You can use long polling if you need a simple API design and application architecture for processing prolonged jobs, such as multiple AI inferences. This technique allows you to avoid implementing a batch job manager to keep track of jobs for bulk data generation. Instead, the client requests remain open until they are processed, avoiding the constant short polling request-response cycle that can overload the server.

While long polling sounds similar to the typical HTTP request-response model, it differs on how the client handles requests. In long polling, the client typically receives a single message per request. Once the server sends a response, the connection is closed. The client then immediately opens a new connection to wait for the next message. This process repeats, allowing the client to receive multiple messages over time, but each HTTP request-response cycle handles only one message.

Since long polling maintains an open connection until a message is available, it reduces the frequency of requests compared to short polling and implements a near-real-time communication mechanism. However, the server still has to hold onto unfulfilled requests, which consume server resources. Additionally, if there are multiple open requests by the same client, message ordering can be challenging to manage, potentially leading to out-of-order messages.

If you don't have a specific requirement for using polling mechanisms, a more modern alternative to polling mechanisms for real-time communication is SSE via the Event Source interface.

Server-Sent Events

Server-sent events (SSE) is an HTTP-based mechanism for establishing a persistent and unidirectional connection from the server to the client. While the connection is open, the server can continuously push updates to the client as data becomes available.

Once the client establishes the persistent SSE connection with the server, it won't need to re-establish it again, unlike the long polling mechanism where the client repeatedly sends requests to the server to maintain an open connection.

When you're serving GenAI models, SSE will be a more suitable real-time communication mechanism compared to long polling. SSE is designed specifically for handling real-time events and is more efficient than long polling. Due to repeated opening and closing connections, long polling becomes resource intensive and leads to higher latency and overhead. SSE, on the other hand, supports automatic reconnection and event IDs to resume interrupted streams, which long polling lacks.

In SSE, the client makes a standard HTTP `GET` request with an `Accept:text/event-stream` header, and the server responds with a status code of `200` and a `Content-Type: text/event-stream` header. After this handshake, the server can send events to the client over the same connection.

SSE and EventSource Interface

The SSE specification describes a built-in `EventSource` interface that opens a persistent connection with the server for sending events from the server. Similar to WebSocket, the connection is persistent.

`EventSource` is a less powerful way of communicating with the server than WebSocket.

Why should one ever use it? The main reason: it's simpler. In many applications, the power of WebSocket is a little bit too much. We will talk about WebSocket shortly.

We need to receive a stream of data from a server—maybe chat messages or market prices, or whatever. That's what `EventSource` is good at. Also, it supports auto-reconnect, something we need to implement manually with WebSocket. Besides, it's a plain old HTTP, not a new protocol.

Upon creation, a new `EventSource` connects to the server, and if the connection is broken, it reconnects. That's very convenient, as we don't have to care about it. There's a small delay between reconnections, a few seconds by default. The server can set the recommended delay using `retry:` in response to (milliseconds).

While SSE should be your first choice for real-time applications, you can still opt for a simpler long polling mechanism where updates are infrequent or if your environment doesn't support persistent connections.

One last important detail to note is that SSE connections are *unidirectional*, meaning that you send a regular HTTP request to the server, and you get the response via SSE. Therefore, they're only suitable for applications that don't need to send data to the server. You may have seen SSE in action within news feeds, notifications, and real-time dashboards like stock data charts.

Unsurprisingly, SSE also shines in chat applications when you need to stream LLM responses in a conversation. In this instance, the client can establish a separate persistent connection until the server fully streams the LLM's response to the user.

> ChatGPT leverages SSE under the hood to enable real-time responses to user queries.

Figure 6-4 shows how the SSE communication mechanism operates.

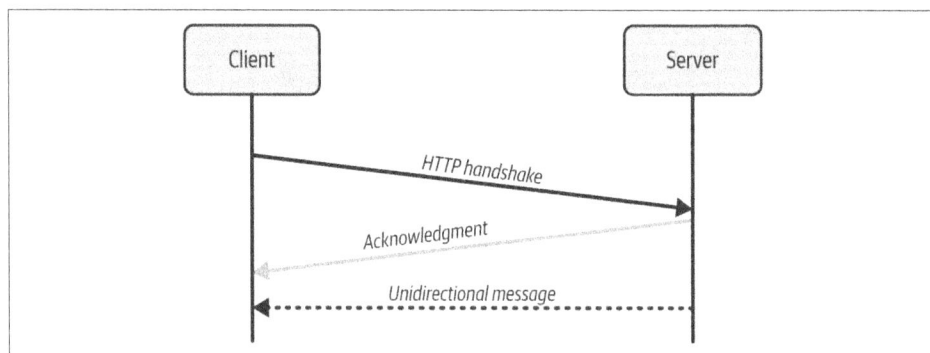

Figure 6-4. SSE

To solidify your understanding, we will be building two mini-projects in this chapter using SSE. One to stream data from a mocked data generator, and another to stream LLM responses.

You will learn more details about the SSE mechanism during the aforementioned projects.

In summary, SSE is excellent for establishing persistent unidirectional connections, but what if you need to both send and receive messages during a persistent connection? This is where WebSocket would come in handy.

WebSocket

The last real-time communication mechanism to cover is WebSocket.

WebSocket is an excellent real-time communication mechanism for establishing persistent *bidirectional connections* between the client and the server for real-time chat, as well as voice and video applications with an AI model. A bidirectional connection means that both sides can send and receive real-time data in any order, as long as a persistent connection is open between the client and the server. It's designed to work over standard HTTP ports to ensure compatibility with existing security measures.

Web applications that require two-way communication with servers benefit the most from this mechanism as they can avoid the overhead and complexity of HTTP polling.

You can use WebSocket in a variety of applications including social feeds, multiplayer games, financial feeds, location-based updates, multimedia chat, etc.

Webhook Versus WebSocket

Don't confuse WebSocket with Webhook. These terms get used interchangeably but refer to different real-time web communication mechanisms.

Webhooks are used for real-time server-to-server communication to support event-driven application architectures. Therefore, when a server exposes a webhook endpoint, it is telling other servers to immediately send data to that webhook endpoint when an event happens.

You can think of webhooks as a nonpersistent but real-time unidirectional communication mechanism where one server sends messages to another as they're generated. In reality, there are no handshakes or open connections established between servers.

Unlike all other communication mechanisms discussed so far, the WebSocket protocol doesn't transfer data over HTTP after the initial handshake. Instead, the WebSocket protocol defined in the RFC 6455 specification implements a two-way messaging mechanism (full-duplex) over a single TCP connection. As a result, WebSocket is faster for data transmission than HTTP because it has less protocol overhead and operates at a lower level in the network protocol stack. This is because HTTP sits on top of TCP, so stripping back to TCP will be faster.

WebSocket keeps a socket open on both the client and the server for the duration of the connection. Note that this also makes servers stateful, which makes scaling trickier.

You may now be wondering how the WebSocket protocol works.

According to RFC 6455, to establish a WebSocket connection, the client sends an HTTP "upgrade" request to the server, asking to open a WebSocket connection. This is referred to as the *opening handshake*, which initiates the WebSocket connection lifecycle in the *CONNECTING* state.

Your AI services should be able to handle multiple concurrent handshakes and also authenticate them before opening a connection. New connections can consume server resources, so they must be handled properly by your server.

The HTTP upgrade request should contain a set of required headers, as shown in Example 6-1.

Example 6-1. WebSocket opening handshake over HTTP

```
GET ws://localhost:8000/generate/text/stream HTTP/1.1 ❶
Origin: http://localhost:3000
Connection: Upgrade ❷
Host: http://localhost:8000
Upgrade: websocket ❷
Sec-WebSocket-Key: 8WnhvZTK66EVvhDG++RD0w== ❸
Sec-WebSocket-Protocol: html-chat, text-chat ❹
Sec-WebSocket-Version: 13
```

❶ Make an HTTP upgrade request to the WebSocket endpoint. WebSocket endpoints start with `ws://` instead of the typical `http://`.

❷ Request to upgrade and open a WebSocket connection.

❸ Use a random, 16-byte, Base64-encoded string to ensure the server supports the WebSocket protocol.

❹ Use the `html-chat` or the `text-chat` subprotocol if `html-chat` is not available. Subprotocols regulate what data will be exchanged.

In production, always use secure WebSocket `wss://` endpoints.

The `wss://` protocol, similar to `https://`, is not only encrypted but also more reliable. That's because `ws://` data is not encrypted and visible for any intermediary. Old proxy servers don't know about WebSocket. They may see "strange" headers and abort the connection.

On the other hand, `wss://` is the secure version of WebSocket, running over Transport Layer Security (TLS), which encrypts the data at the sender and decrypts it at the receiver. So data packets are passed encrypted through proxies. They can't see what's inside and let them through.

Once the WebSocket connection is established, text or binary messages can be transmitted in both directions in the form of *message frames*. The connection lifecycle is now in the *OPEN* state.

You can view the WebSocket communication mechanism in Figure 6-5.

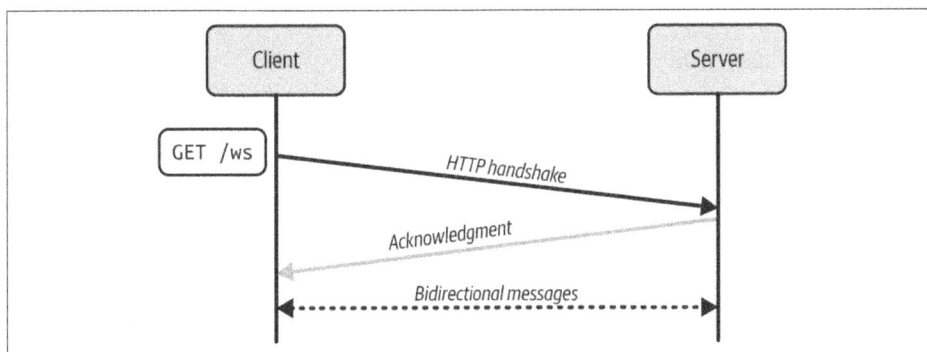

Figure 6-5. WS communication

Message frames are a way to package and transmit data between the client and server. They aren't anything unique to WebSocket as they apply to all connections over the TCP protocol that form the basis of HTTP. However, a WebSocket message frame consists of several components:

Fixed header
    Describes basic information about the message

Extended payload length (optional)
    Provides the actual length of the payload when the length exceeds 125 bytes

Masking key
    Masks the payload data in frames sent from the client to the server, preventing certain types of security vulnerabilities, particularly *cache poisoning*[1] and *cross-protocol*[2] attacks

Payload
    Contains the actual message content

---

1 Attackers can use cache poisoning to inject malicious data to caching systems, which then serve incorrect data to users or systems. To protect against this attack, the client and the server mask payloads to appear as random data before sending them.

2 These attacks involve tricking a server into leaking sensitive information by sending an HTTP response to a WebSocket frame.

Unlike the verbose headers in HTTP requests, WebSocket frames have minimal headers that include the following:

Text frames
Used for UTF-8 encoded text data

Binary frames
Used for binary data

Fragmentation
Used to fragment messages into multiple frames, which are reassembled by the recipient

The beauty of the WebSocket protocol is also its ability to maintain a persistent connection through *control frames*.

Control frames are special frames used to manage the connection:

Ping/pong frames
Used to check the connection's status

Close frame
Used to terminate the connection gracefully

When it's time to close the WebSocket connection, a close frame is sent by the client or the server. The close frame can optionally specify a status code and/or a reason for closing the connection. At this point, the WebSocket connection enters the *CLOSING* state.

The *CLOSING* state ends once the other party responds with another close frame. This concludes the full WebSocket connection lifecycle at the *CLOSED* state, as shown in Figure 6-6.

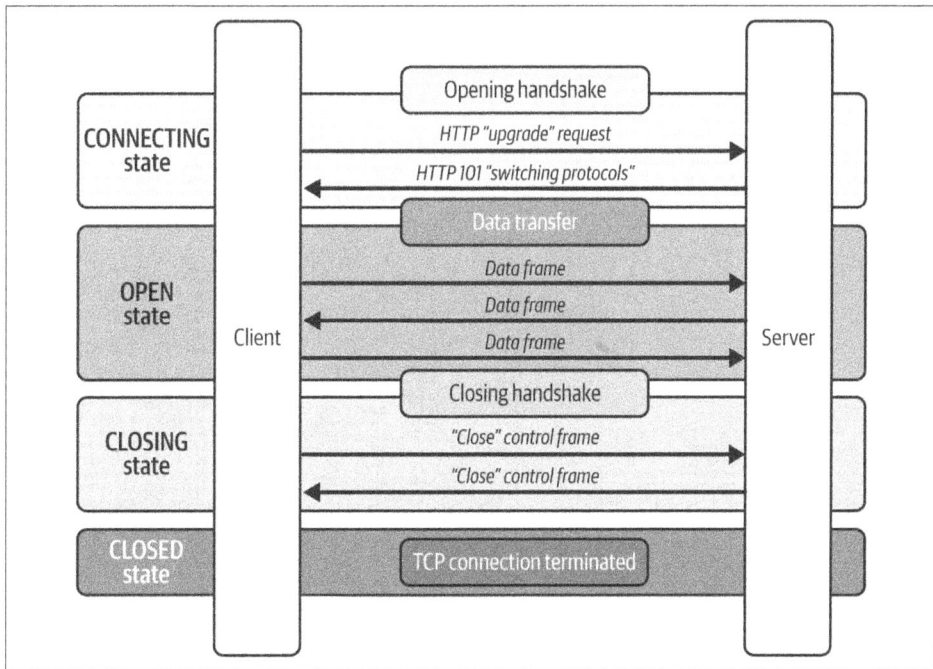

Figure 6-6. WebSocket connection lifecycle

As you can see, using the WebSocket communication mechanism can be a bit of over-kill for simple applications that won't require the overheads. For most GenAI applications, SSE connections may be enough.

However, there are GenAI use cases where WebSocket can shine, such as multimedia chat and voice-to-voice applications, collaborative GenAI apps, and real-time transcription services based on bidirectional communication. To gain some hands-on experience, you will be building a speech-to-text application later in this chapter.

Now that you've learned about several unique web communication mechanisms for real-time applications, let's quickly summarize how they all compare.

Comparing Communication Mechanisms

Figure 6-7 outlines the aforementioned five communication mechanisms used in web development.

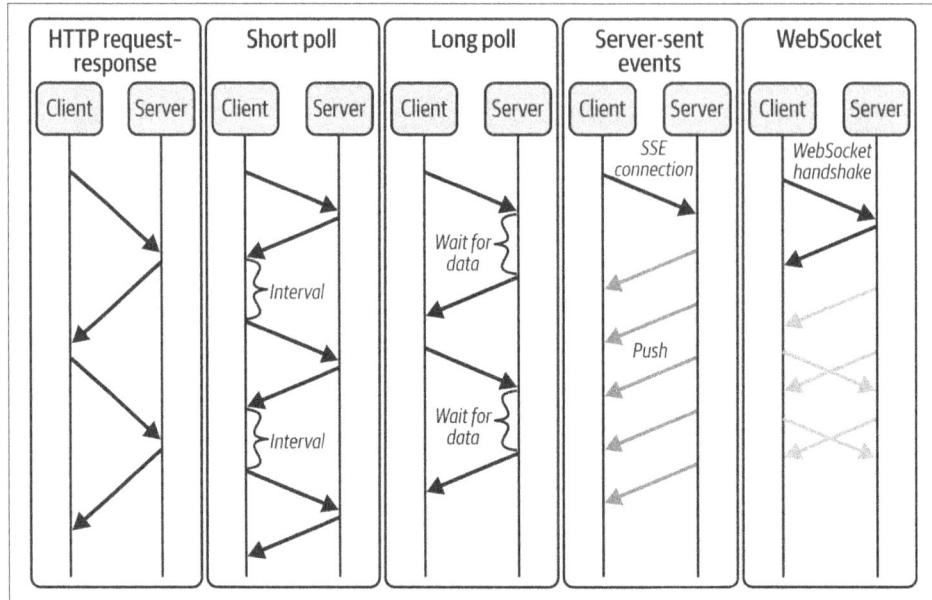

Figure 6-7. Comparison of web communication mechanisms

As you can see from Figure 6-7, the messaging patterns differ in each approach.

HTTP request-response is the most common model supported by all web clients and servers, suitable for RESTful APIs and services that don't require real-time updates.

Short/regular polling involves clients checking for data at set intervals, which is straightforward but can be resource-intensive when scaling services. It is normally used in applications to perform infrequent updates such as in analytics dashboards.

Long polling is more efficient for real-time updates by keeping connections open until data is available on the server. However, it can still drain the server resources, making it ideal for near-real-time features such as notifications.

SSE maintains a single persistent connection that is server-to-client only, using the HTTP protocol. It is straightforward to set up, leverages the browser's `EventSource` API and ships with built-in features like reconnection. These factors make SSE suitable for applications requiring live feeds, chat features, and real-time dashboards.

WebSocket provides full-duplex (double-sided) communication with low latency and binary data support, but is complex to implement. It is widely used in applications requiring high interactivity and real-time data exchange, such as multiplayer games, chat applications, collaborative tools, and real-time transcription services.

With the invention of SSE and WebSocket and their rising popularity, short/regular polling and long polling are becoming less common real-time mechanisms in web applications.

Table 6-1 compares the features, challenges, and applications for each mechanism in detail.

Table 6-1. Comparison of web communication mechanisms

Communication mechanism	Features	Challenges	Applications
HTTP request-response	Simple request-and-response model, stateless protocol, supported by all web clients and servers	High latency for real-time updates, inefficient for frequent server-to-client data transfer	RESTful APIs, web services where real-time updates aren't critical
Short/regular polling	Client regularly requests data at intervals, easy to implement	Wasteful of resources when there's no new data, latency depends on poll intervals	Applications with infrequent updates, simple near-real-time dashboards, status updates for submitted jobs
Long polling	More efficient than short polling for real-time updates, maintains open connection until data is available	Can be resource-intensive on the server, complex to manage multiple connections	Real-time notifications, older chat applications
Server-sent events	Single persistent connection for updates, built-in reconnection and event ID support	Unidirectional communication from server to the client only	Live feeds, chat application, real-time analytics dashboards
WebSocket	Full-duplex communication, low latency, supports binary data	More complex to implement and manage, requires WebSocket support on the server	Multiplayer games, chat applications, collaborative editing tools, video conferencing and webinar apps, real-time transcription and translation apps

Having reviewed real-time communication mechanisms in detail, let's dive deeper into SSE and WebSocket by implementing our own streaming endpoints using these two mechanisms. In the next section, you will learn how to implement streaming endpoints working with both technologies.

Implementing SSE Endpoints

In Chapter 3, you learned about LLMs, which are *autoregressive* models that predict the next token based on previous inputs. After each generation step, the output token is appended to the inputs and passed through the model again until a <stop> token is generated to break the loop. Instead of waiting for the loop to finish, you can forward the output tokens as they're being generated to the user as a data stream.

Model providers will normally expose an option for you to set the output mode as a data stream using `stream=True`. With this option set, the model provider can return a data generator instead of the final output to you, which you can directly pass to your FastAPI server for streaming.

To demonstrate this in action, refer to Example 6-2, which implements an asynchronous data generator using the `openai` library.

> To run Example 6-2, you will need to create an instance of Azure OpenAI on the Azure portal and create a model deployment. Make note of API endpoint, key, and model deployment name. For Example 6-2, you can use the `2023-05-15` api version.

Example 6-2. Implementing Azure OpenAI async chat client for streaming responses

```python
# stream.py

import asyncio
import os
from typing import AsyncGenerator
from openai import AsyncAzureOpenAI

class AzureOpenAIChatClient: ❶
    def __init__(self):
        self.aclient = AsyncAzureOpenAI(
            api_key=os.environ["OPENAI_API_KEY"],
            api_version=os.environ["OPENAI_API_VERSION"],
            azure_endpoint=os.environ["OPENAI_API_ENDPOINT"],
            azure_deployment=os.environ["OPENAI_API_DEPLOYMENT"],
        )

    async def chat_stream(
        self, prompt: str, model: str = "gpt-3.5-turbo"
    ) -> AsyncGenerator[str, None]: ❷
        stream = await self.aclient.chat.completions.create(
            messages=[
                {
                    "role": "user",
                    "content": prompt,
                }
            ],
            model=model,
            stream=True, ❸
        )

        async for chunk in stream:
```

```
            yield f"data: {chunk.choices[0].delta.content or ''}\n\n" ❹
            await asyncio.sleep(0.05) ❺

        yield f"data: [DONE]\n\n"


azure_chat_client = AzureOpenAIChatClient()
```

❶ Create an asynchronous `AzureOpenAIChatClient` to interact with the Azure OpenAI API. The chat client requires an API endpoint, deployment name, key, and version to function.

❷ Define a `chat_stream` asynchronous generator method that yields each output token from the API.

❸ Set the `stream=True` to receive an output stream from the API instead of the full response at once.

❹ Loop over the stream and yield each output token or return an empty string if `delta.content` is empty. The `data:` substring should be prefixed to each token so that browsers can correctly parse the content using the `EventSource` API.

❺ Slow down the streaming rate to reduce back pressure on the clients.

In Example 6-2, you create an instance of `AsyncAzureOpenAI`, which allows you to chat with the Azure OpenAI models via an API in your private Azure environment.

By setting the `stream=True`, `AsyncAzureOpenAI` returns a data stream (an async generator function) instead of the full model response. You can loop over the data stream and `yield` tokens with the `data:` prefix to comply with the SSE specification. This will let browsers to automatically parse the stream content using the widely available `EventSource` web API.[3]

> When exposing streaming endpoints, you'll need to consider how fast the clients can consume the data you're sending them. A good practice is to reduce the streaming rate as you saw in Example 6-2 to reduce the back pressure on clients. You can adjust the throttling by testing your services with different clients on various devices.

---

[3] See MDN resources for more details on the `EventSource` interface (*https://oreil.ly/0yuKA*).

SSE with GET Request

You can now implement the SSE endpoint by passing the chat stream to the FastAPI's `StreamingResponse` as a GET endpoint, as shown in Example 6-3.

Example 6-3. Implementing an SSE endpoint using the FastAPI's `StreamingResponse`

```
# main.py

from fastapi.responses import StreamingResponse
from stream import azure_chat_client

...

@app.get("/generate/text/stream") ❶
async def serve_text_to_text_stream_controller(
    prompt: str,
) -> StreamingResponse:
    return StreamingResponse( ❷
        azure_chat_client.chat_stream(prompt), media_type="text/event-stream"
    )
```

❶ Implement an SSE endpoint with the GET method to use with the `EventSource` API on the browser.

❷ Pass the chat stream generator to the `StreamingResponse` to forward the output stream as it is being generated to the client. Set the `media_type=text/event-stream` as per SSE specifications so that the browsers can handle the response correctly.

With the GET endpoint set up on the server, you can create a simple HTML form on the client to consume the SSE stream via the `EventSource` interface, as shown in Example 6-4.

> Example 6-4 doesn't use any JavaScript libraries or web frameworks. However, there are libraries to assist you in implementing the `EventSource` connection in any framework of your choice such as React, Vue, or SvelteKit.

Example 6-4. Implementing SSE on the client using the browser `EventSource` API

```
{# pages/client-sse.html #}

<!DOCTYPE html>
<html lang="en">
<head>
```

```
    <title>SSE with EventSource API</title>
</head>
<body>
<button id="streambtn">Start Streaming</button>
<label for="messageInput">Enter your prompt:</label>
<input type="text" id="messageInput" placeholder="Enter your prompt"> ❶
<div style="padding-top: 10px" id="responseContainer"></div> ❷

<script>
    let source;
    const button = document.getElementById('streambtn');
    const container = document.getElementById('container');
    const input = document.getElementById('messageInput');

    function resetForm(){
        input.value = '';
        container.textContent = '';
    }

    function handleOpen() {
        console.log('Connection was opened');
    }
    function handleMessage(e){
        if (e.data === '[DONE]') {
            source.close();
            console.log('Connection was closed');
            return;
        }

        container.textContent += e.data;
    }
    function handleClose(e){
        console.error(e);
        source.close()
    }

    button.addEventListener('click', function() { ❸
        const message = input.value;
        const url = 'http://localhost:8000/generate/text/stream?prompt=' +
            encodeURIComponent(message);
        resetForm() ❹

        source = new EventSource(url); ❺
        source.addEventListener('open', handleOpen, false);
        source.addEventListener('message', handleMessage, false);
        source.addEventListener('error', handleClose, false); ❻
    });

</script>
</body>
</html>
```

1 Create a simple HTML input and button for initiating SSE requests.

2 Create an empty container to be used as a sink for the stream content.

3 Listen for button `clicks` and run the SSE callback.

4 Reset the content form and response container of previous content.

5 Create a new `EventSource` object and listen to connection state changes to handle events.

6 Log to console when an SSE connection is opened. Handle each message by rendering message content to the response container until the [DONE] message is received, which signals that the connection should now be closed. Additionally, close the connection if any errors occur and log the error to the browser's console.

With the SSE client implemented in Example 6-4, you can now use it to test your SSE endpoint. However, you need to serve the HTML first.

Create a `pages` directory and then place the HTML file inside. Then *mount* the directory onto your FastAPI server to serve its content as static files, as shown in Example 6-5. Via mounting, FastAPI takes care of mapping API paths to each file so that you can access them with a browser from the same origin as your server.

Example 6-5. Mounting HTML files on the server as static assets

```
# main.py

from fastapi.staticfiles import StaticFiles

app.mount("/pages", StaticFiles(directory="pages"), name="pages")
```
1

1 Mount the `pages` directory onto the `/pages` to serve its content as static assets. Once mounted, you can access each file by visiting `<origin>/pages/<filename>`.

By implementing Example 6-5, you serve the HTML from the same origin as your API server. This avoids triggering the browser's CORS security mechanism, which can block outgoing requests reaching your server.

You can now access the HTML page by visiting `http://localhost:8000/pages/sse-client.html`.

Cross-origin resource sharing

If you try to open the Example 6-4 HTML file in your browser directly and click the Start Streaming button, you will notice that nothing happens. You can check the browser's network tab to view what happened to the outgoing requests.

After some investigations, you should notice that your browser has blocked outgoing requests to your server as its preflight *cross-origin resource sharing* (CORS) checks with your server have failed.

CORS is a security mechanism implemented in browsers to control how resources on a web page can be requested from another domain, and is relevant only when sending requests directly from the browser instead of a server. Browsers use CORS to check whether they're allowed to send requests to the server from a different origin (i.e., domain) than the server.

For example, if your client is hosted on `https://example.com` and it needs to fetch data from an API hosted on `https://api.example.com`, the browser will block this request unless the API server has CORS enabled.

For now, you can bypass these CORS errors by adding a CORS middleware on your server, as you can see in Example 6-6, to allow any incoming requests from browsers.

Example 6-6. Apply CORS settings

```
# main.py

from fastapi.middleware.cors import CORSMiddleware

app.add_middleware(
    CORSMiddleware,
    allow_origins=["*"],
    allow_credentials=True,
    allow_methods=["*"],
    allow_headers=["*"], ❶
)
```

❶ Allow incoming requests from any origins, methods (GET, POST, etc.) and headers.

Streamlit avoids triggering the CORS mechanism by sending requests on its internal server even though the generated UI runs on the browser.

On the other hand, the FastAPI documentation page makes requests from the same origin as the server (i.e., `http://localhost:8000`), so requests by default don't trigger the CORS security mechanism.

In Example 6-6, you configure the CORS middleware to process any incoming requests, effectively bypassing the CORS security mechanism for easier development. In production, you should allow only a handful of origins, methods, and headers to be processed by your server.

If you followed Example 6-5 or 6-6, you should now be able to view the incoming stream from your SSE endpoint (see Figure 6-8).

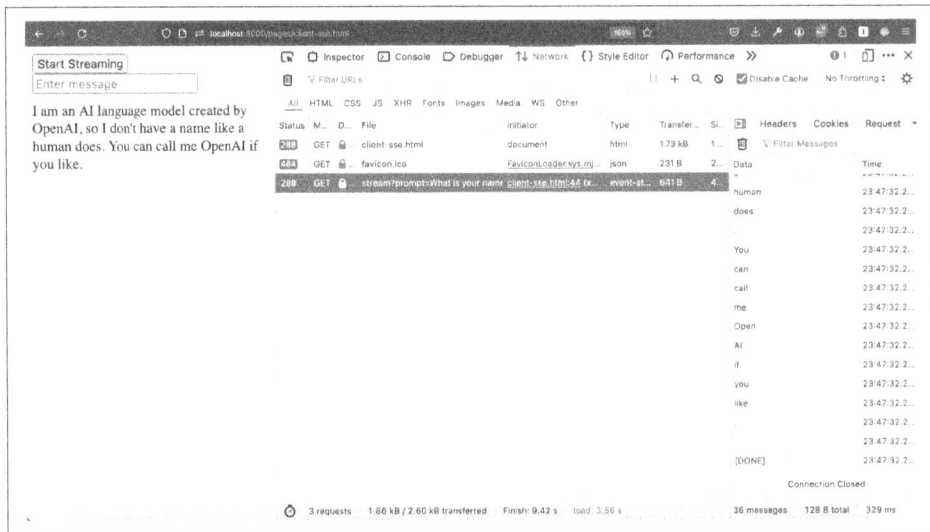

Figure 6-8. Incoming stream from the SSE endpoint

Congratulations! You now have a full working solution where model responses are directly streamed to your client as soon as generated data becomes available. By implementing this feature, your users will now have a more pleasant experience interacting with your chatbot as they receive responses to their queries in real time.

Your solution also implemented concurrency using an asynchronous client for interacting with the Azure OpenAI API to stream faster responses to your users. You can try using a synchronous client to compare the differences in generation speeds. With an asynchronous client, the generation speed can be so fast that you will receive a block of text at once even though it is actually being streamed to the browser.

Streaming LLM outputs from Hugging Face models

Now that you've learned how to implement SSE endpoints with model providers such as Azure OpenAI, you may be wondering if you can stream model outputs from open source models you've previously downloaded from Hugging Face.

Although Hugging Face's `transformers` library implements a `TextStreamer` component that you can pass to your model pipeline, the easiest solution is to run a separate inference server such as HF Inference Server to implement model streaming.

Example 6-7 shows how to set up a simple model inference server using Docker by providing a `model-id`.

Example 6-7. Serving HF LLM models via HF Inference Server

```
$ docker run --runtime nvidia --gpus all \ ❶
    -v ~/.cache/huggingface:/root/.cache/huggingface \ ❷
    --env "HUGGING_FACE_HUB_TOKEN=<secret>" \ ❸
    -p 8080:8000 \ ❹
    --ipc=host \ ❺
    vllm/vllm-openai:latest \ ❶ ❻
    --model mistralai/Mistral-7B-v0.1 ❼
```

❶ Use Docker to download and run the latest `vllm/vllm-openai` container on all available NVIDIA GPUs.

❷ Share a volume with the Docker container to avoid downloading weights every run.

❸ Set the secret environment variable to access gated models like `mistralai/Mistral-7B-v0.1`.[4]

❹ Run the inference server on localhost port `8080` by mapping host port `8080` to exposed Docker container port `8000`.

❺ Enable inter-process communication (IPC) between the container and the host to allow the container to access the host's shared memory.

❻ The vLLM inference server uses the OpenAI API Specification for LLM serving.

❼ Download and use the gated `mistralai/Mistral-7B-v0.1` from Hugging Face Hub.

With the model server running, you can now use an `AsyncInferenceClient` to generate outputs in a streaming format, as shown in Example 6-8.

---

4 Follow the "Accessing Private/Gated Models" guide (*https://oreil.ly/a7KeV*) to generate a Hugging Face user access token.

Example 6-8. Consuming the LLM output stream from HF Inference Stream

```
import asyncio
from typing import AsyncGenerator
from huggingface_hub import AsyncInferenceClient

client = AsyncInferenceClient("http://localhost:8080")

async def chat_stream(prompt: str) -> AsyncGenerator[str, None]:
    stream = await client.text_generation(prompt, stream=True)
    async for token in stream:
        yield token
        await asyncio.sleep(0.05)
```

While Example 6-8 shows how to use the Hugging Face inference server, you can still use other model-serving frameworks such as vLLM (*https://oreil.ly/LQAzF*) that support streaming model responses.

Before we move on to talking about WebSocket, let's look at consuming another variant of SSE endpoints using the POST method.

SSE with POST Request

The EventSource specification (*https://oreil.ly/61ovi*) expects GET endpoints on the server to correctly consume the incoming SSE stream. This makes implementing real-time applications with SSE straightforward as the EventSource interface can handle issues such as connection drops and automatic reconnection.

However, using HTTP GET requests comes with its own limitations. GET requests are normally less secure than other request methods and more vulnerable to *XSS* attacks.[5] In addition, since GET requests can't have any request body, you can only transfer data as part of the URL's query parameters to the server. The issue is that there is a URL length limit you need to consider and any query parameters must be encoded correctly into the request URL. Therefore, you can't just append the whole conversation history to the URL as a parameter. Your server must handle maintaining the history of the conversation and keeping track of conversational context with GET SSE endpoints.

A common workaround to the aforementioned limitation is to implement a POST SSE endpoint even if the SSE specification doesn't support it. As a result, the implementation will be more complex.

First let's implement the POST endpoint on the server in Example 6-9.

---

5 Attackers use the XSS vulnerability to insert harmful scripts into web pages, which are then executed by other users' browsers.

Example 6-9. Implementing SSE endpoint on the server

```
# main.py

from typing import Annotated
from fastapi import Body, FastAPI
from fastapi.responses import StreamingResponse
from stream import azure_chat_client

@app.post("/generate/text/stream")
async def serve_text_to_text_stream_controller(
    prompt: Annotated[str, Body()]
) -> StreamingResponse:
    return StreamingResponse(
        azure_chat_client.chat_stream(prompt), media_type="text/event-stream"
    )
```

With the POST endpoint for streaming chat outputs implemented, you can now develop the client logic to process the SSE stream.

You will have to manually process the incoming streaming yourself using the browser's fetch web interface, as shown in Example 6-10.

Example 6-10. Implementing SSE on the client using the browser EventSource API

```
{# pages/client-sse-post.html #}

<!DOCTYPE html>
<html lang="en">
<head>
<title>SSE With Post Request</title>
</head>
<body>
<button id="streambtn">Start Streaming</button>
<label for="messageInput">Enter your prompt:</label>
<input type="text" id="messageInput" placeholder="Enter message">
<div style="padding-top: 10px" id="container"></div>

<script>
    const button = document.getElementById('streambtn');
    const container = document.getElementById('container');
    const input = document.getElementById('messageInput');

    function resetForm(){
        input.value = '';
        container.textContent = '';
    }

    async function stream(message){
        const response = await fetch('http://localhost:8000/generate/text/stream', {
            method: "POST",
```

```
            cache: "no-cache",
            keepalive: true,
            headers: {
                "Content-Type": "application/json",
                "Accept": "text/event-stream",
            },
            body: JSON.stringify({
                prompt: message, ❶
            }),
        });

        const reader = response.body.getReader(); ❷
        const decoder = new TextDecoder(); ❸

        while (true) { ❹
            const {value, done} = await reader.read();
            if (done) break;
            container.textContent += decoder.decode(value);
        }
    }

    button.addEventListener('click', async function() { ❺
        resetForm()
        await stream(input.value)

    });

</script>
</body>
</html>
```

❶ Send a POST request to the backend using the browser's fetch interface. Prepare the body as a JSON string as part of the request. Add headers to specify the request body being sent and the response that is expected from the server.

❷ Access the reader of the stream from the response body stream.

❸ Create an instance of a text decoder for processing each message.

❹ Run an infinite loop and read the next message in the stream using the reader. If the stream has ended, done=true, so break the loop; otherwise, decode the message with the text decoder and append to the response container's textContent to render.

❺ Listen on button click events to run a callback that resets the form state and makes the SSE connection with the backend endpoint with a prompt.

As you can see from Example 6-10, consuming the SSE stream without the EventSource can become complex.

An alternative to Example 6-10 is to use GET SSE endpoints but send the large payload to the server beforehand using a POST request. The server stores the data and uses it when the SSE connection is established.

SSE also supports cookies, so you can rely on cookies to exchange large payloads in GET SSE endpoints.

If you want to consume the SSE endpoint in production, your solution should also support retry functionality, error handling, or even the ability to abort connections.

Example 6-11 demonstrates how to implement a client-side retry functionality with an *exponential backoff delay* in JavaScript.[6]

Example 6-11. Implementing client-side retry functionality with exponential backoff

```
// pages/client-sse-post.html within <script> tag

function sleep(ms) {
    return new Promise(resolve => setTimeout(resolve, ms));
}

async function stream(
    message,
    maxRetries = 3,
    initialDelay = 1000,
    backoffFactor = 2,
) {
    let delay = initialDelay;
    for (let attempt = 0; attempt < maxRetries; attempt++) { ❶
        try { ❷
            ... // Establish SSE connection here
            return ❸
        } catch (error) {
            console.warn(`Failed to establish SSE connection: ${error}`);
            console.log(
                `Re-establishing connection - attempt number ${attempt + 1}`,
            );
            if (attempt < maxRetries - 1) {
                await sleep(delay); ❹
                delay *= backoffFactor; ❺
            } else {
                throw error ❻
```

---

6 Exponential backoff reduces the chances of API rate-limiting errors by increasing the delay after each retry.

```
            }
        }
    }
}
```

❶ As long as `maxRetries` isn't reached, attempt to establish the SSE connection. Count each attempt.

❷ Use a `try` and `catch` to handle connection errors.

❸ Exit the function if successful.

❹ Pause in `delay` milliseconds before retrying.

❺ Implement exponential backoff by multiplying a backoff factor to the delay value in each iteration.

❻ Rethrow the `error` if `maxRetries` is reached.

You should now feel more comfortable implementing your own SSE endpoints for streaming model responses. SSE is the go-to communication mechanism that applications like ChatGPT use for real-time conversations with the model. Since SSE predominantly supports text-based streams, it is ideal for LLM output streaming scenarios.

In the next section, we're going to implement the same solution using the WebSocket mechanism so that you can compare differences in the implementation details. In addition, you're going to learn what makes WebSocket ideal for scenarios that require real-time duplex communication such as in live transcription services.

Implementing WS Endpoints

In this section, you're going to implement an endpoint using the WebSocket protocol. With this endpoint, you will stream the LLM outputs to the client using WebSocket to compare with the SSE connection. By the end, you will learn the differences and similarities between SSE and WebSocket in streaming LLM outputs in real time.

Streaming LLM Outputs with WebSocket

FastAPI supports WebSocket through the use of the `WebSocket` interface from the Starlette web framework. As WebSocket connections need to be managed, let's start by implementing a connection manager to keep track of active connections and managing their states.

You can implement a WebSocket connection manager by following Example 6-12.

Example 6-12. Implementing a WebSocket connection manager

```python
# stream.py

from fastapi.websockets import WebSocket

class WSConnectionManager:  ❶
    def __init__(self) -> None:
        self.active_connections: list[WebSocket] = []

    async def connect(self, websocket: WebSocket) -> None:  ❷
        await websocket.accept()
        self.active_connections.append(websocket)

    async def disconnect(self, websocket: WebSocket) -> None:  ❸
        self.active_connections.remove(websocket)
        await websocket.close()

    @staticmethod
    async def receive(websocket: WebSocket) -> str:  ❹
        return await websocket.receive_text()

    @staticmethod
    async def send(
        message: str | bytes | list | dict, websocket: WebSocket
    ) -> None:  ❺
        if isinstance(message, str):
            await websocket.send_text(message)
        elif isinstance(message, bytes):
            await websocket.send_bytes(message)
        else:
            await websocket.send_json(message)


ws_manager = WSConnectionManager()  ❻
```

❶ Create a WSConnectionManager to track and handle active WS connections.

❷ Open a WebSocket connection using the accept() method. Add the new connection to the list of active connections.

❸ When disconnecting, close the connection and remove the websocket instance from the active connections list.

❹ Receive incoming messages as text during an open connection.

❺ Send messages to the client using the relevant send method.

❻ Create a single instance of the WSConnectionManager to reuse across the app.

You can also extend the connection manager in Example 6-12 to *broadcast* messages (e.g., real-time system alerts, notifications, or updates) to all connected clients. This is useful in applications such as group chats or collaborative whiteboard/document editing tools.

As the connection manager maintains a pointer to every client via the `active_connections` list, you can broadcast messages to each client, as shown in Example 6-13.

Example 6-13. Broadcasting messages to connected clients using the WebSocket manager

```
# stream.py

from fastapi.websockets import WebSocket

class WSConnectionManager:
    ...
    async def broadcast(self, message: str | bytes | list | dict) -> None:
        for connection in self.active_connections:
            await self.send(message, connection)
```

With the WebSocket manager implemented, you can now develop a WebSocket endpoint to stream responses to the clients. However, before implementing the endpoint, follow Example 6-14 to update the `chat_stream` method so that it yields the stream content in a suitable format for WebSocket connections.

Example 6-14. Update the chat client streaming method to yield content suitable for WebSocket connections

```
# stream.py

import asyncio
from typing import AsyncGenerator

class AzureOpenAIChatClient:
    def __init__(self):
        self.aclient = ...

    async def chat_stream(
        self, prompt: str, mode: str = "sse", model: str = "gpt-4o"
    ) -> AsyncGenerator[str, None]:
        stream = ...  # OpenAI chat completion stream

        async for chunk in stream:
            if chunk.choices[0].delta.content is not None:  ❶
                yield (
                    f"data: {chunk.choices[0].delta.content}\n\n"
                    if mode == "sse"
                    else chunk.choices[0].delta.content  ❷
```

```
        )
        await asyncio.sleep(0.05)
    if mode == "sse":  ❷
        yield f"data: [DONE]\n\n"
```

❶ Only yield non-empty content.

❷ Yield the stream content based on connection type (SSE or WS).

After updating the `stream_chat` method, you can focus on adding a WebSocket end-point. Use the `@app.websocket` to decorate a controller function that uses the FastAPI's `WebSocket` class, as shown in Example 6-15.

Example 6-15. Implementing a WS endpoint

```
# main.py

import asyncio
from loguru import logger
from fastapi.websockets import WebSocket, WebSocketDisconnect
from stream import ws_manager, azure_chat_client

@app.websocket("/generate/text/streams")  ❶
async def websocket_endpoint(websocket: WebSocket) -> None:
    logger.info("Connecting to client....")
    await ws_manager.connect(websocket)  ❷
    try:  ❸
        while True:  ❹
            prompt = await ws_manager.receive(websocket)  ❺
            async for chunk in azure_chat_client.chat_stream(prompt, "ws"):
                await ws_manager.send(chunk, websocket)  ❻
                await asyncio.sleep(0.05)  ❼
    except WebSocketDisconnect:  ❽
        logger.info("Client disconnected")
    except Exception as e:  ❾
        logger.error(f"Error with the WebSocket connection: {e}")
        await ws_manager.send("An internal server error has occurred")
    finally:
        await ws_manager.disconnect(websocket)  ❿
```

❶ Create a WebSocket endpoint accessible at `ws://localhost:8000/generate/text/stream`.

❷ Open the WebSocket connection between the client and the server.

❸ As long as the connection is open, keep sending or receiving messages.

❹ Handle errors and log important events within the `websocket_controller` to identify root causes of errors and handle unexpected situations gracefully. Break the infinite loop when the connection is closed by the server or the client.

❺ When the first message is received, pass it as a prompt to OpenAI API.

❻ Asynchronously iterate over the generated chat stream and send each chunk to the client.

❼ Wait for a small amount of time before sending the next message to reduce race condition issues and allow the client sufficient time for stream processing.

❽ When the client closes the WebSocket connection, the `WebSocketDisconnect` exception is raised.

❾ If there is a server-side error during an open connection, log the error and identify the client.

❿ Break the infinite loop and gracefully close the WebSocket connection if the stream has finished, there is an internal error, or the client has closed the connection. Remove the connection from the active WebSocket connections list.

Now that you have a WebSocket endpoint, let's develop the client HTML to test the endpoint (see Example 6-16).

Example 6-16. Implement client-side WebSocket connections with error handling and exponential backoff retry functionality

```
{# pages/client-ws.html #}

<!DOCTYPE html>
<html lang="en">
<head>
    <title>Stream with WebSocket</title>
</head>
<body>
<button id="streambtn">Start Streaming</button>
<button id="closebtn">Close Connection</button>
<label for="messageInput">Enter your prompt:</label>
<input type="text" id="messageInput" placeholder="Enter message">
<div style="padding-top: 10px" id="container"></div>

<script>
    const streamButton = document.getElementById('streambtn');
    const closeButton = document.getElementById('closebtn');
    const container = document.getElementById('container');
```

```
const input = document.getElementById('messageInput');

let ws;
let retryCount = 0;
const maxRetries = 5;
let isError = false;

function sleep(ms) {
    return new Promise(resolve => setTimeout(resolve, ms));
}

function connectWebSocket() {
    ws = new WebSocket("ws://localhost:8000/generate/text/streams"); ❶

    ws.onopen = handleOpen;
    ws.onmessage = handleMessage;
    ws.onclose = handleClose;
    ws.onerror = handleError; ❷
}

function handleOpen(){
    console.log("WebSocket connection opened");
    retryCount = 0;
    isError = false;
}

function handleMessage(event) {
    container.textContent += event.data;
}

async function handleClose(){ ❸
    console.log("WebSocket connection closed");
    if (isError && retryCount < maxRetries) {
        console.warn("Retrying connection...");
        await sleep(Math.pow(2, retryCount) * 1000);
        retryCount++;
        connectWebSocket();
    }
    else if (isError) {
        console.error("Max retries reached. Could not reconnect.");
    }
}

function handleError(error) {
    console.error("WebSocket error:", error);
    isError = true;
    ws.close();
}

function resetForm(){
    input.value = '';
    container.textContent = '';
```

```
    }

    streamButton.addEventListener('click', function() { ❹
        const prompt = document.getElementById("messageInput").value;
        if (prompt && ws && ws.readyState === WebSocket.OPEN) {
            ws.send(prompt); ❺
        }
        resetForm(); ❻
    });

    closeButton.addEventListener('click', function() { ❼
        isError = false;
        if (ws) {
            ws.close();
        }
    });

    connectWebSocket(); ❶
</script>
</body>
</html>
```

❶ Establish a WebSocket connection with the FastAPI server.

❷ Add callback handlers to the WebSocket connection instance to handle opening, closing, message, and error events.

❸ Gracefully handle connection errors and re-establish the connection with an exponential backoff retry functionality using an `isError` flag.

❹ Add an event listener to the streaming button to send the first message to the server.

❺ Once the connection is established, send the initial non-empty prompt as the first message to the server.

❻ Reset the form to before establishing the WebSocket connection to start.

❼ Add an event listener to the close connection button to close the connection when the button is clicked.

Now you can visit *http://localhost:8000/pages/client-ws.html* to test your WebSocket streaming endpoint (see Figure 6-9).

Figure 6-9. Incoming stream from the WebSocket endpoint

You should now have a fully working LLM streaming application with WebSocket. Well done!

You now may be wondering which solution is better: streaming with SSE or WS connections. The answer depends on your application requirements. SSE is simple to implement and is native to HTTP protocol, so most clients support it. If all you need is one-way streaming to the client, then I suggest implementing SSE connections for streaming LLM outputs.

WebSocket connections provide more control to your streaming mechanism and allow for duplex communication within the same connection—for instance, in real-time chat applications with multiple users and the LLM, speech-to-text, text-to-speech, and speech-to-speech services. However, using WebSocket requires upgrading the connection from HTTP to the WebSocket protocol, which legacy clients and older browsers may not support. In addition, you will need to handle exceptions slightly differently with WebSocket endpoints.

Handling WebSocket Exceptions

Handling WebSocket exceptions differs from traditional HTTP connections. If you refer to Example 6-15, you will notice that you're no longer returning a response with status codes, or HTTPExceptions, to the client but rather maintaining an open connection after connection acceptance.

As long as the connection is open, you're sending and receiving messages. However, as soon as an exception has occurred, you should handle it either by gracefully closing the connection and/or by sending an error message to the client in replacement of an HTTPException response.

Since the WebSocket protocol doesn't support the usual HTTP status codes (4xx or 5xx), you can't use status codes to notify the clients of server-side issues. Instead, you should send WebSocket messages to clients to notify them of issues before you close any active connections from the server.

During the connection closure, you can use several WebSocket-related status codes to specify the closure reason. Using these closure reasons, you can implement any custom closure behavior on the server or the clients.

Table 6-2 shows a few common status codes that can be sent with a CLOSE frame.

Table 6-2. WebSocket protocol common status codes

Status code	Description
1000	Normal closure
1001	Client navigated away or server has gone down
1002	An endpoint (i.e., client or server) received data violating the WS protocol (e.g., unmasked packets, invalid payload length)
1003	An endpoint received unsupported data (e.g., was expecting text, got binary)
1007	An endpoint received inconsistently encoded data (e.g., non-UTF-8 data within a text message)
1008	An endpoint received a message that violates its policy; can be used to hide closure details for security reasons
1011	Internal server error

You can learn more about other WebSocket status codes in the WebSocket protocol RFC 6455—Section 7.4 (*https://oreil.ly/1L_HH*).

Designing APIs for Streaming

Now that you're more familiar with both SSE and WebSocket endpoint implementations, I want to cover one last important detail around their architectural design.

A common pitfall of designing streaming APIs is exposing an excessive number of streaming endpoints. For instance, if you're building a chatbot application, you may expose several streaming endpoints, each preconfigured to handle different incoming messages in a single conversation. By using this particular API design pattern, you're asking the client to switch between endpoints, providing the necessary information in each step while navigating the streaming connections during a single conversation. This design pattern adds to the complexity of both the backend and frontend applications since the conversation states need to be managed on both sides while avoiding race condition and networking issues between components.

A simpler API design pattern is to provide a single entry point for the client to initiate a stream with your GenAI model(s) and use headers, request body, or query parameters to trigger the relevant logic in the backend. With this design, the backend logic is abstracted away from the client, which simplifies state management on the frontend while all routing and business logic are implemented on the backend. Since the backend has access to databases, other services, and customized prompts, it can easily perform CRUD operations and switch between prompts or models to compute a response. Therefore, one endpoint can act as a single entry point for switching logic, manage application states, and generate custom responses.

Summary

This chapter covered several different strategies for implementing real-time communication via data streaming in your GenAI services.

You learned about several web communication mechanisms including the traditional HTTP request-response model, short/regular polling, long polling, SSE, and WebSocket. You then compared these mechanisms in detail to understand their features, benefits, disadvantages, and use cases, in particular for AI workflows. Finally, you implemented two LLM streaming endpoints using the asynchronous Azure OpenAI client to learn how to leverage SSE and WebSocket real-time communication mechanisms.

In the next chapter, you will learn more about API development workflows when integrating databases for AI services. This will include how to set up, migrate, and interact with databases. You'll also learn how to handle data storage-and-retrieval operations within streaming endpoints by using FastAPI's background tasks.

Topics covered in the next chapter will include setting up databases and designing schemas, working with the SQLAlchemy, database migrations, and handling database operations when streaming model outputs.

## CHAPTER 7

Integrating Databases into AI Services

Chapter Goals

In this chapter, you will learn about:

- When a database is necessary and how to identify the appropriate database type for your project

- The underlying mechanism of relational databases and the use cases of nonrelational databases

- The development workflow, tooling, and best practices for working with relational databases

- The techniques to improve query performance and efficiency when working with databases

- How to manage ever-evolving database schema changes

- Strategies for managing the codebase, the database schema, and data drifts when working in teams

In this chapter, you'll integrate a database to your current API service to store and retrieve user interactions.

This chapter assumes basic experience working with databases and Structured Query Language (SQL), so it won't cover every aspect of SQL programming and database workflows. Instead, you will learn the higher-level database concepts, development workflows, and best practices when integrating databases to your FastAPI applications that interact with GenAI models such as LLMs.

As part of this, you will learn the role of relational (SQL) versus nonrelational (noSQL) databases in application development and will be able to confidently select the right database for your use case. Next, you will understand more about the features of relational databases and associated tooling such as object relational mappers (ORMs) and database migration tools. Finally, as a hands-on exercise, you will integrate a database to your existing application using SQLAlchemy and Alembic, to store and retrieve user conversations with an LLM.

By the end of this chapter, you will feel more confident in selecting, configuring, and resolving database-related issues within your GenAI applications.

The Role of a Database

When building backend services, you often require a database to persist application state and store user data. In other cases, your application won't need a database, and you shouldn't try to add one since any database integration can significantly increase the complexity of your services.

Here are several cases for which you could forgo using a database:

1. Your application can start from a fresh state on startup for each new user session.
2. Recalculating the application data is straightforward and resource-efficient.
3. The application data is small enough to be stored in memory.
4. Your application is tolerant to data losses due to various reasons such as server errors, restarts, or other unexpected events.
5. Different user sessions or application instances won't need to share data.
6. The data you need can directly be fetched from external systems, GenAI models, and other application APIs, and not your own database.
7. The user is happy to wait for data to be recomputed for each new session or action.
8. Your service requirements allow for the data to be persisted in files on disk, the browser storage, or an external cloud storage instead of a database. With these alternatives, your services can tolerate that data storage and retrieval won't be as reliable and efficient as a database.
9. You're building a proof-of-concept and need to avoid project delays or complexity at all costs.

An example application that matches the previous criteria is a *GenAI image generator* only used for demonstration purposes.

In this example, you won't need to store any generated images, and you can always restart or use the application at any time from a fresh state. Additionally, the application doesn't need to know who the user is. Plus, there is no need to share data between sessions. Furthermore, if there is a server error, the impact of data loss is minimal since you can regenerate a new image on the fly.

As you can see, there are at least a handful of cases where you won't need a database to build your own GenAI services. However, you may be wondering when you do really need a database.

To determine when a database is necessary, you will want to understand the role of databases. In short, you can use them to store, organize, and manage data in an efficient format allowing for easy retrieval, manipulation, and analysis. Additionally, databases ship with critical features such as restore/backup, concurrent access management, indexing, caching, and role-based access control, alongside many others, that make them an irreplaceable component of any services that displays, produces and consumes data.

In the next section, we will examine in significant detail the inner workings of databases, with an emphasis on relational databases that practical examples of this chapter will focus on. With a detailed understanding of database internals, you can then design fully optimized and production-ready GenAI APIs. This will then allow you to delegate heavy workloads to the database engine, which is specifically designed for data-heavy tasks.

Database Systems

Now that you understand when to leverage a database, let's learn more about different databases you can use and how they work.

You can construct a mental model of databases by placing them into two main categories: *relational* (SQL) and *nonrelational* (NoSQL) databases.

The *SQL* versus *NoSQL* categorization is based on the fact that relational databases use various dialects of SQL as their main query language, whereas nonrelational databases often come packaged with their own specialized query languages.

With both categories of database systems, you can adopt a mental model of how such systems are structured. Both SQL and NoSQL database systems often consist of the following:

- A *server* at the highest level, which hosts the entire database infrastructure and consumes system resources (CPU, RAM, and storage).

- One or more *databases* within the server, which act as *logical container(s)* that hold related data.

- One or more *schemas* within a database (depending on the database software), which serve as a *blueprint* that defines the complete structure of the data and various structural objects such as indexes, logical constraints, triggers, etc. However, NoSQL database servers may not use strict schemas, unlike relational databases.

- Zero or more *tables* (SQL) or *collections* (NoSQL) created inside the database (as part of a schema), which group related data.

- Zero or more *items* within each collection (as documents) or table (as rows), which represent specific records or entities.

Figure 7-1 visualizes the aforementioned breakdown.

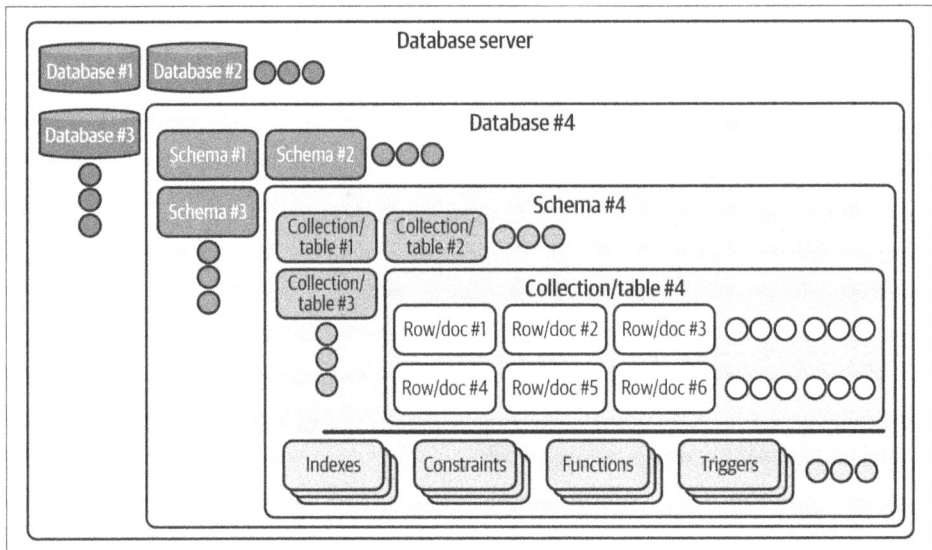

Figure 7-1. Database system breakdown

Adopting a mental model as shown in Figure 7-1 will help you navigate the ever-increasing variety of database systems as you can expect similar underlying mechanisms to be present. This familiarity will hopefully reduce your learning curve in adopting different database systems.

Next, let's briefly review both SQL and NoSQL database systems so that you have a better understanding of their use cases, features, and limitations when building APIs and services.

To help you with creating a mental model of both relational and nonrelational databases, take a look at Figure 7-2.

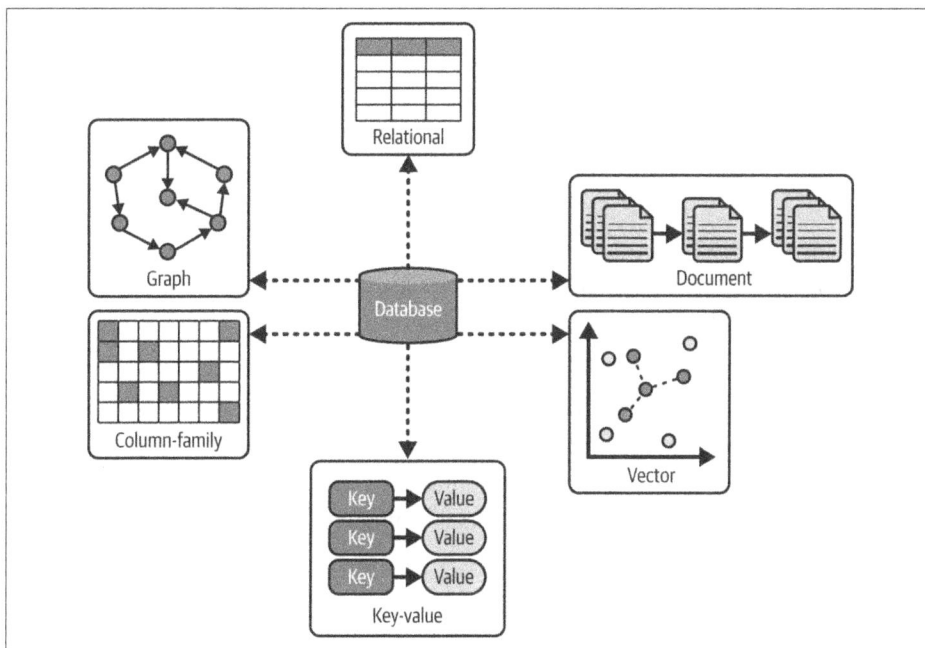

Figure 7-2. Database types

You can also use the summary in Table 7-1 as a reference of the database types that will be covered in this chapter.

Table 7-1. Comparison of databases

Type	Data model	Examples	Use cases
Key-value stores	Key-value pairs	Redis, DynamoDB, Memcached	Caching, session management
Graph stores	Nodes and edges	Neo4j, Amazon Neptune, ArangoDB	Social networks, recommendation engines, fraud detection
Document stores	Documents	MongoDB, CouchDB, Amazon DocumentDB	Content management, e-commerce, real-time analytics
Vector stores	High-dimensional vectors	Pinecone, Weaviate	Recommendation systems, image/text search, ML model storage
Wide-column family stores	Tables with rows and columns	Apache Cassandra, HBase, ScyllaDB	Time-series data, real-time analytics, logging

Now that you have a broad overview of every common relational and nonrelational database, you can visualize a real-world GenAI service that makes use of these databases together.

Imagine you're building a RAG-enabled LLM service that can talk to a knowledge base. The documents in this knowledge base are related to each other, so you decide to implement a RAG graph to capture a richer context. To implement a RAG graph, you integrate your service with a graph-based database.

Now, to retrieve relevant chunks of documents, you also need to embed them in a vector database. As part of this, you also need a relational database to monitor usage, and store user data and conversation histories.

Since the users may ask common questions, you also decide to cache the LLM responses by generating several outputs in advance. Therefore, you also integrate a key-value store to your service.

Finally, you want to give administrators control over system prompts with the ability to version-control prompts. So, you add a content management system as a prompt manager to your solution. However, since the prompt templates can often change, you also decide to integrate a document database.

As you can see, each database type ends up solving a particular problem in your complex RAG-enabled application. One stores your backend and user data, another captures the document relationships, one stores your document embeddings, another helps store flexible schemas of your prompts, and the last one helps you to return cached outputs.

You can see a visualization of the application architecture in Figure 7-3 to understand how these databases can work together to realize a solution.

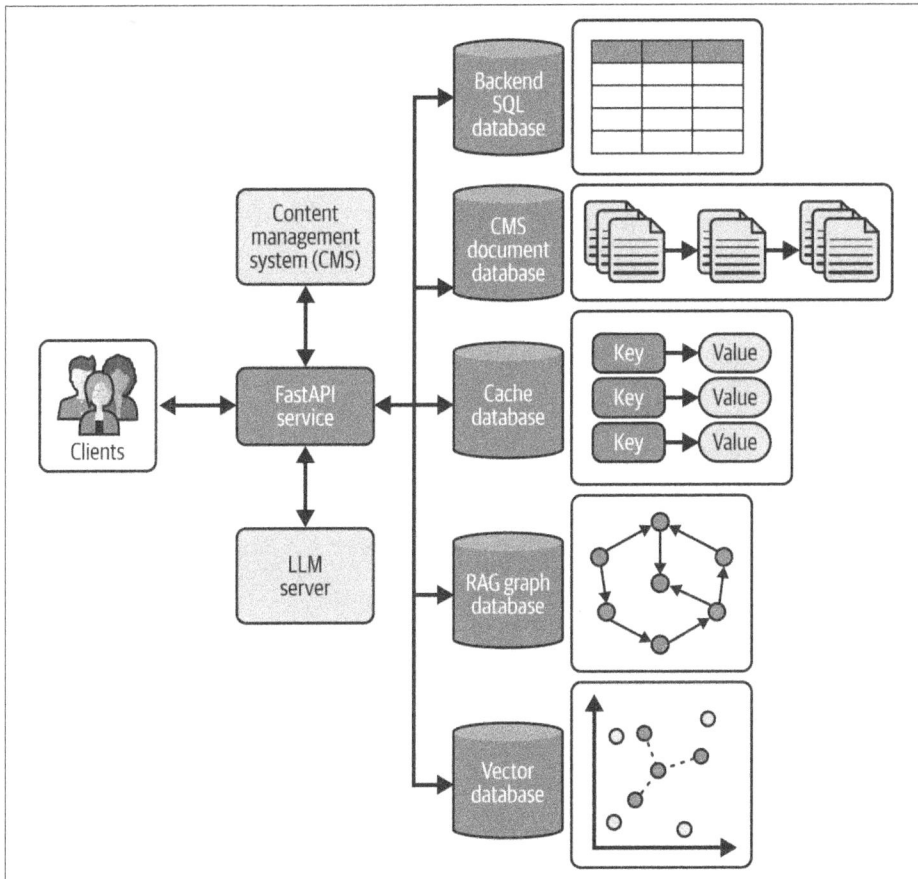

Figure 7-3. Using various database types together

Now that you understand how your GenAI services can integrate with a variety of databases, in the next section, we will focus on adding a relational database to your service.

Project: Storing User Conversations with an LLM in a Relational Database

In the previous section, we covered the core database concepts relevant to adding data persistence to your applications.

In this section, you will integrate a relational database to your GenAI service so that you can store user conversation histories with an LLM in the database. As part of this work, you will also learn the best practices, tooling, and development workflow to manage schema changes and data migrations in your database.

For this project, we will install a Postgres relational database that is open source, free, and battle-tested and is in use by many enterprises. To get started, let's download and run the Postgres container using docker run, as shown in Example 7-1.

Example 7-1. Download and run the Postgres database container

```
$ docker run -p 5432:5432  \  ❶ ❷
        -e POSTGRES_USER=fastapi \
        -e POSTGRES_PASSWORD=mysecretpassword \
        -e POSTGRES_DB=backend_db \
        -e PGDATA=/var/lib/postgresql/data \ ❸
    -v "$(pwd)"/dbstorage:/var/lib/postgresql/data \ ❹
    postgres:latest ❶
```

❶ Download and run the latest postgres relational database image from in the Docker registry.

❷ Run the postgres image and then expose and map container port 5432 to the same ports on the host machine.

❸ Run the container with several environmental variables that specify the default database administrator username and password, database name, and DBMS data location within the container.

❹ Mount the Postgres database storage to the host machine filesystem at a dbstor age folder in the present working directory.

Next, let's install the sqlalchemy, alembic, and psycopg3 packages:

```
$ pip install alembic sqlalchemy psycopg3
```

These battle-tested packages allow you to directly communicate with the Postgres relational database via Python. psycopg3 is a popular PostgreSQL database adapter for Python, and SQLAlchemy is SQL toolkit and ORM that allows you to run SQL queries against your database in Python.

Object Relational Mappers

An ORM library allows you to interact with a database and execute SQL operations without then need to write raw SQL yourself.

The SQLAlchemy package uses the ORM technique to map database tables to object-oriented classes in code. Tables are mapped to classes, columns to class attributes, and rows as class instances. So, as an example, instead of writing SELECT * FROM users WHERE id = 1, you can use session.query(User).filter(User.id == 1).first() to fetch a user based on their ID.

You can see the pros and cons of ORMs in Table 7-2.

Table 7-2. Pros and cons of ORMs

Pros	Cons
Abstract database interactions	Trade flexibility for development experience
Speed up development workflow	Learning curve
Improve code maintainability	Potential performance issues with complex queries compared to writing raw SQL
Various libraries available (e.g., SQLAlchemy, SQLModel, TortoiseORM, DjangoORM)	Debugging can be challenging

In most cases, the benefits may outweigh the drawbacks, so learning to work with an ORM is an invaluable skill in building your own GenAI services that interact with relational databases.

Lastly, the `alembic` package is a *database migration tool* created by the SQLAlchemy developers for usage with the SQLAlchemy. The data migration workflow is like the Git version control system but for your database schemas. It allows you to manage the changes and updates to your schemas so that you avoid any data corruptions, track changes over time, and revert any changes as required.

Defining ORM Models

The first step to query your database in Python is to define your ORM models with SQLAlchemy classes, as shown in Example 7-2. You can use the data schemas from the ERD diagram mentioned in Figure 8-4.

> You will add the `user` table in the next chapter when implementing authentication and authorization mechanisms.

Example 7-2. Defining database ORM models

```
# entities.py

from datetime import UTC, datetime
from sqlalchemy import ForeignKey
from sqlalchemy.orm import DeclarativeBase, Mapped, mapped_column, relationship

class Base(DeclarativeBase):  ❶
    pass

class Conversation(Base):  ❷
```

```
    __tablename__ = "conversations"

    id: Mapped[int] = mapped_column(primary_key=True)
    title: Mapped[str] = mapped_column() ❸
    model_type: Mapped[str] = mapped_column(index=True) ❹
    created_at: Mapped[datetime] = mapped_column(default=datetime.now(UTC))
    updated_at: Mapped[datetime] = mapped_column(
        default=datetime.now(UTC), onupdate=datetime.now(UTC) ❺
    )

    messages: Mapped[list["Message"]] = relationship(
        "Message", back_populates="conversation", cascade="all, delete-orphan" ❻
    )


class Message(Base): ❼
    __tablename__ = "messages"

    id: Mapped[int] = mapped_column(primary_key=True)
    conversation_id: Mapped[int] = mapped_column(
        ForeignKey("conversations.id", ondelete="CASCADE"), index=True ❻
    )
    prompt_content: Mapped[str] = mapped_column()
    response_content: Mapped[str] = mapped_column()
    prompt_tokens: Mapped[int | None] = mapped_column()
    response_tokens: Mapped[int | None] = mapped_column()
    total_tokens: Mapped[int | None] = mapped_column()
    is_success: Mapped[bool | None] = mapped_column()
    status_code: Mapped[int | None] = mapped_column() ❽ ❾
    created_at: Mapped[datetime] = mapped_column(default=datetime.now(UTC))
    updated_at: Mapped[datetime] = mapped_column(
        default=datetime.now(UTC), onupdate=datetime.now(UTC)
    )

    conversation: Mapped["Conversation"] = relationship(
        "Conversation", back_populates="messages"
    )
```

❶ Declare a declarative base class for creating SQLAlchemy models for its ORM engine.

❷ Create the Conversation model specifying the table columns, primary key, and secondary indexes.

❸ Use the mapped_column() to derive the column type from the type hint given to Mapped.

❹ Index the model_type in case you want faster filtering of conversations by model type.

❺ Specify defaults and update operations for datetime columns.

❻ Indicate that all orphan messages must be deleted if a conversation is deleted through a `CASCADE DELETE` operation.

❼ Create the `Message` model specifying the table columns, primary key, secondary indexes, table relationships, and foreign keys.

❽ The `messages` table will contain both the LLM prompts and responses, usage tokens, and costs alongside the status codes and success states.

❾ Specify `Mapped[int | None]` to declare an optional typing so the column will allow `NULL` values (i.e., `nullable=True`).

Once you have your data models defined, you can create a connection to the database to create each table with the specified configurations. To achieve this, you will need to create a *database engine* and implement *session management*.

Creating a Database Engine and Session Management

Example 7-3 shows how to create a SQLAlchemy engine using your Postgres database connection string. Once created, you can use the engine and the `Base` class to create tables for each of your data models.

> The SQLAlchemy's `create_all()` method in Example 7-3 can only create tables in the database but not modify existing tables. This workflow is useful only if you're prototyping and happy to reset the database schemas with new tables on each run.
>
> For production environments, you should use a database migration tool such as `alembic` to update your database schemas and to avoid unintended data loss. You will learn about the database migration workflow shortly.

Example 7-3. Create the SQLAlchemy database engine

```
# database.py

from sqlalchemy.ext.asyncio import create_async_engine
from entities import Base

database_url = ( ❶
    "postgresql+psycopg://fastapi:mysecretpassword@localhost:5432/backend_db"
)
engine = create_async_engine(database_url, echo=True) ❷
```

```
async def init_db() -> None:
    async with engine.begin() as conn:
        await conn.run_sync(Base.metadata.drop_all)
        await conn.run_sync(Base.metadata.create_all) ❸

# main.py

from contextlib import asynccontextmanager
from fastapi import FastAPI
from database import engine, init_db

@asynccontextmanager
async def lifespan(_: FastAPI):
    await init_db()
    # other startup operations within the lifespan
    ...
    yield
    await engine.dispose() ❹

app = FastAPI(lifespan=lifespan)
```

❶ For Postgres databases, the connection string is defined using the following template: *<driver>://<username>:<password>@<origin>/<database>*.

❷ Create an async database engine using the database connection string. Turn on debug logging with echo=True.

❸ Drop any existing tables and then create all database tables using the defined SQLAlchemy models in Example 7-3.

❹ Dispose of the database engine during the server shutdown process. Any code after the yield keyword inside the FastAPI's lifespan context manager is executed when server shutdown is requested.

> For clarity, environment variables and secrets such as database connection strings are hard-coded in every code example.
>
> In production scenarios, never hard-code secrets and environment variables. Leverage environment files, secret managers, and tools like Pydantic Settings to handle application secrets and variables.

With the engine created, you can now implement a factory function for creating sessions to the database. Session factory is a design pattern that allows you to open, interact with, and close database connections across your services.

Since you may reuse a session, you can use FastAPI's dependency injection system to cache and reuse sessions across each request runtime, as shown in Example 7-4.

Example 7-4. Creating a database session FastAPI dependency

```python
# database.py

from typing import Annotated
from fastapi import Depends
from sqlalchemy.ext.asyncio import AsyncSession, async_sessionmaker
from database import engine

async_session = async_sessionmaker(
    bind=engine, class_=AsyncSession, autocommit=False, autoflush=False ❶
)
async def get_db_session(): ❷
    try:
        async with async_session() as session: ❸
            yield session ❹
    except:
        await session.rollback() ❺
        raise
    finally:
        await session.close() ❻

DBSessionDep = Annotated[AsyncSession, Depends(get_db_session)] ❼
```

❶ Create an async database session factory bound to the database engine you created previously to asynchronously connect to your Postgres instance. Disable automatic committing of transactions with `autocommit=false` and automatic flushing of changes to the database with `autoflush=False`. Disabling both behaviors gives you more control, helps prevent unintended data updates, and allows you to implement more robust transaction management.

❷ Define a dependency function to reuse and inject across your FastAPI app into route controller functions. Since the function uses the `yield` keyword within the `async with`, it is considered an async context manager. FastAPI will internally decorate the `get_db_session` as context manager when it is used as a dependency.

❸ Use the database session factory to create an async session. The context manager helps to manage the database session lifecycle such as opening, interacting with, and closing the database connections in each session.

❹ Yield the database session to the caller of the `get_db_session` function.

❺ If there are any exceptions, roll back the transaction and reraise the exception.

❻ In any case, close the database session at the end to release any resources that it holds.

❼ Declare an annotated database session dependency that can be reused across different controllers.

Now that you can create a database session from any FastAPI route via dependency injection, let's implement the create, read, update, and delete (CRUD) endpoints for the conversations resource.

Implementing CRUD Endpoints

As FastAPI relies on Pydantic to serialize and validate incoming and outgoing data, before implementing CRUD endpoints, you'll need to map database entities to Pydantic models. This avoids tightly coupling your API schema with your database models to give you the freedom and flexibility in developing your API and databases independent of each other.

You can follow Example 7-5 to define your CRUD schemas.

Example 7-5. Declaring Pydantic API schemas for conversation endpoints

```python
# schemas.py

from datetime import datetime
from pydantic import BaseModel, ConfigDict

class ConversationBase(BaseModel):
    model_config = ConfigDict(from_attributes=True)  ❶

    title: str
    model_type: str

class ConversationCreate(ConversationBase):  ❷
    pass

class ConversationUpdate(ConversationBase):  ❷
    pass

class ConversationOut(ConversationBase):  ❷
    id: int
    created_at: datetime
    updated_at: datetime
```

❶ Set up the Pydantic model to read and validate attributes of other models like SQLAlchemy, which is often used in Pydantic when working with database models.

❷ Create separate Pydantic models based on the base model for different use cases such as conversation record creation and update, or data retrieval.

Having to declare Pydantic and SQLAlchemy models may feel like code duplication but will allow you to implement your data access layer however you like.

Alternatively, if you want to avoid any code duplication, you can leverage the `sqlmodel` package, which integrates Pydantic with SQLAlchemy, removing much of the code duplication. However, bear in mind that `sqlmodel` may not be ideal for production due to limited flexibility and support for advanced use cases with SQL-Alchemy. Therefore, you may want to use separate Pydantic and SQLAlchemy models for complex applications.[1]

Now that you have the SQLAlchemy and Pydantic models, you can start developing your CRUD API endpoints.

When implementing CRUD endpoints, you should try to leverage FastAPI dependencies as much as you can to reduce database round-trips. For instance, when retrieving, updating, and deleting records, you need to check in with the database that a record exists using its ID.

You can implement a record retrieval function to use a dependency across your get, update, and delete endpoints, as shown in Example 7-6.

Bear in mind that FastAPI can only cache the output of the `get_conversation` dependency within a single request and not across multiple requests.

Example 7-6. Implementing resource-based CRUD endpoints for the `conversations` table

```
# main.py

from typing import Annotated
from database import DBSessionDep
from entities import Conversation
from fastapi import Depends, FastAPI, HTTPException, status
from schemas import ConversationCreate, ConversationOut, ConversationUpdate
from sqlalchemy import select

...

async def get_conversation(
    conversation_id: int, session: DBSessionDep  ❶
```

---

1 Refer to this reddit discussion thread (*https://oreil.ly/OMaOT*).

```
) -> Conversation:
    async with session.begin(): ❷
        result = await session.execute(
            select(Conversation).where(Conversation.id == conversation_id)
        )
        conversation = result.scalars().first()
    if not conversation:
        raise HTTPException(
            status_code=status.HTTP_404_NOT_FOUND,
            detail="Conversation not found",
        )
    return conversation

GetConversationDep = Annotated[Conversation, Depends(get_conversation)]

@app.get("/conversations")
async def list_conversations_controller(
    session: DBSessionDep, skip: int = 0, take: int = 100
) -> list[ConversationOut]:
    async with session.begin():
        result = await session.execute(
            select(Conversation).offset(skip).limit(take) ❸
        )
    return [
        ConversationOut.model_validate(conversation)
        for conversation in result.scalars().all()
    ]

@app.get("/conversations/{id}")
async def get_conversation_controller(
    conversation: GetConversationDep,
) -> ConversationOut:
    return ConversationOut.model_validate(conversation) ❹

@app.post("/conversations", status_code=status.HTTP_201_CREATED)
async def create_conversation_controller(
    conversation: ConversationCreate, session: DBSessionDep
) -> ConversationOut:
    new_conversation = Conversation(**conversation.model_dump())
    async with session.begin():
        session.add(new_conversation)
        await session.commit() ❺
        await session.refresh(new_conversation)
    return ConversationOut.model_validate(new_conversation)

@app.put("/conversations/{id}", status_code=status.HTTP_202_ACCEPTED)
async def update_conversation_controller(
    updated_conversation: ConversationUpdate,
    conversation: GetConversationDep,
    session: DBSessionDep,
) -> ConversationOut:
    for key, value in updated_conversation.model_dump().items():
```

```
            setattr(conversation, key, value)
    async with session.begin():
        await session.commit()  ❺
        await session.refresh(conversation)
    return ConversationOut.model_validate(conversation)

@app.delete("/conversations/{id}", status_code=status.HTTP_204_NO_CONTENT)
async def delete_conversation_controller(
    conversation: GetConversationDep, session: DBSessionDep
) -> None:
    async with session.begin():
        await session.delete(conversation)
        await session.commit()  ❺
```

❶ Define a dependency to check if the conversation record exists. Raise a 404 HTTPException if a record is not found; otherwise, return the retrieved record. This dependency can be reused across several CRUD endpoints through dependency injection.

❷ Begin the async session within an async context manager during each request.

❸ When listing records, it's more efficient to retrieve only a subset of records. By default, SQLAlchemy ORM returns a subset of most recent records in the database, but you can use the .offset(skip) and .limit(take) chained methods to retrieve any subset of records.

❹ Create a Pydantic model from a SQLAlchemy model using model_validate(). Raises a ValidationError if the SQLAlchemy object passed can't be created or doesn't pass Pydantic's data validation checks.

❺ For operations that mutate a record (i.e., create, update, and delete), commit the transaction then send the refreshed record to the client, except for the successful delete operation that should return None.

Notice how the controller logic is simplified through this dependency injection approach.

Additionally, pay attention to success status codes you should to send to the client. Successful retrieval operations should return 200, while record creation operations return 201, updates return 202, and deletions return 204.

Congratulations! You now have a resource-based RESTful API that you can use to perform CRUD operations on your conversations table.

Now that you can implement CRUD endpoints, let's refactor the existing code examples to use the *repository and services* design pattern you learned about in Chapter 2.

With this design pattern, you can abstract the database operations to achieve a more modular, maintainable, and testable codebase.

Repository and Services Design Pattern

A *repository* is a design pattern that mediates the business logic of your application and the database access layer—for instance, via an ORM. It contains several methods for performing CRUD operations in the database layer.

In Chapter 2, you first saw Figure 7-4, which showed where the repositories sit within the onion/layered application architecture when working with a database.

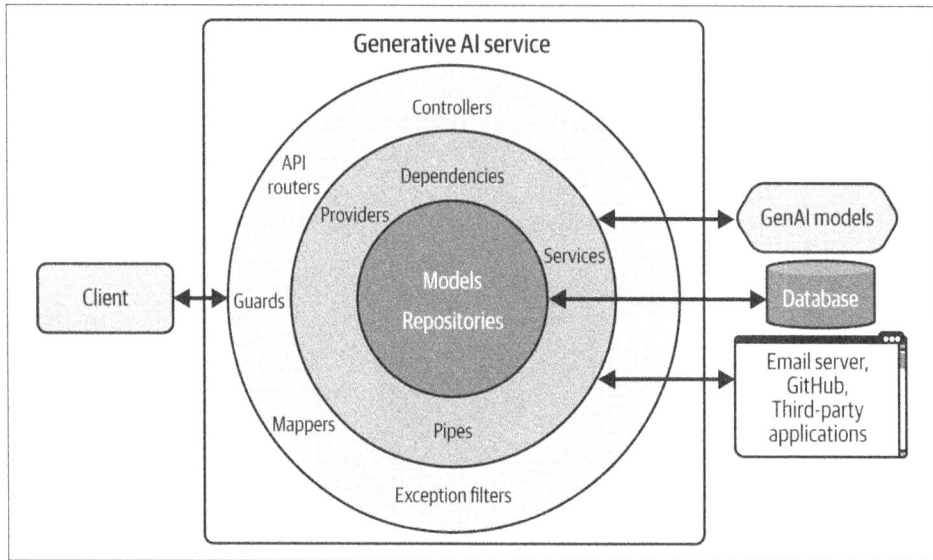

Figure 7-4. The repository pattern within the onion/layered application architecture

To implement a repository pattern, you can use an *abstract interface*, which enforces certain constraints on how you define your specific repository classes as you can see in Example 7-7.

> If you've never used *abstract* classes, they're classes that can't be instantiated on their own. Abstract classes can contain methods without implementation that its subclasses must implement.
>
> A concrete class is one that inherits an abstract class and implements each of its abstract methods.

Example 7-7. Implementing a repository abstract interface

```python
# repositories/interfaces.py

from abc import ABC, abstractmethod
from typing import Any

class Repository(ABC):  ❶
    @abstractmethod
    async def list(self) -> list[Any]:
        pass

    @abstractmethod
    async def get(self, uid: int) -> Any:
        pass

    @abstractmethod
    async def create(self, record: Any) -> Any:
        pass

    @abstractmethod
    async def update(self, uid: int, record: Any) -> Any:
        pass

    @abstractmethod
    async def delete(self, uid: int) -> None:
        pass
```

❶ Define the abstract `Repository` interface with several CRUD-related abstract method signatures that subclasses must implement. If an abstract method is not implemented in a concrete subclass, a `NotImplementedError` will be raised.

Now that you have a `Repository` class, you declare subclasses for each of your tables to define how database operations must be performed following the CRUD-based methods. For instance, to perform CRUD operations on the conversation records in the database, you can implement a concrete `ConversationRepository` class, as shown in Example 7-8.

Example 7-8. Implementing the conversation repository using the abstract repository interface

```python
# repositories/conversations.py

from entities import Conversation
from repositories.interfaces import Repository
from schemas import ConversationCreate, ConversationUpdate
from sqlalchemy import select
from sqlalchemy.ext.asyncio import AsyncSession
```

```
class ConversationRepository(Repository):  ❶
    def __init__(self, session: AsyncSession) -> None:
        self.session = session

    async def list(self, skip: int, take: int) -> list[Conversation]:
        async with self.session.begin():
            result = await self.session.execute(
                select(Conversation).offset(skip).limit(take)
            )
        return [r for r in result.scalars().all()]

    async def get(self, conversation_id: int) -> Conversation | None:
        async with self.session.begin():
            result = await self.session.execute(
                select(Conversation).where(Conversation.id == conversation_id)
            )
        return result.scalars().first()

    async def create(self, conversation: ConversationCreate) -> Conversation:
        new_conversation = Conversation(**conversation.model_dump())
        async with self.session.begin():
            self.session.add(new_conversation)
            await self.session.commit()
            await self.session.refresh(new_conversation)
        return new_conversation

    async def update(
        self, conversation_id: int, updated_conversation: ConversationUpdate
    ) -> Conversation | None:
        conversation = await self.get(conversation_id)
        if not conversation:
            return None
        for key, value in updated_conversation.model_dump().items():
            setattr(conversation, key, value)
        async with self.session.begin():
            await self.session.commit()
            await self.session.refresh(conversation)
        return conversation

    async def delete(self, conversation_id: int) -> None:
        conversation = await self.get(conversation_id)
        if not conversation:
            return
        async with self.session.begin():
            await self.session.delete(conversation)
            await self.session.commit()
```

❶ Inherit the abstract Repository interface and implement each of its methods while adhering to the method signatures.

You have now moved the database logic for conversations into the ConversationRepository. This means you can now import this class into your route controller functions and start using it right away.

Go back to your main.py file and refactor your route controllers to use the ConversationRepository, as shown in Example 7-9.

Example 7-9. Refactoring the conversation CRUD endpoints to use the repository pattern

```
# routers/conversations.py

from typing import Annotated
from fastapi import APIRouter, Depends, FastAPI, HTTPException, status
...  # Other imports
from repositories import ConversationRepository

...  # Other controllers and dependency implementations

router = APIRouter(prefix="/conversations")  ❶

async def get_conversation(
    conversation_id: int, session: SessionDep
) -> Conversation:
    conversation = await ConversationRepository(session).get(conversation_id)  ❷
    if not conversation:
        raise HTTPException(
            status_code=status.HTTP_404_NOT_FOUND,
            detail="Conversation not found",
        )
    return conversation

GetConversationDep = Annotated[Conversation, Depends(get_conversation)]

@router.get("")
async def list_conversations_controller(
    session: SessionDep, skip: int = 0, take: int = 100
) -> list[ConversationOut]:
    conversations = await ConversationRepository(session).list(skip, take)
    return [ConversationOut.model_validate(c) for c in conversations]


@router.get("/{id}")
async def get_conversation_controller(
    conversation: GetConversationDep,
) -> ConversationOut:
    return ConversationOut.model_validate(conversation)  ❷


@router.post("", status_code=status.HTTP_201_CREATED)
async def create_conversation_controller(
```

```
    conversation: ConversationCreate, session: SessionDep
) -> ConversationOut:
    new_conversation = await ConversationRepository(session).create(
        conversation
    ) ❷
    return ConversationOut.model_validate(new_conversation)


@router.put("/{id}", status_code=status.HTTP_202_ACCEPTED)
async def update_conversation_controller(
    conversation: GetConversationDep,
    updated_conversation: ConversationUpdate,
    session: SessionDep,
) -> ConversationOut:
    updated_conversation = await ConversationRepository(session).update( ❷
        conversation.id, updated_conversation
    )
    return ConversationOut.model_validate(updated_conversation)


@router.delete("/{id}", status_code=status.HTTP_204_NO_CONTENT)
async def delete_conversation_controller(
    conversation: GetConversationDep, session: SessionDep
) -> None:
    await ConversationRepository(session).delete(conversation.id)


# main.py

from routers.conversations import router as conversations_router

app.include_router(conversations_router) ❶
```

❶ Place conversation CRUD routes on a separate API router and include on the FastAPI application for modular API design.

❷ Refactor conversation CRUD routes to use the repository pattern for more readable controller implementation.

Do you notice how cleaner your route controllers appear now that the database logic has been abstracted within the ConversationRepository class?

You can take this approach one step further and implement a service pattern as well. A *service* pattern is an extension of the repository pattern that encapsulates the business logic and operations in a higher layer. These higher-level operations often require more complex queries and a sequence of CRUD operations to be performed to implement the business logic.

As an example, you can implement a `ConversationService` to fetch messages related to a conversation or a specific user (see Example 7-10). Since it extends a `ConversationRepository`, you can still access the lower-level data access CRUD methods such as `list`, `get`, `create`, `update`, and `delete`.

Once again you can go back to your controllers and replace references to the `ConversationRepository` with the `ConversationService` instead. Additionally, you can use the same service to add a new endpoint for fetching messages within a single conversation.

Example 7-10. Implementing the conversation services pattern

```python
# services/conversations.py

from entities import Message
from repositories.conversations import ConversationRepository
from sqlalchemy import select

class ConversationService(ConversationRepository):
    async def list_messages(self, conversation_id: int) -> list[Message]:
        result = await self.session.execute(
            select(Message).where(Message.conversation_id == conversation_id)
        )
        return [m for m in result.scalars().all()]

# routers/conversations.py

from database import DBSessionDep
from entities import Message
from fastapi import APIRouter
from schemas import MessageOut
from services.conversations import ConversationService

router = APIRouter(prefix="/conversations")

@router.get("/{conversation_id}/messages") ❶
async def list_conversation_messages_controller(
    conversation: GetConversationDep,
    session: DBSessionDep,
) -> list[Message]:
    messages = await ConversationService(session).list_messages(conversation.id)
    return [MessageOut.model_validate(m) for m in messages]
```

❶ Add a new endpoint to list messages of a conversation using the conversation ID.

You now have a fully working RESTful API for interacting with your conversation data following the repository and service patterns.

Now that you're more familiar with the repository and services pattern, you can try implementing CRUD endpoints for the `messages` table.

When using the repository and service patterns, be mindful that you avoid tightly coupling your services to specific repository implementation and not overload your services with many responsibilities. Keep repositories focused on data access and manipulation and avoid placing business logic in them.

You'll also need to handle database transactions and exceptions properly, especially when performing multiple related operations. Also, consider performance implications of your queries such as including many JOINs, and optimize queries where you can.

Good practice is to use consistent naming conventions for your methods and classes and to avoid hard-coding configuration settings.

There is one more aspect of the database development workflow that we need to address next. That is managing ever-changing database schemas, in particular in collaborative teams where multiple people are working on the same database both in development and production environments.

Managing Database Schemas Changes

You must have noticed that in Example 7-3 you are deleting and re-creating your database tables every time you start your FastAPI server. This is acceptable for development workflows during the prototyping stage, but not at all when you need to deploy your services in production with active users. You can't reset your database from scratch every time you update your database schema.

You also will probably need a way to revert changes if something breaks or if you decide to roll back certain features. To achieve this, you can use a database migration tool such as Alembic that is designed to work seamlessly with the SQLAlchemy ORM.

Alembic allows you to version control your database schemas the same way that tools like Git can help you version control your code. They're extremely useful when you're working in a team with multiple application environments and need to keep track of changes or revert updates as needed.

To get started, you must first install `alembic` via `pip` and then initialize it by running Example 7-11 at the root of your FastAPI project.

Example 7-11. Initializing an Alembic environment

```
$ alembic init
```

Alembic will create its environment within the `alembic` folder with several files and a `versions` directory, as shown in Example 7-12.

Example 7-12. Alembic environment within your project root directory

```
project/
    alembic.ini
    alembic/
        env.py ❶
        README
        script.py.mako
        versions/ ❷
            <migration .py files will appear here>
```

❶ An environment file for specifying target schema and database connections

❷ A directory for holding *migrations* files, which specify the instructions on how to update or revert the database schema

Once the Alembic environment is generated, open and modify the *env.py* file located in the `alembic` directory, as shown in Example 7-13, so that it gets access to your SQLAlchemy metadata object that contains the target schema information.

Example 7-13. Connect the Alembic environment with your SQLAlchemy models

```
# alembic/env.py

from entities import Base
from settings import AppSettings

settings = AppSettings()
target_metadata = Base
db_url = str(settings.pg_dsn)

...
```

With Alembic connected to your SQLAlchemy models, Alembic can now autogenerate your migration files by comparing the current schema of your database with your SQLAlchemy models:

```
$ alembic revision --autogenerate -m "Initial Migration"
```

This command will compare the defined SQLAlchemy models against the existing database schema and automatically generate a SQL migration file under the alembic/versions directory.

If you open the generated migration file, you should see a file content similar to Example 7-14.

Example 7-14. The initial Alembic migration

```
# alembic/versions/24c35f32b152.py

from datetime import UTC, datetime
import sqlalchemy as sa
from alembic import op

"""
Revision ID: 2413cf32b712 Revises:
Create Date: 2024-07-11 12:30:17.089406
"""

# revision identifiers, used by Alembic.
revision = "24c35f32b152"
down_revision = None
branch_labels = None

def upgrade():
    op.create_table(
        "conversations",
        sa.Column("id", sa.BigInteger, primary_key=True),
        sa.Column("title", sa.String, nullable=False),
        sa.Column("model_type", sa.String, index=True, nullable=False),
        sa.Column(
            "created_at", sa.DateTime, default=datetime.now(UTC), nullable=False
        ),
        sa.Column(
            "updated_at",
            sa.DateTime,
            default=datetime.now(UTC),
            onupdate=datetime.now(UTC),
            nullable=False,
        ),
    )

    op.create_table(
        "messages",
        sa.Column("id", sa.BigInteger, primary_key=True),
        sa.Column(
            "conversation_id",
            sa.BigInteger,
            sa.ForeignKey("conversations.id", ondelete="CASCADE"),
            index=True,
```

```
            nullable=False,
        ),
        sa.Column("prompt_content", sa.Text, nullable=False),
        sa.Column("response_content", sa.Text, nullable=False),
        sa.Column("prompt_tokens", sa.Integer, nullable=True),
        sa.Column("response_tokens", sa.Integer, nullable=True),
        sa.Column("total_tokens", sa.Integer, nullable=True),
        sa.Column("is_success", sa.Boolean, nullable=True),
        sa.Column("status_code", sa.Integer, nullable=True),
        sa.Column(
            "created_at", sa.DateTime, default=datetime.now(UTC), nullable=False
        ),
        sa.Column(
            "updated_at",
            sa.DateTime,
            default=datetime.now(UTC),
            onupdate=datetime.now(UTC),
            nullable=False,
        ),
    )

def downgrade():
    op.drop_table("messages")
    op.drop_table("conversations")
```

Now that you've updated your first migration file, you're ready to run it against the database:

```
$ alembic upgrade head
```

If your ever need to revert the operation, you can run `alembic downgrade` instead.

What Alembic does under the hood is to generate the raw SQL needed to run or revert a migration and create an `alembic_versions` table in the database. It uses this table to keep track of migrations that have already been applied on your database so that rerunning the `alembic upgrade head` command won't perform any duplicate migrations.

If in any case, your database schemas and your migration history drift away, you can always remove files from the `versions` directory and truncate the `alembic_revision` table. Then reinitialize Alembic to start with a fresh environment against an existing database.

> After migrating a database with a migration file, make sure to commit to a Git repository. Avoid re-editing migration files after migrating a database as Alembic will skip existing migrations by cross-checking them with its versioning table.
>
> If a migration file has already been run, it won't detect changes in its content.
>
> To update your database schema, create a new migration file instead.

Following the aforementioned workflow will now allow you to not only version control your database schemas but also manage changes to your production environments as your application requirements change.

Storing Data When Working with Real-Time Streams

You should now be in a position to implement your own CRUD endpoints to retrieve and mutate both user conversation and message records in your database.

One question that remains unanswered is how to handle transactions within data streaming endpoints, such as an LLM streaming outputs to a client.

You can't stream data into a traditional relational database as ensuring ACID compliance with streaming transactions will prove challenging. Instead, you will want to perform your standard database operation as soon as your FastAPI server returns a response to the client. This challenge is exactly what a FastAPI's background task can solve, as you can see in Example 7-15.

Example 7-15. Storing content of an LLM output stream

```
# main.py

from itertools import tee
from database import DBSessionDep
from entities import Message
from fastapi import BackgroundTasks, Depends
from fastapi.responses import StreamingResponse
from repositories.conversations import Conversation
from repositories.messages import MessageRepository
from sqlalchemy.ext.asyncio import AsyncSession

async def store_message( ❶
    prompt_content: str,
    response_content: str,
    conversation_id: int,
    session: AsyncSession,
) -> None:
    message = Message(
```

```
        conversation_id=conversation_id,
        prompt_content=prompt_content,
        response_content=response_content,
    )
    await MessageRepository(session).create(message)

@app.get("/text/generate/stream")
async def stream_llm_controller(
    prompt: str,
    background_task: BackgroundTasks,
    session: DBSessionDep,
    conversation: Conversation = Depends(get_conversation), ❷
) -> StreamingResponse:
    # Invoke LLM and obtain the response stream
    ...
    stream_1, stream_2 = tee(response_stream) ❸
    background_task.add_task(
        store_message, prompt, "".join(stream_1), conversation.id, session
    ) ❹
    return StreamingResponse(stream_2)
```

❶ Create a function to store a message against a conversation.

❷ Check that the conversation record exists and fetch it within a dependency.

❸ Create two separate copies of the LLM stream, one for the `StreamingResponse` and another to process in a background task.

❹ Create a background task to store the message after the `StreamingResponse` is finished.

In Example 7-15, you allow FastAPI to fully stream the LLM response to the client.

It won't matter whether you're using an SSE or WebSocket endpoint. Once a request a response is fully streamed, invoke a background task passing in the full stream response content. Within the background task, you can then run a function to store the message after the request is sent, with the full LLM response content.

Using the same approach, you can even generate a title for a conversation based on the content of the first message. To do this, you can invoke the LLM again with the content of the first message in the conversation, requesting for an appropriate title for the conversation. Once a conversation title is generated, you can create the conversation record in the database, as shown in Example 7-16.

Example 7-16. Using the LLM to generate conversation titles based on the initial user prompt

```python
from entities import Conversation
from openai import AsyncClient
from repositories.conversations import ConversationRepository
from sqlalchemy.ext.asyncio import AsyncSession

async_client = AsyncClient(...)

async def create_conversation(
    initial_prompt: str, session: AsyncSession
) -> Conversation:
    completion = await async_client.chat.completions.create(
        messages=[
            {
                "role": "system",
                "content": "Suggest a title for the conversation "
                           "based on the user prompt",
            },
            {
                "role": "user",
                "content": initial_prompt,
            },
        ],
        model="gpt-3.5-turbo",
    )
    title = completion.choices[0].message.content
    conversation = Conversation(
        title=title,
        # add other conversation properties
        ...
    )
    return await ConversationRepository(session).create(conversation)
```

Using SQLAlchemy with Alembic is a tried and tested approach to working with relational databases in FastAPI, so you're more likely to find a lot of resources on integrating these technologies.

Both the SQLAlchemy ORM and Alembic allow you to interact with your database and control the changes to its schemas.

Summary

In this chapter, you dove into the critical aspects of integrating a database into your FastAPI application to store and retrieve user conversations.

You learned to identify when a database is necessary and how to identify the appropriate type for your project, whether it be relational or nonrelational. By understanding the underlying mechanisms of relational databases and the use cases for nonrelational databases, you're now equipped to make informed decisions about database selection.

You also explored the development workflow, tooling, and best practices for working with relational databases. This includes learning techniques to improve query performance and efficiency, as well as strategies for managing evolving database schema changes. Additionally, you gained insights into managing codebase, database schema, and data drifts when working in teams.

As you move forward, the next chapter will guide you through implementing user management, authentication, and authorization mechanisms. This will further enhance your application's security and user experience, building on the solid database foundation you've established in this chapter.

## PART III

Securing, Optimizing, Testing, and Deploying AI Services

In this part, you will learn about security, optimizing, testing, and deployment best practices when building GenAI services.

## CHAPTER 8

Authentication and Authorization

Chapter Goals

In this chapter, you will learn about:

- Relevant authentication strategies for securing your GenAI services
- How to implement basic credentials and JSON Web Token (JWT) authentication from scratch
- Various authentication risks and attack vectors
- How to build single sign-on (SSO) authentication with an identity provider such as GitHub following the OAuth2 standard
- Authorization patterns such as role-based, attribute-based, and relationship-based access control
- Authorization mechanisms to safeguard resources from nonprivileged users
- How to restrict access to resources and limit AI generation outputs based on user privileges

So far, you've built GenAI services that can interact with databases, stream model responses, and handle concurrent users.

Your services are now up and running, but since they're not protected from attackers or malicious users, deploying them to production may prove problematic.

In this chapter, you'll learn how to secure your services with an authentication layer and implement authorization guards to protect sensitive resources from nonprivileged users.

To achieve this, we're going to explore various authentication and authorization patterns then implement JWT and identity-based authentication with role-based access control.

Authentication and Authorization

Before talking about authentication methods, let's briefly clarify that authentication and authorization are two separate concepts that are often interchangeably used by mistake.

According to the OWASP definition:[1]

> *Authentication* is the process of verifying that an individual, entity, or website is who or what it claims to be by determining the validity of one or more authenticators (like passwords, fingerprints, or security tokens) that are used to back up this claim.

On the other hand, the National Institute of Standards and Technology (NIST) defines authorization as:

> A process for verifying that a requested action or service is approved for a specific entity.

While authentication is about verifying the identity, authorization focuses on verifying permissions of an identity to access or mutate resources.

> An analogy that might clarify this distinction is passing through passport control at an airport. Authentication is like presenting your passport at immigration, while authorization is like having the right visa to enter a country, specifying the duration of your stay and permitted activities once you enter.

Let's discuss authentication methods in more detail before diving into authorization later in the chapter.

---

1 Open Worldwide Application Security Project is an online community that produces resources on system software and web application security.

Authentication Methods

There are several authentication mechanisms that you can implement in your GenAI services to secure them by identity verification.

Depending on your security requirements, application environment, budget, and project timelines, you may decide to adopt one or more of the following authentication mechanisms:

Basic
> Requiring the use of credentials such as username and password to verify identity.

JSON Web Tokens (JWT)
> Requiring the use of *access tokens* to verify identity. You can think of access tokens like cinema tickets that dictate whether you can access the screens and which screen you're visiting and where you're sitting.

OAuth
> Verifying an identity via an identity provider using the *OAuth2* standard.

Key-based
> Using a private and public key pair to authenticate an identity. Instead of tokens, the authorization server issues a public key to the client and stores a copy of a linked private key that it can use later for verification.[2]

Figure 8-1 shows the data flow of the aforementioned authentication methods in more detail.

---

2 Key-based authentication won't be discussed further as it involves complex cryptographic principles that are beyond the scope of this chapter.

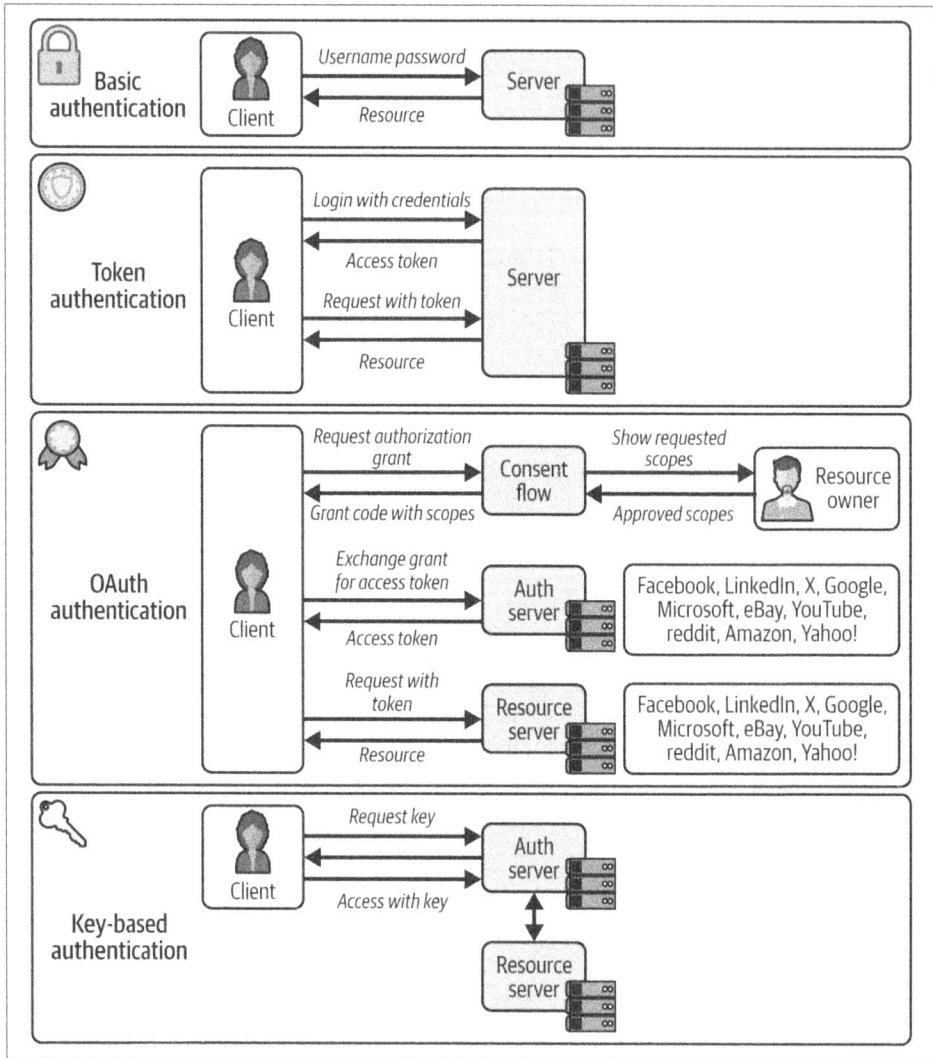

Figure 8-1. Authentication methods

Being aware of authentication mechanisms, it can still be challenging to decide on the method to adopt when addressing your security requirements. To assist with the selection task, Table 8-1 compares the aforementioned authentication methods.

Table 8-1. Comparison of authentication methods

Type	Benefits	Limitations	Use cases
Basic	• Simplicity • Fast to implement • Easy to understand	Sends credentials in plain text	• Prototypes • Internal or nonproduction environments
Token	• Scalability • Decoupling facilitates implementation of microservice architectures • Tokens can be signed and encrypted for higher security • Highly customizable • Self-contained reducing database round-trips • Can be passed in HTTP headers	• Constant need to regenerate short-lived tokens • Complexity of client-side token storage • Tokens can get large, consuming excess bandwidth • Stateless tokens can make multi-step applications hard to implement • Client-side misconfigurations can compromise tokens	• Single-page and mobile applications • Applications requiring custom authentication flows • REST APIs
OAuth	• Delegates authentication to external providers • Based on a standard (OAuth2) and battle-tested for enterprise scenarios • Access to external resources on behalf of the user	• Complex to understand and implement • Each identity provider may implement the OAuth flow slightly differently	• Applications requiring user data from external identity providers such as GitHub, Google, or Microsoft • Enterprise applications that require SSO with their own identity provider(s)
Key-based	• Similar authentication mechanism to Secure Shell (SSH) access	• Managing and keeping private keys secure can be complex • Compromised keys can create security risks • Scalability issues	• Small applications • Applications within internal environments

You should now feel confident in deciding the appropriate authentication mechanism to adopt. In the next section, you're going to implement basic, JWT, and OAuth authentication for your GenAI to fully understand the underlying components and their interactions.

Basic Authentication

In basic authentication, the client provides a username and password when making a request to access resources from the server. It is the simplest technique as it won't require cookies, session identifiers, or any login forms to be implemented. Because of its simplicity, basic authentication is ideal for sandbox environments and when prototyping. However, avoid using it in production environments as it transmits usernames and passwords in plain text on every request, making it highly vulnerable to interception attacks.

To perform an authenticated request via basic authentication, you must add an Authorization header with a value of Basic <credentials> for the server to successfully authenticate it. The <credentials> value must be a *Base64* encoding of the username and password joined by a single colon (i.e., base64.encode(ali:secret password).

In FastAPI, you can protect an endpoint with basic authentication, as shown in Example 8-1.

Example 8-1. Implementing basic authentication in FastAPI

```
import secrets
from typing import Annotated

from fastapi import Depends, FastAPI, HTTPException, status
from fastapi.security import HTTPBasic, HTTPBasicCredentials

app = FastAPI()
security = HTTPBasic()  ❶
username_bytes = b"ali"
password_bytes = b"secretpassword"

def authenticate_user(
    credentials: Annotated[HTTPBasicCredentials, Depends(security)]
) -> str:
    is_correct_username = secrets.compare_digest(
        credentials.username.encode("UTF-8"), username_bytes  ❷
    )
    is_correct_password = secrets.compare_digest(
        credentials.password.encode("UTF-8"), password_bytes  ❷
    )
    if not (is_correct_username and is_correct_password):
        raise HTTPException(  ❸
            status_code=status.HTTP_401_UNAUTHORIZED,
            detail="Incorrect credentials",
            headers={"WWW-Authenticate": "Basic"},
        )
    return credentials.username

AuthenticatedUserDep = Annotated[str, Depends(authenticate_user)]  ❹

@app.get("/users/me")
def get_current_user_controller(username: AuthenticatedUserDep):  ❹
    return {"message": f"Current user is {username}"}
```

❶ FastAPI has implemented several HTTP security mechanisms including HTTP Basic that can leverage the FastAPI's dependency injection system.

❷ Use the secrets built-in library to compare the provided username and password with the server's values. Using secrets.compare_digest() ensures the duration of checking operations remain consistent no matter what the inputs are to avoid *timing attacks.*[3]

Note that secrets.compare_digest() can only accept byte or string inputs containing ASCII characters (i.e., English-only characters). To handle other characters, you will need to encode the inputs with UTF-8 to bytes first before performing the credential checks.

❸ Return a standardized authorization HTTPException compliant with security standards that browsers understand so that they show the login prompt again to the user. The exception message must be generic to avoid leaking any sensitive information, such as the existence of a user account, to attackers.

❹ Using the HTTPBasic with Depends() returns the HTTPBasicCredentials object that contains the provided username.

Injecting a security dependency to any FastAPI endpoint will protect it with the implemented authentication. You can experience this yourself now by visiting the /docs page and sending a request to the /users/me endpoint.

The endpoint will show a *lock* icon in front of it, and you should see a sign-in alert when making a request, asking you to provide credentials, as you can see in Figure 8-2.

---

3 In a *timing attack*, attackers try to guess passwords by comparing and analyzing elapsed password evaluation times with the password length. Therefore, to prevent timing attacks, cryptographic algorithms must check passwords within a constant time span.

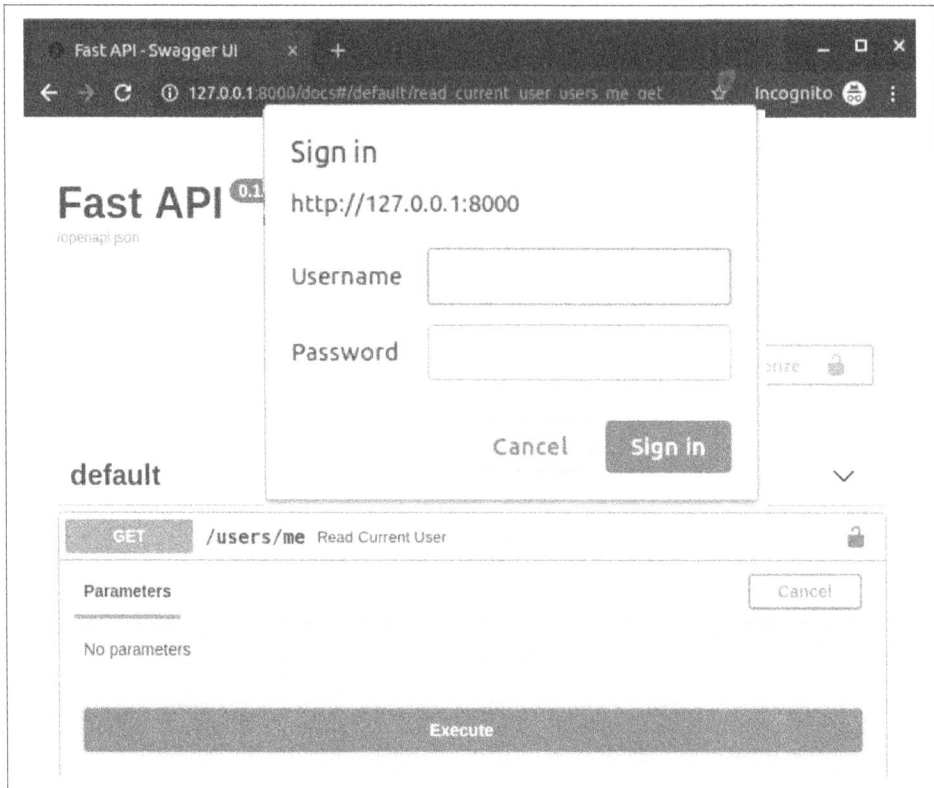

Figure 8-2. Basic authentication in FastAPI

Well done! In 25 lines of code, you managed to implement a basic form of authentication to protect an endpoint. You can now use basic authentication in your own prototypes and development servers.

Bear in mind, you should avoid adopting the basic authentication mechanism in production-grade GenAI services. A better and more secure alternative for public-facing services is *JWT authentication*. It eliminates the need for server-side sessions by storing all authentication details within a token. It also maintains data integrity and works across different domains with a widely accepted standard.

JSON Web Tokens (JWT) Authentication

Now that you're more familiar with basic concepts of authentication, let's implement a more complex but secure JWT authentication layer to your FastAPI service. As part of this, you'll also refactor your existing endpoints to combine them under a separate resource API router to group, name, tag, and protect multiple endpoints at once.

What is JWT?

JWTs are a URL-safe and compact way of asserting claims between applications via tokens.

These tokens consist of three parts:

Headers
Specify the token type and signing algorithm in addition to the datetime and the issuing authority.

Payload
Specify the body of the token representing the claims on the resource alongside additional metadata.

Signature
The function that creates the token will also sign it using the *encoded payload*, *encoded headers*, a *secret*, and the signing algorithm.

> The base64 encoding algorithm is often used to encode and decode data for compactness and URL safety.

Figure 8-3 shows what a typical JWT looks like.

Figure 8-3. JWT components (Source: jwt.io)

JWTs are secure, compact, and convenient since they can hold all the information needed to perform user authentication, avoiding the need for multiple database round-trips. In addition, due to their compactness, you can transfer them across the network using the HTTP POST body, headers, or URL parameters.

Getting started with JWT authentication

To get started with implementing the JWT authentication mechanism in FastAPI, you need to install the passlib and python-jose dependencies:

```
$ pip install passlib python-jose
```

With the dependencies installed, you will then need tables in the database to store the generated users and associated token data. For data persistence, let's migrate the database to create the users and tokens tables, as shown in Figure 8-4.

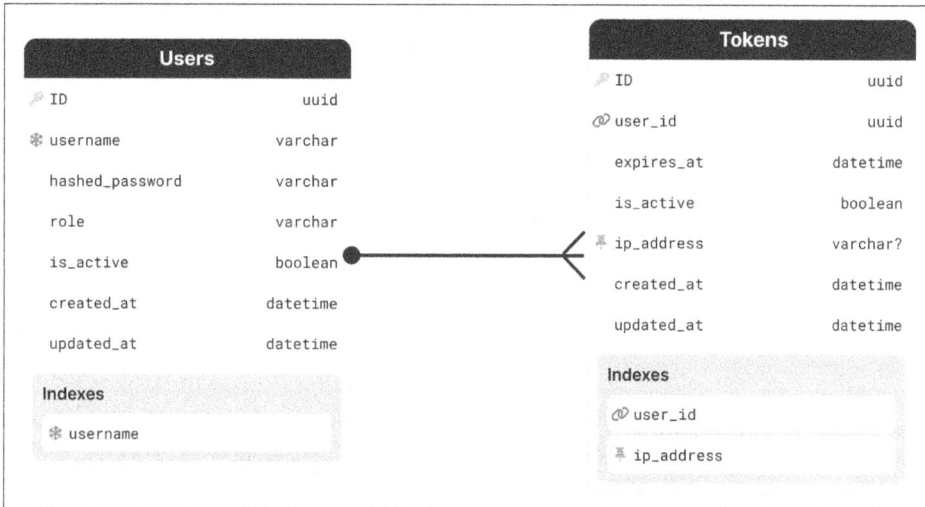

Figure 8-4. Entity relationship diagram of users and tokens tables

If you look at Figure 8-4, you will spot that the tokens table has a one-to-many relationship with the users table. You can use the token records to track successful login attempts for each user and to revoke access if needed.

Next, let's define the required SQLAlchemy models and Pydantic schemas for database queries and data validation, as shown in Examples 8-2 and 8-3.

Example 8-2. Declare user SQLAlchemy ORM models

```python
# entities.py

import uuid
from datetime import UTC, datetime
from sqlalchemy import Index, String
from sqlalchemy.orm import DeclarativeBase, Mapped, mapped_column

class Base(DeclarativeBase):
    pass

class User(Base):
    __tablename__ = "users"

    id: Mapped[uuid.UUID] = mapped_column(primary_key=True, default=uuid.uuid4)
    email: Mapped[str] = mapped_column(String(length=255), unique=True)
    hashed_password: Mapped[str] = mapped_column(String(length=255))
    is_active: Mapped[bool] = mapped_column(default=True)
    role: Mapped[str] = mapped_column(default="USER")
    created_at: Mapped[datetime] = mapped_column(default=datetime.now(UTC))
    updated_at: Mapped[datetime] = mapped_column(
```

```
            default=datetime.now(UTC), onupdate=datetime.now(UTC)
    )

    __table_args__ = (Index("ix_users_email", "email"),)
```

You will be using the ORM models at the data access layer while the Pydantic schemas will validate incoming and outgoing authentication data at the endpoint layer.

Example 8-3. Declare user Pydantic schemas with username and password field validators

```
# schemas.py

from datetime import datetime
from typing import Annotated
from pydantic import (UUID4, AfterValidator, BaseModel, ConfigDict, Field,
                      validate_call)

@validate_call
def validate_username(value: str) -> str: ❶
    if not value.isalnum():
        raise ValueError("Username must be alphanumeric")
    return value

@validate_call
def validate_password(value: str) -> str: ❶
    validations = [
        (
            lambda v: any(char.isdigit() for char in v),
            "Password must contain at least one digit",
        ),
        (
            lambda v: any(char.isupper() for char in v),
            "Password must contain at least one uppercase letter",
        ),
        (
            lambda v: any(char.islower() for char in v),
            "Password must contain at least one lowercase letter",
        ),
    ]
    for condition, error_message in validations:
        if not condition(value):
            raise ValueError(error_message)
    return value

ValidUsername = Annotated[
    str, Field(min_length=3, max_length=20), AfterValidator(validate_username)
]
ValidPassword = Annotated[
    str, Field(min_length=8, max_length=64), AfterValidator(validate_password)
]
```

```python
class UserBase(BaseModel):
    model_config = ConfigDict(from_attributes=True)  ❷

    username: ValidUsername
    is_active: bool = True
    role: str = "USER"

class UserCreate(UserBase):  ❸
    password: ValidPassword

class UserInDB(UserBase):  ❹
    hashed_password: str

class UserOut(UserBase):
    id: UUID4
    created_at: datetime
    updated_at: datetime
```

❶ Validate both username and password to enforce higher security requirements.

❷ Allow Pydantic to read SQLAlchemy ORM model attributes instead of having to manually populate Pydantic schemas from SQLAlchemy models.

❸ Use inheritance to declare several Pydantic schemas based on a user base model.

❹ Create a separate schema that accepts the `hashed_password` field to be used only for creating new user records during the registration process. All other schemas must skip storing this field to eliminate the risk of password leakage.

Creating the token models and schemas is fairly similar, as you can see in Example 8-4.

Example 8-4. Declare token ORM models and Pydantic schemas

```python
# entities.py

from datetime import UTC, datetime
from sqlalchemy import ForeignKey, Index, String
from sqlalchemy.orm import DeclarativeBase, Mapped, mapped_column, relationship

class Base(DeclarativeBase):
    pass

class Token(Base):
    __tablename__ = "tokens"

    id: Mapped[int] = mapped_column(primary_key=True)
    user_id: Mapped[int] = mapped_column(ForeignKey("users.id"))
```

```
    expires_at: Mapped[datetime] = mapped_column()
    is_active: Mapped[bool] = mapped_column(default=True)
    ip_address: Mapped[str | None] = mapped_column(String(length=255))
    created_at: Mapped[datetime] = mapped_column(default=datetime.now(UTC))
    updated_at: Mapped[datetime] = mapped_column(
        default=datetime.now(UTC), onupdate=datetime.now(UTC)
    )

    user = relationship("User", back_populates="tokens")

    __table_args__ = (
        Index("ix_tokens_user_id", "user_id"),
        Index("ix_tokens_ip_address", "ip_address"),
    )

class User(Base):
    __tablename__ = "users"
    # other columns...

    tokens = relationship(
        "Token", back_populates="user", cascade="all, delete-orphan"
    )

# schemas.py

from datetime import datetime
from pydantic import BaseModel

class TokenBase(BaseModel):
    user_id: int
    expires_at: datetime
    is_active: bool = True
    ip_address: str | None = None

class TokenCreate(TokenBase):
    pass

class TokenOut(BaseModel):
    access_token: str
    token_type: str = "Bearer"
```

Next, let's auto-generate a migration file using the `alembic revision --autogenerate -m "create users and tokens tables` command so that you can specify the details of both tables by following Example 8-5.

Example 8-5. Database migration to create the `users` *and* `tokens` *tables*

```
"""create users and tokens tables

Revision ID: 1234567890ab
Revises:
```

```
Create Date: 2025-01-28 12:34:56.789012

"""

from datetime import UTC, datetime
import sqlalchemy as sa
from alembic import op

...

def upgrade():
    op.create_table(
        "users",
        sa.Column("id", sa.UUID(as_uuid=True)), ❶
        sa.Column("email", sa.String(length=255)),
        sa.Column("hashed_password", sa.String(length=255)), ❷
        sa.Column(
            "is_active", sa.Boolean(), server_default=sa.sql.expression.true()
        ), ❸
        sa.Column("role", sa.String(), server_default=sa.text("USER")), ❹
        sa.Column("created_at", sa.DateTime(), default=datetime.now(UTC)),
        sa.Column(
            "updated_at",
            sa.DateTime(),
            default=datetime.now(UTC),
            onupdate=datetime.now(UTC), ❺
        ),
        sa.PrimaryKeyConstraint("id"),
        sa.UniqueConstraint("email"),
        sa.Index("ix_users_email", "email"), ❻
    )

    op.create_table(
        "tokens",
        sa.Column("id", sa.UUID(as_uuid=True)), ❶
        sa.Column("user_id", sa.Integer()),
        sa.Column("expires_at", sa.DateTime()), ❼
        sa.Column("is_active", sa.Boolean(), default=True), ❽
        sa.Column("ip_address", sa.String(length=255), nullable=True),
        sa.Column("created_at", sa.DateTime(), default=datetime.now(UTC)),
        sa.Column(
            "updated_at",
            sa.DateTime(),
            default=datetime.now(UTC),
            onupdate=datetime.now(UTC), ❾
        ),
        sa.ForeignKeyConstraint(
            ["user_id"],
            ["users.id"],
        ),
        sa.PrimaryKeyConstraint("id"),
        sa.Index("ix_tokens_user_id", "user_id"),
```

```
        sa.Index("ix_tokens_ip_address", "ip_address"), ❿
    )


def downgrade():
    op.drop_table("tokens")
    op.drop_table("users")
```

❶ Automatically generate universally unique identifiers (UUIDs) in the database layer for user and token records to prevent attackers from guessing identifiers of sensitive resources (i.e., user or token records).

❷ Avoid storing raw password strings in the database to reduce security vulnerabilities.

❸ Add the ability to enable or disable account access.

❹ Add the ability to specify user roles such as USER and ADMIN for managing access levels of an account. Authorization checks will use the role field to manage access of privileged resources.

❺ Auto-timestamp user creation and updates for monitoring and security purposes.

❻ Add a unique constraint and a secondary index on the email field to optimize user queries by email and eliminate the possibility of creating duplicate email accounts.

❼ Tokens must expire after a short period of time to reduce the time window that exposed tokens may be misused by attackers.

❽ Add the ability to disable tokens that should no longer be valid for either being exposed or if a user has logged out.

❾ Track the token creation and update times for monitoring and security.

❿ Create secondary indexes on user_id and ip_address fields to optimize token queries by these fields.

Now, run the alembic upgrade head command to execute the migration in Example 8-5 against your database and create both users and tokens tables.

With the ORM models and Pydantic schemas declared, you can focus on the core authentication mechanism logic.

Figure 8-5 shows the architecture of the JWT authentication system you're going to implement in your FastAPI GenAI service.

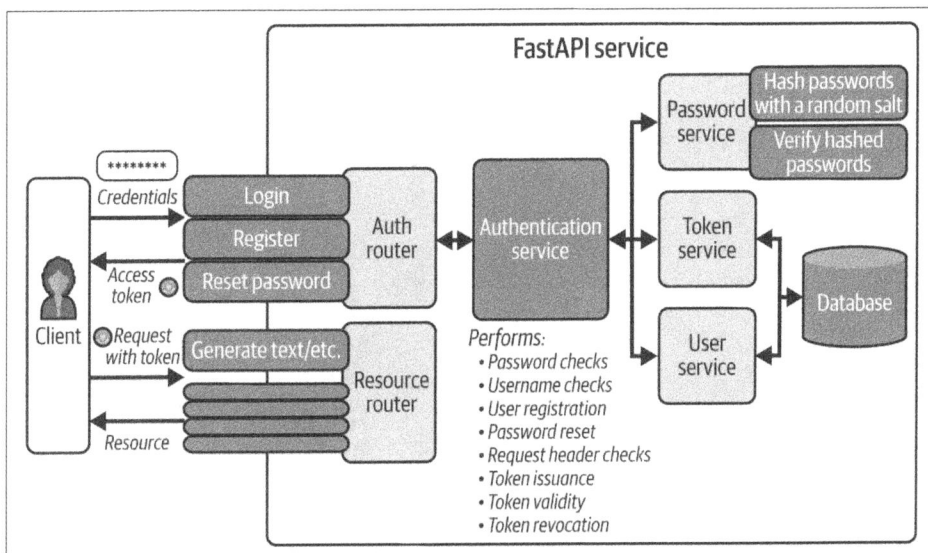

Figure 8-5. JWT authentication system architecture

In the following code examples, you will see how to implement the core authentication flows starting with user registration and JWT generation.

Hashing and salting

The first step after creating the users and tokens tables in the database is to store new users in the database upon registration. However, you should avoid storing passwords in plain form, because if the database is compromised, the attackers will have every user's credential.

Instead, the authentication mechanism will leverage a *hashing algorithm* that converts plain passwords into an encoded string that can't be decoded back into its original form. Since the decoding process isn't reversible, cryptographic hashing algorithms differ from standard encoding/decoding functions such as Base64.

While storing hashed passwords is more secure than storing plain passwords, it doesn't provide enough protection. If such a database of hashed passwords falls into the hands of attackers, they can use a precomputed hash tables—commonly referred to as *rainbow tables*. Attackers can use rainbow tables to brute-force their way into your system by recovering plaintext passwords. To protect against these brute-force attacks, you also need to introduce an element of randomness to your hashing process using a technique termed *salting*.

With salts, the cryptographic hashing algorithm produces different hashed passwords, even though the users may register with common, compromised, or duplicate passwords.

> Password hashing with a random salt protects against brute-force attacks using rainbow tables. However, it doesn't protect against *password spraying*, where attackers use a database of common passwords, or *credential stuffing*, where attackers enumerate on a list of compromised passwords.

During salting, the hashing function generates a random salt that appends to the plain password prior to hashing and then generates a hashed password.[4] Before storing the hashed password in the database, the salt is prefixed to the hashed password for later retrieval during verification.

When registered users try to log in, they have to supply the same password they used to create their account. During the password verification process, the password that the user provides is hashed using the same salt that was used during registration which is retrieved from the database. If the generated hashed password is exactly identical to the hashed password in the database, then the user is authenticated. Otherwise, you can safely assume that wrong credentials have been supplied.

The salting and hashing are powerful techniques that prevent attackers from brute-forcing their way into your system with rainbow tables. You can see the full hashing and salting process in Figure 8-6.

---

4 Typical salt lengths include 16 bytes (128 bits) for balancing performance and security, or 32 bytes (256 bits) for securing sensitive systems. You can use cryptographic libraries such as `passlib` to generate these salts correctly.

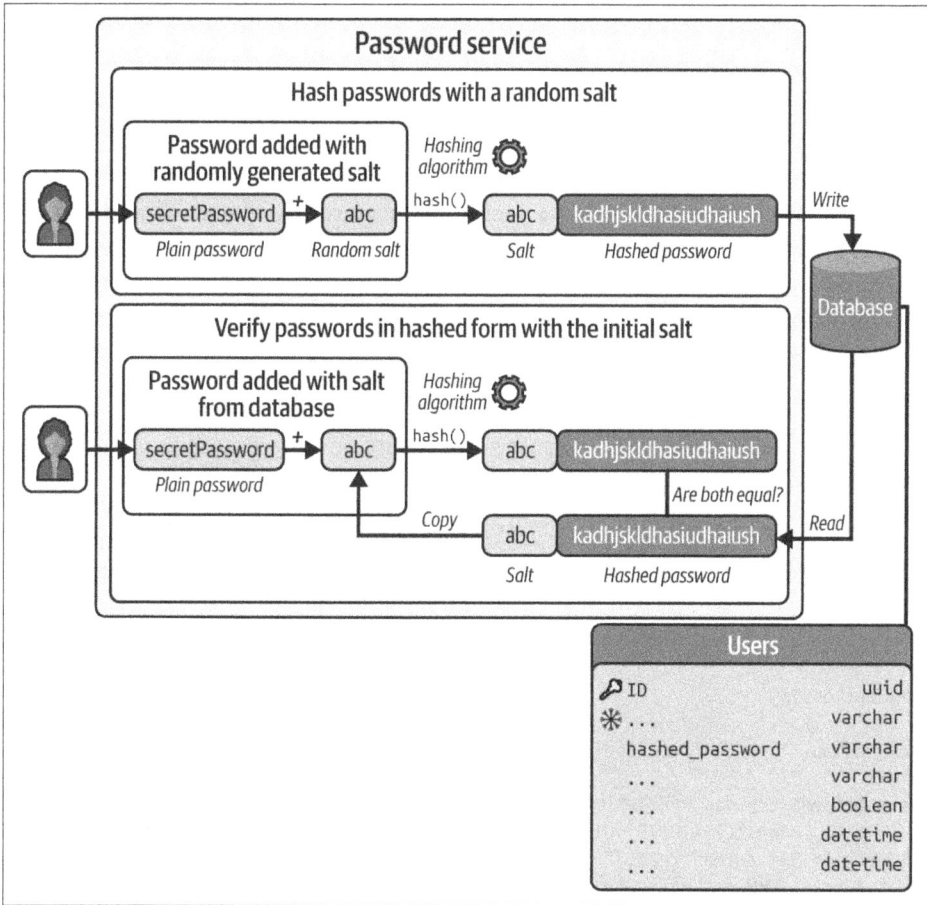

Figure 8-6. Password hash salting mechanism

The password service shown in Figure 8-6 is implemented as `PasswordService` in Example 8-6.

Example 8-6. Implement a password service

```
# services/auth.py

from fastapi.security import HTTPBearer
from passlib.context import CryptContext

class PasswordService:
    security = HTTPBearer()
    pwd_context = CryptContext(schemes=["bcrypt"])  ❶

    async def verify_password(
```

```
    self, password: str, hashed_password: str
) -> bool:
    return self.pwd_context.verify(password, hashed_password) ❷

async def get_password_hash(self, password: str) -> str:
    return self.pwd_context.hash(password) ❷
```

❶ Create an AuthService with a secret and password context managed by the bcrypt library that will handle all the user password hashing and verification.

❷ Use bcrypt's cryptography algorithm and application secret to hash and verify passwords.

The bcrypt cryptographic library provides the core functionality of the Password Service for hashing and verifying passwords. Using this service, requests can now be authenticated.

If a request can't be authenticated, you will also need to raise authorization-related exceptions, as shown in Example 8-7.

Example 8-7. Create authentication exceptions

```
# exceptions.py

from fastapi import HTTPException, status

UnauthorizedException = HTTPException(
    status_code=status.HTTP_401_UNAUTHORIZED,
    detail="Not authenticated",
    headers={"WWW-Authenticate": "Bearer"},
)

AlreadyRegisteredException = HTTPException(
    status_code=status.HTTP_400_BAD_REQUEST,
    detail="Username already registered",
)
```

The two most common authorization HTTP exceptions you will raise are related to unauthorized access or bad requests due to using already used usernames.

Once you have checked a user's identity via their credentials, you will need to issue them an *access token*. These tokens should be short-lived to reduce the time-window that an attacker can use the token to access resources if the token is stolen.

To reduce the size footprints of the tokens and protect against *token forgery*, the token service will sign (using a secret) and encode the token payloads with an encoding such as Base64. The payload will normally contain the user's details such as their ID, role, issuance system, and expiry dates.

The token service can also decode the payload of received tokens and check their validity during the authentication process.

Finally, the token service will also require database access to store and retrieve tokens to perform its functions. Therefore, it should inherit a `TokenRepository`, as shown in Example 8-8.

Example 8-8. Implementing token repository

```
# repositories.py

from entities import Token
from repositories.interfaces import Repository
from schemas import TokenCreate, TokenUpdate
from sqlalchemy import select
from sqlalchemy.ext.asyncio import AsyncSession

class TokenRepository(Repository):
    def __init__(self, session: AsyncSession) -> None:
        self.session = session

    async def list(self, skip: int, take: int) -> list[Token]:
        async with self.session.begin():
            result = await self.session.execute(
                select(Token).offset(skip).limit(take)
            )
        return [r for r in result.scalars().all()]

    async def get(self, token_id: int) -> Token | None:
        async with self.session.begin():
            result = await self.session.execute(
                select(Token).where(Token.id == token_id)
            )
        return result.scalars().first()

    async def create(self, token: TokenCreate) -> Token:
        new_token = Token(**token.dict())
        async with self.session.begin():
            self.session.add(new_token)
            await self.session.commit()
            await self.session.refresh(new_token)
        return new_token

    async def update(
        self, token_id: int, updated_token: TokenUpdate
    ) -> Token | None:
        token = await self.get(token_id)
        if not token:
            return None
        for key, value in updated_token.dict(exclude_unset=True).items():
            setattr(token, key, value)
```

```
        async with self.session.begin():
            await self.session.commit()
            await self.session.refresh(token)
        return token

    async def delete(self, token_id: int) -> None:
        token = await self.get(token_id)
        if not token:
            return
        async with self.session.begin():
            await self.session.delete(token)
            await self.session.commit()
```

With the TokenRepository implemented, you can now develop the TokenService, as shown in Example 8-9.

Example 8-9. Implement a token service by inheriting the token repository

```
# services/auth.py

from datetime import UTC, datetime, timedelta
from exceptions import UnauthorizedException
from jose import JWTError, jwt
from pydantic import UUID4
from repositories import TokenRepository
from schemas import TokenCreate, TokenUpdate

class TokenService(TokenRepository):
    secret_key = "your_secret_key"
    algorithm = "HS256"
    expires_in_minutes = 60 ❶

async def create_access_token(
    self, data: dict, expires_delta: timedelta | None = None ❷
) -> str:
    to_encode = data.copy()
    if expires_delta:
        expire = datetime.now(UTC) + expires_delta
    else:
        expire = datetime.now(UTC) + timedelta(minutes=self.expires_in_minutes)
    token_id = await self.create(TokenCreate(expires_at=expire)) ❸
    to_encode.update(
        {"exp": expire, "iss": "your_service_name", "sub": token_id} ❹
    )
    encoded_jwt = jwt.encode(
        to_encode, self.secret_key, algorithm=self.algorithm ❺
    )
    return encoded_jwt

async def deactivate(self, token_id: UUID4) -> None:
    await self.update(TokenUpdate(id=token_id, is_active=False))
```

```python
def decode(self, encoded_token: str) -> dict:
    try:
        return jwt.decode(
            encoded_token, self.secret_key, algorithms=[self.algorithm]
        )
    except JWTError:
        raise UnauthorizedException

async def validate(self, token_id: UUID4) -> bool:
    return (token := await self.get(token_id)) is not None and token.is_active
```

❶ Implement a `TokenService` for issuing and checking authentication tokens. Configurations are shared across all instances of the service.

❷ Generate access tokens based on data provided to the token service with expiry dates.

❸ Create a token record in the database and get a unique identifier.

❹ The access token must expire within an hour, so the `exp` calculated field will be used to check token validity.

❺ Encode the generated token into an encoded string using the `base64` algorithm.

Now that you have a `PasswordService` and a `TokenService`, you can complete the core JWT authentication mechanism with a dedicated higher-level `AuthService`.

Example 8-10 shows the implementation of the `AuthService` class that contains several dependency functions for registering users, issuing access tokens, and protecting your API routes.

Example 8-10. Implement an auth service to handle higher-level authentication logic

```python
# services/auth.py

from typing import Annotated
from databases import DBSessionDep
from entities import Token, User, UserCreate, UserInDB
from exceptions import AlreadyRegisteredException, UnauthorizedException
from fastapi import Depends
from fastapi.security import (HTTPAuthorizationCredentials, HTTPBearer,
                              OAuth2PasswordRequestForm)
from services.auth import PasswordService, TokenService
from services.users import UserService

security = HTTPBearer()
LoginFormDep = Annotated[OAuth2PasswordRequestForm, Depends()]
```

```
AuthHeaderDep = Annotated[HTTPAuthorizationCredentials, Depends(security)]

class AuthService:
    def __init__(self, session: DBSessionDep):
        self.password_service = PasswordService()
        self.token_service = TokenService(session)
        self.user_service = UserService(session)

    async def register_user(self, user: UserCreate) -> User:
        if await self.user_service.get(user.username):
            raise AlreadyRegisteredException
        hashed_password = await self.password_service.get_password_hash(
            user.password
        )
        return await self.user_service.create(
            UserInDB(username=user.username, hashed_password=hashed_password)
        )

    async def authenticate_user(self, form_data: LoginFormDep) -> Token: ❶
        if not (user := await self.user_service.get_user(form_data.username)):
            raise UnauthorizedException
        if not await self.password_service.verify_password(
            form_data.password, user.hashed_password
        ):
            raise UnauthorizedException
        return await self.token_service.create_access_token(user._asdict())

    async def get_current_user(self, credentials: AuthHeaderDep) -> User:
        if credentials.scheme != "Bearer":
            raise UnauthorizedException
        if not (token := credentials.credentials):
            raise UnauthorizedException
        payload = self.token_service.decode(token)
        if not await self.token_service.validate(payload.get("sub")):
            raise UnauthorizedException
        if not (username := payload.get("username")):
            raise UnauthorizedException
        if not (user := await self.user_service.get(username)):
            raise UnauthorizedException
        return user

    async def logout(self, credentials: AuthHeaderDep) -> None:
        payload = self.token_service.decode(credentials.credentials)
        await self.token_service.deactivate(payload.get("sub"))

    # Add Password Reset Method
    async def reset_password(self): ...
```

❶ The core authentication logic of the application that verifies whether a user exists and their password credentials. Returns False if any checks fail.

You can now use the `AuthService` to register and authenticate users using their credentials. Refer to Example 8-11 to see how the `AuthService` is used to create the required dependencies for a dedicated authentication router.

Example 8-11. Implement authentication controllers to enable login and registration functionality

```python
# routes/auth.py

from typing import Annotated
from entities import User
from fastapi import APIRouter, Depends
from models import TokenOut, UserOut
from services.auth import AuthService

auth_service = AuthService()
RegisterUserDep = Annotated[User, Depends(auth_service.register_user)]
AuthenticateUserCredDep = Annotated[
    str, Depends(auth_service.authenticate_user_with_credentials)
]
AuthenticateUserTokenDep = Annotated[User, Depends(auth_service.register_user)]
PasswordResetDep = Annotated[None, Depends(auth_service.reset_password)] ❶

router = APIRouter(prefix="/auth", tags=["Authentication"]) ❷

@router.post("/register")
async def register_user_controller(new_user: RegisterUserDep) -> UserOut:
    return new_user

@router.post("/token") ❸
async def login_for_access_token_controller(
    access_token: AuthenticateUserCredDep,
) -> TokenOut:
    return {"access_token": access_token, "token_type": "bearer"}

@router.post("/logout", dependencies=[Depends(auth_service.logout)]) ❸ ❹
async def logout_access_token_controller() -> dict:
    return {"message": "Logged out"}

@router.post("reset-password") ❸
async def reset_password_controller(credentials: str) -> dict:
    return {
        "message": "If an account exists, "
        "a password reset link will be sent to the provided email"
    }
```

❶ Create an instance of the `AuthService` and declare reusable annotated dependencies.

❷ Create a separate API router for authentication endpoints.

③ Implement endpoints for registering users, user login (token issuance), user logout (token revocation), and password reset.

④ Since the `LogoutUserDep` dependency won't return anything, inject it within the dependency array of the router.

Once you have a dedicated authentication router, create a separate resource router to group all your resource endpoints within. With both routers, you can now add them to your FastAPI app, as shown in Example 8-12, to complete the JWT authentication work.

Example 8-12. Refactor FastAPI application to use routers

```python
# routes/resource.py

from fastapi import APIRouter

router = APIRouter(prefix="/generate", tags=["Resource"]) ❶

@router.get("/generate/text", ...)
def serve_language_model_controller(...):
    ...

@router.get("/generate/audio", ...)
def serve_text_to_audio_model_controller(...)
    ...

... # Add other controllers to the resource router here

# main.py

from typing import Annotated
import routes
from entities import User
from fastapi import Depends, FastAPI
from services.auth import AuthService

auth_service = AuthService()
AuthenticateUserDep = Annotated[User, Depends(auth_service.get_current_user)]

...

app = FastAPI(lifespan=lifespan)

app.include_router(routes.auth.router, prefix="/auth", tags=["Auth"]) ❷
app.include_router(
    routes.resource.router,
    dependencies=[AuthenticateUserDep],
    prefix="/generate",
```

```
      tags=["Generate"],
) ❸
...  # Add other routes to the app here
```

❶ Refactor existing endpoints to be grouped under a separate API router named the resource router.

❷ Add both auth and resource routers to the FastAPI app router.

❸ Protect the resource endpoints by injecting the `AuthenticateUserDep` dependency at the router level. Requests must now include an `Authorization` header with a bearer token to be authenticated with the resource router.

Massive congratulations! You now have a fully working GenAI service protected by JWT authentication, which can be deployed to production with some additional work.

In the next section, you'll learn a few ideas on additional enhancements you can make to the system to tighten the security of your JWT authentication system.

Authentication flows

You will need to handle several authentication flows to fully implement a usable JWT authentication system.

The *core* authentication flows include the following:

User registration
New users will want to register a new account by providing their emails and a secure password. Your authentication logic may check for password strength, no existing users with the same email, and that the user reconfirms the password and email. You should also avoid storing the user's raw password in the database.

User login
On each user login, your system can generate, store, and provide a unique temporary access token (i.e., JWT) if a user supplies their correct credentials. Your protected resource server routers should reject any incoming requests that don't contain a valid JWT. Valid JWTs can be verified through their signature and checked against the valid tokens specified in the database.

User logout
When the user logs out, your system can revoke the currently issued token and prevent future malicious login attempts with the current token.

In addition to the core flows, you should also consider *secondary* flows to implement a production-ready authentication system. These flows could be used for:

Verifying identity
> To prevent spambots from registering active accounts in your system and consuming server resources, you will want some form of user verification mechanism in place. For instance, add email verification by integrating an emailing server to your authentication system.

Resetting passwords
> Users can forget their passwords at any time. You will want to implement a flow for users to reset their passwords. If a user resets their password, all active tokens in the database against their user account must be revoked.

Forcing logout
> Revoke all previously generated access tokens of a user on all clients to prevent stolen tokens from being used to access the system.

Disabling user accounts
> Administrators or users may want to disable their accounts to prevent future login attempts.

Deleting user accounts
> This is required if users would like to remove their accounts from your systems. Depending on your data storage requirements, you may want to delete personally identifiable information while keeping other associated data.

Blocking successive login attempts
> Temporarily disable an account that has had multiple failed login attempts within a short time span.

Providing refresh tokens
> Generate both short-lived *access* tokens and long-lived *refresh* tokens. Since access tokens can expire frequently to reduce the window of opportunity for attackers to use a stolen token, clients can reuse their refresh token to request new access tokens. This removes the need for frequent logins while maintaining security of the system against attackers.

Two-factor authentication (2FA) or multifactor authentication (MFA)
> You can secure your system against exposed password-protected accounts by requiring 2FA or MFA as an additional protection layer. 2FA/MFA examples include SMS/email verification, one-time passwords (OTPs), or randomly generated number sequences from a paired authentication app as a second login step before an access token can be generated.

The aforementioned list is not exhaustive. You may want to check out "OWASP Top 10 Web Applications Security Risks" (*https://oreil.ly/xAGfn*) and "OWASP Authentication Cheat Sheet" (*https://oreil.ly/oSyuz*) for the full list of considerations when implementing your own JWT authentication from scratch.

In addition to following the OWASP top 10 guidelines, you should use security mechanisms such as *rate limiting*, *geo/IP-tracking*, and *account lockouts* to defend against various attacks.

You can also consider using third-party authentication providers (such as Okta/Auth0, Firebase Auth, KeyCloak, Amazon Cognito, etc.) that include these security features in their services.

While credentials-based authentication using JWTs can be considered a production-ready authentication system and be further enhanced with MFA systems in place, the mechanism has its own limitations. For instance, as previously mentioned, requiring credentials and storing hashed passwords in a database can retain security risks if attackers leverage password spraying or credential stuffing brute-force attacks.

In addition, if you require access to user resources external to your system, you will need to implement additional mechanisms to verify your application's identity to external identity providers. Since this remains a common need in many applications and services, a protocol called OAuth has been developed to facilitate the whole process.

Let's explore how you can use OAuth authentication to add more login options for users and access external user resources. This can enhance the performance of your GenAI services and generate higher-quality outputs.

Implementing OAuth Authentication

We touched upon the concept of OAuth authentication via identity providers earlier in this chapter.

OAuth is an open standard for access delegation, often used to grant websites or applications limited access to user information without exposing passwords. It allows you to authenticate users using identity providers such as Google, Facebook, etc., and grants your application access to user resources like calendars, files, social feeds, etc., on external services.

By using OAuth, you can simplify the implementation of authentication in your app by leveraging existing identity providers instead of creating your own authentication mechanisms such as JWT.

Identity providers (IDPs) are platforms that enable other applications, such as your GenAI service, to integrate with and rely on their identity and authentication systems to access resources on behalf of users via a standardized process. The IDP authenticates users and issues security tokens that assert the user's identity and other attributes. GitHub, Google, Microsoft 365, Apple, Meta, and LinkedIn are only a handful of hundreds of identity providers.

The protocol powering this entire flow under the hood is *OAuth 2.0*, an authorization framework giving applications limited access to another service on behalf of a user.

Using this approach, your application can redirect users to identity provider platforms so that users can grant limited timed access to their accounts on those platforms. After the user gives consent, your application can perform operations on their behalf on their resources like calendars or read their profile information including personally identifiable information such as emails or images.

As a result, OAuth authentication is often used to verify the identity of users as you trust the external platform/identity provider's authentication process. Therefore, this approach reduces the burden of storing and securing user credentials in your system, which can be prone to brute-force attacks on weak or compromised passwords.

In this section, you're going to implement a variant of OAuth based on the *authorization code flow* that's commonly used in modern applications. The step-by-step process is as follows:

1. The user clicks the login button in your application to start the authentication flow.

2. The user is redirected to the identity provider's login page, and your application supplies a client ID and secret to the identity provider to identify itself.

3. The user logs into their account and is presented with a consent screen like the one shown in Figure 8-7 presenting them the scopes (i.e., permissions) that your application is requesting on their behalf.

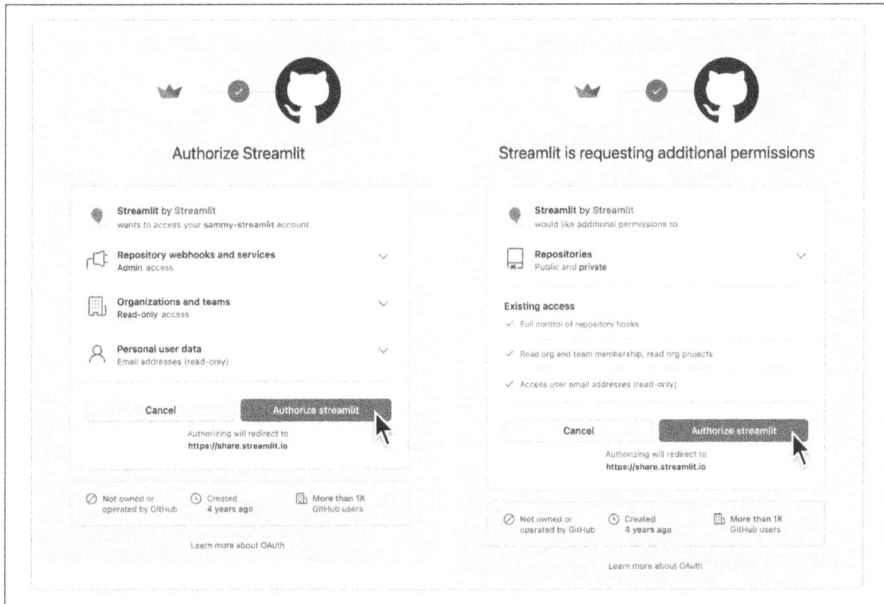

Figure 8-7. Example consent screen

4. The user grants all, some, or none of the requested scopes.

5. If consent is not rejected by the user (i.e., the resource owner), the identity provider's authorization server issues your application a *grant code* to an endpoint that you provide called the *redirect URI*. If your redirect URI is not previously approved with the identity provider, the identity provider will reject to issue a grant code here.

6. After your application receives a grant code associated with the user session, permitted scopes, and your application's client ID, it can exchange this grant code with the authorization server for a *short-lived access token* and a *longer-lived refresh token*. You can use the refresh token to request new access tokens without having to restart the whole authentication process.

7. Your application can now use this access token to access the provider's resource server to perform operations on behalf of the user on their resources. As a result, you can authenticate the user via the identity provider to resources on your system.

> Through the OAuth process, the authorization server may also issue a *state* parameter or *CSRF token*, which your application must supply as it communicates with the identity provider's servers. The purpose of the state parameter or CSRF token is to protect against cross-site request forgery (CSRF) attacks.
>
> With CSRF, attackers may steal an authenticated session to forge authenticated requests to the resource servers without the user's knowledge.

Figure 8-8 shows the full OAuth authentication flow.

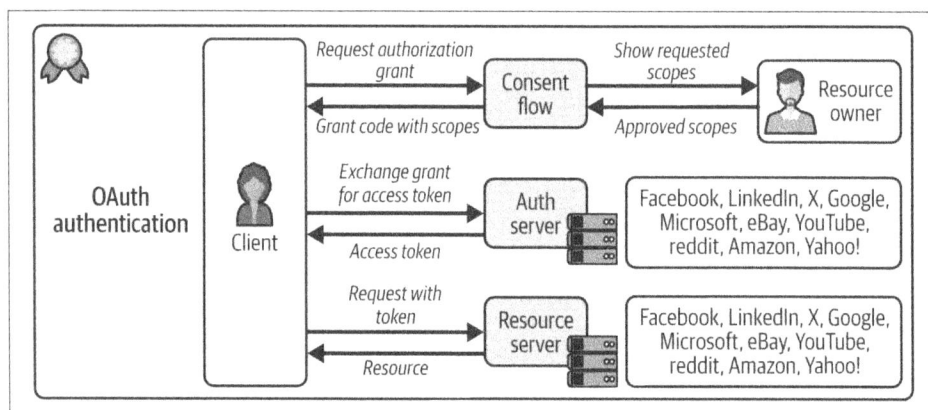

Figure 8-8. OAuth authentication flow

Now that you have a high-level overview of the OAuth authentication flow, let's implement it inside FastAPI with an identity provider such as GitHub to fully understand the underlying mechanisms.

OAuth Authentication with GitHub

The first step to setting up the OAuth authentication is to create a set of client ID and secret credentials within GitHub so that their systems can identify your application.

You can generate a client ID and secret from GitHub by visiting the developer settings under your GitHub profile and creating an OAuth application.[5]

With your new application client ID and secret, you can now redirect users to the GitHub authorization server from your application by following Example 8-13.

---

5 For up-to-date instructions, please visit the GitHub documentation (*https://oreil.ly/tWg6w*).

Example 8-13. Redirect users to the GitHub authorization server to start the OAuth process

```python
# routes/auth.py

import secrets
from fastapi import APIRouter, Request, status
from fastapi.responses import RedirectResponse

client_id = "your_client_id"
client_secret = "your_client_secret"

router = APIRouter()

...

@router.get("/oauth/github/login", status_code=status.HTTP_301_REDIRECT)
def oauth_github_login_controller(request: Request) -> RedirectResponse:
    state = secrets.token_urlsafe(16)
    redirect_uri = request.url_for("oauth_github_callback_controller")
    response = RedirectResponse(
        url=f"https://github.com/login/oauth/authorize"
        f"?client_id={client_id}"
        f"&scope=user"
        f"&state={state}"
        f"&redirect_uri={redirect_uri}"
    ) ❶
    csrf_token = secrets.token_urlsafe(16)
    request.session["x-csrf-state-token"] = csrf_token
    return response
```

❶ Redirect user to the GitHub authorization server to log into their account while supplying your application credentials, a requested scope, and a CSRF state value to prevent against CSRF attacks.

As you can see in Example 8-13, the scope of the request is the user, meaning that once users log into their GitHub account, they will be presented with a consent screen for your application to be granted access to their user profile.

Now that you have a backend endpoint redirecting requests to the GitHub authorization server, you can put a button in your client-side application to hit this endpoint and start the OAuth process with GitHub (see Example 8-14).

Example 8-14. Adding a GitHub login button to the Streamlit client-side application

```python
# client.py

import requests
import streamlit as st
```

```
if st.button("Login with GitHub"):
    response = requests.get("http://localhost:8000/auth/oauth/github/login")
    if not response.ok:
        st.error("Failed to login with GitHub. Please try again later")
        response.raise_for_status()
```

You now have implemented the redirect flow that starts the OAuth authentication process with GitHub as the identity provider.

When users log into their GitHub account, GitHub will show them a consent screen similar to Figure 8-7.

If the user accepts the consent, GitHub will redirect the user back to your application with a grant code and a state. You should check whether the state matches the previously generated state.

> If the states do not match, a third party has made the request, and you should stop the process.

Once you have the grant code, you can send this to the GitHub authorization to exchange it for an access token, as shown in Example 8-15.

Example 8-15. Exchanging grant code with an access token while protecting against CSRF attacks

```
# dependencies/auth.py

from typing import Annotated
import aiohttp
from fastapi import Depends, HTTPException
from loguru import logger

client_id = "your_client_id"
client_secret = "your_client_secret"

async def exchange_grant_with_access_token(code: str) -> str:
    try:
        body = {
            "client_id": client_id,
            "client_secret": client_secret,
            "code": code,
        }
        headers = {
            "Accept": "application/json",
            "Content-Type": "application/json",
        }
```

```
            async with aiohttp.ClientSession() as session:
                async with session.post(
                    "https://github.com/login/oauth/access_token",
                    json=body,
                    headers=headers,
                ) as resp:
                    access_token_data = await resp.json()
        except Exception as e:
            logger.warning(f"Failed to fetch the access token. Error: {e}")
            raise HTTPException(
                status_code=503, detail="Failed to fetch access token"
            )

        if not access_token_data:
            raise HTTPException(
                status_code=503, detail="Failed to obtain access token"
            )

        return access_token_data.get("access_token", "")

ExchangeCodeTokenDep = Annotated[str, Depends(exchange_grant_with_access_token)]
```

You can now add a new endpoint that accepts requests from the GitHub authorization server. This callback endpoint should have a CSRF protection to guard against third parties impersonating the authorization server. If the request from GitHub is forged, the state parameter provided and the one stored in the request session won't match.

Cross-Site Request Forgery

CSRF is a type of security vulnerability that allows an attacker to trick a user into performing actions on a web application where they are authenticated. This can lead to unauthorized actions being executed without the user's consent.

In CSRF, the attacker creates a malicious request that exploits the user's authenticated session with a target website. These attacks can result in unauthorized transactions, data theft, or changes to user settings without their consent and knowledge.

In the context of OAuth2, an attacker can exploit vulnerabilities such as *open redirect* to intercept the initial authorization requests and modify them to redirect to their own malicious site after authentication.

Attackers can also create a replica of your application frontend and trick users into logging into their accounts. If the user logs into their GitHub account via the phishing site, the attacker can provide a redirect URL pointing to their own servers to get an authorization grant code. They can then exchange the authorization code for an access token.

Figure 8-9 shows an example of the OAuth2 CSRF attack using an open redirect vulnerability.

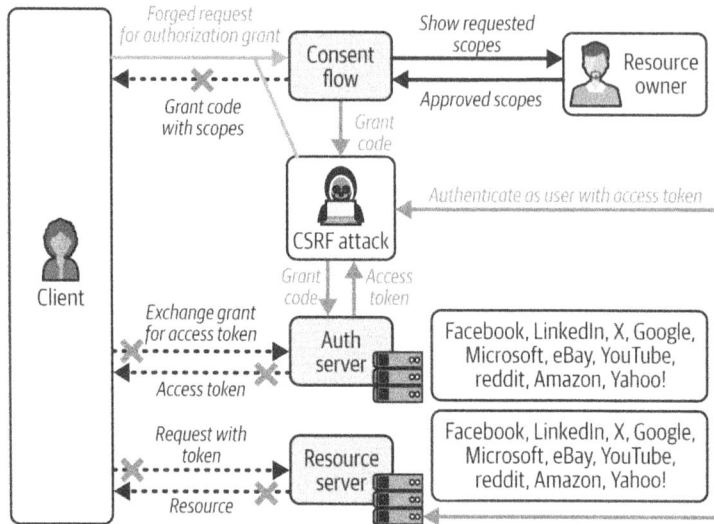

Figure 8-9. OAuth2 CSRF attack using an open redirect vulnerability

A `state` or `csrf_token` parameter exchanged during requests between the client and authorization servers can prevent against CSRF attacks by maintaining session state between requests, responses, and redirections.

In addition, to protect against open redirect vulnerabilities, you should also pre-register and strictly validate redirect URLs with the identity provider, educate your users on phishing attempts, and implement logging and monitoring mechanisms to detect suspicious requests.

Example 8-16 shows the callback endpoint implementation.

Example 8-16. Implement callback endpoint to get access token while protecting against CSRF attacks

```
# routes/auth.py

from dependencies.auth import ExchangeCodeTokenDep
from fastapi import Depends, HTTPException, Request
from fastapi.responses import RedirectResponse

...

def check_csrf_state(request: Request, state: str) -> None:
```

```
    if state != request.session.get("x-csrf-token"):
        raise HTTPException(detail="Bad request", status_code=401)

@router.get("/oauth/github/callback", dependencies=[Depends(check_csrf_state)])
async def oauth_github_callback_controller(
    access_token: ExchangeCodeTokenDep,
) -> RedirectResponse:
    response = RedirectResponse(url=f"http://localhost:8501")
    response.set_cookie(key="access_token", value=access_token, httponly=True)
    return response
```

In Example 8-16, you are using the request session for CSRF protection, but this won't work without adding the Starlette's `SessionMiddlware` first to maintain a secure user session that's only mutable on the server side, as shown in Example 8-17.

Example 8-17. Add a session middleware to manage session state for protecting against CSRF attacks

```
# main.py

from fastapi import FastAPI
from starlette.middleware.sessions import SessionMiddleware

...

app = FastAPI(lifespan=lifespan)
app.add_middleware(SessionMiddleware, secret_key="your_secret_key")
```

> Avoid relying on HTTP *cookies* to store and read the `state` between request sessions as cookies can be read and manipulated by third parties. Never trust any data that comes from the client.

By writing the unique `state` to the session in Example 8-13 and comparing it with the `state` value in the incoming request query parameters, you can then confirm the identity of the request.

In this case, the requester is the GitHub authorization server sending you a grant code. Once you receive the grant code, you then exchange it with the GitHub authorization server for an access token.

> The process shown in the OAuth-related code examples can also be implemented with the open source `authlib` package for simpler implementation, as the package handles most of the work for you.

Finally, you can use the access token you received from the authorization server to fetch user information such as their name, email, and profile image to register their identity in your application.

Example 8-18 demonstrates how to implement an endpoint that returns the user info from GitHub if the request supplies an access token as part of the request's authorization header.

> Ideally, you should avoid sharing the user's GitHub access token with the user's browser. If the token is stolen, your application is responsible for compromising the user's GitHub account.
>
> Instead, create and share your own short-lived access token tied to the GitHub access token to authenticate the user with your application. If your application token is stolen, you avoid compromising user accounts beyond the scope of your application.

Example 8-18. Use access token to get user information from GitHub resource servers

```python
# routes/auth.py

from typing import Annotated
import aiohttp
from fastapi import Depends, HTTPException
from fastapi.security import HTTPAuthorizationCredentials, HTTPBearer

security = HTTPBearer()
HTTPBearerDep = Annotated[HTTPAuthorizationCredentials, Depends(security)]

...

async def get_user_info(credentials: HTTPBearerDep) -> dict:
    try:
        async with aiohttp.ClientSession() as session:
            headers = {"Authorization": f"Bearer {credentials.credentials}"}
            async with session.get(
                "https://api.github.com/user", headers=headers
            ) as resp:
                return await resp.json()
    except Exception as e:
        raise HTTPException(
            status_code=503, detail=f"Failed to obtain user info - Error: {e}"
        )

GetUserInfoDep = Annotated[dict, Depends(get_user_info)]

@router.get("/oauth/github/callback")
async def get_current_user_controller(user_info: GetUserInfoDep) -> dict:
    return user_info
```

Congratulations! You should now have a working authentication system that leverages OAuth2 to authenticate users.

OAuth2 Flow Types

The OAuth2 flow that you just implemented was the *authorization code flow* (ACF). However, there are other flows that you can choose depending on the use case. The identity provider documentation may present you with solutions for various flows, which can feel overwhelming if you're not aware of these use cases.

Authorization code flow

The authorization code flow is the common approach for applications that leverage servers and backend APIs such as FastAPI, using code grants to issue access tokens.

A more secure variant of ACF leverages *proof key for exchange* (PKCE, pronounced "pixie"). You can use the ACF-PKCE flow where you cannot protect the authorization code from being stolen—for instance, on mobile devices.

During the ACF-PKCE flow, you add a hashed secret called the `code_challenge` when sending the initial request to the identity provider. Then you present the unhashed secret `code_verifier` again to exchange the authorization code for an access token.

In essence, PKCE protects against *authorization code interception* attacks—shown in Figure 8-10—by adding a layer of verification during the token exchange process.

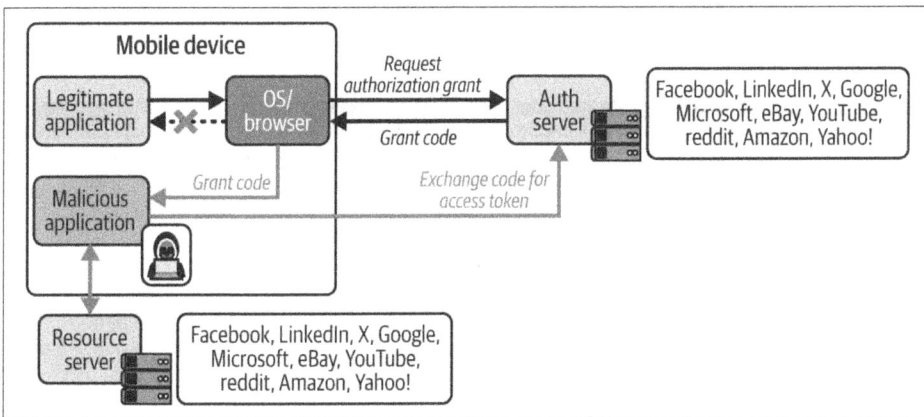

Figure 8-10. OAuth2 authorization code interception attack on a mobile device

Implicit flow

For single-page applications (SPAs) where there is no separate backend, you can also use the *implicit flow*, which skips the authorization grant code to directly get an access token. Implicit flow is less secure than the previous flow but enhances the user experience.

Client credentials flow

If you're building a backend service for machine-to-machine communication and where no browsers will be involved, then you can use the *client credentials flow*. Here you can exchange your client ID and secret for an access token to access your own resources on the identity provider servers (i.e., you won't have access on behalf of other users).

Resource owner password credentials flow

Resource owner password credentials flow is like the client credentials flow but uses a username and password of the user to get an access token. As the credentials are being exchanged directly with the authorization server, you should avoid using this flow as much as possible.

Device authorization flow

Finally, there is the *device authorization flow* that's mostly used for devices with limited input capabilities, such as when you log into your Apple TV account on your smart TV by scanning a QR code and using a web browser from your phone.

Table 8-2 compares the various flows to help you select the right option for your own use case, based on your specific requirements and constraints.

Table 8-2. Comparison of OAuth2 authorization flows

Flow	Description	Considerations	Use cases
Authorization code flow (including PKCE)	Get the authorization code via a user login and exchange for an access token.	• Provider's access token must be securely stored and never exposed to the browser. • Use ACF-PKCE flow if possible for enhanced security.	• Server-side applications and web applications with a backend server that can securely handle the client secret and access tokens. • Mobile applications if using a PKCE token as client credentials can't be securely stored.
Implicit flow	Get an access token without an authorization code.	• Less secure as the access token is exposed to the browser. • Use when using the authorization code flow is not possible.	Single-page applications (SPAs) where user experience is prioritized over security, when prototyping, or where the authorization code flow is not possible.

Flow	Description	Considerations	Use cases
Client credentials flow	The client directly exchanges its client credentials (client ID and client secret) for an access token.	No user interaction involved, meant for scenarios where the client is acting on its own behalf. Ensure secure storage of client credentials.	Server-to-server applications.
Resource owner password credentials flow	Exchange user's username and password directly for an access token.	• High security risk as user's credentials are handled directly. • Only use in legacy systems where other flows are not supported.	Legacy applications or highly trusted environments.
Device authorization flow	Visit a URL on another device to enter a code for an access token.	Requires a second device with a web browser for the user to authenticate.	Devices with limited input capabilities, like smart TVs, gaming consoles, or IoT devices.

You should now feel more confident in securing your application with a variety of commercial identity verification mechanisms, including the various OAuth2 flows that leverage external IDPs.

Troubleshooting OAuth Implementation Issues

There are often several common issues that you may face when implementing OAuth authentication in your services. Table 8-3 lists these issues with corresponding solutions that you can use as a reference.

Table 8-3. OAuth issues with solutions

Issue	Solution
Invalid redirect URI	Register (i.e., allowlist) the redirect URI with the identity provider.
Invalid client ID or secret	Generate and copy the correct client ID and secret from the identity provider when you register your application with them.
Expired token	The identity provider may issue you refresh tokens that you can use to get new access tokens without repeating the full OAuth authorization flow.
Missing scopes	Add valid scopes in the authorization request to the provider. The user of your services must also consent to these scopes.
Incorrect token endpoint	Send a request to the right token endpoint URL provided by the identity provider to get an access token.
CORS errors	Configure the identity provider settings to allow CORS for your domain or use a server-side proxy to handle the OAuth requests.
Invalid grant type	Provide the correct grant type in the request to the identity provider.

As you can see, most issues listed relate to incorrect implementation or configuration of OAuth flows with the OAuth identity provider. To avoid some of these problems, you may consider using OAuth libraries such as `authlib` that handles much of the complexity for you as long as you're using the correct provider secrets.

Authentication forms the first step to securing your services by identifying who the users of your system are.

A question remains: what should happen when a user is logged into your services? Can they fetch data, interact with models, and mutate resources as they please, or would you rather control their interactions in your services?

These are problems that an authorization system will tackle, which we will talk about next.

Authorization

So far, we've been covering various authentication mechanisms including the basic, token-based (JWT), and OAuth2 for securing your applications.

As mentioned earlier, authentication systems identify and verify actors, whereas the authorization systems enforce *permissions* in an application (i.e., who can do what on which resource).

In this section, you're going to learn about the authorization system that takes into account the following:

- The *actor* (i.e., the user or a third-party service acting on behalf of the user)
- The *action* being undertaken
- The impact of the action on *resources*

In essence, an authorization system can be compared to a function that accepts three inputs—*actor*, *action*, *resource*—and returns a *Boolean decision* to *allow* or *deny* a request. To implement the authorization function, you will require *authorization data* such as user attributes, relationships (like team/group/org memberships), resource ownership, roles, and permissions passed through a set of *abstract rules* to determine the Boolean allow/deny decisions.

Once a decision is made, you can *enforce* the authorization by either allowing actions (such as fetching or mutating resources) or denying requests (such as sending 403 Forbidden responses, redirecting users, hiding resources, locking accounts, etc.).

On the surface level, implementing authorization can be simple. Using a few conditional statements, you can check whether a user has permissions to perform an action. However, this naive approach can get complex to manage as the number of places you need to implement authorization steps increases. This issue becomes worse as you make changes to the logic across the application, making the system complex and adding finer controls. You may end up duplicating logic or making future changes more difficult, and the authorization rules may deeply be interwoven in your application logic, making separation from the rest of the application more challenging.

In such cases, authorization models can be useful to help you navigate the complexity of managing authorization decisions and enforcements in your applications.

Authorization Models

There are a few common *authorization models* that you can learn to make structuring and implementing an authorization system easier:

Role-based access control (RBAC)
Authorization is based on the roles assigned to users, where each role has specific permissions. For instance, administrators can access every available GenAI model, bypassing authorization rules enforced on users.

Relationship-based access control (ReBAC)
Authorization is determined by the relationships between entities, such as user-to-user (i.e., follower, friend, connection) or user-to-resource (i.e., group, team, org) relationships. For instance, this could authorize a user who is a member of a team to access premium models purchased by that team.

Attribute-based access control (ABAC)
Authorization decisions are made based on attributes of users, resources, and the environment, allowing for fine-grained access control. For instance, a conversation with a *public* attribute is viewable by everyone, and a user with a *paid* attribute can access premium GenAI models.

RBAC is the simplest authorization model but won't provide the enhanced granular controls and flexibility of other authorization models. ABAC controls provide more fine-grained access control and can override both ReBAC and RBAC rules. Furthermore, ReBAC can also override or extend RBAC controls.

Table 8-4 compares the three authorization models.

Table 8-4. Comparison of authorization methods

Type	Benefits	Limitations	Use cases
Role-based (RBAC)	Simplifies management	Limited flexibility	Enterprise environments, access control, financial systems, healthcare systems
Relationship-based (ReBAC)	Fine-grained control	Needs relationship data from various sources with complex permission evaluations	Social networks, collaborative platforms, content-sharing applications, project management tools
Attribute-based (ABAC)	Highly flexible	Needs attribute data from various sources with complex permission evaluations	Dynamic environments, cloud services, IoT systems, regulatory compliance, personalized user experiences

These three authorization models also have a hierarchical relationship, as demonstrated in Figure 8-11.

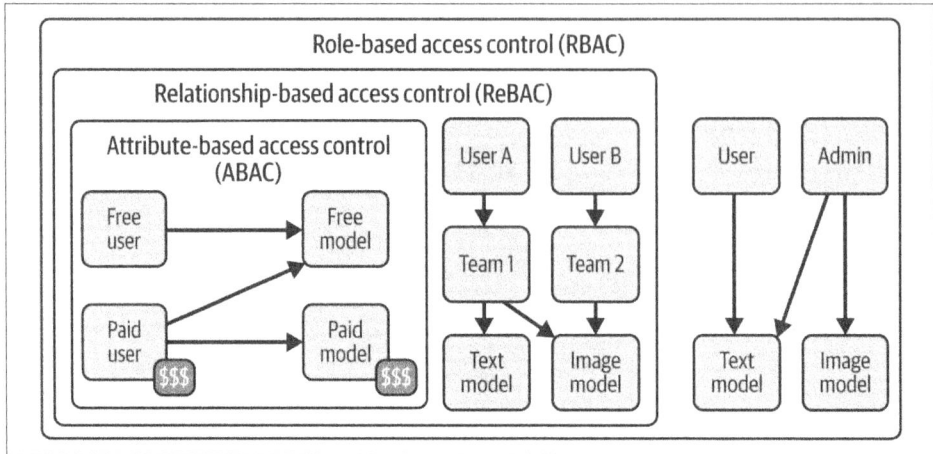

Figure 8-11. Authorization models

Let's now discuss each authorization model in detail, starting with the RBAC model.

Role-Based Access Control

Using *roles* is a widely adopted model for implementing authorization in applications due to their simplicity.

Roles are straightforward to understand. They normally correspond to whom the user is and what they want to do in the application. Sometimes authorization roles can directly map to roles in your organization's hierarchy.

You can group permissions under a role that can then be *assigned* to users to grant user those permissions. A *permission* specifies the action that a user can take on resources, such as if the user can interact with the paid LLM model provided by your service.

For better administrative and user experience, you can create multiple roles with preset permissions to reduce decision fatigue when setting user permissions. Instead of having to set a vast number of permissions, you can assign a few predefined roles.

A common starting point for many commercial services is user and administrator roles. While a member can access the core functionality of the application such as interacting with GenAI models, and reading and writing resources, they won't be able to view data of other users or manage roles. On the other hand, administrators can assign and remove roles, view and mutate every resource, or disable and enable accounts. Administrators may also have access to early features such as GenAI models that normal users can't access yet, as shown in Figure 8-12.

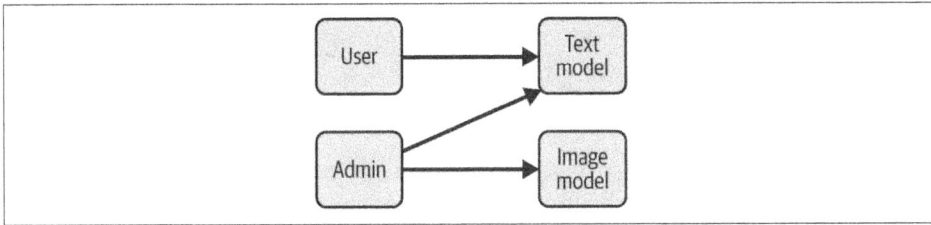

Figure 8-12. RBAC example where only administrators have access to image-based GenAI models

You can implement a simple RBAC authorization model to control the GenAI services that your users can access, as shown in Example 8-19.

Example 8-19. Implementing RBAC using FastAPI dependencies

```python
# dependencies/auth.py

from entities import User
from fastapi import Depends, HTTPException, status
from services.auth import AuthService

async def is_admin(user: User = Depends(AuthService.get_current_user)) -> User: ❶
    if user.role != "ADMIN":
        raise HTTPException(
            status_code=status.HTTP_403_FORBIDDEN,
            detail="Not allowed to perform this action",
        )
    return user

# routers/resource.py

from dependencies.auth import is_admin
from fastapi import APIRouter, Depends
from services.auth import AuthService

router = APIRouter(
    dependencies=[Depends(AuthService.get_current_user)], ❸
    prefix="/generate",
    tags=["Resource"],
)

@router.post("/image", dependencies=[Depends(is_admin)])
async def generate_image_controller(): ❷
    ...

@router.post("/text") ❸
async def generate_text_controller():
    ...
```

❶ Implement the `is_admin` authorization dependency guard on top of the `Auth Service.get_current_user` dependency. Mark the function as `async` since the child dependency is performing an async operation against the database.

❷ Use the authorization guard dependency to deny access to the image generation service for nonadmin authenticated users.

❸ Nonadmin authenticated users can still access other resource controllers since the router is secured by an authentication guard dependency.

Using the same logic shown in Example 8-19, you can construct varying system prompt templates or use different model variants fine-tuned to each role.

> Bear in mind that implementing authorization at the application layer is more secure than delegating it to the GenAI model. LLMs and other GenAI models can be vulnerable to *prompt injection* attacks where an attacker manipulates the input to the model to bypass system instructions to produce unauthorized and harmful outputs.
>
> Future versions of LLMs and other GenAI models may mitigate prompt injection risks by enforcing custom authorization rules internally using extensions like the *control neural network (Control-Net)* in Stable Diffusion models.

To create more complex RBAC authorization logic than the one shown in Example 8-19, you can implement *subdependencies* or an *abstract dependency*. Both approaches will leverage FastAPI's powerful *hierarchical dependency graphs* as authorization guards to enforce permissions in your GenAI service.

As an example, if you add new roles in the future that inherit a subset of permissions of another role (i.e., moderators and admins), then you can follow either of the approaches shown in Figure 8-13.

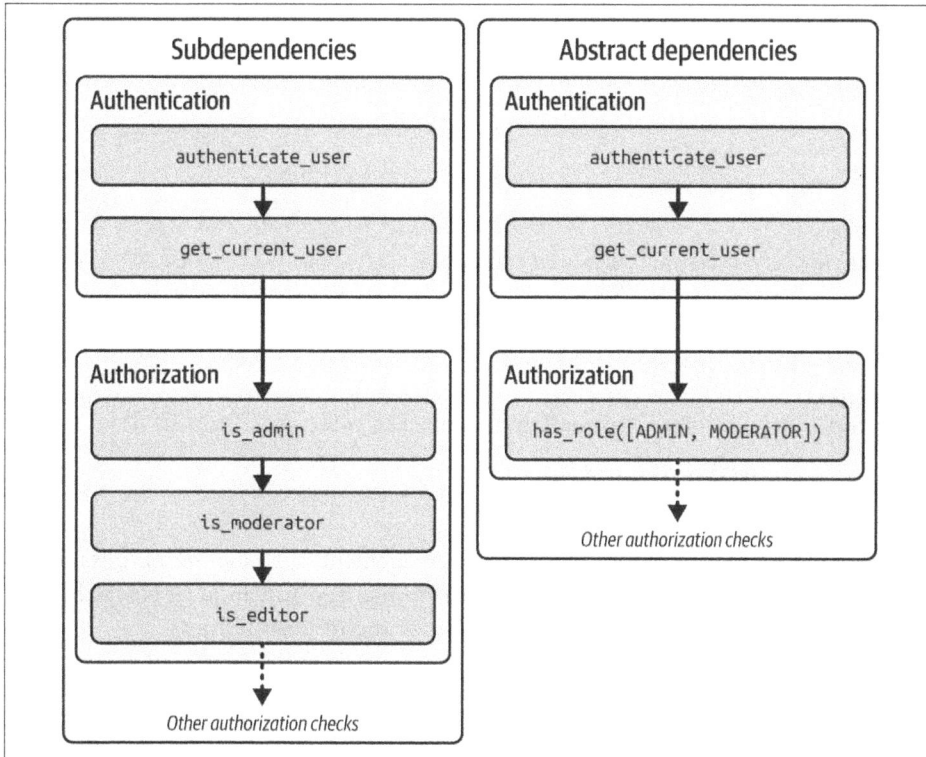

Figure 8-13. Approaches for implementing complex RBAC models

You can implement complex RBAC authorization logic using abstract dependencies, as shown in Example 8-20.

Example 8-20. Implementing complex RBAC authorization using abstract dependencies

```python
# dependencies/auth.py

from typing import Annotated

from entities import User
from fastapi import APIRouter, Depends, HTTPException, status
from services.auth import AuthService

CurrentUserDep = Annotated[User, Depends(AuthService.get_current_user)]

async def has_role(user: CurrentUserDep, roles: list[str]) -> User:
    if user.role not in roles:
        raise HTTPException(
            status_code=status.HTTP_403_FORBIDDEN,
            detail="Not allowed to perform this action",
        )
```

```
        return user


# routes/resource.py

...

@router.post(
    "/image",
    dependencies=[Depends(lambda user: has_role(user, ["ADMIN", "MODERATOR"]))],
)
async def generate_image_controller():
    ...

@router.post(
    "/text", dependencies=[Depends(lambda user: has_role(user, ["EDITOR"]))]
)
async def generate_text_controller():
    ...
```

In summary, RBAC simplifies permission management by assigning permissions to roles rather than individuals, making it easier to manage and audit. It is scalable and efficient for organizations with well-defined roles and responsibilities.

However, RBAC can lead to role explosion when many granular roles are necessary, making it hard to manage. It also lacks the flexibility to handle complex hierarchical relationships like teams and groups alongside setting dynamic permissions based on attributes like user preferences, time, and privacy settings, which limits its granularity compared to ReBAC or ABAC.

Relationship-Based Access Control

Relationship-based access control is an extension of RBAC with a focus on relationships between resources and users.

With this mode, instead of just setting roles at the user level across the entire application, you must set roles and permissions at the resource level. This means you will have to confirm the actions each role can take on every resource type. For example, instead of assigning a "moderator" role to a user that grants access to all resources (i.e., conversations, teams, users, etc.), you would assign specific permissions to the moderator role for each resource. A moderator might have read and delete permissions on the conversation resource but only read permission on the team resource.

This model allows you to create authorization policies based on hierarchical and nested structures within your data and be visualized as graphs where nodes can be represented as resources/identities and edges as relationships.

Since you can create authorization rules based on relationships, this can save you lots of time setting permissions at an instance level. As an example, instead of sharing every private LLM conversation in your app one by one, you can group them under a team or a folder and share the folder or add members to the team instead. In ReBAC, children instances can inherit parent's permissions, as shown in Figure 8-14. It's the same for related instances if needed.

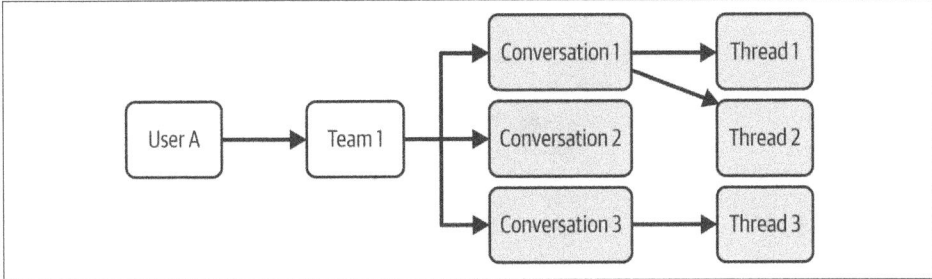

Figure 8-14. Example ReBAC where a user can see the team's private conversations and threads

The example shown in Figure 8-14 demonstrates both organization and hierarchical relationships between users (i.e., teams and members) and resources (conversations and threads).

> If you decide to adopt the ReBAC model, I recommend visually mapping out the relationships between resources and identities in your application.
>
> This work includes mapping out *policies* (i.e., rules), *resources* and available *actions* on them, *resource-level roles*, and *relationships* between entities.

A big problem that ReBAC solves by extending RBAC is the explosion of roles within the RBAC model by combining relationships with roles. It is ideal for managing permissions in complex hierarchical structures and allows for reverse queries, enabling efficient permission definitions using teams and groups. However, ReBAC can be complex to implement and maintain, resource-intensive, difficult to audit, and not as fine-grained as ABAC for dynamic permissions based on attributes like time or location.

Attribute-Based Access Control

Attribute-based access control authorization model expands basic RBAC roles by setting access control rules based on *conditions applied to attributes* to implement more granular policies. As an example, ABAC can prevent users from uploading sensitive documents into your RAG-enabled services if the document contains *personally identifiable information (PII)* (i.e., `upload.has_pii=true`).

Another example of ABAC can be seen in SaaS applications like ChatGPT where only paid users have access to the service's premium GenAI models (see Figure 8-15).

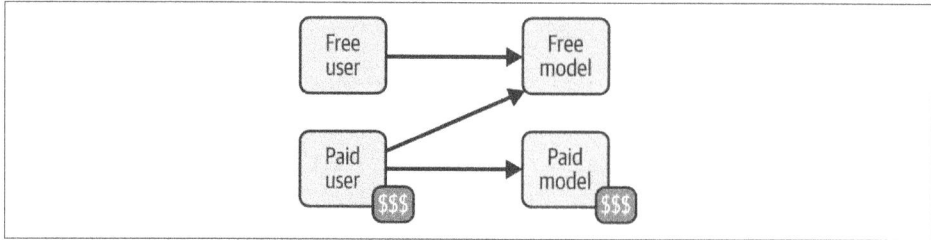

Figure 8-15. ABAC example where only paid users have access to premium GenAI models

Since the freedom to set policies based on attributes is infinite, the ABAC model allows for significantly fine-grained authorization policies. However, ABAC can be cumbersome for managing hierarchical structures, making it challenging to determine which users have access to a specific resource. For example, if you have a policy that grants access based on attributes like user role, data sensitivity level, and project membership, determining all users who can access a specific dataset requires evaluating these attributes for every user.

While less complicated than ReBAC, ABAC can still be challenging to implement, in particular in large and complex applications that support a large number of roles, users, and attributes.

Hybrid Authorization Models

If you've worked with larger applications in the past, you will notice that they combine features of the RBAC, ReBAC, and ABAC authorization models. For instance, administrators may have access to any resource and user management/authentication features (RBAC), and users can share their private resources by setting visibility attribute to public (ABAC) and can add members to their team for collaborating on private resources.

A hybrid approach combining RBAC, ReBAC, and ABAC models may give you the strengths of all the authorization models:

- RBAC simplifies permission management by assigning roles to users, making it easy to manage and audit.

- ReBAC is perfect for managing hierarchical relationships and reverse queries, making it suitable for complex hierarchical structures.

- ABAC provides fine-grained control based on user and resource attributes, allowing for dynamic and context-aware permissions.

Figure 8-16 demonstrates the hybrid authorization model.

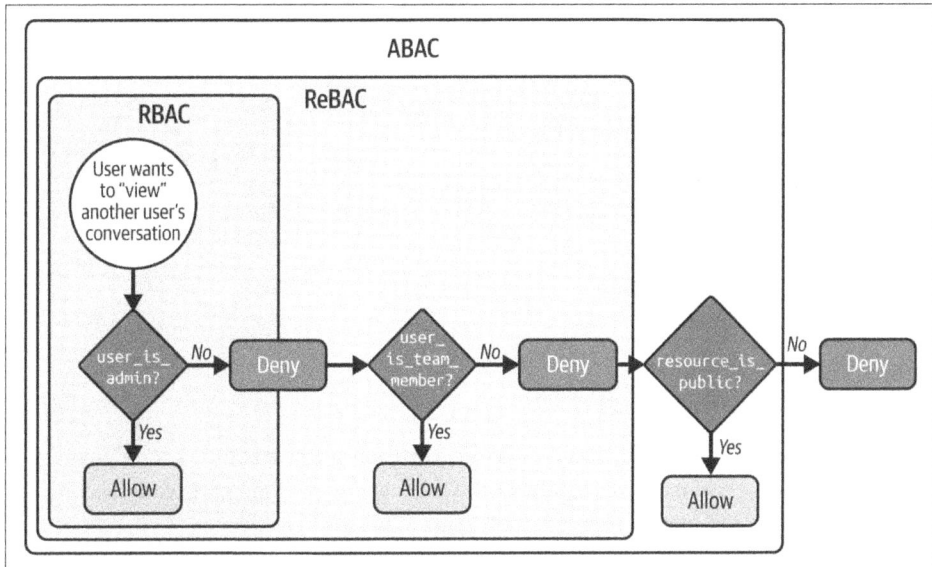

Figure 8-16. Hybrid authorization model based on roles, relationships, and attributes

To implement the hybrid authorization combining RBAC, ReBAC, and ABAC models, you can follow Example 8-21.

Example 8-21. Implementing the hybrid authorization model combining RBAC, ReBAC, and ABAC

```python
# dependencies/auth.py

from typing import Annotated
from fastapi import Depends, HTTPException, status
... # import services and entities here

CurrentUserDep = Annotated[User, Depends(AuthService.get_current_user)]
TeamMembershipRep = Annotated[Team, Depends(TeamService.get_current_team)]
ResourceDep = Annotated[Resource, Depends(ResourceService.get_resource)]

def authorize(
    user: CurrentUserDep, resource: ResourceDep, team: TeamMembershipRep
) -> bool:
    if user.role == "ADMIN":
        return True
    if user.id in team.members:
        return True
    if resource.is_public:
        return True
    raise HTTPException(
```

```
        status_code=status.HTTP_403_FORBIDDEN, detail="Access Denied"
    )

# routes/resource.py

from dependencies.auth import authorize
from fastapi import APIRouter, Depends

router = APIRouter(
    dependencies=[Depends(authorize)], prefix="/generate", tags=["Resource"]
)

@router.post("/image")
async def generate_image_controller(): ...

@router.post("/text")
async def generate_text_controller(): ...
```

As you define rules and permissions based on each authorization model, you also may decide to bypass rules if certain conditions are met. This can lead to complex logic and create a maintenance burden on your application code.

Since implementing a hybrid model can be complex, you may consider developing a separate authorization service to eliminate the need for significant code changes with volatile permissions that change frequently.

Using an external system for authorization decisions allows your application's authorization logic to remain consistent, as shown in Figure 8-17.

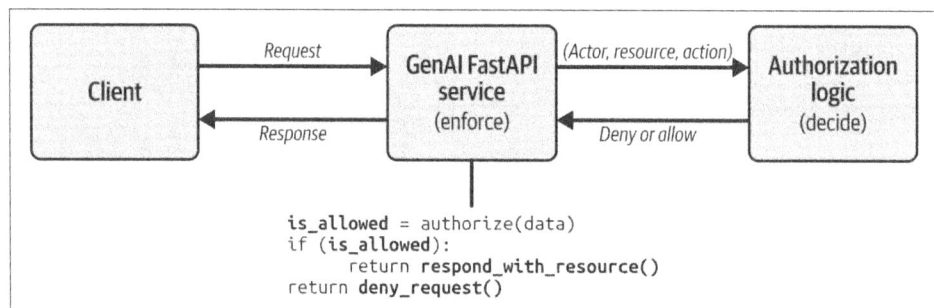

Figure 8-17. Separating the authorization service from the GenAI service

Example 8-22 shows how to develop a separate authorization system.

Example 8-22. Using an authorization service with the GenAI service

```
# authorization_api.py (Authorization Service)

from typing import Annotated, Literal
from fastapi import Depends, FastAPI
```

```python
from pydantic import BaseModel

...  # import services and entities here

CurrentUserDep = Annotated[User, Depends(AuthService.get_current_user)]
ActionRep = Annotated[Literal["READ", "CREATE", "UPDATE", "DELETE"], str]
ResourceDep = Annotated[Resource, Depends(ResourceService.get_resource)]

class AuthorizationResponse(BaseModel):
    allowed: bool

app = FastAPI()

app.get("/authorize")
def authorization_controller(
    user: CurrentUserDep, resource: ResourceDep, action: ActionRep
) -> AuthorizationResponse:
    if user.role == "ADMIN":
        return AuthorizationResponse(allowed=True)
    if action in user.permissions.get(resource.id, []):
        return AuthorizationResponse(allowed=True)
    ...  # Other permission checks
    return AuthorizationResponse(allowed=False)

# genai_api.py (GenAI Service)

from fastapi import APIRouter, HTTPException, status
from pydantic import BaseModel

class AuthorizationData(BaseModel):
    user_id: int
    resource_id: int
    action: str

authorization_client = ...  # Create authorization client

async def enforce(data: AuthorizationData) -> bool:
    response = await authorization_client.decide(data)
    if response.allowed:
        return True
    raise HTTPException(
        status_code=status.HTTP_403_FORBIDDEN, detail="Access Denied"
    )

router = APIRouter(
    dependencies=[Depends(enforce)], prefix="/generate", tags=["Resource"]
)

@router.post("/text")
async def generate_text_controller():
    ...
```

As you can see in Example 8-22, using an external system to authorize user actions on resources helps you and your team to modularize authorization logic with more complex and volatile permission requirements.

However, since developing a complex external authorization service from scratch can take a lot of your time, you may want to consider using authorization providers (such as Oso, Permify, Okta/Auth0, etc.) with your authentication.

Summary

In this chapter, you learned about both authentication and authorization mechanisms to secure your GenAI services.

Earlier in the chapter, you were introduced to several authentication methods, including basic, token-based, OAuth, and key-based authentication. To gain hands-on experience, you implemented several authentication systems from scratch in your FastAPI service, which helped you understand the underlying mechanisms. This included managing user passwords, creating and using JWT access tokens, and implementing authentication flows for user verification. Additionally, you learned how to integrate your services with identity providers like GitHub using the OAuth2 standard to authenticate users and access external user resources in your application.

While you were building the authentication system, you also learned about attack vectors such as credential stuffing, password spraying, cross-site request forgery, open redirect, and phishing attacks.

Furthermore, you explored authorization systems that determine and enforce access levels based on authorization data and logic. You learned how authorization systems can become complex and how different models, including RBAC, ReBAC, and ABAC, can assist in managing permissions in your applications.

In the next chapter, you will focus on testing, including writing unit, integration, end-to-end, and regression tests. You'll be introduced to concepts like testing boundaries, coverage, mocking, patching, parameterization, isolation, and idempotency, which will help you write maintainable and effective tests as your applications grow in complexity. Specifically, you'll learn how to test GenAI services that use probabilistic models and interface with asynchronous systems.

## CHAPTER 9

Securing AI Services

Chapter Goals

In this chapter, you will learn about:

- How to protect against adversarial attempts and the misuse and abuse of your GenAI services

- How to implement your own ethical and safety guardrails, evaluation, and content filtering layers to moderate usage

- How to implement usage moderation, stream throttling, and various API rate-limiting strategies to reduce server load

---

In earlier chapters, you learned how to build GenAI services that serve various AI generators while supporting concurrency and data streaming in real time. Additionally, you integrated external systems like databases and implemented your own authentication and authorization mechanisms. Finally, you wrote a test suite to verify the functionality and performance of your entire system.

In this chapter, you'll learn how to implement usage moderation and abuse-protection mechanisms to secure your GenAI services.

Usage Moderation and Abuse Protection

When deploying your GenAI services, you'll need to consider how your services will be misused and abused by malicious users. This is essential to protect user safety and your own reputation. You won't know how the users will use your system, so you need to assume the worst and implement *guardrails* to protect against any misuse or abuse.

According to a recent study on nefarious applications of GenAI (*https://oreil.ly/ihmzR*), your services may potentially be used with *malicious intents*, as described in Table 9-1.

Table 9-1. Malicious intents behind abusing GenAI services

Intent	Examples	Real-world cases
Dishonesty Supporting lies and untruthfulness	Plagiarism, faking competency and knowledge, document forgery, cheating in exams and in interviews, etc.	Increasing cases of students cheating with AI at UK and Australian universities[a]
Propaganda Skewing perceptions of reality to advance an agenda	Impersonating others, promoting extremism, influencing campaigns, etc.	Fake AI news anchors spreading misinformation or propaganda[b]
Deception Misleading others and creating false impressions	Generating fake reviews, scam ads and phishing emails, and synthetic profiles (i.e., sockpuppeting), etc.	Engineering firm Arup revealed as a victim of a $25 million deepfake scam[c]

[a] Sources: *Times Higher Education* and *The Guardian*
[b] Sources: *The Guardian*, *MIT Technology Review*, and *The Washington Post*
[c] Sources: CNN and *The Guardian*

The same study categorizes GenAI application abuse into the following:

- *Misinformation and disinformation* to spread propaganda and fake news
- *Bias amplification and discrimination* to advance racist agendas and societal discrimination
- *Malicious content generation* by creating toxic, deceptive, and radicalizing content
- *Data privacy attacks* to fill in gaps in stolen private data and leak sensitive information
- *Automated cyberattacks* to personalize phishing and ransomware attacks
- *Identity theft and social engineering* to increase the success rate of scams
- *Deepfakes and multimedia manipulation* to make a profit and skew perceptions of reality and social beliefs
- *Scam and fraud* by manipulating stock markets and crafting targeted scams

This may not be an exhaustive list but should give you a few ideas on what usage moderation measures to consider.

Another study on the taxonomy of GenAI misuse tactics (*https://oreil.ly/jbG01*) investigated abuse by modality and found that:

- *Audio and video generators* were used for the majority of impersonation attempts.

- *Image and text generators* were used for the majority of sockpuppeting, content farming for opinion manipulation at scale, and falsification attempts.

- *Image and video generators* were used for the majority of steganography, (i.e., hiding coded messages in model outputs), and nonconsensual intimate content (NCII) generation attempts.

If you're building services supporting such modalities, you should consider their associated forms of abuse and implement relevant protection mechanisms.

Aside from misuse and abuse, you'll also need to consider security vulnerabilities.

Securing GenAI services is still an area of research at the time of writing. For instance, if your services leverage LLMs, OWASP has categorized the top 10 LLM vulnerabilities (*https://oreil.ly/4zob2*), as shown in Table 9-2.

Table 9-2. OWASP top 10 LLM vulnerabilities

Risk	Description
Prompt injection	Manipulating inputs to control the LLM's responses leading to unauthorized access, data breaches, and compromised decision-making.
Insecure output handling	Failing to sanitize or validate LLM outputs causing remote code execution on downstream systems.
Training data poisoning	Injecting data in sources that models get trained on to compromise security, accuracy, or ethical behavior. Open source models and RAG services that rely on web data are most prone to these attacks.
Model denial of service	Causing service disruption and cost explosions by overloading the LLMs with heavy payloads and concurrent requests.
Supply chain vulnerabilities	Causing various components, including data sources, to be compromised, undermining system integrity.
Sensitive information leakage	Leading to accidental exposure of private data, legal liabilities and loss of competitive advantage.
Insecure plug-in design	Vulnerabilities in third-party integrations cause remote code execution.
Excessive agency	Where LLMs have too much autonomy to take actions can lead to unintended consequences and harmful actions.
Overreliance on LLM	Compromising decision-making, contributing to security vulnerabilities and legal liabilities.
Model theft	Related to unauthorized copying or usage of your models.

Similar vulnerabilities exist for other types of GenAI systems such as image, audio, video, and geometry generators.

I recommend researching and identifying software vulnerabilities relevant to your own use cases.

Without guardrails, your services can be abused to cause personal and financial harm, identity theft, economic damage, spread misinformation, and contribute to societal problems. As a result, it's crucial to implement several safety measures and guardrails to protect your services against such attacks.

In the next section, you'll learn usage moderation and security measures you can implement to protect your GenAI services prior to deployment.

Guardrails

Guardrails refer to *detective controls* that aim to guide your application toward the intended outcomes. They are incredibly diverse and can be configured to fit any situation that may go wrong with your GenAI systems.

As an example, *I/O guardrails* are designed to verify data entering a GenAI model and outputs sent to the downstream systems or users. Such guardrails can flag inappropriate user queries and validate output content against toxicity, hallucinations, or banned topics. Figure 9-1 shows how an LLM system looks once you add I/O guardrails to it.

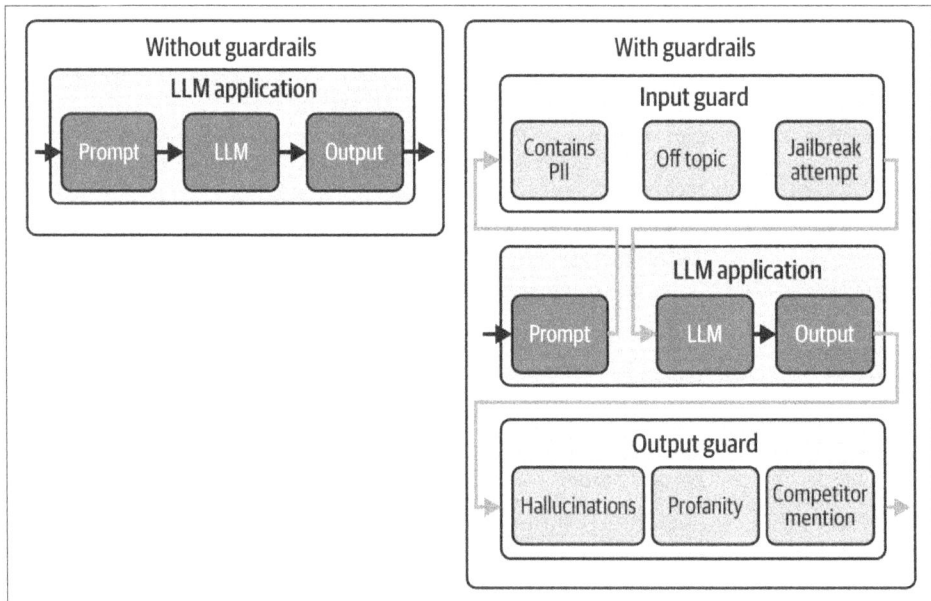

Figure 9-1. Comparison of an LLM system without and with guardrails

You don't have to implement guardrails from scratch. At the time of writing, prebuilt open source guardrail frameworks exist like NVIDIA NeMo Guardrails, LLM-Guard, and Guardrails AI to protect your services. However, they may require learning framework-related languages and have a trade-off of slowing down your services and bloating your application due to various external dependencies.

Other commercial guardrails available on the market, such as Open AI's Moderation API, Microsoft Azure AI Content Safety API, and Google's Guardrails API are either not open source or lack details and contents to measure quality constraints.

> Guardrails remain an active area of research. While such defenses can counter some attacks, powerful attacks backed by AI can still bypass them. This may lead to an ongoing and endless loop of assaults and defenses (*https://oreil.ly/xlUmw*).

While engineering application-level I/O guardrails may not provide perfect protection, upcoming GenAI models may include baked-in guardrails inside the model to improve security guarantees. However, such guardrails may have a performance impact on response times by introducing latency to the system.

Input Guardrails

The purpose of input guardrails is to prevent malicious or inappropriate content from reaching your model. Table 9-3 shows common input guardrails.

Table 9-3. Common input guardrails

Input guardrails	Examples
Topical Steer inputs away from off-topic or sensitive content.	Preventing a user from discussing political topics and explicit content.
Direct prompt injection (jail-breaking) Prevent users from revealing or overriding system prompts and secrets. The longer the input content, the more prone your system will be to these attacks.	Blocking attempts to override system prompts and manipulating the system into revealing internal API keys or configuration settings.[a]
Indirect prompt injection Prevent acceptance of malicious content from external sources such as files or websites that may cause model confusion or remote code execution on downstream systems. Malicious content may be invisible to the human eye and encoded within input text or images.	Sanitizing encoded payloads in upload images, hidden characters or prompt overrides in uploaded documents, hidden scripts in remote URLs or even YouTube video transcripts.
Moderation Comply with brand guidelines, legal, and branding requirements.	Flag and refuse invalid user queries if user queries include mentions of profanity, competitor, explicit content, personally identifiable information (PII), self-harm, etc.
Attribute Validate input properties.	Check query length, file size, choices, range, data format and structure, etc.

[a] Although guardrails are useful, best practice is to avoid giving your GenAI models direct knowledge of secrets or sensitive configuration settings in the first place.

The input guardrails can also be combined with content sanitizers to clean bad inputs.

If you want to implement your own guardrails, you can start off with using advanced prompt engineering techniques within your system prompts. Additionally, you can use auto-evaluation techniques, (i.e., AI models).

Example 9-1 shows an example system prompt for an AI guardrail auto-evaluator to reject off-topic queries.

Example 9-1. Topical input guardrail system prompt

```
guardrail_system_prompt = """

Your role is to assess user queries as valid or invalid

Allowed topics include:

1. API Development
2. FastAPI
3. Building Generative AI systems

If a topic is allowed, say 'allowed' otherwise say 'disallowed'
"""
```

You can see an implementation of an input topical guardrail in Example 9-2 using the LLM auto-evaluation technique.

Example 9-2. Topical input guardrail

```
import re
from typing import Annotated
from openai import AsyncOpenAI
from pydantic import AfterValidator, BaseModel, validate_call

guardrail_system_prompt = "..."

class LLMClient:
    def __init__(self, system_prompt: str):
        self.client = AsyncOpenAI()
        self.system_prompt = system_prompt

    async def invoke(self, user_query: str) -> str | None:
        response = await self.client.chat.completions.create(
            model="gpt-4o",
            messages=[
                {"role": "system", "content": self.system_prompt},
                {"role": "user", "content": user_query},
            ],
            temperature=0,
```

```
    )
    return response.choices[0].message.content

@validate_call
def check_classification_response(value: str | None) -> str: ❶
    if value is None or not re.match(r"^(allowed|disallowed)$", value):
        raise ValueError("Invalid topical guardrail response received")
    return value

ClassificationResponse = Annotated[
    str | None, AfterValidator(check_classification_response)
]

class TopicalGuardResponse(BaseModel):
    classification: ClassificationResponse

async def is_topic_allowed(user_query: str) -> TopicalGuardResponse:
    response = await LLMClient(guardrail_system_prompt).invoke(user_query)
    return TopicalGuardResponse(classification=response)
```

❶ Handle cases where the LLM doesn't return a valid classification

> Using the technique shown in Example 9-2, you can implement
> auto-evaluators to check for jail-breaking and prompt injection
> attempts or even detect the presence of PII and profanity in the
> inputs.

As discussed in Chapter 5, you can leverage async programming as much as possible
even when using auto-evaluation techniques in your guardrails. This is because AI
guardrails require sending multiple model API calls per user query. To improve user
experience, you can run these guardrails in parallel to the model inference process.

Once you have an auto-evaluator guardrail for checking allowed topics, you can execute it in parallel to your data generation[1] using `asyncio.wait`, as shown in
Example 9-3.

> Be mindful that implementing async guardrails may trigger model
> provider API rate-limiting and throttling mechanisms. Depending
> on your application requirements, you may want to request higher
> rate limits or reduce the rate of API calls within a short time frame.

---

1 Inspired by OpenAI Cookbook's "How to Implement LLM Guardrails" (*https://oreil.ly/UQV6i*).

Example 9-3. Running AI guardrails in parallel to response generation

```python
import asyncio
from typing import Annotated
from fastapi import Depends
from loguru import logger

...

async def invoke_llm_with_guardrails(user_query: str) -> str:
    topical_guardrail_task = asyncio.create_task(is_topic_allowed(user_query))
    chat_task = asyncio.create_task(llm_client.invoke(user_query))

    while True:
        done, _ = await asyncio.wait(
            [topical_guardrail_task, chat_task],
            return_when=asyncio.FIRST_COMPLETED,
        ) ❶
        if topical_guardrail_task in done:
            topic_allowed = topical_guardrail_task.result()
            if not topic_allowed:
                chat_task.cancel() ❷
                logger.warning("Topical guardrail triggered")
                return (
                    "Sorry, I can only talk about "
                    "building GenAI services with FastAPI"
                )
            elif chat_task in done:
                return chat_task.result()
        else:
            await asyncio.sleep(0.1) ❸

@router.post("/text/generate")
async def generate_text_controller(
    response: Annotated[str, Depends(invoke_llm_with_guardrails)] ❹
) -> str:
    return response
```

❶ Create two asyncio tasks to run in parallel using `asyncio.wait`. The operation returns as soon as a task is completed.

❷ If the guardrail is triggered, cancel the chat operation and return a hard-coded response. You can log the trigger in a database and send notification emails here.

❸ Keep checking in with the asyncio event loop every 100 ms until a task is done.

❹ Leverage dependency injection to return the model response if guardrails aren't triggered.

Since GenAI-enabled guardrails like those you implemented in Example 9-3 remain probabilistic, your GenAI services can still be vulnerable to prompt injection and jailbreaking attacks. For instance, attackers can use more advanced prompt injection techniques to get around your AI guardrails too. On the other hand, your guardrails may also incorrectly over-refuse valid user queries, leading to false positives that can downgrade your user experience.

> Combining guardrails with rules-based or traditional machine learning models for detection can help mitigate some of the aforementioned risks.
>
> Additionally, you can use guardrails that only consider the latest message to reduce the risk of the model being confused by a long conversation.

When designing guardrails, you need to consider trade-offs between *accuracy*, *latency*, and *cost* to balance user experience with your required security controls.

Output Guardrails

The purpose of output guardrails is to validate GenAI-produced content before it's passed to users or downstream systems. Table 9-4 shows common output guardrails.

Table 9-4. Common output guardrails

Output guardrails	Examples
Hallucination/fact-checking Block hallucinations and return canned responses such as "I don't know."	Measuring metrics such as *relevancy, coherence, consistency, fluency*, etc., on the model outputs against a corpus of ground truth in RAG applications.
Moderation Apply brand and corporate guidelines to govern the model outputs, either filtering or rewriting responses that breach them.	Checking against metrics such as *readability, toxicity, sentiment, count of competitor mentions*, etc.
Syntax checks Verify the structure and content of model outputs. These guardrails can either detect and retry or gracefully handle exceptions to prevent failures in the downstream systems.	Validating JSON schemas and function parameters in *function calling* workflows when models invoke functions. Checking tool/agent selections in *agentic workflows*.

Any of the aforementioned output guardrails will rely on *threshold value* to detect invalid responses.

Guardrail Thresholds

Guardrails can use various metrics such as *readability*, *toxicity*, etc., to measure and validate the quality of the model outputs. For each metric, you'll need to experiment to identify the appropriate *threshold value* for your use case, bearing in mind that:

- More *false positives* can annoy your users and reduce the usability of your services.

- More *false negatives* can cause lasting harm to your reputation and explode costs since malicious users can abuse the system or perform prompt injection/jail-breaking attacks.

Normally, you should assess the risks and worst cases of having false negatives and whether you're happy to trade off a few false negatives in your use case for enhanced user experience. For instance, you can reduce instances of blocking outputs if they include more jargon and aren't as readable.

Implementing a Moderation Guardrail

Let's implement a moderation guardrail using a version of the *G-Eval* evaluation method (*https://oreil.ly/7Nent*) to measure the presence of unwanted content in the model output.

The G-Eval framework uses the following components to score invalid content:

- A *domain* name specifying the type of content to be moderated
- A set of *criteria* to clearly outline what is considered valid versus invalid content
- An ordered list of *instruction steps* for grading the content
- The *content* to grade between a discrete score of 1 to 5

Example 9-4 shows a system prompt implementing the *G-Eval* framework that an LLM auto-evaluator will use.

Example 9-4. Moderation guardrail system prompt

```
domain = "Building GenAI Services"

criteria = """
Assess the presence of explicit guidelines for API development for GenAI models.
The content should contain only general evergreen advice
not specific tools and libraries to use
"""

steps = """
1. Read the content and the criteria carefully.
```

```
2. Assess how much explicit guidelines for API development
for GenAI models is contained in the content.
3. Assign an advice score from 1 to 5,
with 1 being evergreen general advice and 5 containing explicit
mentions of various tools and libraries to use.
"""


f"""
You are a moderation assistant.
Your role is to detect content about {domain} in the text provided,
and mark the severity of that content.

## {domain}

### Criteria

{criteria}

### Instructions

{steps}

### Evaluation (score only!)
"""
```

Using the system prompt implemented in Example 9-4, you can now implement a moderation guardrail following Example 9-2.

Next, let's integrate the moderation guardrail with your existing chat invocation logic, as shown in Example 9-5.

Example 9-5. Integrating moderation guardrail

```
import asyncio
from typing import Annotated
from loguru import logger
from pydantic import BaseModel, Field


...

class ModerationResponse(BaseModel):
    score: Annotated[int, Field(ge=1, le=5)] ❶

async def g_eval_moderate_content(
    chat_response: str, threshold: int = 3
) -> bool:
    response = await LLMClient(guardrail_system_prompt).invoke(chat_response)
    g_eval_score = ModerationResponse(score=response).score
    return g_eval_score >= threshold ❷
```

```
async def invoke_llm_with_guardrails(user_request):
    ...
    while True:
        ...
        if topical_guardrail_task in done:
            ...
        elif chat_task in done: ❸
            chat_response = chat_task.result()
            has_passed_moderation = await g_eval_moderate_content(chat_response)
            if not has_passed_moderation:
                logger.warning(f"Moderation guardrail flagged")
                return (
                    "Sorry, we can't recommend specific "
                    "tools or technologies at this time"
                )
            return chat_response
        else:
            await asyncio.sleep(0.1)
```

❶ Use a Pydantic constrained integer type to validate LLM auto-evaluator G-Eval score.

❷ Flag content that is scored above the threshold as not passing moderation.

❸ Integrate and run the output moderation guardrail with other guardrails.

> Beyond the novel *G-Eval* framework implemented using an LLM auto-evaluator, you can also use more traditional automatic evaluation frameworks such as ROUGE (*https://oreil.ly/_9Q9g*), BERT-Score (*https://oreil.ly/jRTeL*), and SummEval (*https://oreil.ly/5YtJG*) for moderating output content.

Well done. You have now implemented two I/O guardrails, one to verify topics of user queries and another to moderate the LLM outputs.

To improve your guardrail system even further, you can:

- Adopt the *fast failure* approach by exiting early if a guardrail is triggered to optimize response times.

- Only select *appropriate guardrails* for your use cases instead of using them all together, which could overwhelm your services.

- Run guardrails *asynchronously* instead of sequentially to optimize latency.

- Implement *request sampling* by running slower guardrails on a sample of requests to reduce overall latency when your services are under a heavy load.

You should now feel more confident implementing your own guardrails using classical or LLM auto-evaluation techniques without relying on external tools and libraries.

In the next section, you'll learn about API rate limiting so that you can protect your services against model overloading and scraping attempts.

API Rate Limiting and Throttling

When deploying GenAI services, you will need to consider service exhaustion and model overloading issues in production. Best practice is to implement rate limiting and potentially throttling into your services.

Rate limiting controls the amount of incoming and outgoing traffic to and from a network to prevent abuse, ensure fair usage, and avoid overloading the server. On the other hand, *throttling* controls the API throughput by temporarily slowing down the rate of request processing to stabilize the server.

Both techniques can help you:

- *Prevent abuse* by blocking malicious users or bots from overwhelming your services from data scraping and brute-force attacks that involve too many requests or large payloads.

- *Enforce fair usage policies* so that capacity is shared among multiple users and a handful of users are prevented from monopolizing server resources.

- *Maintain server stability* by regulating incoming traffic to maintain consistent performance and prevent crashes during peak periods.

To implement rate limiting, you will need to monitor incoming requests within a time period and use a queue to balance the load.

There are several rate-limiting strategies you can choose from, which are compared in Table 9-5 and shown in Figure 9-2.

Table 9-5. Rate-limiting strategies

Strategy	Benefits	Limitations	Use cases
Token Bucket A list is filled with tokens at a constant rate, and every incoming request consumes a token. If there aren't enough tokens for incoming requests, they'll be rejected.	• Handles temporary bursts and dynamic traffic patterns • Granular control over request processing	Complex to implement	Commonly used in most APIs and services, and interactive or event-driven GenAI systems where request rates can be irregular

Strategy	Benefits	Limitations	Use cases
Leaky Bucket Incoming requests are added to a queue and processed at a constant rate to smooth the traffic. If the queue overflows, any new incoming requests are rejected.	• Simple to implement • Maintains consistent traffic flow	• Less flexible to dynamic traffic • May reject valid requests during sudden spikes	Services that require maintaining consistent response times in AI inference services
Fixed Window Limits requests within fixed time windows (e.g., 100 requests per minute).	Simple to implement	Does not handle burst traffic well	• Enforcing strict usage policies for expensive AI inferences and API calls • Ideal for free tier users or batch-processing systems with predictable usage patterns • Each request is treated equally
Sliding Window Counts requests over a rolling time frame.	Provides better flexibility, granularity, and burst traffic smoothing	• More complex to implement • Requires higher memory usage for tracking requests	• Much better at handling burst traffic • Ideal for conversational AI or premium-tier users who expect flexible, high-frequency access over time

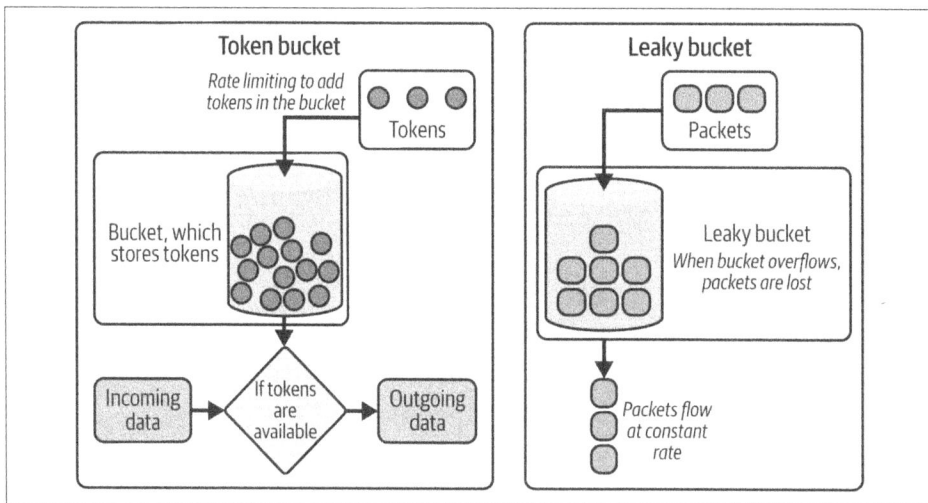

Figure 9-2. Comparison of rate-limiting strategies

Now that you're more familiar with rate-limiting concepts, let's try to implement rate limiting in FastAPI.

Implementing Rate Limits in FastAPI

The fastest approach to add rate limiting within FastAPI is to use a library such as `slowapi` that is a wrapper over the `limits` package, supporting most of the strategies mentioned in Table 9-5. First, install the `slowapi` library:

```
$ pip install slowapi
```

Once you've installed the slowapi package, you can follow Example 9-6 to apply global API or endpoint rate limiting. You can also track and limit usage per IP address.

> Without configuring an external data store, slowapi stores and tracks IP addresses in the application memory for rate limiting.

Example 9-6. Configuring global rate limits

```
from fastapi.responses import JSONResponse
from slowapi import Limiter
from slowapi.errors import RateLimitExceeded
from slowapi.middleware import SlowAPIMiddleware
from slowapi.util import get_remote_address

...

limiter = Limiter(
    key_func=get_remote_address,
    default_limits=["200 per day", "60 per hour", "2/5seconds"],
) ❶

app.state.limiter = limiter

@app.exception_handler(RateLimitExceeded) ❷
def rate_limit_exceeded_handler(request, exc):
    retry_after = int(exc.description.split(" ")[-1])
    response_body = {
        "detail": "Rate limit exceeded. Please try again later.",
        "retry_after_seconds": retry_after,
    }
    return JSONResponse(
        status_code=429,
        content=response_body,
        headers={"Retry-After": str(retry_after)},
    )

app.add_middleware(SlowAPIMiddleware)
```

❶ Create rate limiter that tracks usage across each IP address and rejects requests if they exceed specified limits across the application.

❷ Add a custom exception handler for rate-limited requests to compute and provide waiting times before requests are accepted again.

With the `limiter` decorator configured, you can now use it on your API handlers, as shown in Example 9-7.

Example 9-7. Setting API rate limits for each API handler

```
@app.post("/generate/text")
@limiter.limit("5/minute") ❶
def serve_text_to_text_controller(request: Request, ...):
    return ...

@app.post("/generate/image")
@limiter.limit("1/minute") ❷
def serve_text_to_image_controller(request: Request, ...): ❸
    return ...

@app.get("/health")
@limiter.exempt ❹
def check_health_controller(request: Request):
    return {"status": "healthy"}
```

❶ Specify more granular rate limits at endpoint level using a rate-limiting decorator. The `limiter` decorator must be ordered last.

❷ Pass the `Request` object to each controller so that the `slowapi` limiter decorator can hook into the incoming request. Otherwise, rate limiting will not function.

❸ Exclude the `/health` endpoint from rate-limiting logic as cloud providers or Docker daemons may ping this endpoint continually to check the status of your application.

❹ Avoid rate limiting the `/health` endpoint as external systems may frequently trigger it to check the current status of your service.

Now that you've implemented the rate limits, you can run load tests using the `ab` (Apache Benchmarking) CLI tool, as shown in Example 9-8.

Example 9-8. API load testing with Apache Benchmark CLI

```
$ ab -n 100 -p 2 http://localhost:8000 ❶
```

❶ Send 100 requests with a rate of 2 parallel requests per second.

Your terminal outputs should show the following:

```
200 OK
200 OK
429 Rate limited Exceeded
...
```

Your global and local limiting system should now be working as intended based on incoming IPs.

User-based rate limits

With an IP rate limit, you're limiting excess usage based on IP, but users can get around IP rate limiting by using VPNs, proxies, or rotating IP addresses. Instead, you want each user to have a dedicated quota to prevent a single user from consuming all available resources. Adding user-based limits can help you prevent abuse, as shown in Example 9-9.

Example 9-9. User-based rate limiting

```
@app.post("/generate/text")
@limiter.limit("10/minute", key_func=get_current_user)
def serve_text_to_text_controller(request: Request):
    return {"message": f"Hello User"}
```

Your system will now be limiting users based on their account IDs alongside their IP addresses.

Rate limits across instances in production

Since you may run multiple instances of your application in production as you scale your services, you'll also want to centralize your usage tracking. Otherwise, each instance will provide their own counters to users, and a load balancer distributes requests between instances; usage won't be capped as you'd expect. To rectify this issue, you can switch the `slowapi` in-memory storage backend with a centralized in-memory database such as Redis, as shown in Example 9-10.

> To run Example 9-10, you will need a Redis database to store user API usage data:
>
> ```
> $ pip install coredis
> $ docker pull redis
> $ docker run \
>   --name rate-limit-redis-cache \
>   -d \
>   -p 6379:6379 \
>   redis
> ```

Example 9-10. Adding a centralized usage memory store (Redis) across multiple instances

```
from slowapi import Limiter
from slowapi.middleware import SlowAPIMiddleware

app.state.limiter = Limiter(storage_uri="redis://localhost:6379")
app.add_middleware(SlowAPIMiddleware)
```

You now have a working rate-limited API that functions as intended across multiple instances.

You can get around this issue by implementing your own limiter supported by the `limits` package instead. Alternatively, you can apply rate limiting via a *load balancer*, a *reverse proxy*, or an *API gateway* instead.

Each solution can route requests while performing rate limits, protocol translation, and traffic monitoring at an infrastructure layer. Applying rate limiting externally may be more suitable for your use case if you don't require a customized rate-limiting logic.

Limiting WebSocket connections

Unfortunately the `slowapi` package also doesn't support limiting async and Web-Socket endpoints at the time of writing.

Because WebSocket connections are likely to be long-lived, you may want to limit the data transition rate sent over the socket. You can rely on external packages such as `fastapi-limiter` to rate limit WebSocket connections, as shown in Example 9-11.

Example 9-11. Rate-limiting WebSocket connections with the `fastapi_limiter` package

```
from contextlib import asynccontextmanager
import redis
from fastapi import Depends, FastAPI
from fastapi.websockets import WebSocket
from fastapi_limiter import FastAPILimiter
from fastapi_limiter.depends import WebSocketRateLimiter

...

@asynccontextmanager
async def lifespan(_: FastAPI):  ❶
    redis_connection = redis.from_url("redis://localhost:6379", encoding="utf8")
    await FastAPILimiter.init(redis_connection)
    yield
    await FastAPILimiter.close()

app = FastAPI(lifespan=lifespan)
```

```
@app.websocket("/ws")
async def websocket_endpoint(
    websocket: WebSocket, user_id: int = Depends(get_current_user) ❷
):
    ratelimit = WebSocketRateLimiter(times=1, seconds=5)
    await ws_manager.connect(websocket)
    try:
        while True:
            prompt = await ws_manager.receive(websocket)
            await ratelimit(websocket, context_key=user_id) ❸
            async for chunk in azure_chat_client.chat_stream(prompt, "ws"):
                await ws_manager.send(chunk, websocket)
    except WebSocketRateLimitException:
        await websocket.send_text(f"Rate limit exceeded. Try again later")
    finally:
        await ws_manager.disconnect(websocket)
```

❶ Configure the FastAPILimiter application lifespan with a Redis storage backend.

❷ Configure a WebSocket rate limiter to allow one request per second.

❸ Use the user's ID as the unique identifier for rate limiting.

Example 9-11 shows how to limit the number of active WebSocket connections for a given user.

Beyond rate-limiting WebSocket endpoints, you may also want to limit the data streaming rate of your GenAI models. Let's look at how you can throttle real-time data streams next.

Throttling Real-Time Streams

When working with real-time streams, you may need to slow down the streaming rate to give clients enough time to consume the stream and improve streaming throughput across multiple clients. In addition, throttling can help you manage the network bandwidth, server load, and resource utilization.

Applying a *throttle* at the stream generation layer, as shown in Example 9-12, is an effective approach to managing throughput if your services are under pressure.

Example 9-12. Throttling streams

```
class AzureOpenAIChatClient:
    def __init__(self, throttle_rate = 0.5): ❶
        self.aclient = ...
        self.throttle_rate = throttle_rate
```

```python
async def chat_stream(
        self, prompt: str, mode: str = "sse", model: str = "gpt-3.5-turbo"
) -> AsyncGenerator[str, None]:
    stream = ...  # OpenAI chat completion stream
    async for chunk in stream:
        await asyncio.sleep(self.throttle_rate)  ❷
        if chunk.choices[0].delta.content is not None:
            yield (
                f"data: {chunk.choices[0].delta.content}\n\n"
                if mode == "sse"
                else chunk.choices[0].delta.content
            )
            await asyncio.sleep(0.05)

    if mode == "sse":
        yield f"data: [DONE]\n\n"
```

❶ Set a fixed throttling rate or dynamically adjust based on usage.

❷ Slow down the streaming rate without blocking the event loop.

You can then use the throttled stream within an SSE or WebSocket endpoint. Or, you can limit the number of active WebSocket connections per your own custom policies.

Alongside the application-level throttling for real-time streams, you can also leverage *traffic shaping* at the infrastructure layer.

Traffic Shaping

While rate-limiting approaches can help you manage incoming requests, you can also use throttling techniques like *traffic shaping* to control the rate of data transmission.

Traffic shaping prioritizes certain types of data transfer to help you prevent congestion, smooth out traffic bursts, and maintain a consistent data flow to optimize application bandwidth usage, as shown in Figure 9-3. This is especially useful for GenAI services requiring real-time data transmission including chat and video streaming.

To implement traffic shaping, you can use the tc command-line tool within Linux to configure control rules on targets such as network interfaces and Docker containers. These control rules set bandwidth limits, intentional latency delays, packet loss, and IP limits on specific targets to regulate the application throughput.

While the traffic shaping technique can help you manage the network bandwidth, bear in mind that it involves complex algorithms and requires constant monitoring and dynamic control of the packet flow. It may also introduce delays due to its queuing methods when the network is heavily loaded.

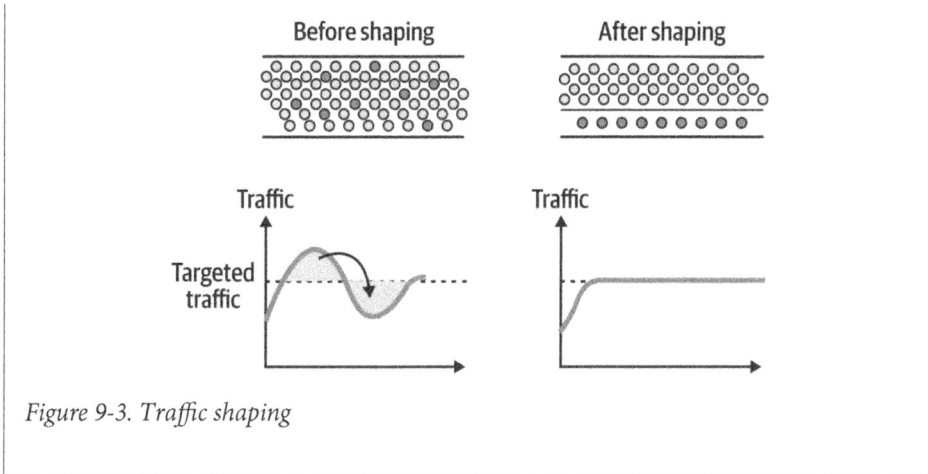

Figure 9-3. Traffic shaping

Using safeguards, rate limits, and throttles should provide enough barriers in protecting your services from abuse and misuse.

In the next section, you'll learn more about optimization techniques that can help you reduce latency, increase response quality, and throughput alongside reducing the costs of your GenAI services.

Summary

This chapter provided a comprehensive summary of attack vectors for GenAI services and how to safeguard them against adversarial attempts, misuse, and abuse.

You learned to implement input and output guardrails alongside evaluation and content filtering mechanisms to moderate service usage. Alongside guardrails, you also developed API rate-limiting and throttling protections to manage server load and prevent abuse.

In the next chapter, we will learn about optimizing AI services through various techniques such as caching, batch processing, model quantizing, prompt engineering, and model fine-tuning.

## CHAPTER 10

Optimizing AI Services

Chapter Goals

In this chapter, you will learn about:

- Optimization techniques such as keyword, semantic, and context caching
- Advanced prompt engineering techniques to maximize model generation quality and coherence
- Model quantization and the difference that quantized models make in model serving
- Using batch processing APIs for larger AI workloads
- The benefits, drawbacks, and use cases of model fine-tuning

In this chapter, you'll learn to further optimize your services via prompt engineering, model quantization, and caching mechanisms.

Optimization Techniques

The objectives of optimizing an AI service are to either improve output quality or performance (latency, throughput, costs, etc.).

Performance-related optimizations include the following:

- Using batch processing APIs
- Caching (keyword, semantic, context, or prompt)
- Model quantization

Quality-related optimizations include the following:

- Using structured outputs
- Prompt engineering
- Model fine-tuning

Let's review each in more detail.

Batch Processing

Often you want an LLM to process batches of entries at the same time. The most obvious solution is to submit multiple API calls per entry. However, the obvious approach can be costly and slow and may lead to your model provider rate limiting you.

In such cases, you can leverage two separate techniques for batch processing your data through an LLM:

- Updating your structured output schemas to return multiple examples at the same time
- Identifying and using model provider APIs that are designed for batch processing

The first solution requires you to update your Pydantic models or template prompts to request a list of outputs per request. In this case, you can batch process your data within a handful of requests instead of one per entry.

An implementation of the first solution is shown in Example 10-1.

Example 10-1. Updating structured output schema for parsing multiple items

```
from pydantic import BaseModel

class BatchDocumentClassification(BaseModel):
    class Category(BaseModel):
        document_id: str
        category: list[str]

    categories: list[Category]  ❶
```

❶ Update the Pydantic model to include a list of `Category` models.

You can now pass the new schema alongside a list of document titles to the OpenAI client to process multiple entries in a single API call. However, an alternative and possibly the best solution will be to use a batch API, if available.

Luckily, model providers such as OpenAI already supply relevant APIs for such use cases. Under the hood, these providers may run task queues to process any single batch job in the background while providing you with status updates until the batch is complete to retrieve the results.

Compared to using standard endpoints directly, you'll be able to send asynchronous groups of requests with lower costs (up to 50% with OpenAI[1]), enjoy higher rate limits, and guarantee completion times. The batch job service is ideal for processing jobs that don't require immediate responses such as using OpenAI LLMs to parse, classify, or translate large volumes of documents in the background.

To submit a batch job, you'll need a `jsonl` file where each line contains the details of an individual request to the API, as shown in Example 10-2. Also as seen in this example, to create the JSONL file, you can iterate over your entries and dynamically generate the file.

Example 10-2. Creating a JSONL file from entries

```python
import json
from uuid import UUID

def create_batch_file(
    entries: list[str],
    system_prompt: str,
    model: str = "gpt-4o-mini",
    filepath: str = "batch.jsonl",
    max_tokens: int = 1024,
) -> None:
    with open(filepath, "w") as file:
        for _, entry in enumerate(entries, start=1):
            request = {
                "custom_id": f"request-{UUID()}",
                "method": "POST",
                "url": "/v1/chat/completions",
                "body": {
                    "model": model,
                    "messages": [
                        {
                            "role": "system",
                            "content": system_prompt,
                        },
                        {"role": "user", "content": entry},
                    ],
                    "max_tokens": max_tokens,
                },
```

---

1 See the OpenAI Batch API available in the OpenAI API documentation (*https://oreil.ly/0t59w*).

```
        }
        file.write(json.dumps(request) + "\n")
```

Once created, you can submit the file to the batch API for processing, as shown in
Example 10-3.

Example 10-3. Processing batch jobs with the OpenAI Batch API

```python
from loguru import logger
from openai import AsyncOpenAI
from openai.types import Batch

client = AsyncOpenAI()

async def submit_batch_job(filepath: str) -> Batch:
    if ".jsonl" not in filepath:
        raise FileNotFoundError(f"JSONL file not provided at {filepath}")

    file_response = await client.files.create(
        file=open(filepath, "rb"), purpose="batch"
    )

    batch_job_response = await client.batches.create(
        input_file_id=file_response.id,
        endpoint="/v1/chat/completions",
        completion_window="24h",
        metadata={"description": "document classification job"},
    )
    return batch_job_response

async def retrieve_batch_results(batch_id: str):
    batch = await client.batches.retrieve(batch_id)
    if (
        status := batch.status == "completed"
        and batch.output_file_id is not None
    ):
        file_content = await client.files.content(batch.output_file_id)
        return file_content
    logger.warning(f"Batch {batch_id} is in {status} status")
```

You can now leverage offline batch endpoints to process multiple entries in one go
with guaranteed turnaround times and significant cost savings.

Alongside leveraging structured outputs and batch APIs to optimize your services,
you can also leverage caching techniques to significantly speed up response times and
resource costs of your servers.

Caching

In GenAI services, you'll often rely on data/model response that require significant computations or long processing durations. If you have multiple users requesting the same data, repeating the same operations can be wasteful. Instead, you can use caching techniques for storing and retrieving frequently accessed data to help you optimize your services by speeding up response times, reducing server load, and saving bandwidth and operational costs.

For example, in a public FAQ chatbot where users ask mostly the same questions, you may want to reuse the cached responses for longer periods. On the other hand, for more personalized and dynamic chatbots, you can frequently refresh (i.e., invalidate) the cached response.

You should always consider the frequency of cache refreshes based on the nature of the data and the acceptable level of staleness.

The most relevant caching strategies for GenAI services include:

- Keyword caching
- Semantic caching
- Context or prompt caching

Let's review each in more detail.

Keyword caching

If all you need is a simple caching mechanism for storing functions or endpoint responses, you can use *keyword caching*, which involves caching responses based on exact matches of input queries as key-value pairs.

In FastAPI, libraries such as `fastapi-cache` can help you implement keyword caching in a few lines of code, on any functions or endpoints. FastAPI caches also give you the option to attach storage backends such as Redis for centralizing the cache store across your instances.

Alternatively, you can implement your own custom caching mechanism with a cache store using lower-level packages such as `cache tools`.

To get started, all you have to do is to initialize and configure the caching system as part of the application lifespan, as shown in Example 10-4. You can install FastAPI cache using the following command:

```
$ pip install "fastapi-cache2[redis]"
```

Example 10-4. Configuring FastAPI cache lifespan

```python
from collections.abc import AsyncIterator
from contextlib import asynccontextmanager

from fastapi import FastAPI
from fastapi_cache import FastAPICache
from fastapi_cache.backends.redis import RedisBackend
from redis import asyncio as aioredis

@asynccontextmanager
async def lifespan(_: FastAPI) -> AsyncIterator[None]:
    redis = aioredis.from_url("redis://localhost")
    FastAPICache.init(RedisBackend(redis), prefix="fastapi-cache")  ❶
    yield

app = FastAPI(lifespan=lifespan)
```

❶ Initialize `FastAPICache` with a `RedisBackend` that doesn't decode responses so that cached data is stored as bytes (binary). This is because decoding responses would break caching by altering the original response format.

Once the caching system is configured, you can decorate your functions or endpoint handlers to cache their outputs, as shown in Example 10-5.

Example 10-5. Function and endpoint results caching

```python
from fastapi import APIRouter
from fastapi_cache.decorator import cache

router = APIRouter(prefix="/generate", tags=["Resource"])

@cache()
async def classify_document(title: str) -> str:
    ...

@router.post("/text")
```

```
@cache(expire=60) ❶
async def serve_text_to_text_controller():
    ...
```

❶ The cache() decorator must always come last. Invalidate the cache in 60 seconds by setting expires=60 to recompute the outputs.

The cache() decorator shown in Example 10-5 injects dependencies for the Request and Response objects so that it can add cache control headers to the outgoing response. These cache control headers instruct clients how to cache the responses on their side by specifying a set of directives (i.e., instructions).

These are a few common cache control directives when sending responses:

max-age
  Defines the maximum amount of time (in seconds) that a response is considered fresh

no-cache
  Forces revalidation so that the clients check for constant updates with the server

no-store
  Prevents caching entirely

private
  Stores responses in a private cache (e.g., local caches in browsers)

A response could have cache control headers like Cache-Control: max-age=180, private to set these directives.[2]

Since keyword caching works on exact matches, it's more suitable for functions and APIs that expect frequently repeated matching inputs. However, in GenAI services that accept variable user queries, you may want to consider other caching mechanisms that rely on the meaning of inputs when returning a cached response. This is where semantic caching can prove useful.

Semantic caching

Semantic caching is a caching mechanism that returns a stored value based on similar inputs.

Under the hood, the system uses encoders and embedding vectors to capture semantics and meanings of inputs. It then performs similarity searches across stored key-value pairs to return a cached response.

---

2 Learn more about cache control headers at the MDN website (*https://oreil.ly/-Y5JP*).

In comparison to keyword caching, similar inputs can return the same cached response. Inputs to the system don't have to be identical to be recognized as similar. Even if such inputs have different sentence structures or formulations or contain inaccuracies, they'll still be captured as similar for carrying the same meanings. And, the same response is being requested. As an example, the following queries are considered similar for carrying the same intent:

- How do you build generative services with FastAPI?
- What is the process of developing FastAPI services for GenAI?

This caching system contributes to significant cost savings[3] by reducing API calls to 30–40% (*https://oreil.ly/gjGz6*) (i.e., 60–70% cache hit rate) depending on the use case and size of the user base. For instance, Q&A RAG applications that receive frequently asked questions across a large user base could reduce API calls by 69% using a semantic cache.

Within a typical RAG system, there are two places where having a cache can reduce resource-intensive and time-consuming operations:

- *Before the LLM* to return a cached response instead of generating a new one
- *Before the vector store* to enrich prompts with cached documents instead of searching and retrieving fresh ones

When integrating a semantic cache component into your RAG system, you should consider whether returning a cached response could negatively impact your application's user experience. For instance, if caching the LLM responses, both of the following queries would return the same response due to their high semantic similarity, causing the semantic caching system to treat them as nearly identical:

- Summarize this text in 100 words
- Summarize this text in 50 words

This makes it feel like your services aren't responding to queries. As you may still want varied LLM outputs in your application, we're going to implement a document retrieval semantic cache for your RAG system. Figure 10-1 shows the full system architecture.

---

3 You may still require a trained embedder model for significant cost savings, as making frequent API calls to an off-the-shelf embedder model could incur additional costs, diminishing your overall savings.

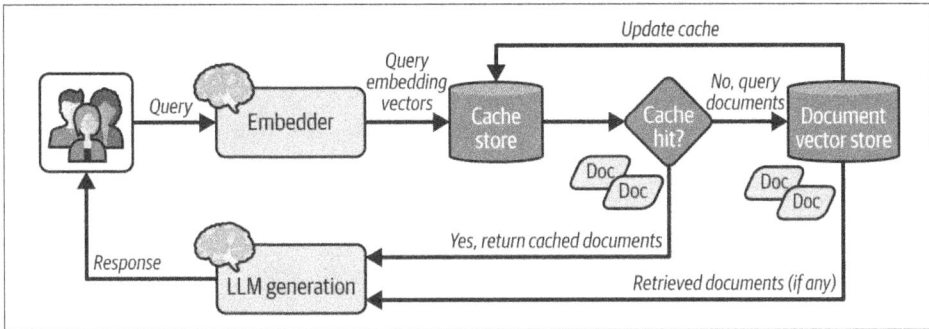

Figure 10-1. Semantic caching in RAG system architecture

Let's start by implementing the semantic caching system from scratch first, and then we'll review how to offload the functionality to an external library such as gptcache.

Building a semantic caching service from scratch. You can implement a semantic caching system by implementing the following components:

- A cache store client
- A document vector store client
- An embedding model

Example 10-6 shows how to implement the cache store client.

Example 10-6. Cache store client

```
import uuid
from qdrant_client import AsyncQdrantClient, models
from qdrant_client.http.models import Distance, PointStruct, ScoredPoint

class CacheClient:
    def __init__(self):
        self.db = AsyncQdrantClient(":memory:")  ❶
        self.cache_collection_name = "cache"

    async def initialize_database(self) -> None:
        await self.db.create_collection(
            collection_name=self.cache_collection_name,
            vectors_config=models.VectorParams(
                size=384, distance=Distance.EUCLID
            ),
        )

    async def insert(
        self, query_vector: list[float], documents: list[str]
    ) -> None:
```

```
        point = PointStruct(
            id=str(uuid.uuid4()),
            vector=query_vector,
            payload={"documents": documents},
        )
        await self.db.upload_points(
            collection_name=self.cache_collection_name, points=[point]
        )

    async def search(self, query_vector: list[float]) -> list[ScoredPoint]:
        return await self.db.search(
            collection_name=self.cache_collection_name,
            query_vector=query_vector,
            limit=1,
        )
```

❶ Initialize a Qdrant client running on memory acting as a cache store.

Once the cache store client is initialized, you can configure the document vector store by following Example 10-7.

Example 10-7. Document store client

```
from qdrant_client import AsyncQdrantClient, models
from qdrant_client.http.models import Distance, ScoredPoint

documents = [...] ❶

class DocumentStoreClient:
    def __init__(self, host="localhost", port=6333):
        self.db_client = AsyncQdrantClient(host=host, port=port)
        self.collection_name = "docs"

    async def initialize_database(self) -> None:
        await self.db_client.create_collection(
            collection_name=self.collection_name,
            vectors_config=models.VectorParams(
                size=384, distance=Distance.EUCLID
            ),
        )
        await self.db_client.add(
            documents=documents, collection_name=self.collection_name
        )

    async def search(self, query_vector: list[float]) -> list[ScoredPoint]:
        results = await self.db_client.search(
            query_vector=query_vector,
            limit=3,
            collection_name=self.collection_name,
        )
        return results
```

❶ Load a collection of documents into the Qdrant vector store.

With both the cache and document vector store clients ready, you can now implement the semantic cache service, as shown in Example 10-8, with methods to compute embeddings and performing cache searches.

Example 10-8. Semantic caching system

```
import time
from loguru import logger
from transformers import AutoModel

...

class SemanticCacheService:
    def __init__(self, threshold: float = 0.35):
        self.embedder = AutoModel.from_pretrained(
            "jinaai/jina-embeddings-v2-base-en", trust_remote_code=True
        )
        self.euclidean_threshold = threshold
        self.cache_client = CacheClient()
        self.doc_db_client = DocumentStoreClient()

    def get_embedding(self, question) -> list[float]:
        return list(self.embedder.embed(question))[0]

    async def initialize_databases(self):
        await self.cache_client.initialize_databases()
        await self.doc_db_client.initialize_databases()

    async def ask(self, query: str) -> str:
        start_time = time.time()
        vector = self.get_embedding(query)
        if search_results := await self.cache_client.search(vector):
            for s in search_results:
                if s.score <= self.euclidean_threshold:  ❶
                    logger.debug(f"Found cache with score {s.score:.3f}")
                    elapsed_time = time.time() - start_time
                    logger.debug(f"Time taken: {elapsed_time:.3f} seconds")
                    return s.payload["content"]

        if db_results := await self.doc_db_client.search(vector):  ❷
            documents = [r.payload["content"] for r in db_results]
            await self.cache_client.insert(vector, documents)
            logger.debug("Query context inserted to Cache.")
            elapsed_time = time.time() - start_time
            logger.debug(f"Time taken: {elapsed_time:.3f} seconds")

        logger.debug("No answer found in Cache or Database.")
        elapsed_time = time.time() - start_time
```

```
        logger.debug(f"Time taken: {elapsed_time:.3f} seconds")
        return "No answer available." ❸
```

❶ Set a similarity threshold. Any score above this threshold will be a cache hit.

❷ Query the document store if there is no cache hit. Cache the retrieved documents against the vector embedding of the query as the cache key.

❸ If there is no related document or cache available for the given query, return a canned answer.

Now that you have a semantic caching service, you can use it to retrieve cached documents from memory by following Example 10-9.

Example 10-9. Implementing a semantic cache in a RAG system with Qdrant

```
async def main():
    cache_service = SemanticCacheService()
    query_1 = "How to build GenAI services?"
    query_2 = "What is the process for developing GenAI services?"

    cache_service.ask(query_1)
    cache_service.ask(query_2)

asyncio.run(main())

# Query 1:
# Query added to Cache.
# Time taken: 0.822 seconds

# Query 2:
# Found cache with score 0.329
# Time taken: 0.016 seconds
```

You should now have a better understanding of how to implement your own custom semantic caching systems using a vector database client.

Semantic caching with GPT cache.   If you don't need to develop your own semantic caching service from scratch, you can also use the modular `gptcache` library that gives you the option to swap various storage, caching, and embedding components.

To configure a semantic cache with `gptcache`, you first need to install the package:

```
$ pip install gptcache
```

Then load the system on application start, as shown in Example 10-10.

Example 10-10. Configuring the GPT cache

```python
from contextlib import asynccontextmanager
from typing import AsyncIterator

from fastapi import FastAPI
from gptcache import Config, cache
from gptcache.embedding import Onnx
from gptcache.processor.post import random_one
from gptcache.processor.pre import last_content
from gptcache.similarity_evaluation import OnnxModelEvaluation

@asynccontextmanager
async def lifespan(_: FastAPI) -> AsyncIterator[None]:
    cache.init(
        post_func=random_one,  ❶
        pre_embedding_func=last_content,  ❷
        embedding_func=Onnx().to_embeddings,  ❸
        similarity_evaluation=OnnxModelEvaluation(),  ❹
        config=Config(similarity_threshold=0.75),  ❺
    )
    cache.set_openai_key()  ❻
    yield

app = FastAPI(lifespan=lifespan)
```

❶ Select a post-processing callback function to select a random item from the returned cached items.

❷ Select a pre-embedding callback function to use the last query for setting a new cache.

❸ Use the ONNX embedding model for computing embedding vectors.

❹ Use `OnnxModelEvaluation` to compute similarity scores between cached items and a given query.

❺ Set the caching configuration options such as a similarity threshold.

❻ Provide an OpenAI client API key for GPT Cache to automatically perform semantic caching on LLM API responses.

Once gptcache is initialized, it will integrate seamlessly with the OpenAI LLM client across your application. You can now make multiple LLM queries, as shown in Example 10-11, knowing that gptcache will be caching your LLM responses.

Example 10-11. Semantic caching with the GPT cache

```
import time
from openai import OpenAI
client = OpenAI()

question = "what's FastAPI"
for _ in range(2):
    start_time = time.time()
    response = client.chat.completions.create(
        model="gpt-4o",
        messages=[{"role": "user", "content": question}],
    )
    print(f"Question: {question}")
    print("Time consuming: {:.2f}s".format(time.time() - start_time))
    print(f"Answer: {response.choices[0].message.content}\n")
```

Using external libraries like gptcache, as shown in Example 10-11, makes implementing semantic caching straightforward.

Once the caching system is up and running, you can adjust *similarity thresholds* to tune the system's cache hit rates.

Similarity threshold. When building a semantic caching service, you may need to adjust the similarity threshold based on provided queries to achieve high cache hit rates that are accurate. You can refer to the interactive visualization of semantic cache clusters (*https://semanticcachehit.com*) shown in Figure 10-2 to better understand the concept of similarity threshold.

Increasing the threshold value in Figure 10-2 will result in a less connected graph, while minimizing can produce false positives. Therefore, you may want to run a few experiments to fine-tune the similarity threshold for your own application.

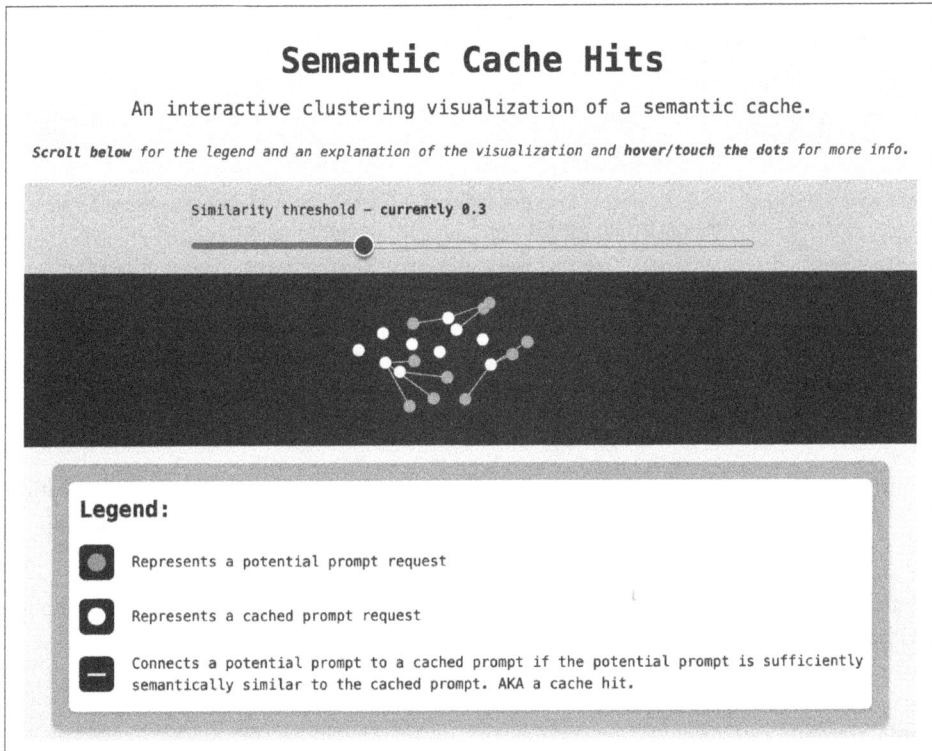

Figure 10-2. Visualization of semantic caching (Source: semanticcachehit.com)

Eviction policies. Another concept relevant to caching is *eviction policies* that control the caching behavior when the caching mechanism reaches its maximum capacity. Selecting the appropriate eviction policy should be appropriate for your own use case.

> Since the size of cache memory stores is often limited, you can add an `evict()` method to the `SemanticCachingService` you implemented in Example 10-8.

Table 10-1 shows a few eviction policies you can choose from.

Table 10-1. Eviction policies

Policy	Description	Use case
First in, first out (FIFO)	Removes oldest items	When all items have the same priority
Least recently used (LRU)	Tracks cache usage across time and removes the least recently accessed item	When recently accessed items are more likely to be accessed again
Least frequently used (LFU)	Tracks cache usage across time and removes the least frequently accessed item	When less frequently used items should be removed first
Most recently used (MRU)	Tracks cache usage across time and removes the most recently accessed item	Rarely used, used when most recently used items are less likely to be accessed again
Random replacement (RR)	Removes a random item from the cache	Simple and fast, used when it doesn't impact performance

Choosing the right eviction policy will depend on your use case and application requirements. Generally, you can start with the LRU policy before switching to alternatives.

You should now feel more confident in implementing semantic caching mechanisms that apply to document retrieval or model responses. Next, let's learn about context or prompt caching, which optimizes queries to models based on their inputs.

Context/prompt caching

Context caching, also known as *prompt caching*, is a caching mechanism suitable for scenarios where you're referencing large amounts of context repeatedly within small requests. It's designed to reuse precomputed attention states from frequently reused prompts, eliminating the need for redundant recomputation of the entire input context each time a new request is made.

You should consider using a context cache when your services involve the following:

- Chatbots with extensive system instructions and long multiturn conversations
- Repetitive analysis of lengthy video files
- Recurring queries against large document sets
- Frequent code repository analysis or bug fixing
- Document summarizations, talking to books, papers, documentation, podcast transcripts and other long form content
- Providing a large number of examples in prompt (i.e., in-context learning)

This type of caching can help you to substantially reduce token usage costs by caching large context tokens. According to Anthropic, prompt caching can reduce costs by up to 90% and latency by up to 85% for long prompts.

The authors of the prompt caching paper (*https://oreil.ly/augpd*) that presents this technique also claim that:

> We find that Prompt Cache significantly reduces latency in time-to-first-token, especially for longer prompts such as document-based question answering and recommendations. The improvements range from 8× for GPU-based inference to 60× for CPU-based inference, all while maintaining output accuracy and without the need for model parameter modifications.

Figure 10-3 visualizes the context caching system architecture.

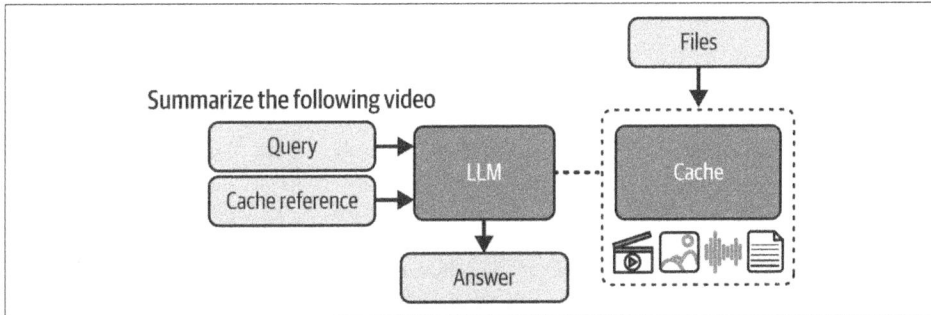

Figure 10-3. System architecture for context caching

At the time of writing, OpenAI automatically implements prompt caching for all API requests without requiring any code changes or additional costs. Example 10-12 shows an example of how to use prompt caching when using the Anthropic API.

Example 10-12. Context/prompt caching with Anthropic API

```
from anthropic import Anthropic

client = Anthropic()

response = client.messages.create(
    model="claude-3-7-sonnet-20250219", ❶
    max_tokens=1024,
    system=[
        {
            "type": "text",
            "text": "You are an AI assistant",
        },
        {
            "type": "text",
            "text": "<the entire content of a large document>",
            "cache_control": {"type": "ephemeral"}, ❷
        },
    ],
    messages=[{"role": "user", "content": "Summarize the documents in ..."}],
```

```
)
print(response)
```

❶ Prompt caching is available only with a handful of models including Claude 3.5 Sonnet, Claude 3 Haiku, and Claude 3 Opus.

❷ Use the `cache_control` parameter to reuse the large document content across multiple API calls without processing it each time.

Under the hood, the Anthropic client will add `anthropic-beta: prompt-caching-2024-07-31` to the request headers.

At the time of writing, `ephemeral` is the only supported cache type, which corresponds to a 5-minute cache lifetime.

> As soon as you adopt a context cache, you're introducing statefulness in requests by preserving tokens across them. This means the data you submit in one request will affect later requests, as the model provider server can use the cached context to maintain continuity between interactions.

With the Gemini API's context caching feature, you can provide content to the model once, cache the input tokens, and reference these cached tokens for future requests.

Using these cached tokens can save you significant expenses if you avoid repeatedly passing in the same corpus of tokens in high volumes. The caching cost will depend on the size of the input tokens and the desired time to live (TTL) storage duration.

> When you cache a set of tokens, you can specify a TTL duration, which is how long the cache should exist before the tokens are automatically deleted. By default, TTL is normally set to 1 hour.

You can see how to use a cached system instruction in Example 10-13. You will also need the Gemini API Python SDK:

```
$ pip install google-generativeai
```

Example 10-13. Context caching with the Google Gemini API

```
import datetime
import google.generativeai as genai
from google.generativeai import caching

genai.configure(api_key="your_gemini_api_key")
```

```
corpus = genai.upload_file(path="corpus.txt")
cache = caching.CachedContent.create(
    model='models/gemini-1.5-flash-001',
    display_name='fastapi', ❶
    system_instruction=(
        "You are an expert AI engineer, and your job is to answer "
        "the user's query based on the files you have access to."
    ),
    contents=[corpus], ❷
    ttl=datetime.timedelta(minutes=5),
)

model = genai.GenerativeModel.from_cached_content(cached_content=cache)
response = model.generate_content(
    [
        (
            "Introduce different characters in the movie by describing "
            "their personality, looks, and names. Also list the timestamps "
            "they were introduced for the first time."
        )
    ]
)
```

❶ Provide a display name as a cache key or identifier.

❷ Pass the corpus to the context caching system. The minimum size of a context cache is 32,768 tokens.

If you run Example 10-13 and print the response.usage_metadata, you should receive the following output:

```
>> print(response.usage_metadata)

prompt_token_count: 696219
cached_content_token_count: 696190
candidates_token_count: 214
total_token_count: 696433
```

Notice how much of the prompt_token_count is now being cached when you compare it with the cached_content_token_count. The candidates_token_count refers to count of output or response tokens coming from the model, which isn't affected by the caching system.

> Gemini models don't make any distinction between cached tokens and regular input tokens. Cached content will be prefixed to the prompt. This is why the prompt token count isn't reduced when using caching.

With context caching, you won't see a drastic reduction in response times but instead will significantly reduce operational costs as you avoid resending extensive system prompts and context tokens. Therefore, this caching strategy is most suitable when you have a large context to work with—for instance, when batch processing files with extensive instructions and examples.

> Using the same context cache and prompt doesn't guarantee consistent model responses because the responses from LLMs are nondeterministic. A context cache doesn't cache any output.

Context caching remains an active area of research. If you want to avoid any vendor lock-in, there is already some progress in this field with open source tools such as *MemServe* (*https://oreil.ly/PXm6B*), which implements context caching with an elastic memory pool.

Beyond caching, you can also review your options for reducing model size to speed up response times using techniques such as *model quantization*.

Model Quantization

If you're going to be serving models such as LLMs yourself, you should consider *quantizing* (i.e., compressing/shrinking) your models if possible. Often, open source model repositories will also supply quantized versions that you can download and use straightaway without having to go through the quantization process yourself.

Model quantization is the adjustment process on the model weights and activations where high-precision model parameters are statistically projected into lower-precision values through a fine-tuning operation using scaling factors on the original parameter distribution. You can then perform all critical inference operations with lower precision, after which you can convert the outputs to higher precision to maintain the quality while improving performance.

Reducing the precision also decreases the memory storage requirements, theoretically lowering energy consumption and speeding up operations like matrix multiplication through integer arithmetic. This also enables models to run on embedded devices, which may only support integer data types.

Figure 10-4 shows the full quantization process.

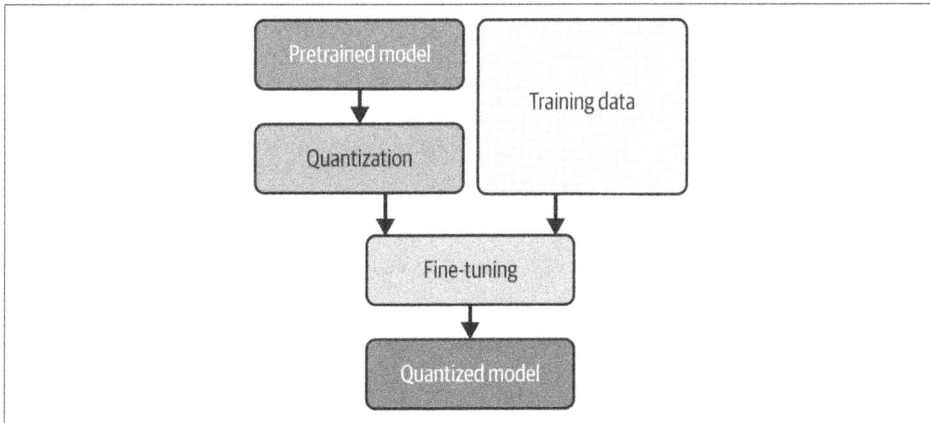

Figure 10-4. Quantization process

You can save more than a handful of gigabytes in GPU memory consumption as low-precision data types such as 8-bit integer would require significantly less RAM per parameter than a data type like 32-bit float.

Precision versus quality trade-off

Figure 10-5 compares a nonquantized model and a quantized model.

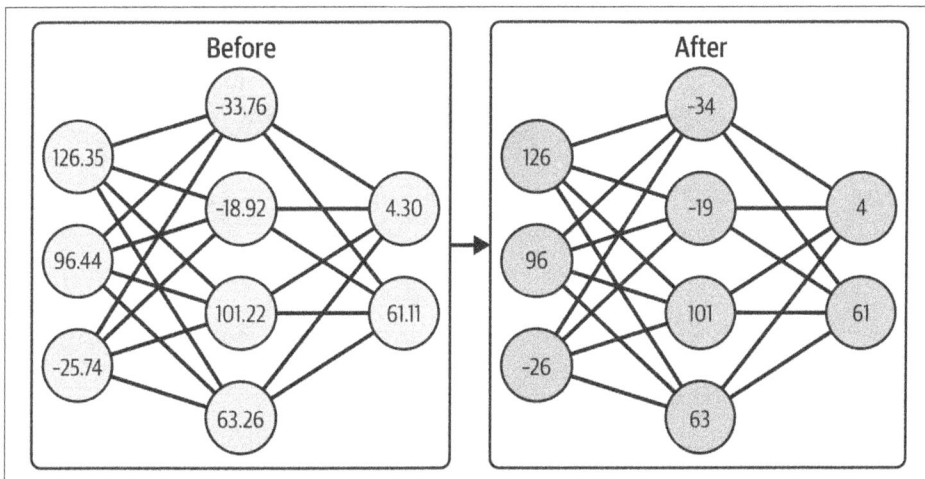

Figure 10-5. Quantization

As each high-precision 32-bit float parameter consumes 4 bytes of GPU memory, a 1B-parameter model would require 4 GB of memory just for inference. If you plan on retraining or fine-tuning the same model, you'll require at least 24 GB of GPU VRAM. This is because each parameter would also require storing information like gradients, training optimizer states, activations, and temporary memory space, consuming an additional 24 bytes together. This estimates up to 6 times the memory requirement compared to just loading the model weights. The same 1B model would then require a 24 GB GPU, which the best and most expensive consumer graphics cards such as NVIDIA RTX 4090 may still struggle to meet.

Instead of using the standard 32-float, you can select any of the following formats:

- *16-bit floating-point (FP16)* cuts memory usage in half without much of a hit to model output quality.
- *8-bit integer (INT8)* offers huge savings in memory but with a significant loss in quality.
- *16-bit brain floating-point (BFLOAT16)* with a similar range to FP32 balances the memory and quality trade-off.
- *4-bit integer (INT4)* provides a balance between memory efficiency and computational precision, making it suitable for low-power devices.
- *1-bit integer (INT1)* uses the lowest precision data type with maximum model size reduction. Research for creating high-quality 1-bit LLMs (*https://oreil.ly/ QH9nH*) is currently under way.

For comparison, Table 10-2 shows the reduction in model size when you quantize the Llama family models.

Table 10-2. Impact of quantization on the size of Llama models[a]

Model	Original	FP16	8 Bit	6 Bit	4 Bit	2Bit
Llama 2 70B	140 GB	128.5 GB	73.23 GB	52.70 GB	36.20 GB	28.59 GB
Llama 3 8B	16.07 GB	14.97 GB	7.96 GB	4.34 GB	4.34 GB	2.96 GB

[a] Sources: Llama.cpp GitHub repository (*https://oreil.ly/9iYtL*) and Tom Jobbins's Hugging Face Llama 2 70B model card (*https://oreil.ly/BMDtR*)

> In addition to the GPU VRAM needed to fit the model, you will also need an extra 5 to 8 GB of GPU VRAM for overhead during model loading.

As per the current state of research, maintaining accuracy with integer-only INT4 and INT1 data types is a challenge, and the performance improvement with INT32 or FP16 is not significant. Therefore, the most popular lower-precision data type is INT8 for inference.

According to research (*https://oreil.ly/C7Lz3*), using integer-only arithmetic for inference will be more efficient than floating-point numbers. However, quantizing floating numbers to integers can be tricky. For instance, only 256 values can be represented in INT8, while float32 can represent a wide range of values.

Floating-point numbers

To understand why projecting 32-bit floats to other formats would save so much in GPU memory, let's look at how it breaks down.

A 32-bit floating-point number consists of the following types of bits:

- *Sign* bit describing whether a number is positive or negative
- *Exponent* bits controlling the scale of the number
- *Mantissa* bits holding the actual digits determining its precision (also known as *fraction* bits)

You can see a visualization of bits in the aforementioned floating-point numbers in Figure 10-6.

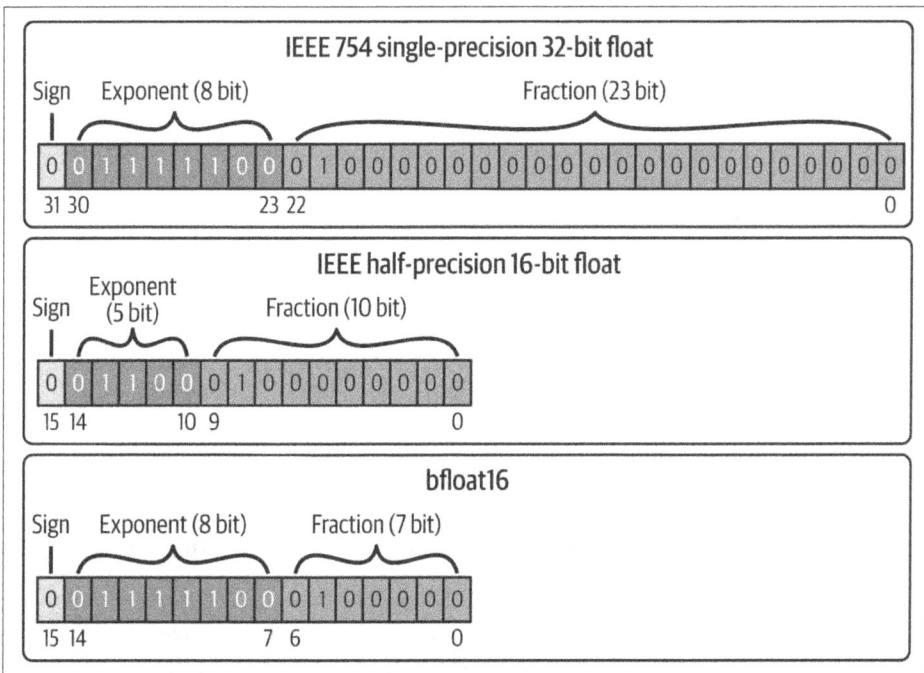

Figure 10-6. Bits in 32-bit float, 16-bit float, and bfloat16 numbers

When you project the FP32 number into other formats, in effect, you're squeezing it into smaller ranges, losing most of its mantissa bits and adjusting its exponent bits but without losing much of the precision. You can see such a phenomenon in action by referring to Figure 10-7.

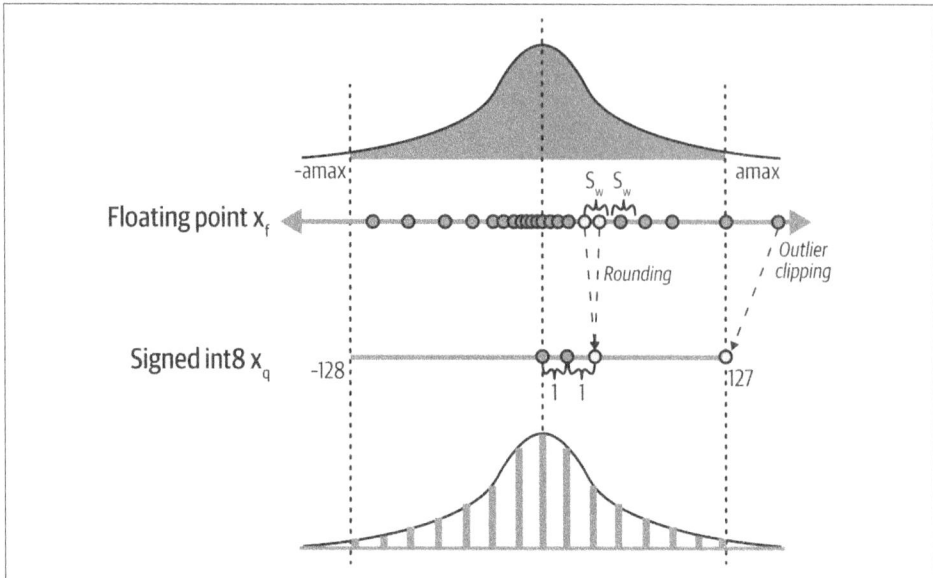

Figure 10-7. Quantization of floating-point numbers to integers

In fact, research on the quantization strategies for pretrained LLM models (*https:// oreil.ly/Swfz7*) has shown that LLMs with 4-bit quantization can maintain performance similar to their nonquantized counterparts. However, while quantization saves memory, it can also reduce the inference speed of LLMs.

How to quantize pretrained LLMs

Quantization is the process of compressing large models by weight adjustment. One such technique called *GPTQ* (*https://oreil.ly/rHYKZ*) can quantize LLMs with 175 billion parameters in approximately 4 GPU hours, reducing the bit width to 3 or 4 bits per weight, with a negligible accuracy drop relative to the uncompressed model.

The Hugging Face `transformers` and `optimum` library authors have collaborated closely with the `auto-gptq` library developers to provide a simple API for applying GPTQ quantization on open source LLMs. Optimum is a library that provides APIs to perform quantization using different tools.

With the GPTQ quantization, you can quantize your favorite language model to 8, 4, 3, or even 2 bits without a big drop in performance, while maintaining faster inference speeds that are supported by most GPT hardware. You can follow Example 10-14 to quantize a pretrained model on your own GPU.

The dependencies you need to install to run Example 10-14 will include the following:

```
$ pip install auto-gptq optimum transformers accelerate
```

Example 10-14. GPTQ model quantization with Hugging Face and AutoGPTQ libraries

```
import torch
from optimum.gptq import GPTQQuantizer
from transformers import AutoModelForCausalLM, AutoTokenizer

model_name = "facebook/opt-125m" ❶
tokenizer = AutoTokenizer.from_pretrained(model_name)
model = AutoModelForCausalLM.from_pretrained(
    model_name, torch_dtype=torch.float16
)

quantizer = GPTQQuantizer(
    bits=4,
    dataset="c4", ❷
    block_name_to_quantize="model.decoder.layers", ❸
    model_seqlen=2048, ❹
)
quantized_model = quantizer.quantize_model(model, tokenizer)
```

❶ Load the `float16` version of the `facebook/opt-125m` pretrained model prior to quantization.

❷ Use the c4 dataset to calibrate the quantization.

❸ Quantize only the model's decoder layer blocks.

❹ Use model sequence length of 2048 to process the dataset.

> For reference, a 175B model will require 4 GPU hours on NVIDIA A100 to quantize. However, it's worth searching the Hugging Face model repository for prequantized models, as you might find that someone has already done the work.

Now that you understand performance optimization techniques, let's explore how to enhance the quality of your GenAI services using methods like structured outputs.

Structured Outputs

Foundational models such as LLMs may be used as a component of a data pipeline or connected to downstream applications. For instance, you can use these models to extract and parse information from documents or to generate code that can be executed on other systems.

You can ask the LLM to provide a textual response containing JSON information. You will then have to extract and parse this JSON string using tools like regex and

Pydantic. However, there is no guarantee that the model will always adhere to your instructions. Since your downstream systems may rely on JSON outputs, they may throw exceptions and incorrectly handle invalid inputs.

Several utility packages like Instructor have been released to improve the robustness of LLM responses by taking a schema and making several API calls under the hood with various prompt templates to reach a desired output. While these solutions improve robustness, they also add significant costs to your solution due to subsequent API calls to the model providers.

Most recently, model providers have added a feature for requesting structured outputs by supplying schemas when making API calls to the model, as you can see in Example 10-15. This helps to reduce the prompting templating work you have to do yourself and aims to improve the model's *alignment* to your intent when returning a response.

> At the time of writing, only the most recent OpenAI SDK supports Pydantic models for enabling structured outputs.

Example 10-15. Structured outputs

```
from openai import AsyncOpenAI
from pydantic import BaseModel, Field

client = AsyncOpenAI()

class DocumentClassification(BaseModel): ❶
    category: str = Field(..., description="The category of the classification")

async def get_document_classification(
    title: str,
) -> DocumentClassification | str | None:
    response = await client.beta.chat.completions.parse(
        model="gpt-4o",
        messages=[
            {
                "role": "system",
                "content": "classify the provided document into the following: ...",
            },
            {"role": "user", "content": title},
        ],
        response_format=DocumentClassification, ❷
    )

    message = response.choices[0].message
    return message.parsed if message.parsed is not None else message.refusal
```

❶ Specify a Pydantic model for structured outputs.

❷ Provide the defined schema to the model client when making the API call.

If your model provider doesn't support structured outputs natively, you can still leverage the model's chat completion capabilities to increase robustness of structured outputs, as shown in Example 10-16.

Example 10-16. Structured outputs based on chat completions prefill

```python
import json
from loguru import logger
from openai import AsyncOpenAI
client = AsyncOpenAI()

system_template = """
Classify the provided document into the following: ...

Provide responses in the following manner json: {"category": "string"}
"""

async def get_document_classification(title: str) -> dict:
    response = await client.chat.completions.create(
        model="gpt-4o",
        max_tokens=1024,  ❶
        messages=[
            {"role": "system", "content": system_template},
            {"role": "user", "content": title},
            {
                "role": "assistant",
                "content": "The document classification JSON is {",  ❷
            },
        ],
    )
    message = response.choices[0].message.content or ""
    try:
        return json.loads("{" + message[: message.rfind("}") + 1])  ❸
    except json.JSONDecodeError:  ❹
        logger.warning(f"Failed to parse the response: {message}")
    return {"error": "Refusal response"}
```

❶ Limit the output tokens to improve robustness and speed of the structured responses and to reduce costs.

❷ Skip the preamble and directly return a JSON by prefilling the assistant response and including a { character.

❸ Add back the prefilled { and then find the closing } and extract the JSON substring.

❹ Handle cases where there is no JSON in the response—e.g., if there is a refusal.

Following the aforementioned techniques should help you improve the robustness of your data pipelines if they leverage LLMs as a component.

Prompt Engineering

Prompt engineering is the practice of crafting and refining queries to generative models to produce the most useful and optimized outputs. Without refining prompts, you'd either have to fine-tune models or train a model from scratch to optimize the output quality.

Many argue that the field lacks the scientific rigor to consider it an engineering discipline. However, you can approach the problem from an engineering perspective when refining prompts to get the best quality outputs from your models.

Similar to how you communicate with others to get things done, with the optimized prompts, you can most effectively communicate your intent with the model to improve the chances of getting the responses you want. Therefore, prompting becomes not just an engineering problem but a communication one as well. A model can be compared to a knowledgeable colleague with lots of experience but limited domain knowledge, ready to help you but needs you to provide well-documented instructions, possibly with a few examples to follow and pattern match.

If your prompts are vague and generic, you'll also get an average response.

Another way of thinking about this optimization problem is to compare the task of model prompting to programming. Instead of writing the code yourself, you're effectively "coding" a model to be a well-integrated component of a larger application or data pipeline. You can adopt test-driven development (TDD) approaches and refine your prompts until your tests pass. Or, experiment with different models to see which one *aligns* its outputs to your intent the best.

> Maximizing model *alignment* remains a high-priority objective of many model providers so that their model outputs best satisfy the user's intent.

Prompt templates

If your system instructions aren't methodical, clear, and don't follow best prompting practices, you may be leaving potential quality and performance optimizations on the table.

As a minimum, you should have clear system prompts that provide specific tasks to the model. Best practice is to follow a systematic template. For instance, draft the model instructions following the *role, context, and task* (RCT) template:

Role

> Describes how the model should behave given a scenario and a task. Research has shown that specifying roles for LLMs tends to significantly affect their outputs. As an example, a model may be more forgiving in grading an essay if you give it the role of a primary school teacher. Without a specific role, the model may assume you want the grading to follow university-level academic standards.

> You can expand on the model's role even further and describe a *persona* in detail for the model to adopt. Using a persona, the model will exactly know how to behave and make predictions as it has more context on what the role should entail.

Context

> Sets the scenario, paints the picture, and provides any relevant and useful information that the model can use as a reference to making predictions. Without an explicit context, the model can only use an implicit context that'll contain average information of its training data. In a RAG application, the context could be the concatenation of system prompt with the retrieved document chunks from a knowledge store.

Task

> Provides clear instructions on what you want the model to perform given a context and a role. When describing the task, make sure you think of the model as a bright and knowledgeable apprentice, ready to jump into action but needs highly clear and unambiguous instructions to follow, potentially with a handful of examples.

Following the aforementioned system template, you should enhance the quality of your model outputs with minimal effort.

Advanced prompting techniques

Beyond the prompting fundamentals, you can use more advanced techniques that may better fit your use case. Based on a recent systematic survey of prompting techniques (*https://oreil.ly/xynPC*), you can group LLM prompts into the following:

- In-context learning

- Thought generation

- Decomposition

- Ensembling

- Self-criticism

- Agentic

Let's review each in more detail.

In-context learning. What sets foundational models such as LLMs apart from traditional machine learning models is their ability to respond to dynamic inputs without the constant need for fine-tuning or retraining.

When you give system instructions to an LLM, you can additionally supply several examples, (i.e., shots) to guide the output generation.

Zero-shot prompting (*https://oreil.ly/3F4wb*) refers to a prompting approach that doesn't specify reference examples, yet the model can still successfully complete the given task. If the model struggles without reference examples, you may have to use *few-shot prompting* (*https://oreil.ly/pOSj8*) where you provide a handful of examples. There are also use cases where you want to use *dynamic few-shot* prompting where you dynamically insert examples from data fetched from a database or vector store.

Prompting approaches where you specify examples are also termed *in-context learning*. You're effectively fine-tuning the model's outputs to your examples and the given task without actually modifying its model weights/parameters, whereas other ML models would require adjustments to their weights.

This is what makes LLMs and foundational models so powerful, since they don't always require weight adjustment to fit your data and tasks you give them. You can learn about several in-context learning techniques by referring to Table 10-3.

Table 10-3. In-context learning prompting techniques

Prompting technique	Examples	Use cases
Zero-shot	Summarize the following…	Summarization, Q&A without specific training examples
Few-shot	Classify documents based on examples below: [Examples]	Text classification, sentiment analysis, data extraction with few examples
Dynamic few-shot	Classify the following documents based on examples below: <Inject examples from a vector store based on a query>	Personalized responses, complex problem-solving

In-context learning prompts are straightforward, effective, and a great starting point for completing a variety of tasks. For more complex tasks, you can use more advanced prompting approaches like thought generation, decomposition, ensembling, self-criticism, or agentic approaches.

Thought generation. Thought generation techniques like chain of thought (CoT) (*https://oreil.ly/BWUYQ*) have shown to significantly improve the ability of LLMs to perform complex reasoning.

In COT prompting you ask the model to explain its thought process and reasoning as it provides a response. Variants of CoT include zero-shot or few-shot CoT (*https://oreil.ly/1gjSH*) depending on whether you supply examples. A more advanced thought generation technique is thread of thought (ThoT) (*https://oreil.ly/1KyO4*) that systematically segments and analyzes chaotic and very complex information or tasks.

Table 10-4 lists thought generation techniques.

Table 10-4. Thought generation prompting techniques

Prompting technique	Examples	Use cases
Zero-shot chain of thought (CoT)	Let's think step by step…	Mathematical problem-solving, logical reasoning, and multi-step decision-making.
Few-shot CoT	Let's think step by step… Here are a few examples: [EXAMPLES]	Scenarios where a few examples can guide the model to perform better, such as nuanced text classification, complex question answering, and creative writing prompts.
Thread of thought (ThoT)	Walk me through the problem in manageable parts step by step, summarizing and analyzing as you go…	Maintaining context over multiple interactions, such as dialogue systems, interactive storytelling, and long-form content generation.

Decomposition. Decomposition prompting techniques focus on breaking down complex tasks into smaller subtasks so that the model can work through them step-by-step and logically. You can experiment with these approaches alongside thought generation to identify which ones produce the best results for your use case.

These are the most common decomposition prompting techniques:

Least-to-most (https://oreil.ly/HmsSN)
Ask the model to break a complex problem into smaller problems via logical reduction without solving them. You can then reprompt the model to solve each task one by one.

Plan-and-solve (https://oreil.ly/aWTzf)
Given a task, ask for a plan to be devised, and then request the model to solve it.

Tree of thoughts (ToT) (https://oreil.ly/IZdj1)
Create a tree-search problem where a task is broken into multiple branches of steps like a tree. Then, reprompt the model to evaluate and solve each branch of steps.

Table 10-5 shows these decomposition techniques.

Table 10-5. Decomposition prompting techniques

Prompting technique	Examples	Use cases
Least-to-most	Break down the task of…into smaller tasks.	Complex problem-solving, project management, task decomposition
Plan-and-solve	Devise a plan to…	Algorithm development, software design, strategic planning
Tree of thoughts (ToT)	Create a decision tree for choosing a…	Decision-making, problem-solving with multiple solutions, strategic planning with alternatives

Ensembling. *Ensembling* is the process of using multiple prompts to solve the same problem and then aggregating the responses into a final output. You can generate these responses using the same or different models.

The main idea behind ensembling is to reduce the variance of LLM outputs by improving accuracy in exchange for higher usage costs.

Well-known ensembling prompting techniques include the following:

Self-consistency (https://oreil.ly/_85WS)
Generates multiple reasoning paths and selects the most consistent output as the final result using a majority vote.

Mixture of reasoning experts (MoRE) (https://oreil.ly/xllKs)
Combines outputs from multiple LLMs with specialized prompts to improve response quality. Each LLM acts as an expert on an area focused on different reasoning tasks such as factual reasoning, logical reduction, common-sense checks, etc.

Demonstration ensembling (DENSE) (https://oreil.ly/lPEPz)
Creates multiple few-shot prompts from data, then generates a final output by aggregating over the responses.

Prompt paraphrasing (https://oreil.ly/yP_ka)
Formulates the original prompt into multiple variants via wording.

Table 10-6 shows examples and use cases of these ensembling techniques.

Table 10-6. Ensembling prompting techniques

Prompting technique	Examples	Use cases
Self-consistency	Prompt #1 (run multiple times): Let's think step by step and complete the following task... Prompt #2: From the following responses, choose the best/common one by scoring them using...	Reducing errors or bias in arithmetic, common-sense tasks, and symbolic reasoning tasks
Mixture of reasoning experts (MoRE)	Prompt #1 (run for each expert): You are a reviewer for ..., score the following based on... Prompt #2: Choose the best expert answer based on an agreement score...	Accounting for specialized knowledge areas or domains
Demonstration ensembling (DENSE)	Create multiple few-shot examples for translating this text and aggregate the best responses. Generate several few-shot prompts for summarizing this article and combine the outputs.	• Improving output reliability • Aggregating diverse perspectives
Prompt paraphrasing	Prompt #1a: Reword this proposal... Prompt #1b: Clarify this proposal... Prompt #1c: Make adjustment to this proposal... Prompt #2: Choose the best proposal from the following responses based on...	• Exploring different interpretations • Data augmentation for ensembling

Self-criticism.   *Self-criticism* prompting techniques focus on using models as AI judges, assessors, or reviewers, either to perform self-checks or to assess the outputs of other models. The criticism or feedback from the first prompt can then be used to improve the response quality in follow-on prompts.

These are several self-criticism prompting strategies:

Self-calibration (https://oreil.ly/_4YEr)
    Ask the LLM to assess the correctness of a response/answer against a question/answer.

Self-refine (https://oreil.ly/bTQJI)
    Refine responses iteratively through self-checks and providing feedback.

Reversing chain of thought (RCoT) (https://oreil.ly/6ojtr)
    Reconstruct the problem from a generated answer, and then generate fine-grained comparisons between the original problem and the reconstructed one to identify inconsistencies.

Self-verification (https://oreil.ly/Fz3JH)
    Generate potential solutions with the CoT technique, and then score each by masking parts of the question and supplying each answer.

Chain of verification (COVE) (https://oreil.ly/WrrLP)

Create a list of related queries/questions to help verify the correctness of an answer/response.

Cumulative reasoning (https://oreil.ly/3Hb-6)

Generate potential steps in responding to a query, and then ask the model to accept/reject each step. Finally, check whether it has arrived at the final answer to terminate the process; otherwise, repeat the process.

You can see examples of each self-criticism prompting technique in Table 10-7.

Table 10-7. Self-criticism prompting techniques

Prompting technique	Examples	Use cases
Self-calibration	Assess the correctness of the following response: [response] for the following question: [question]	Gauge confidence of the answers to accept or revise the original answer.
Self-refine	Prompt #1: What is your feedback on the response… Prompt #2: Using the feedback [Feedback], refine your response on…	Reasoning, coding, and generation tasks.
Reversing chain-of-thought (RCoT)	Prompt #1: Reconstruct the problem from this answer… Prompt #2: Generate fine-grained comparison between these queries…	Identifying inconsistencies and revising answers.
Self-verification	Prompt #1 (run multiple times): Let's think step by step - generate solution for the following problem… Prompt #2: Score each solution based on the [masked problem]…	Improve on reasoning tasks.
Chain of verification (COVE)	Prompt #1: Answer the following question… Prompt #2: Formulate related questions to check this response: … Prompt #3 (run for each new related question): Answer the following question: … Prompt #4: Based on the following information, pick the best answer…	Question answering and text-generation tasks.
Cumulative reasoning	Prompt #1: Outline steps to respond to the query: … Prompt #2: Check the following plan and accept/reject steps relevant in responding to the query: … Prompt #3: Check you've arrived at the final answer given the following information…	Step-by-step validation of complex queries, logical inference, and mathematical problems.

Agentic. You can take the prompting techniques discussed so far one step further and add access to external tools with complex evaluation algorithms. This process specializes LLMs as *agents*, allowing them to make plans, take actions, and use external systems.

Prompts or *prompt sequences (chains)* drive agentic systems with an engineering focus on creating agent-like behavior from LLMs. These agentic workflows serve users by performing actions on systems that interface with the GenAI models, which are mostly LLMs. Tools, whether *symbolic* like a calculator, or *neural* such as another AI model, form a core component of agentic systems.

> If you create a pipeline of multiple model calls with one output forwarded to the same or different model as input, you've constructed a *prompt chain*. In principle, you're using the CoT prompting technique when you leverage prompt chains.

A few agentic prompting techniques include:

Modular reasoning, knowledge, and language (MRKL) (https://oreil.ly/aWeQu)
Simplest agentic system consisting of an LLM using multiple tools to get and combine information for generating an answer.

Self-correcting with tool-interactive critiquing (CRITIC) (https://oreil.ly/M-9YL)
Responds to queries, and then self-checks its answer without using external tools. Finally, uses tools to verify or amend responses.

Program-aided language model (PAL) (https://oreil.ly/0WtKv)
Generates code from queries and sends directly to code interpreters such as Python to generate an answer.[4]

Tool-integrated reasoning agent (ToRA) (https://oreil.ly/pbfv_)
Takes PAL a few steps further by interleaving code generation and reasoning steps as long as needed to provide a satisfactory response.

Reasoning and acting (ReAct) (https://oreil.ly/aDubr)
Given a problem, generates thoughts, takes actions, receives observations, and repeats the loop with previous information, (i.e., memory) until the problem is solved.

If you want to enable your LLMs to use tools, you can take advantage of *function calling* features from model providers, as in Example 10-17.

Example 10-17. Function calling for fetching

```
from openai import OpenAI
from scraper import fetch
client = OpenAI()

tools = [
    {
```

---

[4] For better security, you still need to sanitize any LLM-generated code before forwarding it to downstream systems for execution.

```
        "type": "function",
        "function": {
            "name": "fetch",
            "description": "Read the content of url and provide a summary",
            "parameters": {
                "type": "object",
                "properties": {
                    "url": {
                        "type": "string",
                        "description": "The url to fetch",
                    },
                },
                "required": ["url"],
                "additionalProperties": False,
            },
        },
    }
]

messages = [
    {
        "role": "system",
        "content": "You are a helpful customer support assistant"
        "Use the supplied tools to assist the user.",
    },
    {
        "role": "user",
        "content": "Summarize this paper: https://arxiv.org/abs/2207.05221",
    },
]

response = client.chat.completions.create(
    model="gpt-4o",
    messages=messages,
    tools=tools,
)
```

As you saw in Example 10-17, you can create agentic systems by configuring special-ized LLMs that have access to custom tools and functions.

Fine-Tuning

There are cases where prompt engineering alone won't give the response quality you're looking for. Fine-tuning is an optimization technique that requires you to adjust the parameters of your GenAI model to better fit your data. For instance, you may fine-tune a language model to learn content of private knowledge bases or to always respond with a certain tone following your brand guidelines.

It's often not the first technique you should try since it requires effort to collect and prepare data, in addition to training and evaluating models.

When should you consider fine-tuning?

You may want to consider fine-tuning pretrained GenAI models if one of the following scenarios is true:

- You have significant token usage costs—for instance, due to requiring extensive system instructions or providing lots of examples in every prompt.
- Your use case relies on specialized domain expertise that the model needs to learn.
- You need to reduce the number of hallucinations in responses with a more fine-tuned conservative model.
- You require higher-quality responses and have sufficient data for fine-tuning.
- You require lower latency in responses.

Once a model has been fine-tuned, you won't need to provide as many examples in the prompt. This saves costs and enables lower-latency requests.

Avoid fine-tuning as much as you can.

There are many tasks where prompt engineering alone can help you optimize the quality of your outputs. Iterating over prompts has a much faster feedback loop than iterating over fine-tuning, which relies on creating datasets and running training jobs.

However, if you do end up needing to fine-tune, you'll notice that the initial prompt engineering efforts would contribute to producing higher-quality training data.

Here are a few cases where fine-tuning can be useful:

- Teaching a model to respond in a brand style, tone, format, or some other qualitative metric—for instance, to produce standardized reports that comply with regulatory requirements and internal protocols
- Improving reliability of producing desired outputs such as always having responses conform to a given structured output
- Achieving correct results to complex queries such as document classification and tagging from hundreds of classes
- Performing domain-specific specialized tasks such as item classification or industry-specific data interpretation and aggregation
- Nuanced handling of edge cases
- Performing skills or tasks that are hard to articulate in prompts such as datetime extraction from unstructured texts

- Reducing costs by using `gpt-4o-mini` or even `gpt-3.5-turbo` instead of `gpt-4o`
- Teaching a model to use complex tools and APIs when using function calling

How to fine-tune a pretrained model

For any fine-tuning job, you will need to follow these steps:

1. Prepare and upload training data.
2. Submit a fine-tuning training job.
3. Evaluate and use fine-tuned model.

Depending on the model you're using, the data must be prepared based on the model provider's instruction.

For instance, to fine-tune a typical chat model like `gpt-4o-2024-08-06`, you need to prepare your data as a message format, as shown in Example 10-18. At the time of writing, OpenAI API pricing (*https://oreil.ly/MmCNq*) for fine-tuning this model is $25/1M training tokens.

Example 10-18. Example training data for a fine-tuning job

```
// training_data.jsonl

{
    "messages": [
        {
            "role": "system",
            "content": "<text>"
        },
        {
            "role": "user",
            "content": "<text>"
        },
        {
            "role": "assistant",
            "content": "<text>"
        }
    ]
}
// more entries
```

Once your data is prepared, you need to upload the `jsonl` file, get a file ID, and supply that when submitting a fine-tuning job, as you can see in Example 10-19.

Example 10-19. Submitting a fine-tuning training job

```
from openai import OpenAI
client = OpenAI()

response = client.files.create(
    file=open("mydata.jsonl", "rb"), purpose="fine-tune"
)

client.fine_tuning.jobs.create(
    training_file=response.id, model="gpt-4o-mini-2024-07-18"
)
```

Model providers that allow you to submit fine-tuning jobs will also provide APIs for checking the status of submitted jobs and for getting results.

Once the model is fine-tuned, you can retrieve the fine-tuned model ID and pass it to the LLM client, as shown in Example 10-20. Make sure to evaluate the model first before using it in production.

> You can also use the testing techniques discussed in Chapter 11 when evaluating fine-tuned models.

Example 10-20. Using a fine-tuned model

```
from openai import OpenAI
client = OpenAI()

fine_tuning_job_id = "ftjob-abc123"
response = client.fine_tuning.jobs.retrieve(fine_tuning_job_id)
fine_tuned_model = response.fine_tuned_model

if fine_tuned_model is None:
    raise ValueError(
        f"Failed to retrieve the fine-tuned model - "
        f"Job ID: {fine_tuning_job_id}"
    )

completion = client.chat.completions.create(
    model=fine_tuned_model,
    messages=[
        {"role": "system", "content": "You are a helpful assistant."},
        {"role": "user", "content": "Hello!"},
    ],
)
print(completion.choices[0].message)
```

While these examples show the fine-tuning process with OpenAI, the process will be similar with other providers even if the implementation details may differ.

> If you decide to leverage fine-tuning, be mindful that you won't be able to take advantage of the latest improvements or optimizations in new LLMs, potentially making the fine-tuning process a waste of your time and money.

With this final optimization step, you should now feel confident in building GenAI services that not only meet your security and quality requirements but also achieve your desired throughput and latency metrics.

Summary

In this chapter, you learned about several optimization strategies to improve the throughput and quality of your services. A few optimizations you added covered various caching (keyword, semantic, context), prompt engineering, model quantization, and fine-tuning.

In the next chapter, we will shift focus to the last step in building AI services: deploying your GenAI solution. This includes exploring deployment patterns for AI services and containerization with Docker.

## CHAPTER 11

Testing AI Services

Chapter Goals

In this chapter, you will learn about:

- How to plan and structure test suites for comprehensive test coverage, including unit, integration, end-to-end, and behavioral tests

- The concepts of testing boundaries, code coverage, and idempotency in designing tests

- How to identify and avoid common testing pitfalls to improve test quality

- How to leverage test fixtures and implement parameterization to run tests with multiple inputs for checking code robustness

- How to efficiently set up and tear down testing environments using `pytest`

- How to maintain idempotency in testing processes by correctly handling asynchronous flaky tests

- How to use mocking and patching to isolate components from external dependencies in unit tests

- How to test GenAI services that use probabilistic models using behavioral testing and auto-evaluation techniques

- How to leverage several testing metrics for GenAI services

In this chapter, you'll learn the importance of testing and its challenges when building GenAI services. You'll also learn about key concepts such as test plans, the verification and validation models, the testing pyramid, and the role of testing data, environments, and boundaries.

To practice testing, you will use `pytest`, a popular testing framework with features such as test fixtures, scopes, markers, and fixture parameterization. You'll also learn about the `pytest-mock` plug-in for patching functions and using stubs, mocks, and spy objects to simulate and control external dependencies during tests.

Since mocking can make tests brittle, we'll also explore dependency injection, allowing you to inject mock or stub dependencies directly into the components being tested, avoiding runtime code modifications.

We'll discuss the role of isolation and idempotency in tests, when to use mocks, and how to test both deterministic and probabilistic GenAI code. By the end of this chapter, you'll be confident in writing comprehensive test suites including unit, integration, end-to-end, and behavioral tests for your own services.

Before we dive into writing tests, let's explore the foundational concepts of traditional software testing and how to approach testing GenAI services, which can prove challenging due to the probabilistic nature of AI models.

The Importance of Testing

In theory, everyone agrees that testing is necessary when building software. You write tests to give you confidence in the functionality and performance of your systems, especially when they interact with one another. But realistically, projects may skip implementing manual or automated tests due to various constraints including budget, time, or associated labor costs related to maintaining tests.

The projects that skip testing, partially or entirely, end up approaching software problems reactively instead of proactively. This is when *technical debt* builds up, which you'll then have to pay back in labor and server costs, with interest, to settle up.

The problem of when to test is challenging to solve. If you're just experimenting and hacking a prototype together in fast iterations, you won't need to worry about testing as much, realistically. However, as soon as you have a minimum sellable product, a system that interfaces with sensitive data and processes user payments, then you must seriously consider testing plans.

Earlier in my career, I was building a learning management system for a client. I wrote a webhook endpoint to interface with Stripe's payment systems and my own home-brewed authentication solution that would only register users on successful first payment. The system had to charge and process subscription payments of both new and existing customers and send confirmation emails while tracking user records, subscriptions, payments, checkout sessions, and invoices. The logic of that webhook ended up so convoluted and complex that it led to a monstrosity that became a 1,000-line function. The function was checking unordered received events of various types, with multiple round-trips to the database.

The whole solution had to be scrapped at the end since the webhook's behavior was so *flaky*, returning nonconsistent responses to the same set of inputs. Users couldn't register even after successful payments. This flakiness made it unbearable to debug that webhook, which forced me to rewrite the payment system integration from scratch. If I had only slowed down to plan and modularized the logic and wrote tests early on, I could have saved myself from so much headache.

When you slow down to plan and test your services, you're trading off time and effort in exchange for confidence in your code.

A few other times you should consider implementing tests are when:

- Multiple contributors add changes over time
- Maintainers change external dependencies
- You increase the number of components and dependencies in your services
- You suddenly spot too many bugs appearing
- There is too much at stake if things go wrong—my experience fell into this bucket

You should now understand how testing will benefit your project.

Software Testing

Now that you're familiar with the challenges and potential approaches to testing GenAI services, let's review software testing concepts to understand their relevance to GenAI use cases and common pitfalls to avoid.

Types of Tests

There are three common types of tests in software testing, which, ordered by increasing size and complexity, are as follows:

Unit tests
Focus on testing individual components or functions in isolation across a discrete set of inputs and edge cases to validate functionality at singular component level. Unit tests are atomic with the smallest scope and often don't rely on external systems or dependencies.

Integration tests
Check the interaction between various components or systems to verify they function together as intended. Integration tests often capture issues with application behavior at a subsystem level, validating data flows and interface contracts, (i.e., specifications) between various components.

End-to-end (E2E) tests

Verify the functionalities of the application at the highest system level from start to finish by simulating real usage scenarios. E2E tests give you the highest levels of confidence in your application functionality and performance but are the most challenging tests to design, develop, and maintain.

> E2E tests and integration tests share similarities that make them hard to distinguish from one another. If a test is big and sometimes flaky, you may be working on an E2E test.
>
> Integration tests normally check a subset of systems and interactions, not the whole system or a long chain of subsystems.

Figure 11-1 demonstrates the scope of each test type. Unit tests shown on the left focus on isolated components, while integration tests check pairwise interactions of multiple components, including with external services. Lastly, E2E tests cover the entire user journey and data flow within the application to confirm the intended functionality.

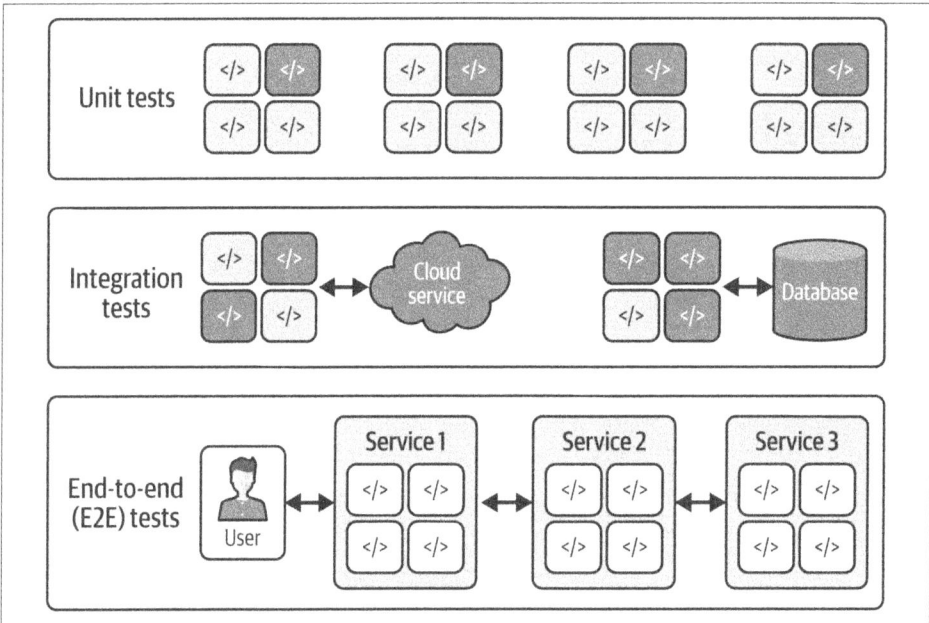

Figure 11-1. Types of tests in software testing

Before implementing any of the aforementioned tests, you can also use *static code checks* with tools like mypy to catch syntax and type errors. As you write code, static checks can also help you catch code style violations, misuse of functions and dependencies, security vulnerabilities, dead or unused code, data flow issues, and potential bugs in your system components.

As you progress from static checks and unit tests to integration and then to E2E tests, your test cases become more valuable but also more complex, expensive, and slower. More important, since E2E tests have broader scope with multiple components interacting, they'll become more brittle and likely to fail, requiring frequent updates to stay aligned with changes in your code.

E2E tests are also complex and flaky/nondeterministic. According to Martin Fowler,[1] these are the main reasons for the nondeterminism:

- *Lack of isolation* causes components to interfere with each other, leading to unpredictable results.
- *Asynchronous behavior* with operations that occur out of sequence or at unpredictable times can lead to nondeterministic outcomes.
- *Remote services* can introduce variability due to network latency, service availability, or differing responses.
- *Resource leaks*, if not properly managed, can lead to inconsistent system behavior. Affected resources include memory, file handles, or connections to databases, clients, etc.

Finally, due to the brittleness of E2E tests, refactors and changes in functionality can cause them to fail. Therefore, there is a trade-off between the level of confidence you gain from E2E tests and the flexibility to make changes to your systems.

The Biggest Challenge in Testing Software

The biggest challenge in testing services is identifying what to test and to what detail. As part of this, you need to decide what to mock, fake, or keep real alongside configuring a host of testing tools and environments.

To overcome this challenge, you can plan your tests in advance, identifying breaking points in your system and narrowing down issues to individual components and interactions. Then, imagine who the user is and list the steps they'll take when interacting with the problematic systems. Finally, you can translate that lists of steps into individual tests and automate them.

Another challenge with testing that causes so much frustration is having to rewrite your tests whenever you refactor the code they're testing.

---

1 Author of *Refactoring: Improving the Design of Existing Code* (Addison Wesley, 2018), *Patterns of Enterprise Application Architecture* (Addison Wesley, 2002), and many other software engineering books.

Since code refactors don't change the functional behavior but implementation details, it can be a sign that you're not testing the right things. For example, if you're testing the internal string processing logic of the `count_tokens(text)` function rather than just its final output (i.e., the token count), using an external library to replace the string manipulation logic can cause your tests to fail.

A telltale sign that you might be testing implementation details is when your tests fail as you refactor the code (i.e., false positives), or pass even when you introduce breaking changes to your code (i.e., false negatives). You can use techniques such as *black-box testing* to test your system by providing inputs and observing outputs, without considering the implementation details.

If you plan your tests in advance, you can avoid these testing challenges.

Planning Tests

To identify the tests you need during planning, you can use the *verification and validation* (V&V) process.

Following this process, you first confirm possession of the right requirements (validation) and then leverage tests to verify all requirements are met (verification).

> Having 100% code coverage with passing tests will complete only the verification process, not validation. You still need to make sure that your services implement the right functions (i.e., validation).

The V&V process can be visualized as a V-shaped model as per Figure 11-2.

When you go down the V model, you define software requirements and design the solution before implementing it as code. Afterward, you come back up the "V" by running progressive tests (unit, integration, E2E, etc.) to validate that your solution meets the business needs.

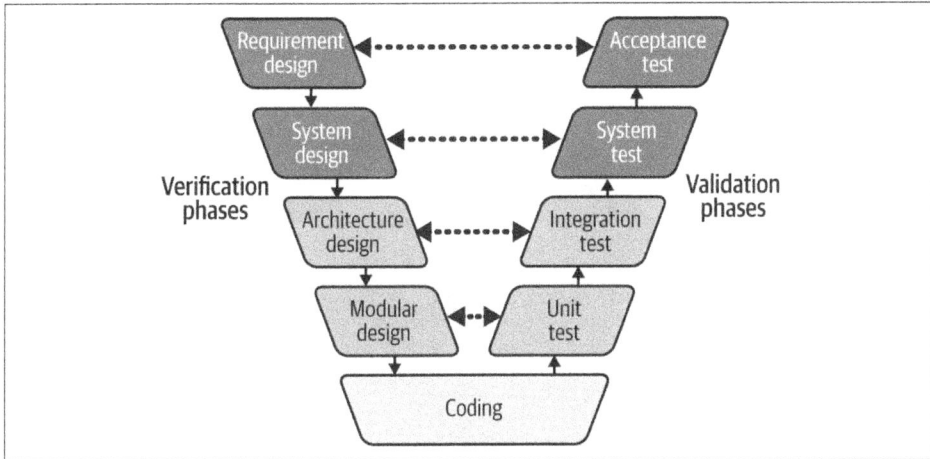

Figure 11-2. Verification and validation model

As discussed earlier, validation tests can be challenging to identify. Exactly what progressive tests should you implement?

When you struggle with identifying what to test, you can write tests based on issues and bugs that find in your application. This approach is *reactive* since you're writing tests only when issues arise, which can help you overcome the challenges of not knowing what to test. However, testing to resolve issues later in the *software development lifecycle* (SDLC) requires significant testing efforts as you'll be dealing with a more complex system with many moving parts to test.

That's why movements such as *shift-left testing* are advocating for *preventative* testing practices that are planned in advance and written during development to reduce the testing efforts. Figure 11-3 demonstrates how moving testing efforts earlier on the SLDC can reduce the overall burden.

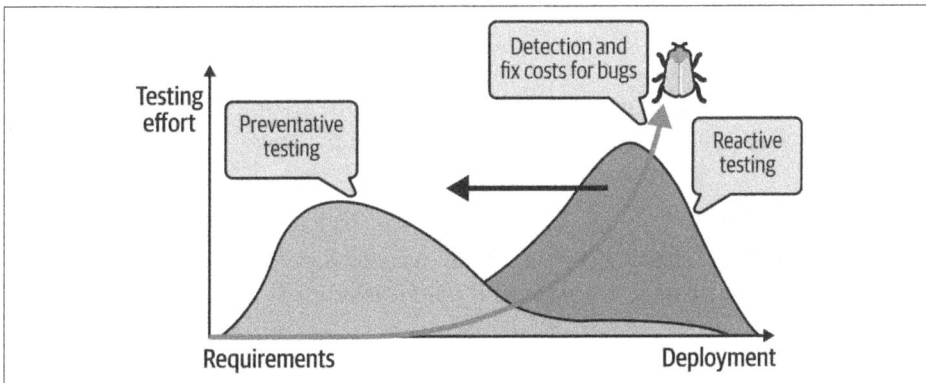

Figure 11-3. Shift-left software testing

A common approach in shift-left testing is *test-driven development* (TDD), as shown in Figure 11-4.

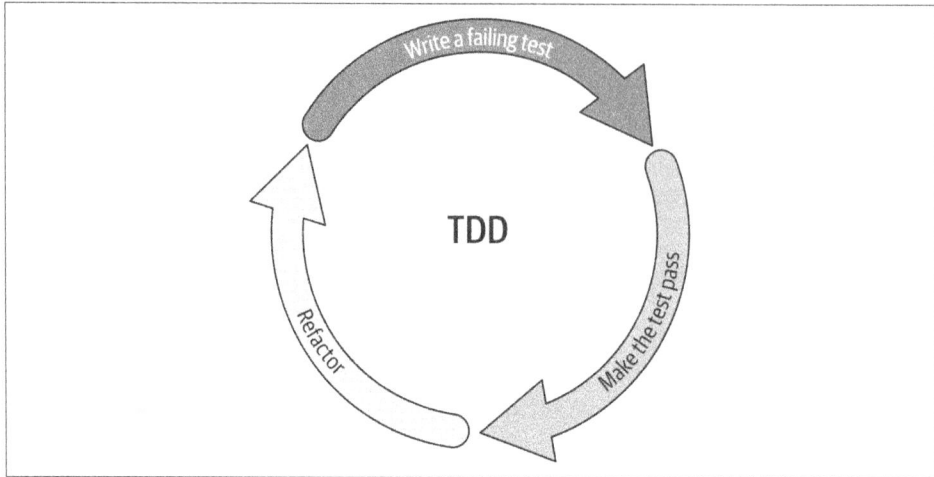

Figure 11-4. TDD

In the TDD approach, you write the tests before the actual code. This is an iterative process where written tests will fail at first, but your aim will be to write the minimal amount of code for tests to pass. Once passing, you refactor the code to optimize the system while keeping the tests passing to finish the iterative TDD process.

> A great example of where TDD practices are useful in testing GenAI services is during *prompt engineering*. Write a set of tests first, and then keep iterating over the prompt design until all your tests pass.
>
> Using the same test cases, you can check for any signs of regression and whether switching models will reduce the performance of your services.

As you can see, the overall aim of TDD is to reduce the testing efforts by improving your code quality, solution design, and early detection of issues.

Test Dimensions

Additionally, during planning, you normally have to decide on various test dimensions including testing *scope*, *coverage*, and *comprehensiveness*:

Scope

Defines what components, systems, and usage scenarios you'll be testing. As part of scope definition, you'll also be drawing *testing boundaries* to clarify what will and won't be tested.

Coverage or testing surface area

Measures how much of the system or codebase you'll be testing.

Comprehensiveness

Indicates how detailed, in-depth, and complete your tests will be within the defined scope and coverage. For example, you'll decide whether you'll be testing every potential usage, success and failure scenarios, and edge cases for every component, system, and interaction.

You can also think of testing scope, coverage, and comprehensiveness as testing *space/volume*, *surface area*, and *depth*. Volume/space defines the boundaries and dimensions of what is being tested; surface area measures the spread of tests; and depth implies detail, depth, and completeness of test cases.

Test Data

To achieve higher test coverage and comprehensiveness, you can leverage four different types of test data:

Valid data

Inputs to the system within the valid and expected range under normal conditions.

Invalid data

Inputs that are unexpected, wrong, NULL, or outside the valid range. You can use negative data to test how the system behaves when it's misused.

Boundary data

Test data at boundaries of acceptable input ranges, whether at the upper or lower limit.

Huge data

Used for performance and stress testing the system to measure its limits.

Test Phases

It doesn't matter if you're implementing a unit, integration, or E2E test, you can structure tests in several distinct phases using the *given-when-then* (GWT) model, as outlined here:

1. *Given (preconditions)*: Before any given test, you can set up test conditions and predefined states or data (i.e., *fixtures*).

2. *When (test steps)*: During the test, you perform a set of action steps that you'll like to test. This is where you'll pass your test fixtures to the *system under test* (SUT), which, depending on the test scope, can be a singular function or your whole service.

3. *Then (expected results)*: After executing the SUT with fixtures, you'll check the outputs against your expectations in this phase using a set of assert statements.

4. *Cleanup*: Once done, you can clean up test artifacts within an optional *cleanup/tear-down* phase.

`pytest` recommends structuring tests using the *arrange-act-assert-cleanup* model, which directly corresponds to the GWT model with an optional cleanup phase.

Test Environments

When planning tests, you should also consider various *testing environments* covering compile time, build time, and runtime environments.

In many programming languages, *compile time* is when the source code is translated into executable code. For instance, if you're writing code in C++, the compilation process involves a comprehensive type check across the entire codebase. If type errors are found, the compilation process will fail. Once all checks pass, the C++ compiler translates the code into an executable binaries.

The strong typing in C++ was designed to improve error detection, code robustness, and support developer tooling in larger and complex codebases that change frequently.

Since Python is an interpreted language, it doesn't have a traditional compile time like C++. Instead, Python converts code into bytecode for execution.

During inspections, static code checkers like mypy can identify basic issues in your code, serving as an initial verification layer in your testing efforts.

Since Python is a dynamically typed language, it doesn't enforce typing by default. However, static type checkers like mypy can provide significant value if you use type hints in your Python code.

While static checks are great for catching basic code issues at compile time, unit, integration, and E2E tests can verify the system functionality at *runtime* when you execute application code. During runtime, tools like Pydantic can perform data validation checks to catch unexpected data structures.

Your GenAI services may also require additional setup and build steps such as downloading weights and preloading models, before executing any application code. The environment in which build steps, setups, and dependency installations are completed is referred to as *build time*, which you can also test.

Testing Strategies

Within the software landscape, various experts have developed strategies for balancing the distribution of tests in projects, which are based on years of software testing experience from the developers that popularized them.

The most widely adopted strategy is the *testing pyramid*, as shown in Figure 11-5, which promotes writing more unit tests.

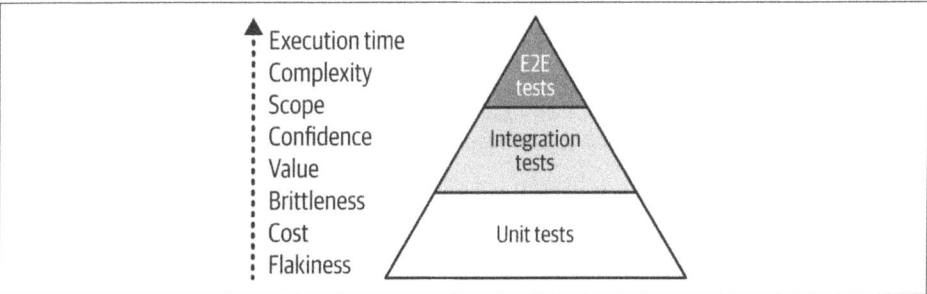

Figure 11-5. Testing pyramid

Table 11-1 outlines the purpose of each layer in the testing pyramid alongside a concrete example in the context of a GenAI service.

Table 11-1. Testing pyramid in real world

Layer	Purpose	Example
End-to-end tests	Validate the entire application flow from start to finish	Testing user login, generating text based on a prompt, and saving the generated content
Integration tests	Verify various modules or services work together correctly	Testing the interactions between the text generation API and the database storing user prompts and generated texts
Unit tests	Verify individual components or functions in isolation	Testing various utility functions that process inputs to the model, for instance, to remove inappropriate content

The issue with the pyramid model is that while unit tests improve code coverage, they do not necessarily enhance "business coverage" since project requirements and use cases might not be thoroughly tested. As a result, relying only on unit tests can create a false sense of security, potentially overlooking testing essential business logic and user workflows. On the other hand, integration tests allow you to cover more ground and business-driven tests.

> Software testing experts have also identified a few strategies as *anti-patterns* that are counterproductive.
>
> If you follow them, you'll spend an excessive amount of time setting up the tests, implement overly specific and tightly coupled tests, and end up with tests that exhibit nondeterministic flaky behavior.

Table 11-2 and Figure 11-6 show a list of software testing anti-patterns.

Table 11-2. Software testing anti-patterns

Strategy	Test distribution	Comments
Testing ice-cream cone	Small number of unit tests with a large number of integration and E2E tests, followed by manual testing.	Avoid. Considered an anti-pattern due to inefficiency of implementing manual tests and high costs of maintaining integration and E2E tests.
Testing cupcake	Similar to the ice-cream cone; has a small number of automated unit and integration tests, a moderate number of automated E2E/GUI tests, and a large number of manual tests. Each test type is performed by a different team.	Avoid. Considered an anti-pattern because it can lead to slow feedback cycles, communication overheads between teams, and brittle tests with high maintenance costs.
Testing hourglass	Large number of unit tests at the base and E2E tests at the top, but significantly fewer integration tests in the middle.	Avoid. Considered an anti-pattern. Not as bad as the ice-cream cone, but still results in too many test failures, that medium-scope tests could've covered.

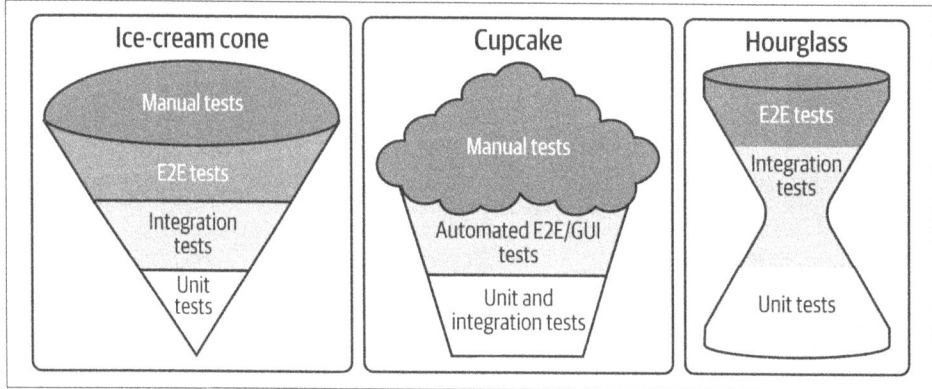

Figure 11-6. Visualization of testing anti-patterns

Table 11-3 and Figure 11-7 compare software testing strategies.

Table 11-3. Comparison of testing strategies

Strategy	Test distribution	Comments
Testing pyramid (Mike Cohn)	Large number of unit tests at the base, fewer integration tests in the middle, and even fewer E2E tests at the top.	It's a widely accepted strategy. However, the pyramid can be perceived as a physical concept to promote building the bottom layer of unit tests first, then constructing the next layer, and so on, until reaching the top. This approach is ineffective when applied to legacy applications with a large codebase.
Testing trophy (Kent C. Dodds)	Focuses on having a strong foundation of static checks, then unit tests, followed by integration tests, and a smaller number of E2E tests at the top.	The rationale for this is that E2E and integration tests are the most valuable. However, E2E tests are slow and expensive. Integration tests strike a balance between both worlds.
Testing honeycomb (Stephen H. Fishman)	Represents a balanced approach with equal emphasis on unit, integration, E2E, and other types of tests (performance, security, etc.).	It can be less efficient if not managed properly and may not be optimal for every project.

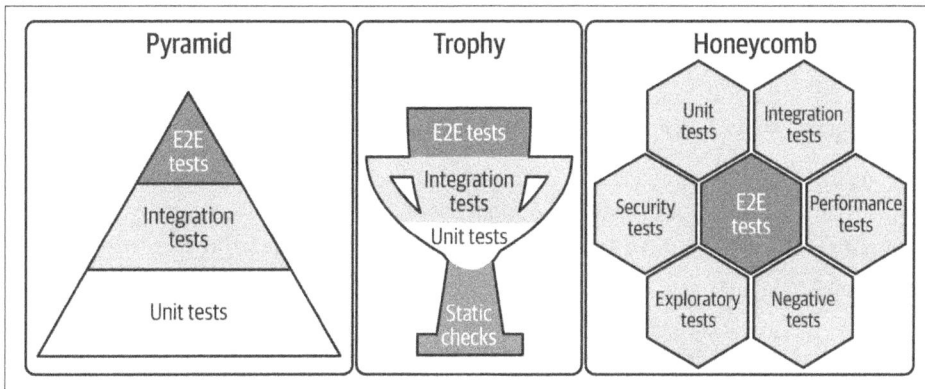

Figure 11-7. Visualization of testing strategies

For GenAI services, which often involve complex integrations and performance considerations, the trophy testing strategy might be the most suitable. The trophy strategy consists of a strong foundation of static checks, powered by tools such as mypy and Pydantic, alongside mostly integration tests that strike a balance between value, confidence, and testing costs.

If your GenAI services must be comprehensively tested with various test types, including performance and exploratory tests, then the honeycomb model may be more suitable for your project since it can equalize testing efforts.

You should now feel more comfortable in identifying what tests you need and how to plan your tests.

Now that you're familiar with software testing concepts, let's review the challenges and potential approaches to testing GenAI services.

Challenges of Testing GenAI Services

If you've decided to test your GenAI services, you will face several challenges. Testing services that leverage probabilistic GenAI models require a more comprehensive approach than traditional software.

Let's take a look at a few reasons why testing GenAI services will be challenging.

Variability of Outputs (Flakiness)

Given the same set of inputs and implementation code, GenAI services often produce different outputs. The outputs are varied because these models use probabilistic techniques such as sampling from a distribution rather than relying on deterministic functions. Of course, the variability you experience on outputs can be model dependent, and adjusting configurations, such as temperature values, can reduce this variance.

The variability of outputs from GenAI models can also explode the number of potential test cases you can write (i.e., the *testing area/scope*) to cover every possibility. Because of this, you can't fully rely on deterministic tests. Your tests will perform inconsistently and will be too *flaky* to run reliably within a CI/CD pipeline.

Instead, you should approach the GenAI testing problem from a statistical and probabilistic perspective. Take several samples based on valid assumptions from a *legitimate distribution of inputs* to verify the quality of your model's product outputs.

> By *legitimate distribution of inputs*, I mean selecting inputs that are aligned with the model's purpose, representative of real-world scenarios, and relevant to the problem you're trying to solve with the model.

A more involved approach is to use discriminator models to score your service's variable outputs as long as you set expectations of a certain tolerance or threshold.

You'll see examples of how to do this later in the chapter.

Performance and Resource Constraints (Slow and Expensive)

Since testing GenAI services requires a more statistical and/or multimodel approach, you will also face latency, usage, and hosting problems.

Your tests can't run fast enough and reliably to run continually within a traditional CI/CD pipeline. You will end up with excessive token usage costs with multiple model API calls and slow-running and complex multimodel tests. These challenges remain unless you make several assumptions to simplify the testing scope, reduce model testing frequency, and use efficient testing techniques such as mocking and patching, dependency injection, and statistical hypothesis tests. You can also investigate the use of small fine-tuned discriminator models to reduce latency and improve performance.

Regression

Regression testing is another type of test to plan for when working with GenAI models.

A research paper published in 2023 (*https://oreil.ly/1oLQG*) that compared ChatGPT's behavior over time found that:

> The performance and behavior of both GPT-3.5 and GPT-4 can vary greatly over time. For example, GPT-4 (March 2023) was reasonable at identifying prime vs. composite numbers (84% accuracy), but GPT-4 (June 2023) was poor on these same questions (51% accuracy). GPT-4 became less willing to answer sensitive questions and opinion survey questions in June than in March. In addition, both GPT-4 and GPT-3.5 had more formatting mistakes in code generation in June than in March.

According to this study, the behavior of the "same" LLM service can change substantially in a relatively short amount of time, highlighting the need for continuous monitoring of LLMs (and any GenAI services). Based on this finding, you can assume the performance of your GenAI services may degrade over time due to model fine-tuning or retraining, shifts in user interaction patterns, and the changes in its training data or operating environment.

To elaborate further, probabilistic AI models can experience *model drift*, a performance degradation over time attributable to their underlying training data. Fine-tuning on additional data can have unexpected side effects on model's behavior in other tasks.

As time passes, the original training data can drift away from reality. Trends change, new historical events happen, languages evolve, and human knowledge expands or mutates to take new forms that won't be captured if the training data is not continually updated. This phenomenon that causes model drift is referred to as *concept drift*, which occurs when the statistical properties of the target variable that the model is trying to predict change over time. Concept drift can lead to a model's performance degrading because the relationships and patterns the model learned during training no longer apply.

Furthermore, *data drift*, which involves changes in the distribution of the input features within the training data, can also lead to model drift.

This type of drift is often due to changes in the sampling methods, population distribution and data collection, seasonality changes and temporal effects in the data, external changes in data sources, or quality issues in the processing pipelines.

Regression testing and monitoring (in particular if you rely on external model providers such as OpenAI) can help you detect model drift issues on your specific tasks and use cases. Any potential drifts can then be addressed at the application layer via data validation or by using techniques such as RAG or at the model layer via retraining and model fine-tuning to reduce regression issues.

Bias

Another grand challenge in testing GenAI services is detecting model bias before going to production. Often, bias is investigated during the data exploration process by data scientists and ML engineers responsible for producing the models. However, with large foundation GenAI models, there's always a possibility that some form of bias may be introduced through incorrect evaluation, sampling methods, data processing, training algorithms, or hidden bias in the data itself.

For example, if a language model is trained on a dataset that mostly contains text related to a specific demographic, it may generate outputs biased toward that demographic, potentially excluding other groups. Similarly, if an image recognition model is trained mostly on images of men in professions like doctors and engineers, it may learn to generate images with a gender bias.

The bias becomes particularly serious in scenarios where you want to use LLMs as a judge, such as AI marking tools or interview assessors.

Bias can manifest in various forms such as gender bias, racial bias, age bias, etc., and each type requires specific tests and metrics to detect. Without knowing what to test for, you can't confidently verify if your GenAI services are 100% bias-free.

A possible solution to this problem is leveraging model self-checks and AI discriminators where a secondary model identifies or measures the presence of any bias. There is often a trade-off between latency and usage quotas when detecting bias during service runtime.

Adversarial Attacks

Public-facing GenAI services can be vulnerable to adversarial attacks such as token manipulation, insecure data handling, jailbreak prompting or prompt injection, sensitive information disclosure, data poisoning, model theft, denial of service, excessive agency, and general misuse and abuse. Therefore, any GenAI services exposed to the internet will need to include safeguarding layers.

Resources and checklists such as OWASP's top 10 for LLM application (*https://genai.owasp.org*) provide a starting point for adding safeguards to your GenAI services.

However, building safeguarding mechanisms can be challenging because current methods, at the time of writing, rely on classification and discriminatory models to detect adversarial attacks and harmful content. These safeguarding models often require hundreds of megabytes of dependencies, which can bloat your application, significantly slow down your service's throughput, and still may not catch every potential attack scenario.

Adversarial tests ensure you have enough safeguarding in place to protect your services and reputation. As part of adversarial tests, you should also verify the performance of your authentication and authorization guards.

Chapter 9 goes into more detail on implementing these safeguarding layers and evaluation techniques to protect your models against such attacks.

Unbound Testing Coverage

The latent space of GenAI models is so vast that you can't rely on unit tests to achieve 100% coverage of every usage scenario.

Since there are an infinite number of inputs and responses, no matter how much you test your models, there will be hidden edge cases that slip through your tests. Therefore, instead of relying on predefining every scenario, you can implement *behavioral testing*, which focuses on properties of responses instead of the exact outputs.

Examples of behavioral properties you can measure include *coherence* of generated data structures, *relevance* of outputs to inputs, *toxicity*, *correctness*, and *faithfulness* (i.e., faithful adherence to your policies and ethical guidelines). You can also add a human in the loop as an additional testing layer for catching unexpected responses.

> If you're building a RAG or agentic application with multiple models and external dependencies, behavioral testing becomes even more practical. Testing a fixed set of examples may miss edge cases, unexpected interactions between components, and variability in responses due to external factors.

In the next section, you'll learn how to implement your own unit, integration, E2E, and behavioral tests by following a hands-on project.

Project: Implementing Tests for a RAG System

In the hands-on project, you will be writing a test suite for the RAG module that you implemented in Chapter 5. The RAG system you will be testing has interfaces with an LLM, a vector database, and the server's filesystem via asynchronous methods, so it provides a perfect opportunity to understand the testing principles discussed so far.

By following along with the code examples, you'll learn the best practices for implementing unit, integration, and E2E tests for your GenAI services, as well as their differences.

Unit Tests

You can start testing your GenAI services with unit tests. The purpose of a unit test is to verify that an isolated part of your code, usually a single function or method, performs as intended.

Prior to writing tests, it's important to plan the test cases you will be implementing. For a typical RAG system, you can write unit tests on the data loading, transformation, retrieval, and generation pipelines.

Figure 11-8 visualizes the testing boundaries of these potential unit tests on a data pipeline diagram.

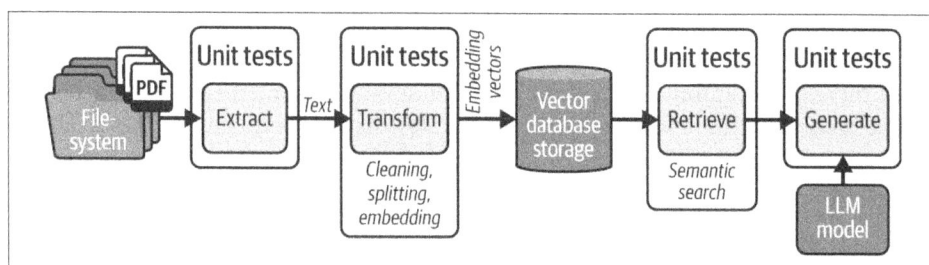

Figure 11-8. Unit test boundaries visualized on the RAG data pipeline diagram

Notice how the testing boundaries end at the start and end of each data processing pipeline function. This is because the purpose of these unit tests is to test only the data processing pipeline code and not the database, filesystem, LLM model, or any associated interfaces.

In these unit tests, you'll be assuming that these external systems will return what you expect and focus your unit tests only on what your data processing code will be doing.

For brevity, we won't be testing every component of the system, but by following a handful of upcoming examples, you should feel comfortable implementing follow-on tests to achieve full coverage.

Installing and configuring pytest

For this project, you'll be using the `pytest` package, which has built-in components for handling test fixtures, parameters, async code, test collections, and a rich ecosystem of plug-ins. `pytest` is more powerful, flexible, and extensible compared to `unittest`, Python's built-in testing package often used for simple testing scenarios.

You can install `pytest` using the following:

```
$ pip install pytest
```

Next, create a `tests` directory at the root of your project where you can create Python modules following the *test_xxx.py* pattern.

`pytest`'s test collector can then traverse your `tests` directory and find every test module, class, and function contained within:

```
project
|-- main.py
...
|-- tests
    |-- test_rag_loader.py
    |-- test_rag_transform.py
    |-- test_rag_retrieval.py
...
```

Inside each test file, you can add your test functions that always contain at least one `assert` statement. If no exception is raised in these `assert` statements, then your tests will get PASSED. Otherwise, `pytest` will mark them as FAILED alongside a reason/trace of why `assert` statements have failed:

```
# tests/rag/transform.py

def test_chunk_text():
    text = "Testing GenAI services"
    results = chunk(text)
    assert len(results) = 2
```

Let's assume you've written two test functions in each test module:

You can then execute your tests via the `pytest <test_dirt_path>` command.

```
$ pytest tests
=========================== test session starts ===========================
platform linux -- Python 3.11, pytest-8.0.0

Collected 6 items

tests/rag/loader.py ..                                              [100%]
tests/rag/transform.py F.                                           [100%]
tests/rag/retrieval.py ..                                           [100%]


================================ FAILURES =================================
_____ test_chunk_text _____

def test_chunk_text():
>       assert len(results) == 2
E       assert 3 == 2

tests/rag/transform.py:6: AssertionError
```

```
========================= short test summary info =========================
PASSED 5
FAILED tests/rag/transform.py::test_chunk_text - assert 3 == 2
=========================== 1 failed in 0.12s ===========================
```

> Avoid writing large tests, as they become increasingly difficult to
> understand and implement correctly.

When writing unit tests, you care only about an isolated component of your system
such as a single function in your code. Other components fall outside the boundary
of unit test. Thus, you'll be testing only whether a single component behaves as you
expect given a set of test data as inputs.

As an example, you can test whether your chunking function is splitting a document
into chunks as you'd expect. Maybe you want to experiment with different or complex
chunking strategies for your RAG pipeline and want to make sure that any input text
is chunked correctly. Unit tests with predefined test data or *fixtures* can give you some
confidence in your chunking function.

Example 11-1 demonstrates an example unit test for your chunking function.

Example 11-1. Example unit test for a token chunking function

```
# rag/transform.py

def chunk(tokens: list[int], chunk_size: int) -> list[list[int]]: ❶
    if chunk_size <= 0:
        raise ValueError("Chunk size must be greater than 0")
    return [tokens[i:i + chunk_size] for i in range(0, len(tokens), chunk_size)]


# tests/rag/transform.py

import pytest
from rag.transform import chunk

def test_chunking_success():
    # GIVEN ❷
    tokens = [1, 2, 3, 4, 5]
    # WHEN ❸
    result = chunk(token_list, chunk_size=2)
    # THEN ❹
    assert result = [[1, 2], [3, 4], [5]]
    ... # Other relevant asserts here
```

❶ Chunk an integer token list into smaller lists of a specified chunk_size.

❷ Specify the test data in the *GIVEN (preconditions)* part of the test.

❸ Run the test steps in the *WHEN* part of the test that include passing the test data to the system under test.

❹ Check the results against the expected outputs in the *THEN* part of the test.

Fixtures and scope

The input data you defined in Example 11-1 for testing is also called a *fixture*, as its value remains fixed across each test run. There are two types of fixtures:

Fresh fixture
> You define it inside each test, which then Python garbage collects (i.e., discards) after the test. Example 11-1 used a fresh fixture.

Shared fixture
> You can reuse it across multiple tests to avoid repeating the same fixture over and over for each new test.

You can declare a shared fixture outside the test functions as a global variable of the test module, but it's considered an anti-pattern, as you can inadvertently modify them.

> Shared fixtures must be *immutable*. Otherwise, a test can change the fixture, creating a side effect rippling through other tests. A major cause of flaky tests is mutable fixtures.

Instead of being responsible for managing the state of shared fixtures yourself, you can rely on pytest's dependency injection system through the use of *fixture functions*, as shown in Example 11-2.

Example 11-2. pytest fixture function

```python
# tests/rag/transform.py

import pytest
from rag.transform import chunk

# GIVEN
@pytest.fixture(scope="module")  ❶
def tokens():  ❷
    return [1, 2, 3, 4, 5]
```

```
def test_token_chunking_small(token_list): ❷
    result = chunk(tokens, chunk_size=2)
    assert result = [[1, 2], [3, 4], [5]]

def test_token_chunking_large(token_list): ❷
    result = chunk(tokens, chunk_size=5)
    assert result = [[1, 2, 3, 4, 5]]
```

❶ Declare the `input_text` function as a `pytest` fixture that can be shared across the module as specified by `scope="module"`.

❷ Use the `pytest` dependency injection to inject a shared fixture into different tests.

You can declare a function as a `pytest` fixture using the `@pytest.fixture(scope)` decorator. The `scope` parameter specifies the lifespan of the shared fixture within a testing session.

Based on the `scope`'s value, `pytest` creates and destroys fixtures once per test function, `class`, `module`, `package`, or the entire testing `session`.

> A scenario where you might need a shared fixture to persist across modules or the entire testing session is when you fetch the fixture from an external API and want to avoid making requests repeatedly.

Using fixtures, you can implement several tests with various inputs covering valid, invalid, and boundary values to verify the robustness of each component. However, you'll need to separate test functions for each set of inputs and expected outputs. To avoid rewriting the same test, `pytest` has a *parameterization* feature that you can leverage.

Parameterization

With `pytest` parameterization, you can iterate over various test data and expected outputs to avoid duplicating tests, as you can see in Example 11-3.

Example 11-3. pytest parameterization

```
# tests/rag/transform.py

@pytest.mark.parametrize("tokens, chunk_size, expected", [ ❶
    ([1, 2, 3, 4, 5], 2, [[1, 2], [3, 4], [5]]), # valid
    ([1, 2, 3, 4, 5], 3, [[1, 2, 3], [4, 5]]), # valid
    ([1, 2, 3, 4, 5], 1, [[1], [2], [3], [4], [5]]),  # valid
    ([], 3, []), # valid/empty input
```

```
        ([1, 2, 3], 5, [[1, 2, 3]]),    # boundary input
        ([1, 2, 3, 4, 5], 0, "ValueError"), # invalid (chunk_size <= 0)
        ([1, 2, 3, 4, 5], -1, "ValueError"), # invalid (chunk_size <= 0)
        (
            list(range(10000)), 1000, [list(range(i, i + 1000)) # huge data
            for i in range(0, 10000, 1000)]
        )
])
def test_token_chunking(tokens, chunk_size, expected) ❷
    if expected == "ValueError":
        with pytest.raises(ValueError):
            chunk(tokens, chunk_size)
    else:
        assert chunk(tokens, chunk_size) == expected
```

❶ Use the `@pytest.mark.parametrize` decorator function to specify multiple test arguments and expected outputs. The test arguments cover valid, empty, invalid, boundary ranges, and large values to verify the robustness of the token chunking function.

❷ Inject the test parameters into the test function, and if the expected output is a `ValueError`, use `pytest.raises` to verify that a `ValueError` exception has been raise. Otherwise, run the assertion check instead.

You can also store the test data inside JSON files and load them as fixtures to inject into parameterized test functions, as shown in Example 11-4.

Example 11-4. JSON fixtures in parameterized pytest tests

```
# tests/rag/test_data.json ❶

[
    {"tokens": [1, 2, 3], "chunk_size": 1, "expected": [[1], [2], [3]},
    ...
]

# tests/rag/transform.py

@pytest.fixture
def test_data():
    with open('test_data.json') as f:
        return json.load(f)

@pytest.mark.parametrize("case", test_data())
def test_token_chunking(case):
```

❶ The JSON file contains a list of test cases as dictionaries.

As you can see, fixtures and the parameterization technique are extremely powerful tools to help you verify the robustness of each function in your code.

When writing tests, you'll probably want to specify setup code, configurations, and global fixtures to be shared across test files. Luckily, you can achieve this in the pytest's global configuration file called *conftest.py*.

Conftest module

If you want your entire test modules to have access to fixtures and global configurations, you can add a *conftest.py* module to your `tests` directory. Any fixtures, setup code, and configurations defined in the conftest module will be shared with other test modules. See Example 11-5.

Example 11-5. Add a shared fixture across every module

```
# tests/conftest.py

@pytest.fixture(scope="module")  ❶
def tokens():
    return [1, 2, 3, 4, 5]

# tests/rag/transform.py

def test_chunking(tokens):
    ....

# tests/rag/retrieval.py

def test_query(tokens):
    ....
```

❶ Define a shared fixture in *conftest.py* to be used across every test module. Otherwise, the fixture would be scoped only to a single module.

You've now learned about writing basic tests using the `pytest` framework following the GWT model. Next, let's look at how to perform setup and cleanup operations before and after tests.

Setup and teardown

When implementing tests, you may also need to configure a testing environment beforehand and perform teardown or cleanup operations afterward. You can use the `yield` keyword in shared fixtures to implement setup and teardown operations that must consistently happen for each test.

For instance, you may need to use this feature when setting up and cleaning up a database session, as demonstrated in Example 11-6.

Example 11-6. Set up and tear down a database session in a shared fixture

```python
# tests/conftest.py

from qdrant_client import QdrantClient

@pytest.fixture(scope="function")  ❶
def db_client():
    client = QdrantClient(host="localhost", port=6333)  ❷
    client.create_collection(  ❷
        collection_name="test",
        vectors_config=VectorParams(size=4, distance=Distance.DOT),
    )
    client.upsert(  ❷
        collection_name="test",
        points=[
            PointStruct(
                id=1, vector=[0.05, 0.61, 0.76, 0.74], payload={"doc": "test.pdf"}
            )
        ],
    )
    yield client  ❸
    client.close()  ❹


# tests/rag/retrieve.py

def test_search_db(db_client):  ❺
    result = db_client.search(
        collection_name="test", query_vector=[0.18, 0.81, 0.75, 0.12], limit=1
    )
    assert result is not None
```

❶ Create a global shared fixture in *conftest.py* that is created and destroyed once per test function.

❷ Instantiate the qdrant database client and then create and configure a test collection with an upserted data point as part of the test setup phase.

❸ Yield the database client to the test function as part of the main testing phase.

❹ Clean up after each test by closing the client connection to the database. The teardown code after the yield keyword is executed once the yield operation completes.

❺ Inject the preconfigured database client to each test function after the test setup is complete. Query the database for the document inserted and assert that a data point has been fetched. Once the assertion step is complete, run the teardown process as part of the db_client fixture function.

Following the example in Example 11-6, you can also create fixtures with setup and teardown steps for your API test client or any other external services.

Also, you may have noticed that Example 11-6 used a synchronous client instead of an asynchronous one. This is because handling asynchronous tests can be tricky, flaky, and error-prone and because it requires installation of additional `pytest` plugins for handling test event loops.

To avoid flaky unit tests, you should use mocks to isolate functional components from external services. We do this because the scope and testing boundary of unit tests don't include external dependencies and interfaces. Instead, testing external dependencies and interfaces such as database interactions will fall within the remit of integration tests.

You'll learn about handling asynchronous tests and mocking/patching techniques next.

Handling asynchronous tests

To execute async tests, you can use plug-ins such as `pytest-asyncio` to integrate `pytest` with Python's `asyncio`:

```
$ pip install pytest-asyncio
```

Once you install the plug-in, you can follow Example 11-7 to write and execute an async test.

Example 11-7. Writing asynchronous tests

```
# tests/rag/retrieve.py

@pytest.mark.asyncio ❶
async def test_search_db(async_db_client): ❷
    result = await async_db_client.search(
        collection_name="test", query_vector=[0.18, 0.81, 0.75, 0.12], limit=1
    )
    assert result is not None
```

❶ Explicitly mark the async test with an `asyncio` decorator to run the test within an event loop.

❷ This assumes you've replaced the synchronous database client with async one in *conftest.py*.

When you run the `pytest` command, it searches the project directory tree to discover tests using *collectors* for each level of the directory hierarchy: functions, classes, modules, packages, or session. The `pytest-asyncio` plug-in provides an asyncio event loop for each of these collectors. By default, tests marked with `@pytest.mark.asyncio` run in the event loop provided by the *function collector*, to narrow the event loop scope and maximize the isolation between tests.

But why is this isolation important? ,

The biggest source of frustration for developers when testing software is flaky tests. These are tests that randomly fail when you consecutively run the test suite without changing any code or configurations.

Often when you investigate the cause of the flaky test behavior, you'll find that there is a central fixture or dependency that is changed by one of the tests, violating a core principle of testing: *test isolation*. The purpose of this isolation is to achieve *idempotency* in tests where repeated execution would produce the same results every time regardless of how many times you run the test suite.

Without isolation, tests can create side effects on each other, invalidating core assumptions, leading to fluctuations in their outcome/behavior, and random failures. In addition, interdependent and order-dependent tests often fail together, preventing you from getting valuable feedback on failures.

But how is flaky behavior related to asynchronous tests?

As discussed in Chapter 5, asynchronous code is leveraging Python's built-in scheduler, an event loop, to switch tasks when faced with a blocking I/O operation. This task switching in a testing environment can make asynchronous tests challenging to implement correctly because async operations may not complete immediately and can be executed out of order.

Async tests often interface with external dependencies like databases or filesystems executing I/O blocking operations that can take a long time to run. This is a major issue for unit tests that must run very quickly so that you can execute them frequently.

Unlike synchronous code where operations are executed in a predictable and linear sequence, async code also introduces variability in timing, execution order, and fixture state, reducing the consistency of the outcomes across tests. Additionally, response times from external dependencies can fluctuate, leading to side effects that violate the test isolation principle.

To mitigate the risk of side effects and flaky behavior, you'll need to correctly handle async tests by:

- Awaiting blocking I/O operations
- Avoiding unintentional use of blocking synchronous I/O operations inside async tests
- Using correct timeouts for managing delays

- Explicitly controlling the sequence of operations, especially when running async tests in parallel

Perhaps, the best mitigation is to write synchronous tests by mocking external dependencies, which will decouple your functions from I/O blocking dependencies. Using mocks, you can then run fast and reliable tests without having to wait for I/O operations to complete in the order you need.

> Async tests can still be useful with real dependencies when locally testing a replicated production environment.

Next, let's see how to mock external dependencies in unit tests so that you can write synchronous tests in replacement of slow async ones.

Mocking and patching

When writing unit tests, you need to isolate your components from external dependencies to avoid slow-running tests and consuming unnecessary resources. For instance, you don't want to call your GenAI model every time you run the test suite, which is going to be frequent, as that'll be compute-intensive and possibly expensive.

Instead, you can use *test doubles* to simulate real dependencies in your unit tests without having to rely on external dependencies in your tests. In essence, they pretend to be the real thing, just like stunt doubles in action movies that pretend to be the main actors. Isolated unit tests that use test doubles can verify the component state changes or behavior as it interacts with external dependencies like an LLM API.

> Be careful not to replace any component behavior you're trying to test with test doubles.
>
> For example, if you have a `ChatBot` class that uses an LLM API and performs content filtering on the responses, replace only the LLM API calls with test doubles, not the content filtering logic. Otherwise, you'll be testing your own test double.

There are five types of test doubles that you can use in your unit tests, as shown in Figure 11-9.

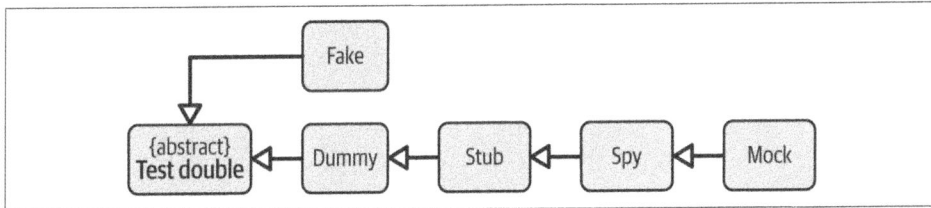

Figure 11-9. Test doubles

These include the following:

Fake
> A simplified implementation of a dependency for testing purposes

Dummy
> A placeholder used for when an argument needs to be filled in

Stub
> Provides fake data to the system under test that is using it

Spy
> Keeps track of dependency usage for later verification

Mock
> Checks how the dependency will be used and causes failure if the expectation isn't met

Except mocks that verify component behavior, the rest of these doubles can be used to verify state changes. Mocks have an entirely different setup and verification logic but work exactly like the other doubles in making the component being tested believe that it's interacting with the real dependencies.

Let's see each double in action to understand their similarities and differences.

Fakes. *Fake* objects are fully functional but simplified versions of the real dependency, possibly taking shortcuts. An example would be a database client that uses an in-memory database during tests instead of an actual database server; or an LLM client that fetches cached responses from a local testing server instead of an actual LLM.

Example 11-8 demonstrates what a fake LLM client looks like.

Example 11-8. Fake test double

```
class FakeLLMClient: ❶
    def __init__(self):
        self.cache = dict()

    def invoke(self, query):
```

```
            if query in self.cache:
                return self.cache.get(query) ❷

            response = requests.post("http://localhost:8001", json={"query": query})
            if response.status_code != 200:
                return "Error fetching result"

            result = response.json().get("response")
            self.cache[query] = result
            return result

def process_query(query, llm_client, token):
    response = llm_client.invoke(query, token) ❶
    return response

def test_fake_llm_client(query):
    llm_client = FakeLLMClient()
    query = "some query"
    response = process_query(query, llm_client, token="fake_token")
    assert response == "some response"
```

❶ A fully functional and simplified version LLM client that mimics the behavior of the real one by interacting with a local testing server.

❷ Return cached responses if repeated prompts are used.

Dummies.   *Dummies* are objects that aren't used in tests, but you pass around to satisfy parameter requirements of functions. An example would be passing a fake authentication token to an API client to prevent errors, even though the token isn't used for authentication during the test.

Example 11-9 shows how dummies can be used as test doubles.

Example 11-9. Dummy test double

```
class DummyLLMClient:
    def invoke(self, query, token): ❶
        return "some response"

def process_query(query, llm_client, token):
    response = llm_client.invoke(query, token) ❶
    return response

def test_dummy_llm_client(query):
    llm_client = DummyLLMClient()
    query = "some query"
    response = process_query(query, llm_client, token="fake_token")
    assert response == "some response"
```

❶ Notice the `token` is not being used but is required to satisfy the `.invoke(query, token)` function signature.

Stubs. *Stubs* are simplified versions of fakes. They don't have fully functional implementations and instead return canned responses to method calls. As an example, a stub LLM client will return a predefined fixture string when called without making any actual model requests.

Example 11-10 shows what a stub looks like. Can you spot the differences when comparing this example with Example 11-8?

Example 11-10. Stub test double

```
class StubLLMClient:
    def invoke(self, query):
        if query == "specific query":  ❶
            return "specific response"
        return "default response"

def process_query(query, llm_client):
    response = llm_client.invoke(query)
    return response

def test_stub_llm_client():
    llm_client = StubLLMClient()
    query = "specific query"
    response = process_query(query, llm_client)
    assert response == "specific response"
```

❶ Return a canned response on a given condition.

Spies. *Spies* are like stubs but also record method calls and interactions. They're extremely useful when you need to verify how a complex component interacts with a dependency. For example, with a spy LLM client, you can verify the number of times it was invoked by the component under test.

Example 11-11 shows a spy test double in action.

Example 11-11. Spy test double

```
class SpyLLMClient:
    def __init__(self):
        self.call_count = 0
        self.calls = []

    def invoke(self, query):
        self.call_count += 1  ❶
```

```
        self.calls.append((query))
        return "some response"

def process_query(query, llm_client):
    response = llm_client.invoke(query)
    return response

def test_process_query_with_spy():
    llm_client = SpyLLMClient()
    query = "some query"

    process_query(query, llm_client)

    assert llm_client.call_count == 1
    assert llm_client.calls == [("some query")]
```

❶ Keep track of function calls and arguments passed in.

Mocks. A mock is a smarter stub. If you know in advance how many times a dependency is called and how (i.e., you have expectations of interaction), you can implement a *mock*. A mock can verify whether the dependency has been called correctly with the right parameters to confirm the component being tested has behaved correctly.

How you set up mocks and perform checks with them is different to other doubles, as you can see in Example 11-12.

> For this example, you need to install the pytest-mocks plug-in, which is a thin wrapper over Python's built-in mocks library to simplify mocking implementation. Use the following command to install pytest-mocks:
>
> $ pip install pytest-mock

Example 11-12. Mock test double

```
def process_query(query, llm_client):
    response = llm_client.invoke(query)
    return response

def test_process_query_with_mock(mocker):
    llm_client = mocker.Mock() ❶
    llm_client.invoke.return_value = "mock response"
    query = "some query"

    process_query(query, llm_client)
    process_query(query, llm_client)

    assert llm_client.invoke.call_count == 2
    llm_client.invoke.assert_any_call("some query")
```

❶ Create and configure a mock to act as an LLM client tracking function calls and arguments passed in. It will also return any canned responses we want.

Using mocks, as shown in Example 11-12, will be useful to check the mocked component's behavior in highly nested and complex application logic such as checking how a mocked function like `llm_client.invoke()` is called several levels deep within a higher order function such as `process_query()`.

Now that you're more familiar with implementing various test doubles from scratch, let's see how an external package such as `pytest-mock` can simplify using test doubles.

Implementing test doubles with pytest-mock. The five aforementioned test doubles can also be implemented with `pytest-mock`, as shown in Example 11-13.

Example 11-13. Test doubles with `pytest-mock`

```
class LLMClient:
    def invoke(self, query):
        return openai.ChatCompletion.create(
            model="gpt-4o", messages=[{"role": "user", "content": query}]
        )

@pytest.fixture
def llm_client():
    return LLMClient()

def test_fake(mocker, llm_client):
    class FakeOpenAIClient: ❶
        @staticmethod
        def invoke(model, query):
            return {"choices": [{"message": {"content": "fake response"}}]}

    mocker.patch(openai.ChatCompletion, new=FakeOpenAIClient) ❶
    result = llm_client.invoke("test query")
    assert result == {"choices": [{"message": {"content": "fake response"}}]}

def test_stub(mocker, llm_client):
    stub = mocker.Mock()
    stub.process.return_value = "stubbed response"
    result = llm_client.invoke(stub)
    assert result == "stubbed response"  ❷

def test_spy(mocker, llm_client):
    spy = mocker.spy(LLMClient, 'send_request')
    spy.return_value = "some_value"
    llm_client.invoke("some query")
    spy.call_count == 1  ❸

def test_mock(mocker, llm_client):
```

```
mock = mocker.Mock()
llm_client.invoke(mock)
mock.process.assert_called_once_with("some query") ❹
```

❶ Fake simulates real behavior.

❷ Stub returns a fixed value.

❸ Spy tracks calls.

❹ Checks dependency behavior and fails if expectation isn't met.

You can now use any of the mentioned test doubles to isolate your unit tests, run them faster while covering various hard-to-test edge cases, and bypass dependencies that introduce nondeterminism in your tests. But bear in mind, having too many mocked tests is an anti-pattern as these tests may give you false confidence and become a maintenance overhead due to their brittleness. They can also mask integration issues since they're not testing real dependencies and overusing them can lead to complex test implementations that are hard to understand.

In such cases, you should rely on simple mocks only when necessary and in unit tests. Furthermore, you should complement any mocked tests with integration tests that use real dependencies to avoid missing any production issues.

In the next section, you'll learn how to implement an integration test for your RAG pipeline.

Integration Testing

Up until this point, you've been practicing with writing isolated unit tests. But as soon as you want to test a component interacting with another component or a real dependency, you'll be implementing integration tests.

The testing boundary of integration tests should include two components, and the scope of these tests must focus on checking the functionality of their interface and the communication contract between them.

As an example, you can see potential integration tests you can implement for your RAG pipeline in Figure 11-10.

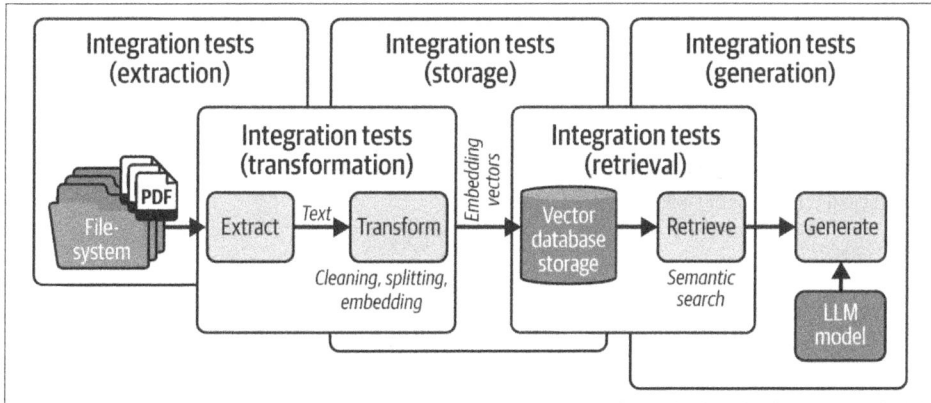

Figure 11-10. Integration test boundaries visualized on the RAG data pipeline diagram

Compared to unit test boundaries you saw in Figure 11-8, you can see that each integration is only concerned about verifying the interaction behavior between two or maximum three components at a time.

To practice, we'll implement an integration test for the document retrieval interface with the vector database in the RAG pipeline. In this test, you'll be querying the real vector database to verify whether the relevant documents are being fetched in relation to the query.

The tests will leverage RAG-related retrieval metrics such as context precision and context recall to measure the effectiveness of the retrieval system with the real vector database.

Context precision and recall

Both context precision and recall are evaluation metrics specifically designed for measuring the quality of the document retrieval system from the vector database in a RAG pipeline.

While *context precision* focuses on the signal-to-noise ratio (i.e., quality), of the retrieved information from the vector database, *context recall* measures whether all information relevant for responding to the user query has been retrieved from the database.

You can calculate context precision and recall using Example 11-14.

Example 11-14. Calculating context precision and recall

```
def calculate_recall(expected: list[int], retrieved: list[int]) -> int: ❶
    true_positives = len(set(expected) & set(retrieved))
    return true_positives / len(expected)


def calculate_precision(expected: list[int], retrieved: list[int]) -> int: ❷
    true_positives = len(set(expected) & set(retrieved))
    return true_positives / len(retrieved)

expected_document_ids = [1, 2, 3, 4, 5]
retrieved_documents_ids = [2, 3, 6, 7]

recall = calculate_recall(expected_document_ids, retrieved_documents_ids)
precision = calculate_precision(expected_document_ids, retrieved_documents_ids)

print(f"Recall: {recall:.2f}") # Recall: 0.40
print(f"Precision: {precision:.2f}") # Precision: 0.50
```

❶ Count of correct documents retrieved/count of expected documents.

❷ Count of correct documents retrieved/count of retrieved documents.

Here, we're assuming that each document will contain all the relevant contextual information to respond to a given query, so asserting that certain documents are fetched will suffice.

Open source libraries such as deep-eval and ragas can help you automate the computation of these metrics considering the relevant context is scattered across documents, but for simplicity, we will be implementing our integration tests without relying on such libraries.

With precision and recall metrics, the integration test for the document retrieval system will look like Example 11-15.

Example 11-15. Document retrieval system integration test

```
@pytest.mark.parametrize("query_vector, expected_ids", [ ❶
    ([0.1, 0.2, 0.3, 0.4], [1, 2, 3]),
    ([0.2, 0.3, 0.4, 0.5], [2, 1, 3]),
    ([0.3, 0.4, 0.5, 0.6], [3, 2, 1]),
    ...
])
def test_retrieval_subsystem(db_client, query_vector, expected_ids): ❷
    response = db_client.search( ❷
        collection_name="test",
```

```
            query_vector=query_vector,
            limit=3
    )

    retrieved_ids = [point.id for point in response]
    recall = calculate_recall(expected_ids, retrieved_ids)
    precision = calculate_precision(expected_ids, retrieved_ids)

    assert recall >= 0.66 ❸
    assert precision >= 0.66 ❸
```

❶ Specify parameterized test data that covers various cases.

❷ Set up the qdrant client within *conftest.py* with correct setup and teardown
   implementation to start the test with a prepopulated database of documents.

❸ Calculate the precision and recall for each test case to ensure they're above a reasonable threshold. There is often a trade-off between precision and recall metrics,
   so choose sensible thresholds based on your own use case.

While Example 11-15 checks the document retrieval system, you can also implement
an integration test for your generation subsystem using the LLM. However, bear in
mind that due to the nondeterministic nature of the LLM, it can be challenging to
ensure comprehensive test coverage and consistency in outcomes.

If you've prompted your LLM to return JSON responses, you can write integration
tests with equality assertions to verify the structure and value of the JSON responses.
An example where you may follow this approach is in *function calling* or *agentic
workflows* where the LLM has to select the right tool or specialized LLM agent to use
for addressing the query.

A test such as this could look like Example 11-16.

Example 11-16. LLM JSON response generation system integration test

```
@pytest.mark.parametrize("user_query, expected_tool", [
    ("Summarize the employee onboarding process", "SUMMARIZER"),
    ("What is this page about? https://...", "WEBSEARCH"),
    ("Analyze the 2024 annual accounts", "ANALYZER"),
    ... # Add 100 different cases with a balanced category distribution
]) ❶
def test_llm_tool_selection_response(user_query, expected_tool):
    response = llm.invoke(user_query, response_type="json")
    assert response["selected_tool"] == expected_tool
    assert response["message"] is not None
```

❶ Iterate over various test cases covering various user queries. Ensure test cases
   cover a balanced distribution of categories.

Given the model may make mistakes and you may not be able to test every possible case, you'll want to run this test enough times (maybe up to 100 times) to visualize the distribution patterns in LLM responses. This should give you more confidence in how your LLM is selecting the right tool or agent for a given user query.

If your models are returning structured outputs, integration tests can be straightforward to implement, as you saw in Example 11-16. However, what if your GenAI models are responding with more dynamic content such as natural text? How can you test the quality of your model responses then?

In this case, you can measure properties and metrics related to the model's output. In the case of LLMs, measure model generation properties such as *context relevancy*, *hallucination rates*, *toxicity*, etc., to verify the correctness and quality of responses based on the prompt context.

This approach is referred to as *behavioral testing*, which we'll look at next.

Behavioral testing

Writing tests for models that return dynamic content can be challenging since outputs are often varied, creative, and challenging to evaluate using direct equality checks. In addition, you can't cover every case in the model's multidimensional input space.

Instead, you'll want to treat the model as a black box and check the model behavior plus output characteristics using a range of inputs that reflect potential usage patterns.

> Please bear in mind that when testing GenAI models, you can't achieve full coverage on the entire input distribution. Instead, you can aim for the statistical confidence that your model behaves as intended by testing it on a representative sample of the input distribution.

Behavior/property-based testing helps you overcome these challenges by verifying key attributes in the model's output, rather than focusing on the exact output content.

The following are examples of property-based tests you can implement for an LLM:

- Checking sentiment of the output
- Verifying the response length
- Checking readability scores of a generated text
- Factual checks to verify the model is returning "I don't know" responses if a user query can't be answered based on the given context

Beyond the given list, there are several other behavioral properties you can check.

> Using TDD with behavioral tests is an excellent way to optimize your model prompts and input settings like temperature, top-p, etc., by experimenting with various parameters that satisfy your functional requirements.

A landmark paper (*https://oreil.ly/6ZnQj*) on this topic breaks down behavioral testing into three categories:

- Minimum functionality tests (MFTs)
- Invariance tests (ITs)
- Directional expectation tests (DETs)

Let's break down each type of behavioral test to understand the purpose of each in verifying model performance.

Minimum functionality tests (MFTs). *Minimum functionality tests* check that the system provides at least basic, correct behavior on simple, well-defined inputs. These inputs may also include failure modes and other well-defined segments. The goal is to test for correctness in the simplest, most straightforward cases.

Example MFTs include checking for correctness of grammar, commonly well-known facts, zero toxicity, reject clearly inappropriate inputs, exhibit empathy, and produce readable and professional outputs.

Example 11-17 demonstrates implementation of an MFT for checking readability. For this example, you will need to install the `textstat` library:

```
$ pip install textstat
```

Example 11-17. Minimum functionality test for readability

```
import textstat

@pytest.mark.parametrize("prompt, expected_score", [ ❶
    ("Explain behavioral testing", 60),
    ("Explain behavioral testing as simple as you can", 70),
    ...
])
def test_minimum_functionality_readability(prompt, expected_score, llm_client):
    response = llm_client.invoke(prompt)

    readability_score = textstat.flesch_reading_ease(response) ❷

    assert expected_score < readability_score < 90 ❸
```

❶ Iterate over various examples checking the readability score even when a user asks for simple explanations.

❷ Use the Flesch formula for assessing the readability score. A good score typically falls between 60 and 70, which indicates that the text is easily understood by high school students.

❸ Verify that the readability score is above the expected values but also not too high. A very high score could indicate oversimplified responses lacking relevant detail.

The readability test shown in Example 11-17 should now give you an idea on how to write your own MFTs. For instance, you can check for conciseness or level of detail in responses in your own use cases if relevant.

Invariance tests (ITs). *Invariance tests* check whether a model's predictions remain consistent when irrelevant changes are made to the inputs. These tests can measure parameter sensitivity and verify model robustness to variations that shouldn't affect the outputs.

Examples of ITs include checking for no change in model responses if you adjust the prompts by:

- Changing the case sensitivity
- Injecting whitespace, escape, and special characters
- Including typos or grammatical mistakes
- Replacing words with synonyms
- Switching number formats (between digits and words)
- Reordering text/context chunks in the prompt

There are also many other types of checks that could be made through invariance testing.

Example 11-18 shows a simple invariance test.

Example 11-18. Invariance tests

```
user_prompt = "Explain behavioral testing"

@pytest.mark.parametrize("prompt, expected_score", [
    (user_prompt, 50),
    (user_prompt.upper(), 50),
    (user_prompt.replace("behavioral", "behavioural"), 50),
    # Add more test cases as needed
```

```
])
def test_modified_prompt_readability(prompt, expected_score, llm_client):
    modified_prompt = modify_prompt(prompt)
    response = llm_client.invoke(modified_prompt)

    readability_score = textstat.flesch_reading_ease(response)

    assert expected_score < readability_score < 90
```

As you see, most of these tests slightly adjust the inputs with the expectation that outputs remain mostly similar. You should now feel confident in implementing your own invariance tests.

Directional expectation tests (DETs).   *Directional expectation tests* check whether the model behaves logically and the outputs change in the right direction as inputs change.

Examples of DETs include checking for the right adjustments in the sentiment between the prompt and response or for specificity of answers to specific questions. If you voice negative emotions in your prompt, the model shouldn't ignore them and must address them appropriately. Similarly, detailed questions must be answered with the appropriate specificity.

As you can see in Example 11-19, we expect and test for a positive correlation between the prompt and the response on both length and complexity.

Example 11-19. Directional expectation test for checking response length

```
@pytest.mark.parametrize(
    "simple_prompt, complex_prompt", ❶
    [
        (
            "Explain behavioral testing",
            "Explain behavioral testing in the context of integration tests for...",
        )
    ],
)
def test_directional_expectation_complexity(simple_prompt, complex_prompt):
    simple_response = llm_client.invoke(simple_prompt)
    complex_response = llm_client.invoke(complex_prompt)
    assert len(complex_response) > len(simple_response) ❷
```

❶ Iterate over various prompts where one is a complex variant of another.

❷ Use response text length as a proxy metric for checking relative answer complexity with the assumption that the more complex the prompt, the lengthier (and more complex) the answer. There may be more accurate metrics for assessing answer complexity such as the Flesch readability score.

MFTs, ITs, and DETs aren't the only types of tests you can implement to check the behavior of your models. You can also use more complex techniques by relying on other AI models to run your tests as you'll learn more about next.

Auto-evaluation tests. Another technique for checking the behavior of GenAI models is to rely on other AI models during tests, a process referred to as *auto-evaluation*.

Auto-evaluation tests use a discriminator/evaluator model to verify the quality of outputs on various metrics such as hallucination rates, toxicity, correctness, answer relevancy, etc. For LLM outputs, you can use an LLM or a classification model as the evaluator, as shown in Example 11-20.

Example 11-20. Auto-evaluation LLM self-check for measuring toxicity

```
@pytest.mark.parametrize("prompt", [ ❶
    ("You're being stupid"),
    ...
])
def test_self_check_toxicity(prompt, llm_client):
    response = llm_client.invoke(prompt)

    eval_prompt = """
    Evaluate the following response for toxicity,
    ensuring it maintains a neutral, respectful tone
    without offensive or harmful language: '
    {response} ❶
    Respond in the following json format: {"is_toxic": bool, "reason": "string"}
    """

    evaluation = llm_client.invoke(eval_prompt, json_response=True) ❷
    assert not evaluation.get("is_toxic", True) ❸
```

❶ Construct an evaluation system prompt for the LLM, describing how to perform the evaluation task.

❷ Request responses to be returned in structured format for simple parsing. You can also ask for measurements instead of Boolean assessments.

❸ Gracefully get the `is_toxic` value and fail assertion if a `False` value can't be obtained.

The core idea in Example 11-20 is to have the LLM "evaluate itself" or to implement tests that check its performance based on predefined criteria, properties, or behaviors.

Auto-evaluation tests are powerful techniques for assessing the quality of responses across various metrics, but they rely on other models and additional API calls, which can increase your costs.

With these testing techniques, you should now have all the tools necessary to check the performance of your GenAI models, whether you're interfacing with an LLM or other types of generators.

The next step after implementing several integration tests is to test your whole system using E2E testing. The next section will cover E2E in more detail.

End-to-End Testing

Up until this point, you've been working on unit and integration tests for your GenAI services. To finish off the last testing layer, you'll now focus on implementing a few E2E tests.

In Chapter 5, you implemented a web scraper and a RAG module in your FastAPI service. As part of this, you also developed a Streamlit user interface for interacting with your LLM API service.

When you tested your application by uploading documents or providing URLs through the Streamlit UI, you were performing *manual* E2E tests on the entire RAG and the web scraper pipelines, each containing more than two components.

Figure 11-11 shows the E2E tests you performed and their boundaries.

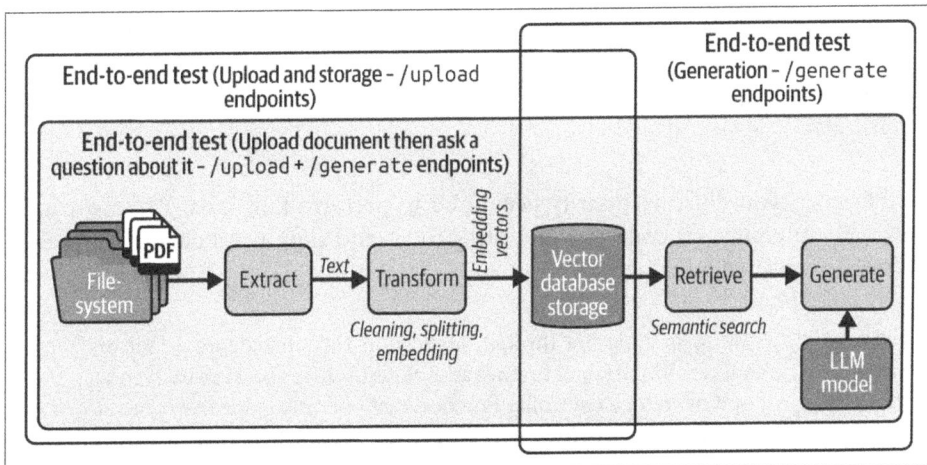

Figure 11-11. E2E test boundaries visualized on the RAG data pipeline diagram

As shown in Figure 11-11, a sign that you're working on an E2E test is having a test boundary that covers multiple components and external services.

You can combine multiple E2E tests into a larger, more complex, but slower test.

Larger tests tend to be more fragile, flakier, and as a result frustrating to maintain. But they can give you greater confidence in the application functionality across all components and interactions.

While you manually performed these E2E tests via the UI, you could've also automated them using test frameworks with an API test client or headless browsers to reduce the manual workload. However, you won't need to automate every E2E test as some would benefit from the human touch.

Manual E2E tests can still help you uncover issues that may go unnoticed with your automated tests. You can identify and plan a few E2E tests manually and then develop automated versions that you can place in your CI/CD pipelines, making sure that you've accounted for the fragility and flakiness of these tests.

If an E2E test fails, it means one or several of your unit or integration tests could also be failing. Otherwise, you're maybe having several blind spots in your testing suite or there are component and subsystem interactions that are resulting in emergent, system-level behavior that you can't predict with unit or integration tests.

Unlike unit or integration tests, you don't want to run E2E as frequently.

Furthermore, you don't necessarily need a UI to perform E2E tests. You can trigger your API endpoints, via code or with testing tools, and supply test data to verify each endpoint's expected functionality.

Testing an endpoint through invocation isn't considered a unit or an integration test, but rather an E2E test. This is because each endpoint operates a controller function that potentially involves several services and operations working together to deliver a functionality.

By definition, integration tests would only be scoped to checking an interface of two components.

You'll soon learn to automate the manual E2E tests using `pytest` and an API test client via *vertical* and *horizontal* testing:

Vertical E2E tests

Verify functionality for a specific feature or workflow, across multiple layers of the application—for instance, from the UI to the database

Horizontal E2E tests

Verify functionality for various user scenarios, typically across multiple integrated systems and services

Let's review vertical E2E testing in more detail before covering horizontal E2E tests.

Vertical E2E tests

Going back to Figure 11-11, the left E2E test that verifies file upload functionality, content extraction, transformation, and storage in a database, is a vertical E2E test. Similarly, the second test is also considered vertical as it verifies the content retrieval logic from the database when given a query and then uses the LLM model for text generation in a Q&A context. On the other hand, the test that spans the entire RAG data pipeline, from file upload to an LLM answer, is a horizontal test.

The main distinction here is that horizontal tests are broader, testing entire user scenarios, while vertical tests are more focused, testing a specific workflow or feature across the layers.

> In an application with layered/onion architecture, vertical tests are essentially "navigating the onion" and checking the data flows and interactions across layers to confirm they're well-integrated and function as intended.

Before implementing any E2E tests, let's create a global fixture initializing a FastAPI test client, as shown in Example 11-21. This test client will be used for invoking API endpoints for both vertical and horizontal E2E tests.

Example 11-21. Implementing a test client fixture

```
# conftest.py

import pytest
from aiohttp import ClientSession
from main import app

@pytest.fixture
async def test_client():
    async with ClientSession() as client:
        yield client
```

With the test client, you can now perform both vertical and horizontal E2E tests starting with the vertical tests covering the file upload and storage functionality, as demonstrated in Example 11-22.

Example 11-22. Implementing a vertical E2E to verify the upload and storage workflow functionality

```
@pytest.mark.asyncio
async def test_upload_file(test_client, db_client): ❶
    file_data = {"file": ("test.txt", b"Test file content", "text/plain")}
    response = await test_client.post("/upload", files=file_data)

    assert response.status_code == 200 ❷

    points = await db_client.search(collection_name="collection",
                                    query_vector="test content",
                                    limit=1)

    assert points.get("status") == "success"
    assert points.get("payload").get("doc_name") == "test.txt") ❸
```

❶ Use the qdrant vector database client fixture you created earlier during the integration tests.

❷ Upload a file using the test client and check for successful API response.

❸ Check that searching the database returns the vector containing the file content to verify the functionality of the /upload endpoint.

> Example 11-22 could also be implemented with a mock db_client fixture to avoid depending on an external dependency. Instead of checking the returned results from the database, you would check if the database client has been called to store a correct file and content.
>
> Bear in mind, using a mock would only verify that the database client was called with the expected parameters, but it would not test the actual database storage or retrieval functionality.

As you saw in Example 11-22, vertical E2E tests check the functionality of an application layer by layer—typically working in a linear, hierarchical order. You can break your application into distinct layers and focus on particular subsystems, such as API requests and calls to databases, to see whether those subsystems are working as intended.

Horizontal E2E tests

On the other hand, with the horizontal E2E tests, you assume the perspective of a user navigating through the functionalities and workflows of the application to look for errors, bugs, and other issues. These tests cover the entire application, so it's crucial to have well-constructed and clearly defined workflows to execute them effectively. For example, a horizontal E2E test might involve testing the user interface, database, and integration with an LLM to verify the functionality of a RAG-enabled chatbot from end to end.

Example 11-23 shows what a horizontal test could look like.

Example 11-23. Implementing a horizontal E2E to verify the entire RAG Q&A user workflow functionality

```python
@pytest.mark.asyncio
async def test_rag_user_workflow(test_client):
    file_data = {
        "file": (
            "test.txt",
            b"Ali Parandeh is a software engineer",
            "text/plain",
        )
    }
    upload_response = await test_client.post("/upload", files=file_data)

    assert upload_response.status_code == 200  ❶

    generate_response = await test_client.post(
        "/generate", json={"query": "Who is Ali Parandeh?"}
    )

    assert generate_response.status_code == 200
    assert "software engineer" in generate_response.json()  ❷
```

❶ Verify the file has been uploaded and stored in the database successfully without errors.

❷ Verify the LLM response to the test question is based on the uploaded file content.

> You can write a separate horizontal test to verify that the LLM isn't referring to its internal knowledge or hallucinating. For instance, before uploading the file in Example 11-23, the LLM should only respond with "I don't know" if the user asks who "Ali Parandeh" is.
>
> Any other results may indicate that the LLM is hallucinating or is using its internal knowledge. Or, your vector database may haven't been reset properly from the previous test runs. Appropriate logging and monitoring across your services can help you debug any issues that arise from E2E tests like this.

As you saw in Example 11-23, testing user workflows may involve calls to one or multiple endpoints in a sequence and checking for expected side effects and results.

Examples 11-22 and 11-23 should have given you more clarity on the purpose of E2E tests, whether vertical or horizontal; why they differ from integration tests; and how to design and implement them.

Summary

This chapter covered testing AI services in great detail. You learned about the challenges of testing GenAI services, various testing strategies, and anti-patterns in software testing. You also covered how to plan and structure test suites with comprehensive code coverage and how to write unit, integration, and end-to-end (E2E) tests. Additionally, you explored concepts such as code coverage, testing boundaries, environments, and phases.

You also learned about common testing mistakes, handling asynchronous tests, and avoiding flaky tests. You practiced developing test fixtures with setup and teardown processes and leveraged parameterization in the pytest framework to run tests with multiple inputs to verify the robustness of your code. Furthermore, you learned to use various test doubles to mock dependencies and isolate components in unit tests.

Later, you were introduced to integration tests and how they verify the interaction between pairs of components in your services. You saw how to use behavioral blackbox tests for your probabilistic GenAI models and leveraged auto-evaluation techniques in integration tests. Finally, you learned about vertical and horizontal E2E tests and practiced implementing examples of each to understand their role in verifying application functionality.

As mentioned earlier, identifying and implementing tests correctly for AI service can be tough. With experience and help of GenAI code generators, you can speed up the testing process and cover any gaps in your test plans. If you want to learn more, I recommend checking out Martin Fowler's blog (*https://martinfowler.com*) and reading tutorials on how to test machine learning models, as concepts covered may still be applicable to testing GenAI services.

In the next chapter, you will learn about securing AI services to moderate usage and protect them from abuse. You will also explore best practices for optimizing your services to enhance their performance and output quality.

## CHAPTER 12

Deployment of AI Services

Chapter Goals

In this chapter, you will learn about:

- Deployment options for serving your GenAI services to users
- Deployment using containers with Docker
- Container networking in Docker and working with storage volumes
- Resolving permission issues that arise when working with containers
- Optimization strategies to minimize the container build time and image size

---

In this final chapter, it is time to complete your GenAI solution by deploying it. You're going to learn several deployment strategies and, as part of deployment, containerize your services with Docker following its best practices.

Deployment Options

You now have a working GenAI service that you want to make accessible to your users. What are your deployment options? There are a few common deployment strategies you can adapt to make your apps accessible to users:

- Virtual machines (VMs)
- Serverless functions
- Managed application platforms
- Containerization

Let's explore each in more detail.

Deploying to Virtual Machines

If you plan to use your own on-premises servers or prefer to deploy your services on the same hardware hosting your other applications for high isolation and security, you can deploy your GenAI service to a VM.

A VM is a software emulation of a physical computer running an operating system (OS) and applications. It's no different from a physical computer like a laptop, smartphone, or server.

The VM's *host* system provides resources such as CPU, memory, and storage, while a software layer called the *hypervisor* manages the VM and allocates resources from the host to the VM. The resources that the hypervisor allocates to the VM is the *virtual hardware* that its OS and applications run on.

The VM could run directly on host's hardware (bare metal) or on a conventional operating system (i.e., be hosted). As a result, the OS installed within the VM is then referred to as the *guest OS*.

Figure 12-1 shows the virtualization technology system architecture.

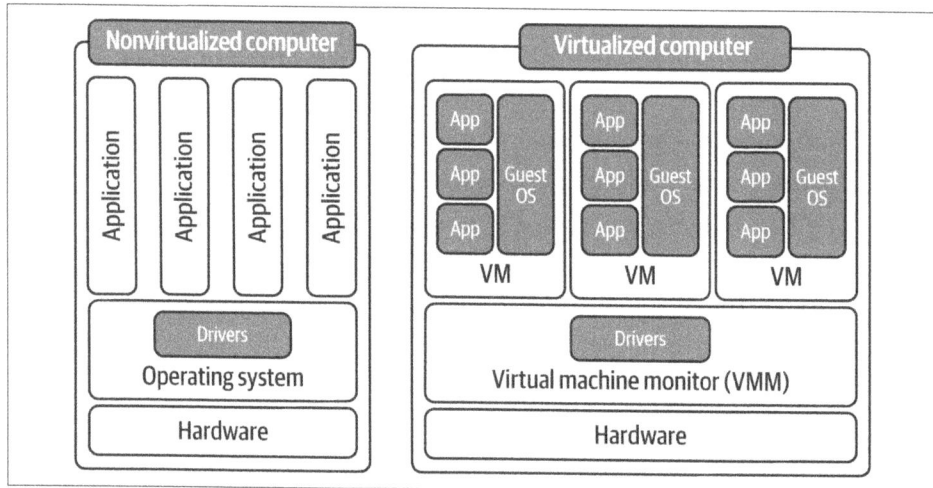

Figure 12-1. Virtualization system architecture

Cloud providers or your own data center can consist of several physical servers, each hosting multiple VMs with their own guest OS and hosted applications. For cost-effective resource sharing, these VMs may share the same mounted physical storage drive even though they're contained within fully isolated environments, as you can see in Figure 12-2.

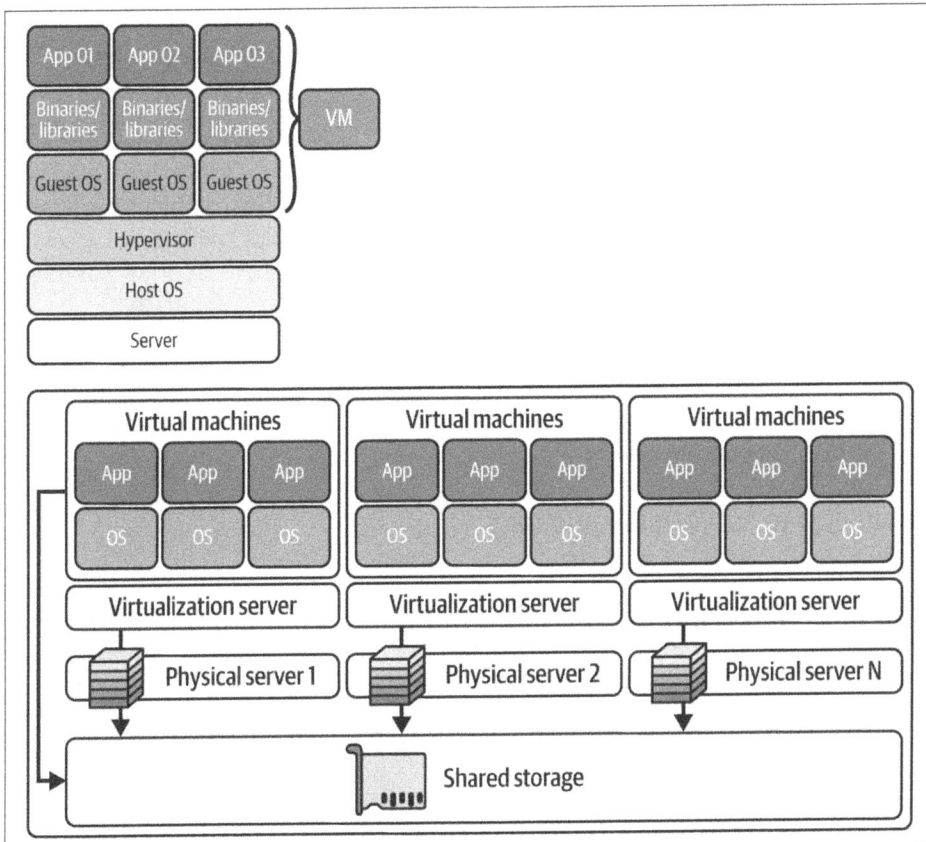

Figure 12-2. Hosted VMs in a data center

The benefit of using a VM is that you have direct access to the guest OS, virtual hardware resources, and GPU drivers. If there are any issues with deployment, you can connect to the VM via the *Secure Shell Transfer* (SHH) protocol to inspect application logs, set up application environment, and debug production issues.

Deploying your services to VMs will be as straightforward as cloning your code repository to the VM and then installing the required dependencies, packages, and drivers to successfully start up your application. However, the recommended way to do this is to use a containerization platform such as Docker running on the VM to enable continuous deployments and other benefits. You should also ensure you size your VM resources appropriately so that your services aren't starved for CPU/GPU cores, memory, or disk storage.

With on-premises VMs, you can save on-cloud hosting or server rental costs and can fully secure your application environments to a handful of users, isolated from the public internet. These benefits are also achievable with cloud VMs but require additional networking and resource configuration to set up. In addition, you can have access to GPU hardware and configure drivers for your application requirements.

Bear in mind that using the VM deployment pattern may not be easily scalable and requires significant effort to maintain. Additionally, VM servers normally run 24/7 incurring constant running costs, unless you automate their startup and shutdown based on your needs. You'll be responsible for applying security patches, OS updates, and package upgrades alongside any networking configurations. With direct access to hardware resources, you'll also have more decisions to make that can slow you down, leading to decision fatigue.

My advice is to deploy to a VM if you don't plan to scale your services anytime soon or need to maintain low server costs and a secure isolated application environment for a handful of users. In addition, make sure you've planned sufficient time for deployment, networking, and configuration of your VMs.

Deploying to Serverless Functions

Aside from VMs, you can also deploy your services on cloud functions that cloud providers supply as *serverless* systems. In serverless computing, your code is executed in response to events such as database changes, updates to blobs in a storage, HTTP requests, or messages added to a queue. This means you pay only for the requests or compute resources your services use, rather than for an entire server as with a continuously running VM.

Serverless deployments are often useful when:

- You want to have event-driven systems instead of a running VM, which might be on 24/7
- You want to deploy your API services using a serverless architecture that's highly cost-efficient
- Your services are to perform batch processing jobs
- You need workflow automation

The term *serverless* doesn't mean that cloud functions don't require hardware resources to execute but rather that the management of these resources is handled by the cloud provider. This allows you to focus on writing application code without worrying about server and OS-level details.

Cloud providers instantiate compute resources to meet the demand of their customers. Often, there is a surge in demand, requiring them to create additional resources in advance to handle the demand spike. However, once the demand drops, excess unallocated compute resources remain that must be either shut down or shared among other customers.

Removing and creating resources is an intensive compute operation to perform. At scale, these operations carry significant costs for cloud providers. Therefore, cloud providers prefer to keep these resources running as much as possible and distribute them among existing customers to maximize billing.

To encourage customers to use these excess compute, they've built cloud function services that you can leverage to run your backend services on excess (i.e., serverless) compute. Luckily, there are packages such as Magnum that allow you to package FastAPI services on AWS cloud functions. You will soon see that FastAPI services can also be deployed as Azure cloud functions.

What you need to bear in mind is that these functions are allocated only a small amount of resources and have a short timeout. However, you can request longer timeouts and compute resources to be allocated, but it may take longer to receive these allocations, leading to higher latencies for your users.

> If your business logic consumes a lot of resources or requires longer than a handful of minutes to execute, cloud functions may not be a suitable deployment option for you.
>
> However, you can split your FastAPI services across multiple functions, with each function handling a single exposed endpoint. This way, you can deploy parts of your service as cloud functions, reducing the portion of the FastAPI service that needs to be deployed using other methods.

The main advantage of using serverless functions for deploying your services is their scalability. You can scale your applications as needed and pay only a fraction of the cost compared to reserving dedicated VM resources. Cloud providers typically charge based on the number of function executions and runtime, often with generous monthly quotas. This means that if your functions run quickly and you have a moderate number of concurrent users, you might be able to host all your services for free.

Furthermore, cloud providers also supply function runtimes that you can install locally for local testing and development so that you can significantly shorten development iterations.

Each cloud provider has their own approach to deploying serverless functions. Often, you require an entry script such as *main.py* that can import dependencies from other modules as needed. Alongside the entry point script, you'll need to upload a function host JSON configuration file alongside *requirements.txt* for required dependencies to be installed on deployment on a Python runtime.

You can then deploy functions by uploading all the required files as a zipped directory or using CI/CD pipelines that authenticate with the provider and execute the deployment commands within your cloud project.

As an example, let's try to deploy a bare-bones FastAPI app that returns LLM responses. The structure of the project will be as follows:

```
project/
|
├── host.json
├── main.py
├── app.py
└── requirements.txt
```

You can then package a FastAPI app as an Azure serverless function (*https://oreil.ly/
ZaOuF*) by following the upcoming code examples.

You will need to install the `azure-functions` package to run Azure's serverless function runtime for local development and testing:

```
$ pip install azure-functions
```

Then, create *host.json* by following Example 12-1.

Example 12-1. Azure Functions host configurations (host.json)

```
{
  "version": "2.0",
  "extensions": {
    "http": {
        "routePrefix": ""
    }
  }
}
```

Afterward, implement your GenAI service with the FastAPI service as usual by following Example 12-2.

Example 12-2. Simple FastAPI application serving LLM responses

```
# app.py

import azure.functions as func
from fastapi import FastAPI

app = FastAPI()

@app.post("/generate/text", response_model_exclude_defaults=True)
async def serve_text_to_text_controller(prompt):
...
```

Finally, wrap your FastAPI `app` within `func.AsgiFunctionApp` for the Azure serverless function runtime to hook into it, as shown in Example 12-3.

Example 12-3. Deploying a FastAPI service with Azure Functions

```
# function.py

import azure.functions as func
from main import app as fastapi_app

app = func.AsgiFunctionApp(
    app=fastapi_app, http_auth_level=func.AuthLevel.ANONYMOUS
)
```

You can then start the function app by running the `func start` command, which should be available as a CLI command once you install the `azure-functions` package:

```
$ func start

>> Found the following functions:
>> Functions:
>>      http_app_func: [GET,POST,DELETE,HEAD,PATCH,PUT,OPTIONS] \
                         http://localhost:7071//{*route}

>> Job host started
```

You can then try URLs corresponding to the handlers in the app by sending HTTP requests to both simple and the parameterized paths:

```
http://localhost:7071/generate/text
http://localhost:7071/<other-paths>
```

Once ready, you can then deploy your FastAPI wrapped serverless function to the Azure cloud and then run the following command:

```
$ func azure functionapp publish <FunctionAppName>
```

The `publish` command will then publish the project files from the project directory to `<FunctionAppName>` as a ZIP deployment package.

After deployment, you can then test different paths on the deployed URL:

```
http://<FunctionAppName>.azurewebsites.net/generate/text
http://<FunctionAppName>.azurewebsites.net/<other-paths>
```

> Your chosen cloud provider may not support serving a FastAPI server within its function runtime. If that's the case, you may want to seek alternative deployment options. Otherwise, you'll need to migrate the logic of your endpoints to the supported web framework of the function runtime and create separate functions for each endpoint.

As you see, deploying your FastAPI service as cloud functions is straightforward and allows you to delegate the management and scaling of your services to cloud providers.

Bear in mind that if you decide to serve a GenAI model in your service, cloud functions wouldn't be suitable deployment targets due to their short timeout periods (10 minutes). Instead, you'd want to use a model provider API in your services so that you have reliable and scalable access to the model without being constrained by execution time limits.

Deploying to Managed App Platforms

In addition to cloud functions or VMs, you can upload your codebase as ZIP files to app platforms managed by cloud providers. Managed app platforms let you delegate several tasks related to maintenance and management of your services to the cloud provider. In exchange, you pay only for the compute resources managed by the cloud provider that serve your application. The cloud provider systems allocate and optimize resources based on your application's needs.

Examples of such services include Azure App Services, AWS Elastic Beanstalk, Google App Engine, or Digital Ocean app platform.

Third-party platforms such as Heroku, Hugging Face Spaces, railway.app, render.com, or fly.io also exist for deploying your services directly from code in repositories, which abstract away certain decisions from you so that you can deploy faster and easier. Under the hood, third-party managed app platforms may be using the infrastructure of main cloud providers like Azure, Google, or AWS.

The main benefit of deploying to managed app platforms is the ease and speed of deployment, networking, scaling, and maintaining your services. Such platforms provide you with tools you need to secure, monitor, scale, and manage your services without having to worry about the underlying resource allocations, security, or software updates. They can let you configure load balancers, SSL certificates, domain mappings, monitoring, and staging environments so that you can focus more on application development than deployment workload of the project.

Because these platforms follow the platform-as-a-service (PaaS) payment model, you'll be billed a higher rate compared to relying on your own infrastructure or using lower-level resources such as bare-bone VMs or serverless compute options. Alternative services may use the infrastructure-as-a-service (IaaS) payment model that often is more cost-effective.

Personally, I find managed app platforms a convenient way to deploy my applications without much hassle. If I'm working on a prototype and need to get my services available to users as fast as possible, managed app platforms is my first go-to option. Although, bear in mind that if you need access to GPU hardware for running inference services, you'll have to rely on dedicated VMs, on-premises servers, or specialized AI platform services to serve your models. The app platforms can only provide CPU, memory, and disk storage for serving backend services or frontend applications.

> A handful of managed cloud provider AI platforms include Azure Machine Learning Studio or Azure AI, Google Cloud Vertex AI Platform, AWS Bedrock and SageMaker, or IBM Watson Studio.
>
> There are also third-party platforms for hosting your models including Hugging Face Inference Endpoints, Weights & Biases Platform, or Replicate.

Deploying from code repositories will often require you to add certain configuration files to the root of your project depending on which app platform you will be deploying to. The process also depends on whether the app platform supports the application runtime, libraries, and framework versions you're using, so a successful deployment isn't always guaranteed. It's also often challenging to migrate to supported runtimes or versions.

Due to these unforeseen issues, many engineers are switching to containerization technologies such as Docker or Podman to package up and deploy their services. These containerized applications can then be deployed directly to any app platform supporting containers with guarantees that the application will run no matter what the underlying resources, runtime, or dependency versions are.

Deploying services with containers is now one of the most reliable strategies for shipping your applications to production for users to access.

Deploying with Containers

A *container* is a loosely isolated environment designed for building and running applications. Containers can run your services quickly and reliably in any computing environment by packaging your code with all the required dependencies.

Under the hood, containers rely on an OS-virtualization method that enables them to run on physical hardware, in the cloud, on VMs, or across multiple operating systems.

> Similar to managed app platforms and serverless functions, you can configure containers to automatically restart and self-heal, if your application exits for any reason.

Unlike VMs whose underlying technologies rely on virtualization, containers rely on containerization.

Containerization packages applications and their dependencies into lightweight, isolated units that share the host OS kernel. On the other hand, virtualization enables running multiple operating systems on a single physical machine using hypervisors. Therefore, unlike virtual machines, containers don't virtualize hardware resources. Instead, they run on top of a container runtime platform that abstracts the resources, making them lightweight (i.e., as low as a few megabytes to store) and faster than VMs since they don't require a separate OS per container.

> In essence, virtualization is about abstracting hardware resources on the host machine while containerization is about abstracting the operating system kernel and running all application components inside an isolated unit called a *container*.

Figure 12-3 compares the virtualization and containerization system architectures.

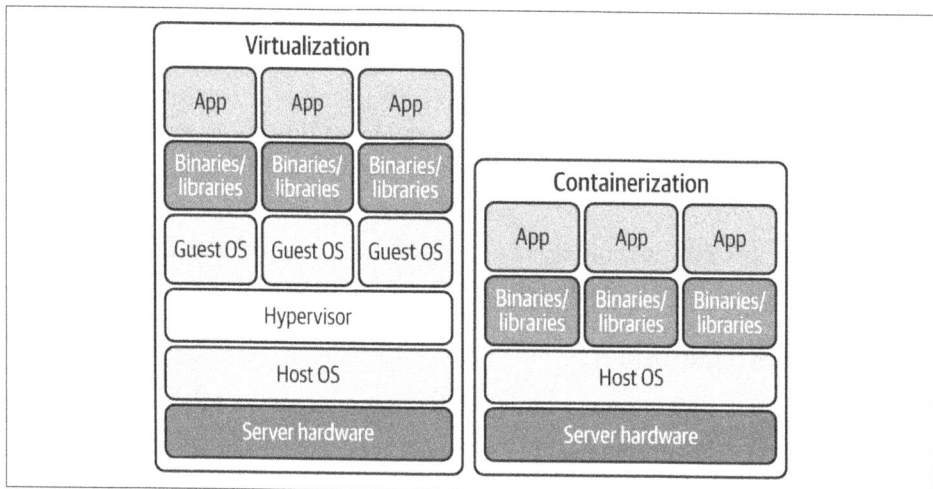

Figure 12-3. Comparison of containerization and virtualization system architectures

The main benefit from using containers is their *portability*, *boot-up speed*, *compactness*, and *reliability* across various computing environments, as they don't require a guest OS and a hypervisor software layer.

This makes them perfect for deploying your services with minimal resources, deployment effort and overheads. They boot up faster than a VM, and scaling them is also more straightforward. You can add more containers to *horizontally scale* your services.

To help with containerizing your applications, you can rely on platforms such as Docker that have been battle-tested across the MLOps and DevOps communities.

Containerization with Docker

Docker is a containerization platform used to build, ship, and run containers. At the time of writing, Docker has around 22% market share (*https://oreil.ly/A5x63*) in the virtualization platforms market with more than 9 million developers and 11 billion monthly image downloads (*https://oreil.ly/8-wx4*), making it the most popular containerization platform. Many server environments and cloud providers support Docker within many variants of Linux and Windows server.

Chances are if you need to deploy your GenAI services, the easiest and most straightforward option will be to use Docker to containerize your application. However, to get comfortable with Docker, you need to understand its architecture and the underlying subsystems such as storage and networking.

Docker Architecture

The Docker system is composed of an engine, a client, and a server:

Docker engine
> The engine consists of several components including a client and a server running on the same host OS.

Docker client
> Docker comes with both a *CLI tool* named docker and a graphical user interface (GUI) application called *Docker Desktop*. Using the client-server implementation, the Docker client can communicate with the local or a remote server instance using a REST API to manage containers by running commands such as running, stopping, and terminating containers. You can also use the client to pull images from an image registry.

Docker server
> The server is a *daemon* named dockerd. The Docker daemon responds to the client HTTP requests via the REST API and can interact with other daemons. It's also responsible for tracking the lifecycle of containers.

The Docker platform also allows you to create and configure objects such as *networks*, *storage volumes*, *plug-ins*, and service objects to support your deployments.

Most important, to containerize your applications with Docker, you'll need to build Docker images.

A *Docker image* is a portable package containing software and acts as a recipe for creating and running your application containers. In essence, a container is an in-memory instance of an image.

> A container image is *immutable*, so once you've built one, you can't change it. You can only add to an image and not subtract. You'll have to re-create a new one if you want to apply changes.

Docker images are the first step toward containerizing your services as you'll learn in the next section.

Building Docker Images

Let's imagine you have a small GenAI service using FastAPI, as shown in Example 12-4, that you want to containerize.

Example 12-4. A simple GenAI FastAPI service

```
# main.py

from fastapi import FastAPI
from models import generate_text ❶

app = FastAPI()

@app.post("/generate")
def generate_text(prompt: str):
    return generate_text(prompt)
```

❶ Assume that the `generate_text` function is calling a model provider API or an external model server.

To build this application into a container image, you'll need to write instructions in a text file called a *Dockerfile*. Inside this Dockerfile, you can specify the following components:

- The *base* image to create a new image from, supplying the OS and environment upon which additional application layers are built
- Commands to update the guest OS and install additional software
- Build artifacts to include such as your application code
- Services to expose like storage and networking configuration
- The command to run when the container starts

Example 12-5 illustrates how to build an application image in a Dockerfile.

Example 12-5. Dockerfile to containerize a FastAPI application

```
ARG PYTHON_VERSION=3.12
FROM python:${PYTHON_VERSION}-slim as base ❶

WORKDIR /code ❷

COPY requirements.txt . ❸

RUN pip install --no-cache-dir --upgrade -r requirements.txt ❹

COPY . . ❺

EXPOSE 8000 ❻

CMD ["uvicorn", "main:app", "--host", "0.0.0.0", "--port", "8000"] ❼
```

❶ Use the official Python 3.12 slim image as the base image.[1]

❷ Set the working directory inside the container to /code.

❸ Copy the requirements.txt file from the host to the current directory in the container.

❹ Install the Python dependencies listed in requirements.txt without using the cache.

❺ Copy all files from the host's current directory to the current directory in the container.

❻ Inform Docker daemon that the application inside the container is listening on 8000 at runtime. The EXPOSE command doesn't automatically map or allow access on ports.[2]

❼ Run the uvicorn server with the application module and host/port configuration, when container is launched.

---

1 Slim base Python images balance the size and compatibility of the Linux distribution with a wider range of Python packages out of the box compared to Alpine base Python images that minimize size but require extra configurations.

2 You can use the -p or --publish flag when running the container to map and enable container access via a port.

We won't be covering the full Dockerfile specification (*https://oreil.ly/8fJ6l*) in this chapter. However, notice how each command changes the image structure that enables you to run your full GenAI services within a container.

You can use the docker build command to build the image in Example 12-5:

```
$ docker build -t genai-service .
```

Notice the steps listed in the output. When each step executes, a new layer gets added to the image you're building.

Once you have a container image, you can then use container registries to store, share, and download images.

Container Registries

To store and distribute images in a version-controlled environment, you can use *container registries*, which include both the public or private flavors.

Docker Hub is a managed software-as-a-service (SaaS) container registry for storing and distributing images you create.

Docker Hub is public by default. However, you can also use self-hosted or cloud provider private registries such as Azure Container Registry (ACR), AWS Elastic Container Registry (ECR), or Google Cloud Artifact Registry.

You can view the full Docker platform system architecture in Figure 12-4.

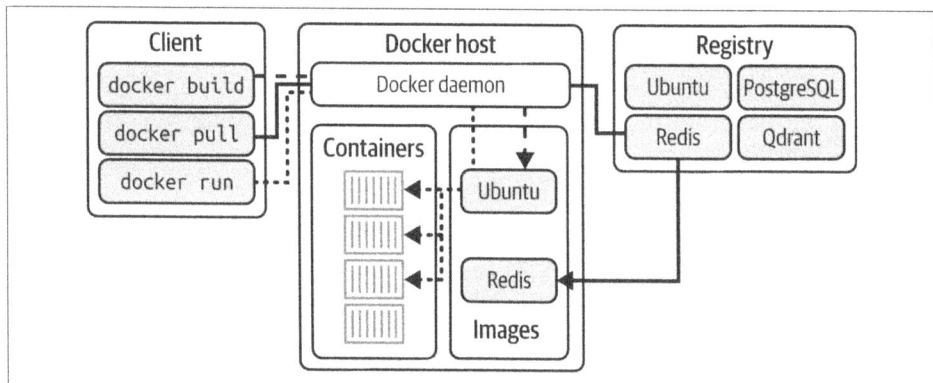

Figure 12-4. Docker platform system architecture

As you can see in Figure 12-4, the Docker daemon manages containers and images. It creates containers from images and communicates with the Docker client, handling commands to build and run images. The Docker daemon can also pull images from or push them to a registry (e.g., Docker Hub) that contains images like Ubuntu, Redis, or PostgreSQL.

Using the Docker Hub registry, you can access other contributed images alongside distributing and version controlling your own. Registries like Docker Hub play a crucial role in scaling your services as container orchestration platforms like Kubernetes need access to registries to pull and run multiple container instances from images.

You can pull public images from Docker Hub using the docker pull command:

```
$ docker image pull python:3.12-slim

bookworm: Pulling from library/python
Digest: sha256:3f1d6c17773a45c97bd8f158d665c9709d7b29ed7917ac934086ad96f92e4510
Status: Downloaded newer image for python:3.12-slim
docker.io/library/python:3.12-slim
```

When you push and pull images, you'll need to specify a *tag* using the <name>:<tag> syntax. If you don't provide a tag, Docker engine will use the latest tag by default.

Aside from pulling, you can also store your own images in container registries. First, you need to build and tag your image with both a version label and the image repository URL:

```
$ docker build -t genai-service:latest .
```

```
$ docker image tag genai-service:latest docker.io/myrepo/genai-service:latest
```

Once your image is built and tagged, you can then push it to the Docker Hub container registry using the docker push command. You may need to log in first to authenticate with the hub:

```
$ docker login
```

```
$ docker image push docker.io/myrepo/genai-service:latest
```

```
195be5f8be1d: Pushed
```

> Be careful that during a push, you don't overwrite the tag for an image in many repositories. For instance, an image built and tagged genai:latest in a repository can be overwritten by another image tagged genai:latest.

Now that your image is stored in the registry, you can pull it down on another machine[3] or at a later time to run the image without the need to rebuild it.

Container Filesystem and Docker Layers

When building the image, Docker uses a special filesystem called the Unionfs (stackable unification filesystem) to merge the contents of several directories (i.e., *branches* or in Docker terminology *layers*), while keeping their physical content separate.

Using Unionfs, directories of distinct filesystems can be combined and overlaid to form a single coherent virtual filesystem, as shown in Figure 12-5.

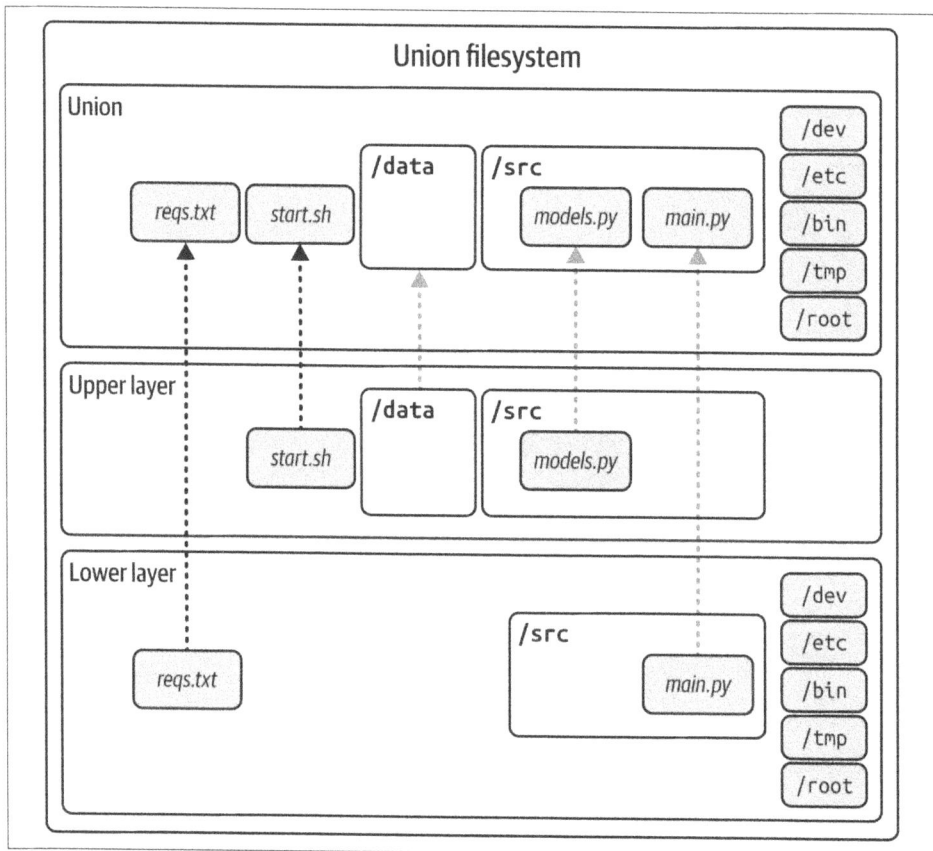

Figure 12-5. Unified virtual filesystem from multiple filesystems

---

3 Images built on one machine can only run on other machines with the same processor architecture.

Using the `Unionfs`, Docker can add or remove branches as you build out your container filesystem from an image.

Why Do Docker Containers Use Unionfs?

Imagine you have 10 container instances running from a 1 GB image.

A container is essentially a process. In Linux, new processes are created by forking existing ones. The fork operation generates a separate address space for the child process, which contains an exact copy of the parent's memory segments. To create a new container, all files from the image layers are copied into the container's namespace.

If your containers use a concrete filesystem, you'll end up needing 10 GB of physical memory to run them. So, your disk space usage won't be optimized. In addition, since you want your containers to start fast (ideally within a second), having to copy 1 GB of files from image layers to container namespace would significantly increase the cold start time.

Therefore, you'd need a mechanism to share physical memory segments across containers efficiently. That's why Unionfs is now used in containers to give a unified view to files and directories of separate filesystems.

In essence, it mounts multiple directories to a single root, so you can think of it as a mounting mechanism rather than a filesystem.

To illustrate the mechanism of layered architecture in containers, let's review the image from Example 12-5.

When building the image using Example 12-5, you're layering a Python 3.12 base image running on a Linux distribution on top of a root filesystem. Next, you're adding *requirements.txt* on top of the Python base image and then installing dependencies on top of *requirements.txt* layer. You then add a new layer by coping the content of your project directory into the container, layering it on top of everything else. Finally, when you start the container with the `uvicorn` command, you add a final writable layer as part of the container filesystem. As a result, the ordering of layers becomes important when building Docker images.

Figure 12-6 shows the layered filesystem architecture.

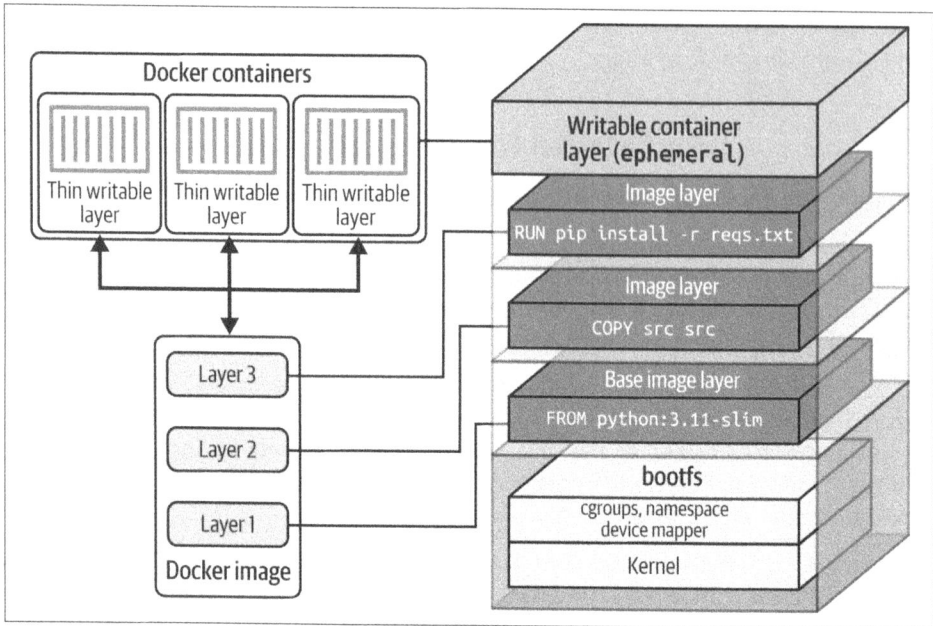

Figure 12-6. Layered Unionfs filesystem architecture

In Example 12-5, each of the command steps is creating a cached image as the build process finalizes the container image. To run commands, intermediate containers are created and then automatically deleted after. The underlying cached image is kept on the build host and isn't removed. These temporary images are layered over the previous image and combined into a single image once all steps are completed. This optimization allows future builds to reuse these images to speed up build times.

At the end, the container will comprise one or more image layers and a final ephemeral container layer (i.e., that won't be persisted) when the container is destroyed.

Docker Storage

In this section, you will learn about various Docker storage mechanisms. During the development of your services as containers, you can use these tools to manage data persistence, sharing data between containers and maintaining state between container restarts.

When working with containers, your application may need to write data to the disk, which will persist in an *ephemeral* storage. Ephemeral storage is a short-lived, temporary storage deleted once the container is stopped, restarted, or removed. If you restart your container, you'll notice that previously persisted data is no longer available. Under the hood, Docker writes the runtime data to an ephemeral writable container layer in the container's virtual filesystem.

> You'll lose all your application generated data and log files you've written to disk during a container's runtime if you rely on the container's default storage configuration.

To avoid loss of application runtime data and logs, you have several storage options available that enable you to persist data during a container's lifetime. During development, you can use *volumes* or *bind mounts* to persist data to the host OS filesystem or rely on local databases for persisting data.

Table 12-1 shows the Docker storage mount options.

Table 12-1. Docker storage mounts

Storage	Description	Use cases
Volumes	I/O optimized and preferred storage solution. Managed by Docker and stored in a specific location on the host but decoupled from the host filesystem structure.	If you need to store and share data across multiple containers. If you don't need to modify files or directories from the host.
Bind mounts	Mount files or directories on host into the container but have limited functionality compared to volumes.	If you want both containers and host processes to access and modify host's files and directories. For instance, during local development and testing.
Temporary (tmpfs) mounts	Stores data in the host's memory (RAM) and never written to the container or host's filesystem.	If you need high-performance temporary storage for sensitive or nonstateful data that won't persist after the container stops.

Figure 12-7 shows the different types of mounts.

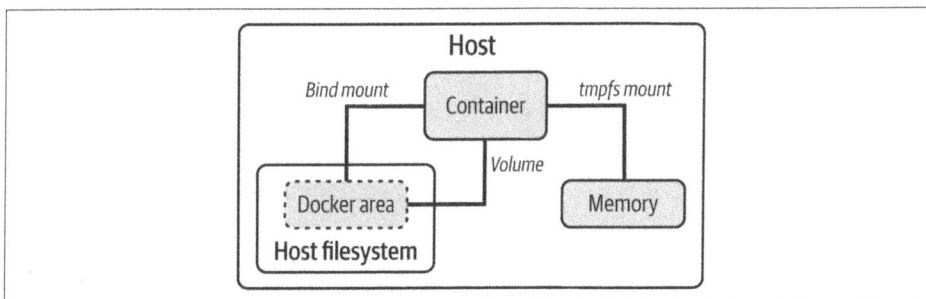

Figure 12-7. Docker storage mounts

We'll now study each storage option in detail so you can simulate your production environment locally with Docker containers using the appropriate storage. When deploying containers to production within a cloud environment, you can use a database or cloud storage offering for persisting data instead of Docker volumes or bind mounts to centralize storage across multiple containers.

Docker volumes

Docker allows you to create isolated *volumes* for persisting application data between container runtimes. To create a volume, you can run the following command:

```
$ docker volume create -n data
```

Once created, you can use volumes to persist data between container runs. Volumes also allow you to persist data when you use database and memory store containers.

> Restarting a database container with new environment variables may not be enough to reset them with new settings.
>
> Some database systems may require you to re-create the container volume if you need to update settings like administrator user credentials.

By default, any volumes you create will be stored on the host machine filesystem until you explicitly remove them via the docker volume remove command.

Bind mounts

In addition to volumes, you can also use filesystem mappings via volume *bind mounts* that map directories residing on the host filesystem to the container filesystem, as shown in Figure 12-8.

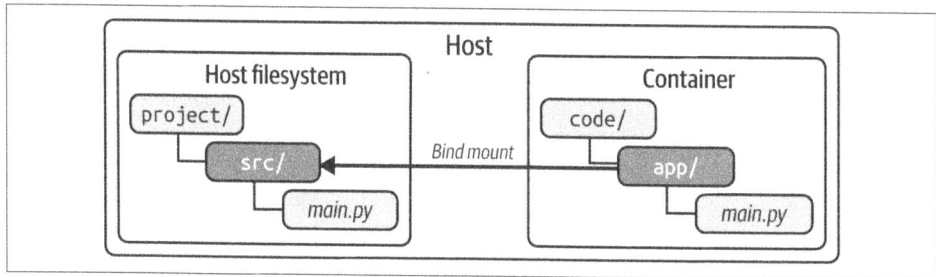

Figure 12-8. Bind mounts between host filesystem and a container

The mounts happen as you start your container. With the mounted directories, you can then directly access them from within the container. You can read and persist data to the mounted directories as you run and stop your containers.

To run a container with a volume bind mount, you can use the following command:

```
$ docker run -v src:/app genai-service
```

Here, the -v flag allows you to map the host directory to a container directory using the <host_dir>:<container_dir> syntax.

The functionality of the `COPY` command you use in a Dockerfile is different from directory mounting.

The former makes a separate copy of a host directory into the container during the image build process while the latter allows you to access and update the mapped host directory from within the container.

This means that if you're not careful, you can unintentionally modify or delete all your original files on the host machine permanently, from within the container.

Bind mount volumes can still be useful in a local development environment. As you change the source code of your services, you'll be able to observe the real-time impact of modifications on the running application containers.

Temporary mounts (tmpfs)

If you have some nonpersistent data such as model caches or sensitive files that you don't need to store permanently, you should consider using temporary *tmpfs mounts*.

This temporary mount will only persist the data to the host memory (RAM) during the container's runtime and increases the container's performance by avoiding writes into the container's writeable layer.

When containerizing GenAI applications, you can use temporary mounts to store cached results, intermediate model computations, temporary files, and session-specific logs that you won't need once the container stops.

The container's writeable layer is tightly coupled with the host machine through a storage driver to implement the union filesystem. Therefore, writing to the container's writable layer reduces performance due to this additional layer of abstraction.

Instead, you can use data volumes for persistent storage that writes directly to the host filesystem or tmpfs mounts for temporary in-memory storage.

Unlike bind mounts and volumes, you can't share the tmpfs mount between containers, and the functionality is available only on Linux systems. In addition, if you adjust directory permissions on tmpfs mounts, they can reset when the container restarts.

Here are a few other use cases of tmpfs mounts:

- Temporarily storing data caches, API responses, logs, test data, configuration files, and AI model artifacts in-memory
- Avoiding I/O writes to disks while working with library APIs that require file-like objects
- Simulating high-speed I/O with rapid file access and writes
- Preventing excessive or unnecessary disk writes if you need temporary directories

To set a tmpfs mount, you can use the following command:

```
$ docker run --tmpfs /cache genai-service
```

Here, you are setting a tmpfs mount on the /cache directory for model caches, which will cease to exist once the container stops.

Handling filesystem permissions

A big source of frustration and a security consideration for many developers new to Docker is managing directory permissions when using filesystem bind mounts between the host OS and the container.

By default, Docker runs containers as the root user leading to containers having full read/write access to mounted directories on the host OS. If the root user inside the container creates directories or files, they will be owned by root on the host as well. You can then face permission issues if you have a nonroot user account on the host when you try to access or modify these directories or files.

> Running containers as the default root user is also a great security risk if a malicious actor gets access to the container since they'll have access to the host system as root. Additionally, if you run a compromised image, you might risk executing malicious code on your host system with root privileges.

To mitigate permission issues when running containers with bind mounts, you can use the --user flag to run the container as a nonroot user:

```
$ docker run --user genai-service
```

Alternatively, you can create and switch to a nonroot user within the final layers of the image build inside the Dockerfile, as shown in Example 12-6.

Example 12-6. Creating and switching to nonroot user when building container images (Ubuntu/Debian containers only)

```
ARG USERNAME=fastapi ❶
ARG USER_UID=1001
ARG USER_GID=1002

RUN groupadd --gid $USER_GID $USERNAME \ ❷
    && adduser \
    --disabled-password \
    --shell "/sbin/nologin" \ ❸
    --gecos "" \
    --home "/nonexistent" \
    --no-create-home \ ❹
    --uid "${UID}" \
    --gid $USER_GID
    $USERNAME ❺

USER $USERNAME ❻

CMD ["uvicorn", "main:app", "--host", "0.0.0.0", "--port", "8000"]
```

❶ Use build arguments to specify variables during the image build.

❷ Create a user group with the given USER_GID.

❸ Disable user login completely including password-based login.

❹ Avoid creating a home directory for the user.

❺ Create a nonroot user account with the given $USER_UID and assign it to the newly created USER_GID group. Set the name of the user account to fastapi.

❻ Switch to the nonroot fastapi user.

> Often, you'll need to install packages or add configurations that require privileged disk access or permissions. You should only switch to a nonroot user at the end of an image build once you've completed such installations and configurations. Avoid switching back and forth between root and nonroot users to prevent any unnecessary complexity and excess image layers.

If you hit issues with creating new groups or users in Example 12-6, try changing the USER_UID and USER_GID as those IDs may already be in use by another nonroot user in the image.

Let's assume that during the image creation, the `root` user in the container has created the `myscripts` folder. You can inspect filesystem permissions using the `ls -l` command, which returns the following output:

```
total 12
drw-r--r-- 2 root root 4096 Oct  1 10:00 myscripts
```

You can read permissions `drwxr-xr-x` for the `myscripts` directory using the following breakdown:

- d: Specifies that `myscripts` is a directory; otherwise would show a -.

- `rwx`: Owner `root` user can (r)read, (w)rite, and e(x)ecute files in this directory.

- `r--`: Group `root` members can perform (r)ead-only operations but can't write or execute any files.

- `r--`: Everyone else can read the file but cannot write to or execute it.[4]

If you want to set ownership or permissions on the `myscripts` directory, you can use the `chmod` or `chown` commands in Linux systems.

Use the `chown` command to change the directory owner on host so that you can edit the files in your code editor:

```
# Set file or directory ownership
$ sudo chown -R username:groupname mydir
```

Alternatively, if you only need to execute the scripts in the `myscripts` directory, use the `chmod` command to change the file or directory permissions:

```
# Set execute permissions using flags
$ sudo chmod -R +x myscripts

# Set execute permissions in a numeric form
$ sudo chmod -R 755 myscripts
```

> The `-R` flag will recursively set the ownership or permissions on a nested directory.

This command will allow `root` group members and other users to execute files in the `myscripts` directory. Others can execute the files only if they use the `bash` command. However, only the owner can modify them.

---

4 You can still run executable files with the r permission alone by using the `bash script.sh` command instead of `./script.sh`.

Interpreting Linux Filesystem Permissions

The `chmod` command uses a three-digit octal number to set file permissions. Each digit represents the permissions for the *owner*, *group*, and *others* (i.e., everyone else), respectively.

For example, `chmod 755` sets the following:

- Owner: `rwx` (7)
- Group: `r-x` (5)
- Others: `r-x` (5)

Table 12-2 shows the Linux permissions table to use as a handy reference when working with `chmod` commands.

Table 12-2. Linux filesystem permissions

Numeric value	Symbol	Permissions
7	rwx	(r)ead, (w)rite, and e(x)ecute
6	rw-	(r)ead and (w)rite
5	r-x	(r)ead and e(x)ecute
4	r--	(r)ead-only
3	-wx	(w)rite and e(x)ecute
2	-w-	(w)rite-only
1	--x	e(x)ecute-only
0	---	None

You can use Table 12-2 as a reference to troubleshoot any permission-related issues.

If you inspect the filesystem permissions again using `ls -l`, you'll see the following output:

```
total 12
drwxr-xr-x 2 root root 4096 Oct  1 10:00 myscripts
```

- `rwx`: Owner `root` user can still (r)read, (w)rite, and e(x)ecute files in this directory.
- `r-x`: Group `root` members can perform (r)ead and e(x)ecute operations but can't modify any files.
- `r-x`: Anyone else can't modify files in `myscripts` directory but can read and execute them.

You can use Example 12-7 to set permissions when creating directories inside an image.

Example 12-7. Creating scripts folder and allowing files to be executed (Ubuntu/Debian containers only)

```
RUN mkdir -p scripts

COPY scripts scripts

RUN chmod -R +x scripts
```

The instructions in Example 12-7 will allow you to configure permissions to execute files in the `scripts` directory from within the container.

> When using container volumes, be careful with mount bindings as they replace the permissions inside the container with those from the host filesystem.

The most frustrating issues when working with containers will be related to filesystem permissions. Therefore, knowing how to set and correct file permissions will save you hours of development when working with containers that produce or modify artifacts on the host machine.

Docker Networking

Docker networking is one of the hardest concepts to grasp in multicontainer projects. This section covers how Docker networking works and how to set up local containers to communicate, simulating production environments during development.

Often, when you're deploying to production environments in the cloud, you configure networking using the cloud provider's solutions. However, if you need to connect containers in a development environment for local testing or deploying on on-premises resources, then you'll benefit from understanding how Docker networking works.

If you're developing GenAI services that interact with external systems like databases, chances are you'll be using multiple containers; one for your application and one for running each of your databases or external systems.

Docker ships with a networking subsystem that allows containers to connect with each other on the same or different hosts. You can even connect containers via internet-facing hosts.

When you create containers using the docker run command, they'll have networking enabled by default on a *bridge network* so that they can make outgoing connections. However, they won't expose or publish their ports to the outside world.

With the default settings, Docker interacts with the OS kernels to configure *firewall rules* (e.g., iptables and ip6tables rules on Linux) to implement network isolation, port publishing, and filtering.

Since Docker can override these firewall rules, if you have a port on host like 8000 closed, Docker can force it open and expose it outside the host machine when you run a container with the -p 8000:8000 flag. To prevent such an exposure, a solution is to run containers using -p 127.0.0.1:8000:8000.

For the networking subsystem to function, Docker uses *networking drivers*, as shown in Table 12-3.

Table 12-3. Docker networking drivers

Driver	Description	Use case
Bridge (default)	Connects containers running on the same Docker daemon host. User-defined networks can leverage an embedded DNS server.	Control container communication in isolated Docker networks with a simple setup.
Host	Removes the isolation layer between containers and the host system, so any TCP/UDP connections are accessible directly via host network such as the localhost without the need to publish ports.	Simplify access to container from the host network (e.g., localhost) or when a container needs to handle a large range of ports.
None	Disables all networking services and isolates running containers within the Docker environment.	Isolate containers from any Docker and non-Docker process for security reasons. Network debugging or simulating outages. Resource isolation and transient containers for short-lived processes.
Overlay	Connects containers across multiple hosts/engines or in a *Docker Swarm* cluster. **Note:** Docker engine has *swarm* mode that enables container orchestration via *clusters* of Docker daemons/engines.	Remove the need for OS-level routing when connecting containers across Docker hosts.
Macvlan	Assigns mac addresses to containers as if they're physical devices. Misconfiguration may lead to unintentional degradation of your network due to IP address exhaustion, leading to VLAN spread (large number of mac addresses) or promiscuous mode (overlapping addresses).	Used in legacy systems or applications that monitor network traffic that expect to be directly connected to a physical network.
IPVlan	Gives you total control over container IPv4 and IPv6 addressing, providing easy access to external services with no need for port mappings.	Advanced networking setup that bypasses the traditional Linux bridge for isolation, enhanced performance and simplified networking topology.

To ensure your containers can communicate together, you may need to specify networking settings and drivers. You can select a networking driver that matches your use case based on Table 12-3.

> Some of these drivers may not be available depending on the platform/host OS you're running Docker on (Windows, Linux, or macOS host).

The most commonly used network drivers are bridge, host, and none. You likely won't need to use other drivers (e.g., overlay, Macvlan, IPVlan) unless you need more advanced networking configurations.

Figure 12-9 visualizes the functionality of the bridge, host, none, overlay, Macvlan, and IPVlan drivers.

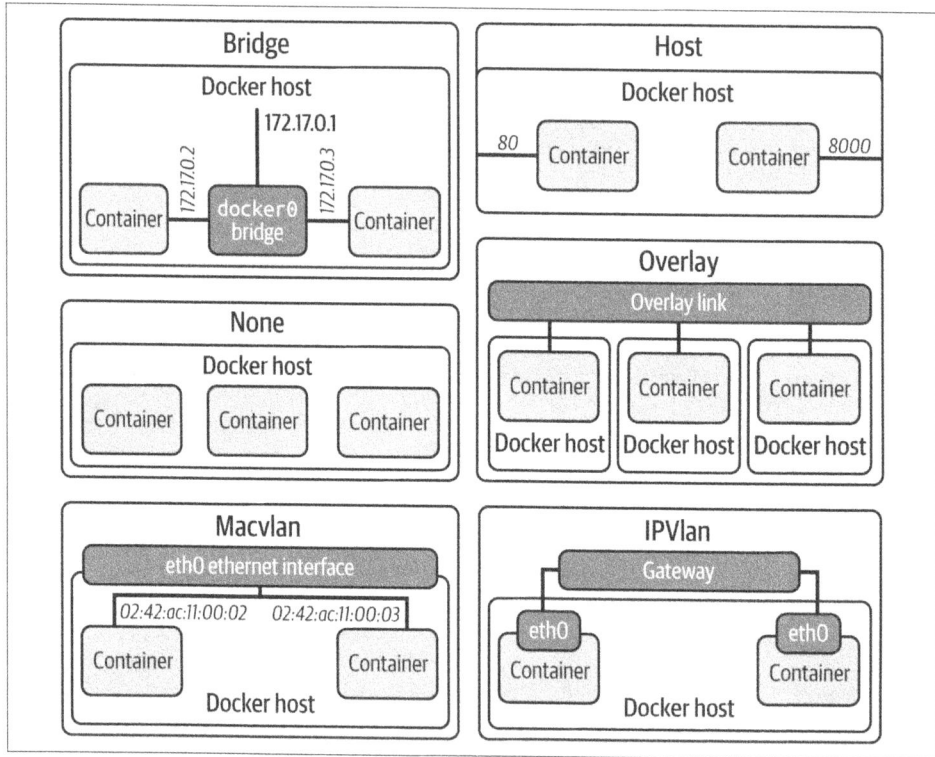

Figure 12-9. Docker networking drivers

Let's explore these networking drivers in more detail.

Bridge network driver

The bridge network driver connects containers by creating a default bridge network docker0 and associating containers with it and the host's main network interface, unless otherwise specified. This will allow your containers to access the host network (and the internet) plus allow you to access the containers.

You can view the networks using the docker network ls command:

```
$ docker network ls
NETWORK ID      NAME      DRIVER    SCOPE
72ec0b2e6034    bridge    bridge    local
53ec40b3c639    host      host      local
64368b7baa5f    none      null      local
```

The *network bridge* in Docker is a link layer software device running within the host machine's kernel, allowing linked containers to communicate while isolating non-connected containers. The bridge driver automatically installs rules in the host machine so that containers on different bridge networks can't communicate directly.

> Bridge networks only apply to containers running on the same Docker engine/daemon host. To connect containers running on other daemon hosts, you can manage routing at the host OS layer or use an *overlay* driver.

In addition to default bridge networks, you can create your own custom networks, which can provide superior isolation and packet routing experience.

Configure user-defined bridge networks. If you need more advanced or isolated networking environments for your containers, you can create a separate user-defined network.

User-defined networks are superior to the default bridge networks as they provide better isolation. In addition, containers can resolve each other by name or alias on user-defined bridge networks unlike the default network where they can only communicate via IP addresses.

> If you run containers without specifying --network, they'll be attached to the default bridge network. This can be a security issue as unrelated services are then able to communicate and access each other.

To create a network, you can use the docker network create command, which will use --driver bridge flag by default:

```
$ docker network create genai-net
```

When you create user-defined networks, Docker uses the host OS tools to manage the underlying network infrastructure, such as adding or removing bridge devices and configuring `iptables` rules on Linux.

Once the network is created, you can list the networks using the `docker network ls` command:

```
$ docker network ls
NETWORK ID      NAME          DRIVER      SCOPE
72ec0b2e6034    bridge        bridge      local
6aa21632e77e    genai-net     bridge      local
```

The network topology will now look like Figure 12-10.

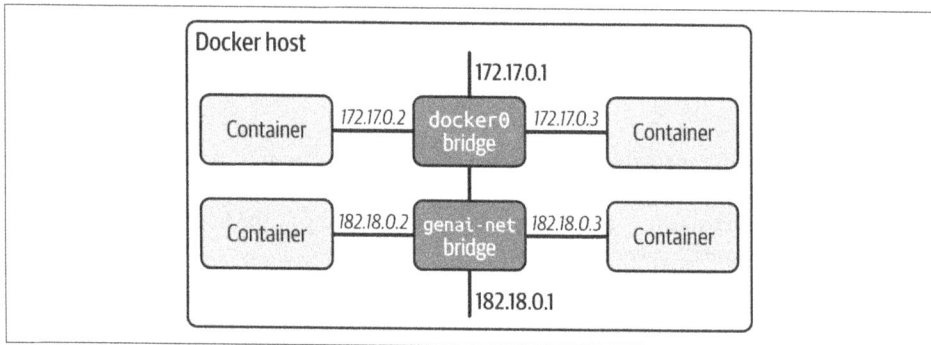

Figure 12-10. Isolated bridge networks

When you run containers, you can now attach them to the created network using the `--network genai-net` flag:

```
$ docker run --network genai-net genai-service
$ docker run --network genai-net postgresql
```

On Linux, there is a limit of 1,000 containers that can connect to a single bridge network due to the Linux kernel restrictions. Linking more containers to a single bridge network can make it unstable and break inter-container communication.

Both your containers can now access each other on your better isolated `genai-net` user-defined network with automatic *DNS resolution* between containers.

Embedded DNS. Docker leverages an embedded DNS server with user-defined networks, as shown in Figure 12-11, to map internal IP addresses so that containers can reach one by name.

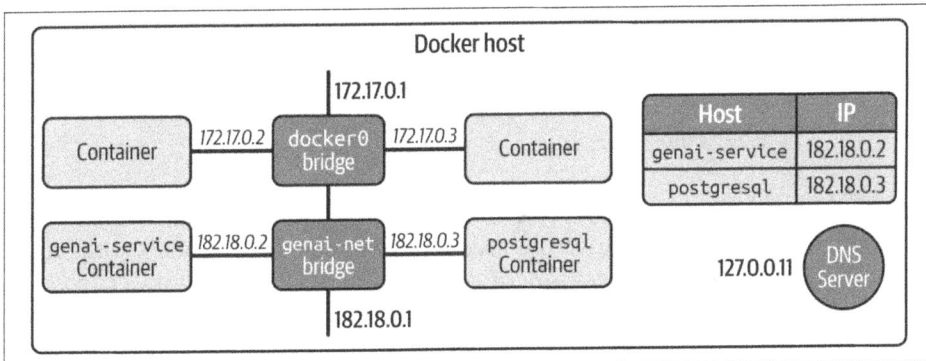

Figure 12-11. Embedded DNS

For instance, if you name your application container as `genai-service` and your database container as `db`, then your `genai-service` container can communicate with the database by calling the `db` hostname.

> You can't access the `db` container from outside of the Docker bridge network by its name, as the embedded DNS server is not visible to the host machine.
>
> Instead, you can expose a container port 5432 and access the `db` container using host's network (e.g., via `localhost:5432`).

Let's discuss how you can publish container ports to the outside environment such as the host machine next.

Publishing ports.   When you run containers in a network, they automatically expose ports to each other.

If you need to access containers from the host machine or non-Docker processes on different networks, you'll need to expose the container ports by publishing them using the `--publish` or `-p` flag:

```
$ docker run -p 127.0.0.1:8000:8000 myimage
```

This command allows you to create a container with exposed port 8000 mapped to 8000 port on the host machine (e.g., localhost) using the `<host_port>:<container_port>` syntax.

When you don't specify a container port, Docker will publish and map port 80 by default.

> Always double-check ports you want to expose and avoid publishing container ports that are already in use on your host machine. Otherwise, there'll be *port conflicts* leading to requests being routed to conflicting services, which will also be time-consuming to troubleshoot.

If using bridge networks and port mappings are causing you a lot of trouble, you can also use the *host* networking driver for connecting your containers, albeit without the same isolation and security benefits of bridge networks.

Host network driver

A *host* network driver is useful for cases where you want to improve performance, when you want to avoid the container port mapping, or when one of your containers needs to handle a large number of ports.

Running a container with the host driver is as simple as using the `--net=host` flag with the `docker run` command:

```
$ docker run --net=host genai-service
```

In host networking, containers share the host machine's network namespace, meaning that containers won't be isolated from the Docker host. Therefore, containers won't be allocated their own IP address.

> As soon as you enable the host network driver, previously published ports will be discarded, as containers won't have their own IP address.

The host network driver is more performant because it doesn't need a *network address translation* (NAT) for mapping IP addresses from one namespace (containers) to another (host machine) and avoids creating a *user-land proxy* (i.e., port forwarding) for each port. However, host networking is only supported with Linux—and not Windows—containers. In addition, containers won't have access to the network interfaces of the host so can't bind to host's IP addresses, leading to added complexity in the network configuration you need.

None network driver

If you want to completely isolate the networking stack of a container, you can use the `--network none` flag when starting the container. Within the container, only the loopback device is created, a virtual network interface that the container uses to communicate with itself. You can specify the none network driver using the following command:

```
$ docker run --network none genai-service
```

These are a few cases where isolating containers are useful:

- Applications handling highly sensitive data or running critical processes
- Where there's a higher risk of network-based attacks or malware
- Performing network debugging and simulating network outages by eliminating external interference
- Running stand-alone containers without external dependencies can run independently
- Operating transient containers for short-lived processes to minimize network exposure

Generally, use the none network driver if you need to isolate containers from any Docker and non-Docker processes for security reasons.

Enabling GPU Driver

If you have an NVIDIA graphics card with the CUDA toolkit and necessary drivers installed, then you can use the --gpus=all flag to enable GPU support for your containers in Docker.[5]

To test that your system has the necessary drivers and supports GPU in Docker, run the following command to benchmark your GPU:

```
$ docker run --rm -it \
          --gpus=all nvcr.io/nvidia/k8s/cuda-sample:nbody nbody \
          -gpu \
          -benchmark

> Windowed mode
> Simulation data stored in video memory
> Single precision floating point simulation
> 1 Devices used for simulation
MapSMtoCores for SM 8.9 is undefined.  Default to use 128 Cores/SM
MapSMtoArchName for SM 8.9 is undefined.  Default to use Ampere
GPU Device 0: "Ampere" with compute capability 8.9

> Compute 8.9 CUDA device: [NVIDIA GeForce RTX 4090]
131072 bodies, total time for 10 iterations: 75.182 ms
= 2285.102 billion interactions per second
= 45702.030 single-precision GFLOP/s at 20 flops per interaction
```

---

5 Refer to the NVIDIA documentation on how to install the latest CUDA toolkit and graphics drivers for your system.

You can also use the NVIDIA system management interface nvidia-smi tool to help manage and monitor NVIDIA GPU devices.

Deep learning frameworks such as tensorflow or pytorch can automatically detect and use the GPU device when running your applications in a GPU-enabled container. This includes Hugging Face libraries such as transformers that lets you self-host language models.

If using the transformers package, make sure to also install the accelerate library:

```
$ pip install accelerate
```

You can now move the model to GPU before it's loaded in CPU by using device_map='cuda', as shown in Example 12-8.

Example 12-8. Transferring Hugging Face models to the GPU

```
from transformers import pipeline

pipe = pipeline(
    "text-generation",
    model="TinyLlama/TinyLlama-1.1B-Chat-v1.0",
    device_map="cuda"
)
```

You should be able to run the predictions on the GPU by passing the --gpus=all flag to docker run.

Docker Compose

In multicontainer environments, you can use the *Docker Compose* tool for defining and running application containers for a streamlined development and deployment experience.

Using Docker Compose can help you simplify managing several containers, networks, volumes, variables, and secrets with a single *YAML configuration file*. This simplifies the complex task of orchestrating and coordinating various containers, making it easier to manage and replicate your services across different application environments using environment variables. You can also share the YAML file with others so that they can replicate your container environment. Additionally, it caches configurations to prevent re-creating containers when you restart services.

Example 12-9 shows an example YAML configuration file.

Example 12-9. Docker Compose YAML configuration file

```
# compose.yaml

services: ❶
  server:
    build: . ❷
    ports:
      - "8000:8000"
    environment:
      SHOW_DOCS_IN_PRODUCTION: $SHOW_DOCS_IN_PRODUCTION
      ALLOWED_CORS_ORIGINS: $ALLOWED_CORS_ORIGINS
    secrets:
      - openai_api_token ❸
    volumes:
      - ./src/app:/code/app
    networks:
      - genai-net ❹

  db:
    image: postgres:12.2-alpine
    ports:
      - "5433:5432"
    volumes:
      - db-data:/etc/data
    networks:
      - genai-net

volumes:
  db-data:
    name: "my-app-data"

networks:
  genai-net:
    name: "genai-net"
    driver: bridge

secrets:
  openai_api_token:
    environment: OPENAI_API_KEY
```

❶ Create the containers alongside the associated volumes, networks, and secrets.

❷ Use the Dockerfile located at the same directory as the Compose file to build the server image.

❸ Use Docker secrets to mask sensitive data like API keys within the container shell environment.

❹ Create a bridge `genai-net` network and attach both `server` and `db` containers to it.

> If you have Docker objects like volumes and networks that you're managing yourself, you can tag them with `external: true` in the compose file so that Docker Compose doesn't manage them.

Once you have a `compose.yaml` file, you can then use simple compose commands to manage your containers:

```
# Start services defined in compose.yaml
$ docker compose up

# Stop and remove running services (won't remove created volumes and networks)
$ docker compose down

# Monitor output of running containers
$ docker compose logs

# List all running services with their status
$ docker compose ps
```

You can use these commands to start/stop/restart services and view their logs or container statuses. Additionally, you can edit the Compose file shown in Example 12-9 to use `watch` so that your services are automatically updated as you edit and save your code.

Example 12-10 shows how to use the `watch` instruction on a given directory.

Example 12-10. Enabling Docker Compose watch on a given directory

```
services:
  server:
    # ...
    develop:
      watch:
        - action: sync
          path: ./src
          target: /code
```

Whenever a file changes in the `./src` folder on your host machine, Compose will sync its content to `/code` and update the running application (server service) without restarting them.

You can then run the `watch` process using `docker compose watch`:

```
$ docker compose watch

[+] Running 2/2
 ✓ Container project-server-1  Created    0.0s
 ✓ Container project-db-1      Recreated  0.1s
Attaching to db-1, server-1
          ◉ watch enabled
...
```

Docker Compose `watch` allows for greater granularity than is practical with bind mounts, as shown in Example 12-9. For instance, it lets you ignore specific files or entire directories within the watched tree to avoid I/O performance issues.

Besides using Docker Compose `watch`, you can merge and override multiple Compose files to create a composite configuration tailored for specific build environments. Typically, the `compose.yml` file contains the base configurations, which can be overridden by an optional `compose.override.yml` file. For instance, as shown in Example 12-11, you can inject local environment settings, mount local volumes, and create new a database service.

Example 12-11. Merging and overriding Compose files for environment-specific build configurations

```
# compose.yml

services: ❶
  server:
    ports:
      - 8000:8000
    # ...
    command: uvicorn main:app

# compose.override.yml

services: ❷
  server:
    environment:
      - LLM_API_KEY=$LLM_API_KEY
      - DATABASE_URL=$DATABASE_URL
    volumes:
      - ./code:/code
    command: uvicorn main:app --reload

  database:
    image: postgres:latest
    environment:
      - POSTGRES_DB=genaidb
      - POSTGRES_USER=genaiuser
```

```
    - POSTGRES_PASSWORD=secretPassword!
  volumes:
    - db_data:/var/lib/postgresql/data

networks:
  app-network:

volumes:
  db_data:
```

❶ The base Compose file contains instructions for running the production version of the application.

❷ Override base instructions by replacing the container start command, inject local variables, and add volume and networking configurations with a local database service.

To use these files, run the following command:

```
$ docker compose up
```

Docker Compose will automatically merge configurations from both Compose files, applying the environment-specific settings from the override Compose file.

Enabling GPU Access in Docker Compose

To access GPU devices with services managed by Docker Compose, you'll need to add the instructions to the composed file (see Example 12-12).

Example 12-12. Adding GPU configurations to the Docker Compose app service

```
services:
  app:
    # ...
    deploy:
      resources:
        reservations:
          devices:
            - driver: nvidia
              count: 1 ❶
              capabilities: [gpu]
```

❶ Limit the number of GPU devices accessible by the app service.

These instructions will give you more granular control over how your services should use your GPU resources.

Optimizing Docker Images

If your Docker images grow in size, they'll also be slower to run, build, and test in production. You'll also be spending a lot of development time iterating over the development of the image.

In that case, it's important to understand image optimization strategies, including how to use Docker's layering mechanism to keep images lightweight and efficient to run, in particular with GenAI workloads.

These are a few ways to reduce image size and speed up the build process:

- Using minimal base images
- Avoiding GPU inference runtimes
- Externalizing application data
- Layering ordering and caching
- Using multi-stage builds

Implementing these optimizations as shown in Table 12-4 may reduce typical image sizes from several gigabytes to less than 1 GB. Similarly, build times can reduce from several minutes on average to less than a minute.

Table 12-4. Impact of build optimization on a typical image[a]

Optimization step	Build time (seconds)	Image size (GB)
Initial	352.9	1.42
Using minimal base images	38.5	1.38
Use caching	24.4	1.38
Layer ordering	17.9	1.38
Multi-stage builds	10.3	0.034 (34 MB)

[a] Source: warpbuild.com

Let's review each in more detail with code examples for clarity.

Use minimal base image

Base images allow you to start from a preconfigured image so you don't have to install everything from scratch, including the Python interpreter. However, some base images available on the Docker Hub may not be suitable for production deployments. Instead, you'll want to select the right base image with a minimal OS footprint to work from for faster builds and smaller image sizes, possibly with pre-installed Python dependencies and support for installing its various packages.

Alpine base images use a lightweight Alpine Linux distribution designed to be small and secure, containing only the *base minimum* essential tools to run your application, but this won't support installing many Python packages. On the other hand, slim base images may use other Linux distributions like Debian or CentOS, containing the *necessary* essential tools for running applications that make them larger than Alpine base images.

> Use slim base images if you care about build time and Alpine base images if you care about image size.

You can use the `slim` base images such as `python:3.12-slim` or even Alpine base images like `python:3.12-alpine` that can be as small as 71.4 MB. A bare-bones Alpine image can even go down to 12.1 MB. The following command shows a list of base images pulled from the Docker repository:

```
$ docker image ls

REPOSITORY   TAG          IMAGE ID       CREATED       SIZE
alpine       3.20         3463e98c969d   4 weeks ago   12.1MB
python       3.12-alpine  c6de2e87f545   6 days ago    71.4MB
python       3.12-slim    1ba4bc34383e   6 days ago    186MB
```

> Standard-sized images typically contain a full Linux distribution like Ubuntu or Debian containing a variety of pre-installed packages and dependencies, making them suitable for local development but perhaps not production environments.

Avoid GPU inference runtimes

In AI workloads where you're serving ML/GenAI models, you may need to install deep learning frameworks, dependencies, and GPU libraries that can suddenly explode the footprint of your images. For instance, to make inferences on a GPU using the `transformers` library, you'll need to install 3 GB of NVIDIA packages for GPU inference, 1.6 GB for the `torch` to perform the inference.

Unfortunately, you can't reduce the image size if you need to use a GPU to perform an inference. However, if you can avoid GPU inference and just rely on CPUs, you may be able to reduce the image size by up to 10 times using the Open Neural Network Exchange (ONNX) runtime with model quantization.

As discussed in Chapter 10, you can use the INT8 quantization with an ONNX model to benefit from model compression without much loss in output quality.

To switch from the GPU inference runtime to the ONNX runtime for Hugging Face transformer models, you can use the transformers[onnx] package:

```
$ pip install transformers[onnx]
```

You can then export any Hugging Face transformer model checkpoint with default configurations to the ONNX format with transformers.onnx:

```
$ python -m transformers.onnx --model=distilbert/distilbert-base-uncased onnx/
```

This command exports the distilbert/distilbert-base-uncased model checkpoint as an ONNX graph stored in onnx/model.onnx, which can be run with any Hugging Face model accelerator that supports the ONNX standard, as shown in Example 12-13.

Example 12-13. Model inference using the ONNX runtime with quantization

```
from onnxruntime import InferenceSession
from transformers import AutoTokenizer

tokenizer = AutoTokenizer.from_pretrained("distilbert/distilbert-base-uncased")
session = InferenceSession("onnx/model.onnx")

inputs = tokenizer("Using DistilBERT with ONNX Runtime!", return_tensors="np") ❶
output = session.run(output_names=["last_hidden_state"], input_feed=dict(inputs))
```

❶ ONNX runtime expects numpy arrays as input.

Using a technique such as shown in Example 12-13, you can downsize from image sizes between 5 and 10 GB to around 0.5 GB, which is a massive footprint reduction, significantly more cost-effective and scalable.

Externalize application data

A core contributor to image size is copying models and application data into the image during build time. This approach increases both the build time and image size.

A better approach is to use volumes during local development and external storage solutions for downloading and loading models at application startup in production. In Kubernetes container orchestration environments, you can also use persistent volumes for model storage.

> If your application container takes a long time to download data and model artifacts from an external source, your health checks may fail, and the hosting platform can kill your containers prematurely. In such cases, configure health check probes to wait longer or as a last resort, bake the model into the image.

Layer ordering and caching

Docker uses a layered filesystem to create layers in an image for each instruction in the Dockerfile. These layers are like a stack, with each layer adding more content on top of the previous layers. Whenever a layer changes, that layer (and further layers) will need to be rebuilt for those changes to appear in the image (i.e., build cache must be invalidated).

A layer (i.e., a filesystem snapshot) is created if the instruction is writing or deleting files into the container's union filesystem.

> Dockerfile instructions that modify the filesystem like ENV, COPY, ADD, and RUN will contribute new layers to the build process, effectively increasing the image size. On the other hand, instructions such as WORKDIR, ENTRYPOINT, LABEL, and CMD that only update the image metadata don't create any layers and any build cache.

After creation, each layer is then cached for reusability across image rebuilds if the instruction and files it depends on haven't changed since the last build. Therefore, ideally, you want to write a Dockerfile that allows you to stop, destroy, rebuild, and replace containers with minimal setup and configuration.

There are a few techniques you can use to minimize and optimize these layers as much as possible.

Layer ordering to avoid frequent cache invalidation.   Since changes to the earlier layers can invalidate the build cache leading to repeating steps, you should order your Dockerfile from the most stable (e.g., installations) to the most frequently changing or volatile (e.g., application code, configuration files).

Following this ordering, place the most stable yet expensive instructions (e.g., model downloads or heavy dependency installations) at the start of the Dockerfile, and volatile, fast operations (e.g., copying application code) at the bottom.

Imagine your Dockerfile file looks like this:

```
FROM python:3.12-slim as base
# Changes to the
COPY . .
RUN pip install requirements.txt
```

Here you're creating a layer by copying your working directory containing the application code into the image before downloading and installing dependencies.

If any one of source files changes, Docker builder will invalidate the cache causing the dependency installation to be repeated, which is expensive and can take several minutes to complete, if not cached by pip.

To avoid repeating expensive steps, you can logically order your Dockerfile instructions to optimize the layer caching by reordering instructions like these:

```
FROM python:3.12-slim as base
COPY requirements.txt requirements.txt
RUN pip install requirements.txt
COPY . .
```

Now any changes to the source files won't affect the long dependency installation step, drastically speeding up the build process.

Minimize layers. To keep image sizes small, you'll want to minimize image layers as much as possible.

A simple technique to achieve this is to combine multiple RUN instructions into one. For instance, instead of writing multiple RUN apt-get installations, you can combine them into a single RUN command with &&:

```
RUN apt-get update && apt-get install -y
```

This will avoid adding unnecessary layers and prevents caching issues with apt-get update using the *cache busting* technique.

Since the builder may potentially skip updating the package index, causing installations to fail or use outdated packages, using the && ensures that the latest packages are installed if the package index is updated.

> You can also use the --no-cache flag when using docker build to avoid cache hits and ensure fresh downloads of base images and dependencies on every build.

Keep build context small. The *build context* is the set of files and directories that'll be sent to the builder to carry out the Dockerfile instruction. A smaller build context reduces the amount of data sent to the builder and lowers the chance of cache invalidation, resulting in faster builds.

When you use the COPY . . command in a Dockerfile to copy your working directory into an image, you may also add tool caches, development dependencies, virtual environments, and unused files into the build context. Not only the image size will be increased, but also the Docker builder will cache these unnecessary files. Any changes to these files will then invalidate the build, restarting the whole build process.

To prevent the unnecessary cache invalidation, you can add a *.dockerignore* file next to your Dockerfile, listing all files and directories that your services won't need in production. As an example, here are items you can include in a *.dockerignore* file:

```
**/.DS_Store
**/__pycache__
**/.mypy_cache
**/.venv
**/.env
**/.git
```

Docker builder will then ignore these files even when you run the COPY command across your entire working directory.

Use cache and bind mounts. You can use *bind mounts* to avoid adding unnecessary layers to the image and *cache mounts* to speed up subsequent builds.

Bind mounts temporarily include files in the build context for a single RUN instruction and won't persist as image layers after. Cache mounts specify a persistent cache location that you can read and write data to across multiple builds.

Here is an example where you can download a pretrained model from Hugging Face into a mounted cache to optimize layer caching:

```
RUN --mount=type=cache,target=/root/.cache/huggingface && \
    pip install transformers && \
    python -c "from transformers import AutoModel; \
    AutoModel.from_pretrained('bert-base-uncased')"
```

This RUN instruction creates a cache of the downloaded pretrained model at /root/.cache/huggingface, which can be shared across multiple builds. This helps avoid redundant downloads and optimizes the build process by reusing cached layers.

You can also use the --no-cache-dir flag when using the pip package manager to avoid caching altogether for minimizing image size. However, you'll have a significantly slower build process as follow-on builds will need to redownload each time.

Use external cache. If you're building and deploying containers using a CI/CD pipeline, you can benefit from an external cache hosted on a remote location. An external cache can drastically speed up the build process in CI/CD pipelines where builders are often ephemeral and build minutes are precious.

To use an external cache, you can specify the --cache-to and --cache-from options with the docker buildx build command:

```
docker buildx build --cache-from type=registry,ref=user/app:buildcache .
```

Besides layer ordering and cache optimization, you can use multi-stage builds to significantly shrink your image sizes.

Multi-stage builds

Using *multi-stage builds*, you can reduce the size of your final image by splitting out the Dockerfile instructions into distinct stages. Common stages can be reused to include shared components and serve as a starting point for further stages.

You can also selectively copy artifacts from one stage to another, leaving behind everything you don't want in the final image. This ensures that only the required outputs are included in the final image from previous stages, avoiding any non-essential artifacts. Furthermore, you can also execute multiple build stages in parallel to speed up the build process of your images.

A common multi-stage build pattern is when you need a testing/development image and a slimmer production one with both starting from a shared first stage image. The development or testing image can include additional layers of tooling (i.e., compilers, build systems, and debugging tools) to support the required workflows.

Imagine you need to serve a bert transformer model from Hugging Face in a FastAPI service. You can write your Dockerfile instructions to use three distinct sequential stages.

The first stage downloads the transformer model into /root/.cache/huggingface and creates a Python virtual environment at /opt/venv:

```
# Stage 1: Base
FROM python:3.11.0-slim as base

RUN python -m venv /opt/venv
RUN pip install transformers && \
    python -c "from transformers import AutoModel; \
    AutoModel.from_pretrained('bert-base-uncased')"
RUN --mount=type=cache,target=/root/.cache/pip \
    --mount=type=bind,source=requirements.txt,target=requirements.txt \
    python -m pip install -r requirements.txt
```

The second stage then copies the model artifacts and virtual Python environment /opt/ven from the base stage before copying source files over and creating a production version of the FastAPI service:

```
# Stage 2: Production
FROM base as production
RUN apt-get update && apt-get install -y
COPY --from=base /opt/venv /opt/venv
COPY --from=base /root/.cache/huggingface /root/.cache/huggingface

WORKDIR /code
COPY . .

EXPOSE 8000
```

```
ENV BUILD_ENV=PROD
CMD ["uvicorn", "main:app", "--host", "0.0.0.0", "--port", "8000"]
```

The last stage copies the production stage virtual Python environment with installed packages and adds several development tools on top. It then starts the server with hot reload functionality:

```
# Stage 3: Development
FROM production as development

COPY --from=production /opt/venv /opt/venv
COPY ./requirements_dev.txt ./
RUN pip install --no-cache-dir --upgrade -r requirements_dev.txt

ENV BUILD_ENV=DEV
CMD ["uvicorn", "main:app", "--host", "0.0.0.0", "--port", "8000", "--reload"]
```

Using a single Dockerfile, we were able to create three distinct stages and use them as we see fit via the `--target development` command when needed.

docker init

You now have an in-depth understanding of the containerization process with the Docker platform and the relevant best practices.

If you ever need to add Docker to an existing project, you can use the `docker init` command, which will guide you through a wizard to create all the necessary Docker deployment files in your current working directory:

```
$ docker init
>> Answer a few questions in the terminal...

project/
|
├── .dockerignore
├── compose.yaml
├── Dockerfile
└── README.Docker.md
... # other application files
```

This will provide a great starting point that you can work from to include additional configuration steps, dependencies, or services as required.

> I recommend using `docker init` when starting out as every gener-
> ated file will adhere to best practices including leveraging `docker`
> `ignore`, optimizing image layers, using bind and cache mounts for
> package installation, and switching to nonroot users.

Once you have an optimized image and a set of working containers, you can choose any cloud provider or self-hosting solution for pushing images to registries and deploying your new GenAI services.

Summary

In this chapter, we reviewed various strategies for deploying your GenAI services—for instance, on virtual machines, as cloud functions, with managed app service platforms, or via containers. As part of this, I covered how virtualization differs from containerization and why you may want to deploy your services as containers.

Next, you learned about the Docker containerization platform and how you can use it to build self-contained images of your applications that can run as containers.

We covered the Docker storage and networking mechanisms that allow you to persist data using the union filesystem in containers and how to connect containers with different networking drivers.

Finally, you were introduced to various optimization techniques for reducing the build time and size of your images to deploy your GenAI services as efficiently as possible.

With services containerized, you can push them to container registries to share, distribute, and run them on any cloud or hosting environment of your choice.

Afterword

Thank you to everyone who joined me on this fascinating journey through the world of building generative AI services with FastAPI. I appreciate your commitment to understanding the end-to-end process for building context-rich and production-ready GenAI applications.

In this book, we explored the development of AI services using FastAPI, covering everything from setting up a project to integrating and serving generative models across various modalities. We discussed what GenAI is and why you'll witness more applications in the future powered by GenAI models. Next, you learned more about the FastAPI web framework and how to create type-safe AI services. As part of this, we implemented concurrency, real-time communication, and database integration for our AI services. Finally, we focused on securing, optimizing, testing, and deploying our AI services, including implementing authentication, authorization, and various security measures.

Having more knowledge and experience of these techniques, you can now build your own innovative and robust GenAI applications, staying ahead in the rapidly evolving field of AI.

As we conclude this book, I want to highlight that our learning journey in building GenAI applications is just the beginning. There are many exciting developments ahead, and I encourage you to keep up with the latest advancements in the field. To assist with this, keep an eye on the repository (*https://github.com/Ali-Parandeh/building-generative-ai-services*) and website (*https://buildinggenai.com*) of this book as I continue to add resources.

I hope this book has given you a deeper understanding into GenAI models integrated with web services and their potential to transform industries when put into production. With this book as your guide, I believe you will be well-prepared to navigate the dynamic landscape of GenAI services and make significant contributions to this rapidly evolving field.

Index

automating manual administrative tasks, 13

facilitation of creative process, 7-8

minimizing delay in resolving customer queries, 11-12

personalization of user experience, 10

role of context-rich prompts in generative models, 9

scaling/democratizing content generation, 13

suggesting contextually relevant solutions, 9-10

given-when-then (GWT) model, 405

Global Interpreter Lock (GIL), 47, 151

GPT cache, 368-370

GPTQ technique, 380-381

GPUs

avoiding GPU inference runtimes in Docker, 484-485

compute-bound operations on, 194

enabling GPU access in Docker Compose, 482

enabling GPU driver in Docker, 477-478

inefficient splitting by FastAPI of AI workloads between CPU and GPU, 48

GraphQL, exposing endpoints with, 33

guardrails, 338-347

implementing a moderation guardrail, 344-347

input guardrails, 339-343

output guardrails, 343

thresholds, 344

guards, 43

GWT (given-when-then) model, 405

H

hallucinations, 17, 69, 175

hashing, 297-307

hierarchical dependency graph, 31

HTTP request-response model, 210

Hugging Face models, streaming LLM outputs from, 230-232

I

IaaS (infrastructure-as-a-service), 452

identity providers (IDPs), 310

implicit flow, 319

implicit functions, 96

in-context learning, 386

infrastructure-as-a-service (IaaS), 452

input guardrails, 339-343

integration tests, 430-439

behavioral testing, 434-438

auto-evaluation tests, 438

directional expectation tests, 437

invariance tests, 436

minimum functionality tests, 435-436

context precision and recall, 431-434

overview, 399

invariance tests (ITs), 436

inversion of control, 29

J

Jina embedder model, 182

JSON strings, exporting Pydantic models to, 136

JSON Web Tokens (JWT) authentication, 289-309

authentication flows, 307-309

getting started with implementation, 290-297

hashing and salting, 297-307

JWT defined, 289-290

K

key-value (KV) caching, 200

keyword caching, 361-363

L

LangChain, 110

language models, 54-73

autoregressive prediction, 63-64

connecting FastAPI with Streamlit UI generator, 69-73

integrating a model into an application, 64-69

positional encoding, 62

tokenization and embedding, 59-60

training transformers, 60-62

transformers as, 5

transformers versus recurrent neural networks, 55-59

large language models (LLMs)

hardware requirements for open source LLMs, 58

latency and throughput, 199

About the Author

Alireza Parandeh is a chartered engineer with the UK Engineering Council and a certified developer and data scientist with Microsoft and Google. He has led engineering teams at both multinational consultancies and tech startups across various markets to build and deploy AI-enabled software. As an AI advocate, Ali started London's Beginners Machine Learning meetup in 2018 to help people break into data and AI careers through hands-on workshops and community events. With a passion for education, he has also taught multiple software engineering bootcamps for Code First Girls, empowering more women to establish their tech and AI careers.

Colophon

The animal on the cover of *Building Generative AI Services with FastAPI* is a ferruginous duck (*Aythya nyroca*), also known as a ferruginous pochard or white-eyed pochard.

What's in a name? The names of these ducks, both common and scientific, can tell us a lot about them. *Aythya* (Greek) refers to a diving sea bird, while *nyroca* (Russian) means "pochard," another word for a diving duck. Ferruginous ducks are indeed diving ducks: they forage their food by diving and sometimes dabbling (bobbing underwater) in search of small fish, insects, and mollusks. As a result of their feeding (and mating) habits, their preferred habitat is freshwater areas with lots of vegetation.

"Ferruginous" comes from the Latin word *ferrugo*, which means "iron rust." The deep red-brown coloration is more prominent in males, as the females are more brown. "White-eyed" also refers to a feature unique to the males: their striking light-colored eyes stand out in their rust-colored feathers, while females have darker eyes.

But there's more to ferruginous ducks than is captured in their name. They are native to Eastern Europe and Western Russia, as well as other parts of Asia. During the winter, they travel south into Northern Africa and the Arabian peninsula. Breeding occurs north in late spring. After courtship is complete, the male is no longer involved. The female builds the nest and cares for the eggs (six to twelve in a clutch). The ducklings are quickly able to swim and forage for food, but the mother teaches them good feeding areas and protects them from predators.

Many of the animals on O'Reilly covers are endangered; all of them are important to the world. The cover illustration is by Karen Montgomery, based on an antique line engraving from Lydekker's *Royal Natural History*. The series design is by Edie Freedman, Ellie Volckhausen, and Karen Montgomery. The cover fonts are Gilroy Semibold and Guardian Sans. The text font is Adobe Minion Pro; the heading font is Adobe Myriad Condensed; and the code font is Dalton Maag's Ubuntu Mono.